Washington Island Through the Years

by

Hannes M. Andersen

Best Wishes 8/19/07

Hannes

Westman Islands,
Heimay

Published by:

Jackson Harbor Press
845 Jackson Harbor Road
Washington Island, WI 54246

Printed in the Canada

ISBN Number 1-890352-21-7

CONTENTS

Our Family (taken in late 20s)
(L. to R.) Olivia, Louise, Ma, Hannes, Dad, Sis, Marvin

That's me
Hannes

FAMILY

Halloween night, 1917, I was born in the farmhouse across from what is now the Washington Island School. It is said that Dr. Boucsein was drunk at the time and his watch was fast, therefore my birthday was recorded for All Saints Day. Dad was 67 and mother was 43 years old.

My earliest memory of Dr. Bouscein was when he scratched my arm to vaccinate against small pox, with a resulting scar that I have carried since age four. Boucseins had the house where Jack Cornell now resides; there was also farm land with it. I remember the Dr. visiting our home to buy dairy products. He drove an old car that was enclosed in the winter by using glass accessories to help shut out the weather. Some Islanders did likewise with their cars, but some rebelled against that. Bachelor Jake Bowman, who lived where Sylvia Jorgenson now does, utterly refused to ride in a “glass cage”. He swore that a person would get "consumption (TB)" and die in "two weeks" if they rode in one.

Dr. Boucsein graduated from medical college in Germany with such high honors that the officials told him if he ever had son(s) who wished to enter the medical profession they would offer scholarships for them. One son, August, became a Veterinarian and practiced in southern Minnesota. The other son, Ernest, after sailing on the Lakes for years became our rural mail carrier. As a young man, one day Ernie was replacing all the fenceposts in the large field west of the Boucsein house when old man Roen came along. Roen was emphatic that Ernie should make all post tops exactly the same height. Ernie asked about the wisdom of that, whereupon Roen said, "I did that in a field and one morning I found a crow sitting on each fencepost. So I got my rifle lined up and fired just one shot killing 99 crows." Ernie quipped, "Why didn't you make it 100 crows?" Roen retorted, "I wouldn't lie for the sake of one crow. "

Ernie married Ruby Foss and they lived where Dave Johnson, Sr. now resides. Every Thursday night the two of them would come to our farm for dairy products and to spend the evenings. He had a delightful sense of humor and all of us looked forward to Thursday evening. Summer afternoons he would gather up all the youngsters in our neighborhood and drive out to Gislason's dock (now Munao’s) for swimming. He was an excellent swimmer and instructor. Normally I had chores to do so could only enviously watch them go.

John Malloch, who lived at Main and Detroit Harbor Rds., was the rural mail carrier before Ernie. He and wife, Annie, had a large family. John's droll wit occasionally surfaced. One day Annie was carrying fresh laid eggs in her apron from the barn when one dropped. She remarked, "Oh, John, I dropped an egg." His quick response was, “Why don't you cackle, Annie?” John loved children and did many nice things for them. At that time the Post Office was in the small room facing south on the lower level in John’s house. In winter he used a single horse pulling a covered sleigh and delivered mail to half of the Island each day. He kept his horse in his own barn, but would pasture it across the road where the Laundromat now is. In the late 20s spinster Weideman rented Bill Engleson's house, now owned by Sawoskos. She loved to raise plants and very soon had picked up all the "horse apples" where John's horse grazed. We youngsters were certain that she followed the horse around and sometimes caught the steaming "meadow muffins” before they hit the ground. She was successful in getting Dad to agree to sell a little over an acre of ground for a building site along Old West Harbor Road. We youngsters were very unhappy because this was a favorite playing spot. She had a home built where Lee Engstrom now resides. As a nature lover she was fascinated with birds and consequently we nicknamed her “Chickadee" and the name stuck.

People today who have grown up with so many comforts cannot fathom the hardships that were endured by early settlers. While attending grade school I learned that some of the boys apparently wore the same suit of long underwear all winter and by spring they became quite rank. While we had to resort to "sponge" baths with a wash cloth and a bowl of warm water, all of us bathed at least once a, week in the months when we could not go swimming. One of my early recollections is when I was less than four years old and mother was bathing me near the old "box" stove, which was our main source of winter heat. I rebelled against having my ears scrubbed and inadvertently backed into the red hot stove. The result was a temporary branding of part of "Patent Pending" on my behind.

Of course, that stove and kitchen range demanded a good supply of wood which was cut during the winter in cordwood lengths, then allowed to air dry in piles until the next fall when it was hauled by wagon to the farm. Then it was sawed into stove lengths and stacked into the wood shed. However, we always tried to burn only wood which had already spent at least one winter in the shed and thus was much drier and created less creosote in the chimney. Still beads of creosote would form in the flue and occasionally we would see flames standing out the chimney top with the interior wall getting so hot you could not hold your hand on it.

At a young age it became my job to refill the large wood box in the kitchen each day after school. One day my brother was working in the woodshed so, for the hell of it, I decided to lock him in. When he learned what had happened he started pitching pieces of wood at the door. The latch came loose and the door opened as he, with back to the door, continued tossing. Wood was falling outside and I thought that was easier than having to go inside so I bent to pick some up and the next piece bonked me right on top of the head. I ran bawling into the house where Sis was complaining about being hungry until she lifted my cap off and blood streamed down the sides of my face. There went her appetite.

Daily chores were heavier in winter than summer. First was rising about six AM and milking cows before breakfast. Then mash was mixed using ground grain from the granary which was placed in large, wooden candy pail that had been given by the local grocer after emptying the hard candy out. Water from the kitchen range reservoir was added to the mash and it was allowed to steam until noon feeding. Next all animals were fed hay and cleaning barns began.

If there was no wind to drive the windmill it was necessary to pump all the water for the animals by hand into the trough. In cold weather we first skimmed the ice off the top, then added hot water to the trough in addition to the well water. Before noon all animals were let out of the barn to drink and exercise while bedding was spread in the stalls and food was placed in the mangers. Corn, which was brought from the fields in shocks, had been cut like silage ahead of time and was placed in each cow's manger. Then the right amount of mash was smeared over this corn. Cows took to this like it was chocolate ice cream. After the noon meal the time was spent either repairing things or cutting cordwood in the woods. Before supper cows were again milked.

Of course, at both morning and evening the milk was run through the cream separator and then cream and whole milk was stored in a cool place. Some skim milk was placed in a barrel to sour and be fed to pigs and chickens, while the surplus was fed to some cows who would drink it, or to the horses. Pigs could only tolerate either whey or sour milk as they had no rennin in their digestive juice to curdle the milk. Sweet skim milk would go right through without hardly changing color.

There were actually four communities on the Island in the 20s. Detroit Harbor, Washington Harbor, Jackson Harbor and Eastside had their own separate grade schools. Eastside (Lucke) School was one room. This is now the Gunnerson residence & former store. The one room Jackson Harbor school is now part of Sievers; while the two room Washington Harbor School now houses the Art and Nature Center. Detroit Harbor had a two room grade school plus a lower room that was rented by parents sending their children to a private high school. This high school had one teacher who taught the essential 9th and 11th grade subjects one year and the 10th and 12th classes the other year. Participating parents paid the amount of tuition required to cover the teacher's salary, room rent and necessary supplies. Students bought their own books which were later sold to succeeding class members. While it was not an accredited high school an excellent education was received. Graduates had no trouble going on to higher learning institutions.

Two outstanding teachers were Olga Wickman from Ellison Bay and Clara (Kieper) Jessen who was my teacher for three years. She started the practice of having the senior class publish an Annual which is continued to the present day.

When the Island was consolidated into one school district all grade level children attended the former Detroit Harbor school while high school was conducted at the former Washington Harbor site. Finally, after considerable additions to the grade school, high school was also incorporated under that roof. The old Detroit Harbor school, which was built during WW I, fell to the "headache" ball when the new K through 12 school was constructed just to the rear.

The teacher during my first HS year was a small man named J.P.Hill. One day my brother, Marvin, suddenly broke into the room shouting, "Mann's Store is on fire!" Six foot Emery

Hansen, seated in the farthest corner was out of his seat and almost past Hill's desk before Hill could stand up and stop him. Hill's only words were, "Be careful". So we all piled into cars and sped to the scene where some of us helped carry goods out of the burning building. The Baptist Church parsonage, just to the south, was threatened, so its contents were also removed to a safe spot. One man carefully carried a feather bed out, but then later threw a mirror from the second story. Fred and Lettie Mann had been living in the parsonage. After the fire that building was moved to its present location across from the REA and Mann's garage was built on that site.

Harry and Reggie Hanson, who built what is now Karly's, offered the dance hall as a temporary store which was used until the new store was constructed.

In those days most people phoned their grocery orders to the stores, who then delivered the order to one's house. The stores extended credit. As no one locked their houses the grocery deliverer would first knock and then if there was no answer, he would enter and place the groceries on the kitchen table. One day, when Fred Mann encountered no response to his knock, he entered to find a very fat woman taking a sponge bath by the kitchen stove. He set the groceries down, tipped his hat and left. Of course, the story was told when he got back to the store. An inquisitive clerk asked, "What did you see?" His response was, “Acres and acres of fat!" Lawrence Gislason had the store which was started by his father, John. This was north of the "Red Barn" and later became a tavern and then the first Community Center before it was razed. His favorite expression if he was out of an item was, "It's coming on the next boat."

When the Detroit Harbor school was built the old one-room school building was moved to Washington Harbor and Ted Gudmundson ran a store there for many years. Later Emory Hanson and then Ruth and Bonnie Boniface operated the store. Emory wore size thirteen shoes and Arni's mother, Maggie Richter, nick-named him "Oliver Spreadfoot". The Vagabond now operates in the old "Ted's Store".

In September 1923 I entered the First Grade at Detroit Harbor School which was right across the road from our farm. My teachers throughout my 12 years were:

First grade - Marjorie Gustafson

2nd & 3rd - Ruth Knudsen
4th - Violet Shirkey (married Harvey Cornell)
5th - Harvey Cornell (later, Co. Superintendent)
6th - Lester Olson (later, Egg Harbor Postmaster)
7th & 8th - Conrad Anderson
9th - J.0. Hill (never found out what "J.O." meant).
10th thru 12th - Clara (Kieper)Jessen

Today I don't know why, but then I envied the pupils who brought their lunch to school and could socialize during the noon break. I was always expected to come home for lunch. If I hurried through the meal and had no chores to do I could get back in time to play some baseball before the 1 o'clock bell rang for reassembly in the classroom.

In those days the curriculum was set up by the State Superintendent and supervised through the County Superintendent and his assistant whose title was Supervising Teacher. They visited each Door County school several times a year, observed the teaching and sent written reports to the local school boards regarding what they had observed.

On occasions, the Parent-Teacher (PTA) evening meetings were held and a program was presented by the students. Each school always had **a** Christmas program which was well attended by families. In our school we set up a temporary stage--complete with curtains that could be drawn. A decorated Christmas tree and evergreen boughs were placed about the room. After reaching the fifth grade it was my annual job to go back in our woods to cut the Christmas tree. On that date I was the most popular lad in the classroom as I got to choose who would accompany me and we were excused from classes so we could perform this task.

It was expected that the teacher would present each pupil with a box of goodies at the Christmas program. All the ingredients could be purchased either at the local store or from the mail order company's wonderful Christmas catalog. The decorated cardboard boxes measured about 6" x **4"** x 2 1/2". They were filled with peanuts, mixed nuts and hard candy. Everyone looked forward to these treats especially children from the poorer families.

The program consisted of several carols, appropriate poems and skits in which nearly all of the school enrollment had some part. I don't know when this practice ceased but it was still done during my three years of teaching at Appleport School (east of Sister Bay) from 1938 to 1941.

Each year the eighth grade classes throughout the county vied for the prizes in the "SAA" contest involving written exams in Spelling, Arithmetic and Achievement. Achievement included questions from most of the other school subjects.

Philip Ellefson, Washington Harbor School, and I, of Detroit Harbor School, were the top contestants from the Island. Conrad Anderson drove both of us to Sturgeon Bay to compete in the county contest. Philip took first place while I, who missed one arithmetic answer, took third place. I still remember spending the night at Conrad's parents' farm in Carnot and his mother introducing us to the wonders of Norwegian lefse. She fried it right on top of the old kitchen wood-fired range. I thought it was great.

Most schools had active 4H clubs, which had a primary interest in agriculture. Annually the members presented demonstrations with the hope of earning prizes on a county level. Warren Richter and I chose testing milk to show butterfat content. Shortly before we were to compete for the Island prize, Warren visited our farm one evening while I was milking.

He was dressed in new tan trousers and a light tan sweater. We discussed our forthcoming demonstration as I "pulled teats." The cow had just made a generous deposit behind her. Even though her hind leg was slipping on the wet barn floor, Warren did not pay much heed to it. Suddenly the foot shot out through the fresh "doilie" spraying juicy dung all over Warren as well as the wall. He had to return home to bathe and change clothes before he could go on to the party he was planning to attend.

During the warm summer months most of our family tried to find enough time between the daily field work and evening milking to grab our swimming suits and either head for Detroit Harbor, or through the woods to West Harbor.After our first dip in the water we lathered up with a bar of Ivory soap that floated and thus was not easily lost. Then through swimming and playing in the water we were thoroughly rinsed. Of course, my close pal, cousin Allen Cornell, and I always had to try out Detroit Harbor near the bayou in May while the water was still quite frigid. Usually we were able to keep it a secret from our parents. While there were make-shift dressing shelters at West

Harbor and Earl Richter's beach,we never worried about privacy when changing clothes as long as a convenient clump of bushes was nearby. While still at a very tender age,one day I fell off the make-shift raft near Richter's beach and swallowed a lot of water before regaining the surface. After that it took a lot of courage to get my head or face under the water.

When weather was not conducive to cleansing by swimming, or the opportunity did not afford itself, we took "sponge baths". At each corner of our house we had rain barrels that caught the water that came from the eaves. We much preferred to use that"soft" water rather than the well water which had about 30 grains of hardness in it and was difficult to form a lather in. Mother also used rain water to wash clothes. "Sponge bath" water was heated on the old,wood cook stove.Each of us normally waited till everyone else had gone to bed. Thus we had the nice, warm spot next to the stove all to ourselves.In summer my underclothes were boxer shorts and sleeveless undershirts,while in winter I donned the one-piece Union suit with the overlapping flap on the back.

During the late 30s our cousin, Leslie Cornell, gave us an old double-acting bilge pump from a fish tug. Marvin & I repaired it and decided that we could use it to pump into a water pressure tank and pipe some running water into the farm house. There was a small "milk" room in the NW corner of the house.Here we concreted the shallow cellar to form a cistern to receive the rain water. Then we mounted the pump with suction from the cistern and discharge into a pressure tank. From Sears we got a water heating plate that fit into the firebox of the wood cook stove. A nearby storage tank for hot water was placed in the kitchen, a wash basin was installed with necessary galvanized piping and lo we had running water. After I began teaching school in Sister Bay I bought a bath tub. Marvin and I converted a closet under the stairway into space to receive the tub. Unfortunately the space was so limited that we had to have a tub of less than normal length. As my brother and I were each six feet tall we had to be somewhat of a contortionist to get in and out. Besides the stairway above the tub gave very limited overhead room. Still, it was luxurious to be able to soak in nice, hot water. In order to make a complete bathroom, we sacrificed space from what had originally been a "front hall", which had never been used for anything but storage. We dug a hole under this area to receive a sort of septic tank and installed a special toilet which accompanied the septic tank. Drain piping was run outside into a "dry well". No longer did we have to make visits to the outside "Chick Sale" where the icy winds blew up through the hole.Luxurious conveniences had arrived on the farm. Of course, we still had to hand pump the water into the supply tank.

While I was still in grade school,my brother got the job of being janitor at the Detroit Harbor School, which was right across the road from our farm. On cold winter mornings he would usually go to the school before beginning the milking chores. The fire, which had been "banked" the night before, was stirred up and fresh, soft coal was added to begin warming the classrooms. "Banking" the fire was done by heaping fresh coal on the glowing embers and then covering this with ashes while all the draft dampers were then closed. A second trip after early morning chores assured that the rooms would be warm when the teachers and pupils arrived. Sweeping and scrubbing floors, tending the toilets and making minor repairs were also the janitor's responsibility. For this he received $25 per month. I was enlisted to sweep floors daily at a stipend of 25 cents a week. I continued doing this until I graduated from high school. In those days it was common to use “sweeping compound” to keep the dust down. This mixture of sawdust, sand,light oil and red or green coloring was spread at the back of each aisle. Then I swept forward around all the seats and desks finishing at the front of the room where the dirt and compound was gathered in a dust pan to be thrown into the furnace. With the oil in the compound it burned merrily.

About once a month we scrubbed the hard maple floors.Also,on regular occasions we "burned out" the toilets. Remember, this school and many like it were built during WW I. In each toilet there were three stools enclosed in "modesty panels". The cast iron toilets with hardwood seats were bolted to large, steel diamond plates. Under the toilets were steel T bars which supported a decking of red bricks. Under each toilet hole was placed an "Indian style" stack of dry,hard maple wood. In the girl's toilet both urine and feces fell onto this pile of wood. In the boy's toilet there was an open urine trough cast in the concrete floor. Often during lunch hour some of us would heat a furnace poker red hot,take it into the boy's room and urinate on it. This would quickly empty the room.

Under the toilets was a large,concrete lined air duct which led to the chimney to vent off odors and smoke when we "burned" the toilets.Today at the old Sunnypoint school on Highway 42 you can still see the oversized chimney that accommodated both the furnace flue and the venting from the toilet system. When the time arrived to do the "burning out" we first poured a considerable amount of kerosene down each hole and then ignited this. It took several hours to complete the burning. Afterwards we had to individually lift each steel plate and toilet, then descend into the space to scoop up what remained and dispose of it. Another "Indian style" pile of wood was placed under each hole, the plates were lowered and the toilets were again ready for use.

Later this system was abandoned and large,tarred steel tanks with large holes extending up to the floor line were installed. These had special toilets placed above each hole with a small vent pipe leading to the outside. They had no flushing handles,but on regular occasions the janitor poured buckets of water down each hole. Bacteria worked in the tanks and the overflow was piped to a "dry well". As the ground around the school was either clay or "hardpan" it did not absorb much moisture. The"dry well" had walls of flat,open stone with a concrete capping laid over the top. This technological advance was greeted by both of us as we no longer had to do that messy job of "burning out" toilets.

At an early age I learned to "pull teats" as we called milking cows.The first job was to thoroughly wash the cow's udders and teats. Then we sat on the right side of the cow's udder on a three-legged stool, secured the milk pail between our thighs, just above the knees and began squeezing the teats.The proper action was to close tightly with thumb and fore finger around the upper part and then progressively tighten the fingers on down to the little one. When that part of the udder was nearly empty we would use just the thumb and forefinger held closely together to "strip" the last milk from those two quarters of the udder.

Some cows were what we called “kickers” and occasionally the pail of milk would land in the ditch and we might be tumbled off the stool onto the barn floor. We had a remedy for that. Sears sold "leg hobbles".These were made of two pieces of galvanized steel in a shape that would hook around the cows "hocks".There was a chain linking the two parts and we could tighten that to where the "kickers" hind legs were brought right together.

Normally we would have both adult cats and kittens in the barn to use as “mousers”. We had a small trough that we placed fresh, warm milk in to feed both the cats and our dog. They would often stand side-by-side lapping out of the same vessel. Many cats learned to sit near us and beg for milk. We youngsters loved to squirt milk in their faces.They would open their mouths to receive it,but usually most of it landed on their faces. Then,using a paw,they would wipe off the milk and lick it from their paws.

When new calves were born, we never let them nurse from the mother. However,we saved that first milk to feed them later. It had special nourishment to start the calf off right including a laxative to get the bowels moving. Teaching a calf to drink from a pail was often my job. With warm milk in the bucket, I would dip my finger into the milk then insert it into the calf's mouth. The animal would immediately begin urgent sucking. With the free hand I would force the calf's head down to where it could get milk from around my fingers. After a few such lessons the youngster would take over on its own without the aid of my finger.

Unfortunately,when the weather had warmed to where we could place the calves in a small pasture with a sheltering shed for night time, they would occasionally refuse to drink from the pail. Then the teaching process had to be repeated.I encountered one very stubborn calf while I was in high school.So I collared it, straddled its neck to force the head down into the pail.This one decided it wanted no part of that procedure, so it took off on a run. This placed me at an extreme disadvantage as the creature was tall enough that my legs were in the air most of the time. Gradually I slipped back onto its rump and then fell to the ground and dislocated my spine. As I entered the house walking like an 80 year old man, Ma said, "What's the matter with you?" I told her what had happened and she said I had to immediately get to Dr. Farmer, O.D. There I was greeted by Farmer's usual "Heh-heh" laugh and told to get on the table. For a dollar he put my spine back into alignment. Dr. Farmer served the Island for many years and was a great "bone cracker".Later,while going to college

I got a "cold" in my back and was thankful when Christmas vacation arrived and I could once more attain relief through his ministrations.

Pastimes on the Island were simple and few. A young lad could catch girls, but upon catching one it was only to yell, "Tag! You're,it!" Or, he could give smoking a try.

The means by which we could get cigarettes at an early age were very limited. Even though a package of "Wings" only cost ten cents we had to turn to some of nature's products.

Dried corn silk, while very mild, was considered "smart" when rolled in a small piece of last week's Door County Advocate. My first attempt was not successful. Later I learned from veteran "corn silkers" that I had failed to create enough saliva to seal the quarter page of.the newspaper. Also, an. eighth-pager would not have caused the,flare-up that sent my cousin (a fellow smoker) scurrying.

Not until the next'day did my taste-buds resume their proper function and my voice return to its normal soprano pitch. The burn spots on my overalls were explained by the fact that it was fall and I had been burning leaves.

A simpler and more successful venture was to gather the seeds of burdock weed. These we called "Indian tobacco" and smoked them in whatever type of pipe we could fashion. Late in the summer we would search under the oaks for large acorns. Carefully the "lid" was loosened and pried off to be saved for the eventual pipe cover. Then we carefully removed the "meat" from inside'the acorn. Usually the pipe stem was fashioned from a piece of rye straw, although sometimes we found stiffer, more satisfactory weed stems in the barnyard.

After tamping the "Indian tobacco" firmly into the acorn pipe, we lighted it and immediately placed the acorn cover on it so the "tobacco" would not burn too rapidly. Without the advantage of the pipe lid, one often got blisters in one's mouth from the hot gasses.

Of course, my cousin and I always hoped that someday we could get a real pipe and some real tobacco. One year, after the threshing crew had finished with the grain and left the farm, to my amazement and delight I discovered one of the workers had left a corncob pipe and some Prince Albert tobacco in a can. We couldn't wait to try this out.

Of course, to do this authentically, we had to have, some of the old sulphur, strike-anywhere matches. I gathered a supply of these from the dispenser on the wall in our kitchen right next to the old wood cook stove. Off we went to the "back forty" woods to feast on the marvelous find. Strangely we soon found that Prince Albert was not anything like the milder corn silk or "Indian tobacco." What a bite it had! Soon my tongue felt like it was afire and the rest of my respiratory system was badly in need of a soothing treatment of Mentholatum salve. How we managed to avoid throwing up I don't know, but perhaps it was because it had been hours since we'd had our last meal. At one fell swoop my cousin and I lost all interest in smoking.

Over the years I wonder how many thousands of dollars I have saved by never buying cigarettes. Each time I pass a cigarette counter and see a price of nearly fifteen dollars a carton, I am thankful I learned my lesson at an early age. What a pity that so many young people are smoking today and think it is smart. The smart ones were those who never started or learned to quit at an early age.

Dr. Koop, retired U.S. Surgeon General, often started his speeches by saying, "Ten thousand Americans quit smoking today. Their funerals will be held in the next couple days."

The old kitchen stove that I first remember at the farm had solid sheet metal on the outside extending all the way to the floor. On occasion one of us children was given the task of applying black stove polish to make it shine. We were thankful when a new kitchen range with a baked porcelain finish was purchased. This one rested on four legs and is still in use in the old farm house where I grew up.

Our cats and dog liked the new stove much better, for on cold days they could crawl under there to sleep.

The old stove was sold to Thora Paulsen and was moved to her small cottage on the corner of West Harbor and Old West Harbor Roads, just across from Gibson's Resort.

A nice feature on the new stove was a built-in thermometer in the oven door. When using the old stove, Ma judged the temperature of the oven either by feeling into it with her hand or by determining how hot the fire was.

I cannot recall a morning breakfast that did not include oatmeal. The old-fashioned kind was purchased in large gunny sacks that were stored in a small room on the second floor.

Before going to bed Ma always prepared the oatmeal in the doubleboiler, which then sat on the kitchen stove all night. In the morning, as soon as the fire was lighted, the double-boiler was moved to the hot part of the stove so the meal could be heated and would finish cooking while we milked the cows. Rich, creamy milk was liberally applied to the dish of oatmeal after sprinkling it with white or brown sugar.

Besides the oatmeal, we usually. had toast from homemade bread on which we placed our homemade butter. If lucky, we might have jam or jelly to spread on the toast. Since we were all milk drinkers we did not have coffee with breakfast. Coffee was normally reserved for when company came.

The noon day meal was the main one of the day. Following that meal I would lie down on the hardwood floor in the living room and nap for about fifteen minutes before returning to work. I have followed that practice quite consistently over the years and still find that it really refreshes me.

The evening meal was a light one. Sometimes it included smoked fish, if our cousins had given us lawyers or possibly a trout to smoke.

In those days most Islanders looked down on lawyers and did not realize what a delicacy they are. Of course, all of the fish's oil is stored in its liver and the flesh is dry when smoked. At first, after skinning them, we would coat them with lard to make the smoked flesh juicier. Then my brother and I got the bright idea of just leaving the fat-rich liver hanging in the carcass. This allowed just enough of the oil to be rendered into the flesh to do a great job.

One evening two of the Malloch girls, who lived where Myrtle Boese did, had come to the farm for dairy products. They spied a plate of smoked fish resting on the kitchen table in preparation for our evening meal. Both fell to eating this with gusto and were admiring its flavor. Finally one asked what kind of fish it was. When told it was a lawyer they quit eating and looked with disdain at the remaining portions.

Ma, like my sister Sylvia, was a wonderful bread baker. However, we could never understand why she would not let us cut a slice of bread off the hot loaf that had just emerged from the oven and smelled so great! We always had pumpernickel bread made from rye meal, not rye flour. We raised our own rye and had it ground at Peter Jensen's grist mill where Kirby Foss now lives. I am sure Peter did not look forward to this task since he had to completely clean the mill of any traces of the former grindings which were normally a mixture of grains for cattle feed.

Like other sourdoughs, Ma kept a small amount from each batch as a starter for the next time. This was placed in an old china cup with a broken handle. It was liberally covered with salt and left in the warming oven of the kitchen range to be used as yeast for the following batch.

Often she would be removing the baked loaves from the oven just as our neighbor, Frank Richter, arrived to buy dairy products. I remember one of his comments to Ma. "Gertie, you know that storebought bread tastes just like eating fog."

On rare occasions Ma made cinnamon rolls or raised doughnuts, which we greatly appreciated. She was not inclined to make too many cakes, however. As Sylvia grew older she became the cake maker in the family.

The year she finished high school she prepared to go to Door-Kewaunee Normal School in Algoma to launch a teaching career. She got me aside and said, "If you want cake from now on, you are going to have to learn how to bake them yourself."

Well, I was all ear's, since I loved cake. Of course, in those days, there was no such thing as buying a package cake mix at the store. So, we started from scratch with the recipe and all the ingredients. I dutifully followed her instructions to the letter and then placed the cake in the oven. While it was baking I licked the dough pan clean as this always tasted mighty good to me.

Finally, after sticking a toothpick into the center of the cake and having it come out clean, Sis declared the cake was done. Peering into the oven I thought it was the most beautiful Devil's food cake I had ever seen.

I guess Sis didn't trust me to remove the cake from the oven, because while using a pair of cloth pads, she grasped the pan and out it came. To the dismay of both of *us,* somehow the cake slipped from her hands and landed upside down on the kitchen floor. Well I knew I could now bake a good cake but it was little consolation that night when my mouth had been all prepared for chocolate cake.

Another dish that Ma made almost daily was boiled rice in the double-boiler. Dad had grown accustomed to this in Denmark and really.looked forward to it at least once a day.

Hans Hansen, who owned the farm where the potato operation was later headquartered, remarked one day to Dad, "Martin, didn't you get enough of that grout in the old country?" But Dad had not.

The rice was served in a shallow bowl with cinnamon and sugar spread over the top. Sometimes lumps of butter were added and then rich milk was poured over it.

We looked forward to the rice pudding Ma made from leftover rice-- especially when she added raisins. She never cooked rice in water but always used milk as the liquid. That made it much richer. Frequently our meals were topped off with homemade fruit sauce that came from either tame or wild fruits.

After a long work day on the farm we were so tired that we never noticed the uneven, lumpy mattresses when we crawled into bed for a night's sleep. There was no such thing as the luxury of a "box spring" with an inner spring mattress above it. Instead the early beds on our farm, and most others, had a very different type of spring.

A checkerboard network of thin steel straps extended from side to side and top to bottom of the bed with short coil springs attached to these straps on one end and secured to the hardwood frame on the other end. Later some beds had lighter gauge coil springs extending from one side to the other. There was little springiness in this framework.

The mattress consisted of a large casing of "bed ticking" - a heavy coarse cotton material with blue striping. On some beds this mattress was stuffed with corn husks. Naturally every time I moved in bed the corn husks made a distinct rustling noise.

It was a real treat in the summer, after haying was finished, to get the opportunity to go with Dad on the hay wagon down Lobdell's Point Road to about where the north end of Green Bay Road now joins the Point Road. There we turned off to the east to go into the land owned by brother Chris where we would cut fine swamp grass.

Dad cut it with a scythe in the open area west of Arni's bayou. We children then raked it and it was placed on the hay wagon to be taken home, spread in a field to dry and finally stuffed into the mattress ticking. This made a bed that was a good deal softer than the corn husks and it was quiet when I moved about at night.

On top of the mattress, double, flannel, cotton sheets formed the part that we nestled down into. Our early quilts were of cotton batting covered with percale and did not provide much insulation from the cold on wintery nights. When our pet sheep began to provide enough wool from his shearing to make a woolen quilt, we then encountered a good, light weight insulation on top of us.

Of course with just enough wool coming from that sheep each year to make one quilt batt, it was years before I, as the youngest member of the family, could finally crawl under a woolen comforter at night. In fact, this did not happen until several of the older family members were no longer residing at home.

Still, with no heat in the upper rooms of the farm house, a person never tarried in undressing at night, but leapt into bed, pulled the covers overhead and let one's breath take the chill off the cold flannel sheets.

We did not have any single beds in our house, but many were what was called "three-quarter" beds. They were in between single and double beds in width. Two adults sleeping in this, size bed had to do it in a very cozy manner.

Sometimes, when there were extra relations staying with us someone had to sleep at the foot of the bed. As the youngest and smallest, usually I was selected to occupy that position. It meant sleeping crosswise at the foot and on very cold nights just letting -my nose project from under covers. If one of My bed partners had not bathed their feet recently, there was no way I was going to put my head under the covers.

Occasionally I would get to fill the hot water bottle with hot water and place that at my feet when retiring. Still, while this was luxurious to begin with, touching it in the early hours of the morning when it was icy cold caused a rude awakening.

Some people heated bricks wrapped them in cloths and warmed the foot of the bed in this manner. Unfortunately we had no spare bricks around our farm so I never was able to learn how satisfactory this method was. Even though we always placed storm windows throughout the house before winter, still at night our breath moisture would condense on the cold window panes.

Often in the morning we were amazed by the ornate patterns in the windows, which we accredited to "Jack Frost."

I had hoped to find a copy of the poem "Sleeping at the Foot of the Bed," but have not found it. If I run across it later I will publish it for you.

Modern conveniences have completely altered children's way of life and removed from their daily routine a number of chores. They never have to do the things I did as a farm boy on a regular basis, such as: Pitching hay and manure. Daily cleaning barns and occasionally also cleaning the chicken coop and pig pen. Mending fences. Milking cows by hand. Assisting in difficult calf births. Currying horses. Cutting fresh hay with a scythe to feed horses. Smoking hams and sausage after curing them. Slopping pigs and feeding chickens. Hunting eggs in the barnyard. Butchering, scalding and then picking feathers from chickens as well as cleaning out the insides. Daily filling the wood box. Shaking down ashes in the stoves and then carrying them out to spread in the garden. Trimming wicks on kerosene lights and lanterns. Replacing mantles on Coleman gas lights, then filling with fuel and pumping up the tank before lighting. Setting a broody hen to raise chickens. Playing "Andy Over" on the granary roof. Playing tag and "One-o-Cat" and "Two-o-Cat" ball at school. Following a team of horses behind a plow or other farm implements.

Inconveniences they will miss which I accepted in simpler days include: Walking on muddy roads. Sitting in a two-holer in subzero weather. Shelling corn for chickens by hand. Taking a weekly bath on Saturday night using a wash basin on the kitchen stove. Wearing hand-knitted woolen stockings over long underwear. Wearing hand-knitted woolen mittens inside leather ones when doing outside chores. Sleeping on a mattress stuffed with corn husks in a bedroom with no heat in winter with thick layers of frost festooning the window panes. Finding the cow's water tank dry and no breeze to turn the windmill. Cranking the Model T Ford. Sleeping on the floor in front of the open door in summer when the upstairs bedroom heat is unbearable. Daily driving the cows to pasture in the morning and home in the evening in summer.

They will never know the simple joys of: Going to a Chautauqua tent show in Charley Jensen's field, about where the

Community Center now is, and spending a whole twobits for a highly touted jacknife. (It never did hold a sharp edge.) Smoking corn silk and chewing wintergreens. Listening to singers like Vernon Dalhart on the wind-up phonograph. Dipping the braids of the girl in front of you at school in the inkwell.

They will not hear: The sound of an old well pump handle moving up and down. The striking of an old eight-day clock. The whistle of the threshing machine or the sound of a reaper. The bell in the belfry at school calling everyone in, for class time. The early morning sound of roosters crowing. The bells on cows coming home from pasture. The satisfied grunts of pigs devouring slop.

They will never enjoy the treasured memories of: Evening gatherings at the kitchen table to play simple games or cards under a kerosene light. Giving the Christmas program at school on a stage with a variety of sheets and blankets for curtains. Venturing forth into the woods to cut and drag home the Christmas tree .Popping corn on the kitchen wood-fired stove, then stringing it to decorate the Christmas tree. Saving lead tinsel from year to year to ornament the tree. The joys of summer evenings outside with family and neighbors gathered there. The delight in receiving a nickel for doing someone a favor. Making homemade toys and creating games to play with friends before TV, VCR, Nintendo, computers and ready-made entertainment. And, never, ever being bored.

Christmas to me as a young lad holds simple memories. Of course the school program was well attended by the parents and the big event was when Santa arrived and dispensed boxes of candy and nuts to all the students.The teachers provided candy and nuts which they had purchased either from a local store or by mail order from Sears. We then had three grocery stores on the Island. Mann's, Ted's (now Vagabond) and Gislason's (across from Gislason's Beach). All three stores took orders by crank telephone and delivered right to the kitchen.

At that time we had lots of young balsam and balsam fir trees growing along Old West Harbor Road. When Dad was alive, prior to 1928, he would take us with him to select the tree and we would help to bring it home. Tree ornaments were very simple. We got out the box of decorations and first carefully separated and hung the "tinfoil" which was very thin strips of shiny metal about 2 feet long and cut into pieces less than 1/4 inch wide. These were hung throughout the tree to resemble ice cycles. Tinsel was draped from bough to bough as was threaded popcorn. The corn had been placed in a wire screen popper with a tin-coated lid on top. With a hearty fire blazing in the kitchen cook stove the popper was constantly shaken back and forth until all the good kernels had popped. With a needle and fine thread the popcorn was strung into long lengths. We had a few wooden, painted ornaments to put in place. Lastly the candle holders were very carefully clipped near the ends of the branches. They had large,alligator-type clips on the bottom with an expandable candle holder and wax drip pan on top. Candles were about 3/8" diameter and about 4 or 5 inches long. For fire safety reasons the candles were always placed so they could not accidentally start something above them on fire. Also they were never allowed to burn without an older person present in the room.

Even though Dad was always the hard,outdoor worker, before Christmas he would take over in the kitchen and make and bake a large batch of "Pfeffernusse" (A German Christmas cookie meaning 'pepper nuts'). The recipe called for six different spices and they were mighty tasty. Dad also made the Christmas coffee cakes.It was traditional to "kill the old, red rooster" which Dad stuffed with prunes and Mom baked it in the oven. This was the meat dish for Christmas Day.

In the early days gifts were non-existent, later usually the gifts were in the form of needed clothing. My sister's dolls were from cloth prints of the doll's front and back which Mom stitched together,then stuffed with cotton batting. Inside the bottom was a stiff piece of cardboard, thus the doll could be stood up. In May, 1927 Lindbergh made his solo flight across the Atlantic and we followed this closely. I think it was the next Christmas that I received a tin toy model of his "Spirit of St. Louis". When it was rolled across the floor its noisemaker sounded somewhat like an airplane engine. Another Christmas I received Lindbergh's book "WE" telling of his preparation and flight. A gift I wore and cherished for many years was an aviator's type, leather helmet. It was lined with sheepskin and had flaps that could be snapped under the chin in cold weather or worn pointing upward in warmer weather. On the front was a leather visor which could be turned downward when "bucking" into a snowstorm. That fine gift was worn for many years.

Laundry day in the 1920s was traditionally on Monday. Early in the morning the copper wash boiler, which held nearly 10 gallons of water, was placed on the wood-fired kitchen stove. When well heated, this water, plus warm water from the stove reservoir, was used for laundering clothes. A stand that held two wash tubs was set in place in the small attached shed on the rear of the farm house. As this shed was not heated, in winter the work was done in the farm kitchen. A hand operated clothes wringer was mounted on the stand in between the wash tubs. (One of these stands can be seen at the Farm Museum.)

Corrugated metal washboards were leaned into the tub. They had a recess at the top to hold the bar of laundry soap which was either white P & G soap or yellow Fels Naptha. As hot water was at a premium, usually the cleaner clothes were washed first, then the dirtier, farm togs came last. Several pieces would be placed in the tub to soak, then an item was selected and placed on the washboard where the bar of soap was run up and down it. Then the rubbing all sides of the garment vigorously up and down the corrugated part of the board began. After an inspection to make sure it was clean, it was cranked through the wringer to remove the soapy water and it dropped into the other wash tub which contained clear rinse water. After all the clothes were in the rinse tub some bluing was added to make these appear whiter. This was before the days of Chlorox. Sometimes very dirty or greasy clothes had to be additionally cleaned using a stiff scrub brush. We nicknamed this the "Armstrong" method of doing laundry.

Early washing machines had a hand crank, gears and an agitator that was fastened through the lid. Most of it was made of wood and the agitator resembled a small, four-legged milk stool.

Our first Sears machine was powered by a one-cylinder, air-cooled gasoline engine. This was started by rapidly stepping down on a pedal. Levers controlled the engaging of the agitator or the wringer which was mounted on top. A flexible, metal exhaust pipe ran through the floor to the outdoors. As this was quite noisy, my brother and I later buried a 30 gallon steel drum in the ground to serve as a muffler.

Bar soap, shaved into small pieces, was placed in the wash water. Still, because of the limited supply of hot water, cleaner things were washed first and the same water was then used for dirtier items. Early gasoline powered washers that I remember include Sears, Maytag and Haig that had a copper tub.

Sometimes the rinsing was done in a separate washtub, but often the wrungout , soapy clothes were set aside and when all the washing was finished, the machine was filled with clear, rinse water and the clothes were given a short rinse cycle before they went through the wringer again.

Summer and winter the clothes were hung on an outside line to dry. In summer the weather was watched closely and before a rain storm began, the partially dried items were gathered in a basket and taken indoors to be rehung after the storm passed. In winter working outside was a miserable job. Ma used a pair of woolen gloves that left the finger tips exposed. With complete gloves, it would have been very awkward to pin clothes on the line. Of course, in cold winter time everything quickly froze shortly after hanging, but with the help of wind and sunshine it was amazing that a lot of the garments dried. Still, eventually some things like overalls had to be taken indoors and draped about to complete the drying.

A far cry from the luxuries of automatic washers and dryers which are enjoyed today.

Kerosene lights were the first I remember as being used for night illumination. 55 gallon drums of kerosene came to the Island on freighters. The local general stores transferred it to cans which they delivered to homes along with groceries. We had a gallon can with a very small spout to pour the fluid directly into glass lamp reservoir. In fact the whole lamp, other than the wick mechanism was made of clear glass. We did have one fancy parlor lamp of milk glass with flower patterns on it. The wick extended from the bottom of the kerosene to the top of the burner. At regular intervals this had to be trimmed to just the right contour so the flame would burn with little or no smoke. Still, quite often the thin glass chimneys had to have the soot washed out so the lamp would furnish good light.

The hanging light over the kitchen was the fanciest in the house. It was suspended from a hook in the ceiling and could be adjusted up or down as needed. The light had a large milk glass shade with a brass, crown-type ring on the top. Two small chains that supported the lamp were fastened to wheels in the upper mechanism. These wheels had counter springs which allowed the lamp to remain at any given level.

Dietz metal lanterns with glass chimneys were used in the barn and other places away from the house. However, we always tried to get our chores done before night came. If we needed to go to the barn at night we always immediately hung the lantern on a nail so there would be no chance of it being tipped over and accidentally starting a fire.

The Coleman white-gasoline lamps ware a great improvement over the kerosene ones. We only had one, therefore, the older lamps were still used to a large degree. The pressurized base of the Colemans was nade of plated metal. The gas was poured into this part, the cap was tightly sealed and an external pump was used to pressurize this part. The active part had two silk mantles with a generator between them. To light the lamp, first two ignited,large strike-anywhere matches were placed by the generator to preheat it. Soon the gas valve was cracked open and gas vapors reached the mantles where it ignited. At first the generator wasn't hot enough to fully vaporize the gas, so flames would flare up, but soon this was corrected and then the fuel valve could be opened fully and the lamp was put in its proper place, usually on a hook in the ceiling of the room, where it would be used. An open, large milk glass shade surrounded the mantle area and a long wire hanger extended above this to provide a safe distance between the lamp and the ceiling so the heat would not cause any damage above.

The mantles occasionally had to be replaced as they *were* fragile. Actually they were the ash of the silk mantles. To do this job, first the old remains were removed. Then a new cloth mantle was draped and firmly tied to the mantle base. The cloth was carefully burned using a large natch. Then the 1amp was lighted and the flame forced the mantle into a full expanded state which then lasted as long as the mantle did.

Some homes installed central Coleman lighting systems with one large, pressurized tank and small copper piping leading to each lamp. Usually the lamps were mounted in the ceilings. To light these lamps the same technique was used as for the individual ones previously discussed.

Our first radio was a gift from cousin, Leslie Cornell, a commercial fisherman. He had bought a more modern radio, so he gave us his old Atwater-Kent. The main part was in a wooden enclosure about 30" long, 10" high and 12" deep. To power this unit required three batteries; a 6 volt auto type, a "B" type and a small "C" type to furnish power to the various parts. (By this time, Thordarson had invented transformers and Leslie's new radio only needed a single battery to operate. A Chicago mail-order company named Allied Radio was soon selling Thordarson's and many other manufacturer's radio parts.) To tune in a station a person had to carefully adjust each of the three black dials on the front to exactly the station's frequency. There were individual condensers behind each dial. A long, double wire antenna was strung outside in a SE to NW direction to get the best reception. Still the programs would fade and we would hastily adjust the dials to try to recover the sound. A separate round speaker stood on top of the radio. It was about 12" diameter and was made of stamped metal with gold colored cloth over the front.

When John Esperson came back and began selling Zenith radios we soon upgraded to one of those. This was a console model with a single dial and it was powered by a single 6 volt auto-type battery. Along with it we got a "Wincharger" generator to mount on the peak of the house roof with wires running down to the battery. This charger could be activated whenever the wind blew. No longer did we have to worry about removing the battery to charge it. However,if the battery's specific gravity was not carefully watched, the charger could overcharge, which would shorten the battery's life considerably. Therefore, we changed to an Edison battery which could not be damaged by overcharging. Instead of an acid electrolyte as in auto cells, this battery used a sal ammoniac solution. The positive plates were of flaked nickel covered with perforated metal, while the negative ones were iron oxide and also metal shielded. Each cell produced 1.2 volts rather than 2 volts, so there were 5 cells. It was claimed that the only way an Edison battery could be destroyed was to take a sledge hammer to it. They were widely used by the Coast Guard and Lighthouse Service.

With this new radio a whole world opened up to us. Besides now getting news as things happened we could enjoy WLS (Sears-World's Largest Station), WGN(Tribune's World's Greatest News) WMAQ and even WMAM from Marinette & Menominee. WLS presented an excellent weekly cowboy country type show. Early performers included Gene Autry, Roy Rogers, Dale Evans, Lulubell and 'Skyland' Scotty, Andy Divine and many others. Of course the humorous Amos and Andy show with Kingfish and attorney J. Algonquin Calhoun was seldom missed. Sunday afternoon we listened to "Who knows what evil lurks in the hearts of men, The Shadow knows" which was followed by a sinister laugh and a chilling story. The Green Hornet's programs were of a similar theme. Wayne King, The Waltz King, was always one of my favorites and Guy Lombardo's "Auld Lang Syne" was ushering in the New Years even then.

The Hit Parade, featuring singer Snooky Lamson, kept us up-to-date on the ten top tunes in the country.

Fibber McGee and Molly from "Wistful Vista" and their associated characters could not be missed, nor could Jack Benny with Mary Livingston and Rochester and Dennis Day. George Burns and Gracie Allen added to our amusement. Many excellent comedies and tragedies were presented regularly. What a blessing the radio was!

It was an exciting day on the Island when the red-stacked Goodrich boat would arrive at Johnny Young's dock in Washington Harbor. Usually it was the steamship "Carolina," but sometimes the "Georgia" or the "Christopher Columbus" would appear.

The Columbus was a whaleback steamer. Not too many of these types were built. The only one I know that remains on the lakes is a museum-piece ore-carrier in Superior, Wisconsin. Since the sides were rounded with no distinct gunwale, the inventor thought they would perform better in rough seas.

The Goodrich line began operating combination passenger and freight service on Lake Michigan in the 1800s. Some of their early steamers were propelled by paddlewheels on either side. Throughout the summer season they maintained a regularly scheduled service. They traveled from Chicago to Mackinac Island with stops at all Door County ports on the Green Bay side from Sturgeon Bay northward.

As they passed the west side of the Island, the deep-throated whistle was sounded to announce the imminent arrival at Washington Harbor. This gave Islanders who were expecting friends or freight a chance to get to the dock about the time of the vessel's docking. Much freight was brought to the Island that way. I recall seeing old Sears Roebuck furniture with shipping instructions via the "Goodrich line" written on the bottom.

I believe our Island library still has an interesting book about the Goodrich Line. I think it's entitled "Red Stacks Over the Horizon."

My half-sister, Mary, who was born in Denmark, had married Arthur Johnson, a one-time Island teacher. Arthur had become paymaster at Marshal Field's store in Chicago. In those days all employees were paid in cash. It was his job to count and hand out each employee's wages. I learned from him that money can be very dirty. On paydays he wore black gauntlets over his shirtsleeves to keep them clean. Still, his hands would be filthy by the time the pay period ended.

The Johnsons lived on Harding Street in northwest Chicago. It was a flat owned by the church that was on the same block.

Half-brother, Carl, was custodian in that church. Until about 1930, when Carl bought a new Chrysler 66 sedan, the family always came to the Island for vacation via the Goodrich boat. If I was very lucky, I got to ride all the way to Washington Harbor to greet the relatives and to see the "wonderful" steamship!

Once, I was denied permission because Dad did not think there would be enough seating room in the fringed surrey on the return trip. However, I outfoxed him by hiding behind the back seat. This led to some disciplining afterward though. In fact, if I remember correctly, I think my brother-in-law, Art, suggested "stick him in a cow flop." When he turned from being an office man to a "gentleman farmer" for two weeks, this was his favorite disciplinary suggestion. But it was never carried out.

Once however, Art and Mary's daughter, Goldie, brother Anton's children, Emma and Edward, were exploring the farm together. I wanted to show them something in the granary.

We all mounted the narrow, raised "stoop" or deck at the doorway, unlatched the door and stepped back as the door opened outward. This caused the furthest child to lose his footing. As he began to fall off the stoop, he grabbed the person in front of him. That led to a chain-reaction, with all of us tumbling to the ground. To our misfortune, a huge, recently deposited "cow doily" was right at that landing location.

When our parents discovered our plight, they barred us from the house until we had stripped off the old clothes and washed and donned clean garments.

Not only did half-sister, Mary, and family arrive on the Goodrich steamer, but also occasionally my half-brother, Anton, would come with his family from Africa. He was a missionary in the Belgian Congo and was a graduate of Moody Bible Institute.

Early in his life he had fallen in love with Viola Prinzing, whose parents from Palatine, IL were very religious. Their first pilgrimage to the Congo was to an area where missionaries had previously been. However, Anton's second "tour of duty" was into the wilds where Christianity was unknown.

As a very young lad, I was utterly fascinated by the tales he told about hunting and experiences with the natives. He killed all sorts of big game with his standard issue Winchester .405 caliber rifle. The rifle had a recoil about the same as firing both barrels of a 12 gauge shotgun at the same time.

On one occasion he had killed a deer for family meat and hung it just outside the hut where they lived. After sunset he could hear something chewing on the carcass. Thinking it was the family dog, he ordered it to come back into the house, only to find the dog already cowering under the bed. Next morning he saw leopard pug marks on the partly eaten remains. So, he left it hanging and before sunset he determined about where to aim from the hut's opening to strike the cat if it returned.

Shortly after darkness settled, the leopard was back. So Anton carefully aimed and fired. This was followed by a fierce scream from the cat. It would have been foolhardy to venture from the hut in darkness so he waited till morning. At daybreak, having heard the shot the previous evening, the whole village was assembled. They were waiting to learn what had happened. With the aid of a blood trail and native trackers, Anton made his way into the deep jungle. Finally the trail to the cat's lair narrowed down in the thorn bush. There he was forced to travel on hands and knees.

With the thick jungle foliage, his only light was a battery-operated one strapped to his forehead so he could see directly ahead. About the time that his light picked up the leopard's shining eyes, the cat let out a scream. From a prone position, Anton aimed between the eyes and fired, killing the cat.

The natives waiting outside the thornbush figured the cat had gotten Anton when it emitted the scream. They all ran back to the village to inform Viola that she was now a widow.

Anton had to drag the cat out by himself and in the process the thornbush tore most of his clothing off. It thoroughly lacerated his skin as well. His exit from the cat's lair was further complicated by the fact that, in firing from a prone position, the heavy recoil had dislocated his shoulder.

After hearing this story, I always felt that my brother had such a firm Christian belief that he felt the Lord was right by his side on these ventures.

He brought the tanned leopard skin back to the Island. What a wondrous thing for me to see at about age six.

Other "goodies" included an elephant's hoof and the tip of its tail, the hairs of which were stiffer than a coarse whisk broom.

Antelope horns and a huge python snake skin were among other mementos.

Anton often hunted with the natives. White ants (termites) built huge colony shelters that somewhat resembled haystacks and stood as high as 8 to 10 feet. If the natives found an active nest they feasted on the ants, first pinching the heads off with their fingernails. They said the ants tasted somewhat like peanuts.

One day, while looking for ants, they discovered an 18 foot python sleeping in an abandoned nest. Their jabbering awoke the creature that started emerging, whereupon one husky native seized it behind the head. Soon another sank a spear into the snake, killing it. Of course the villagers had a great feast and Anton became the possessor of the hide.

As a missionary in Africa's Belgian Congo, brother Anton in early days used a WW I surplus Harley-Davidson motorcycle to go from village to village to preach the Gospel and tend the sick. As there were no roads, he traveled on elephant trails through the jungle. At least half of his day was spent administering to ill natives. After having gained their friendship and respect he began training some of them to preach and convert others to Christianity. When he first arrived there the government officials told him he had to converse with the natives either in Belgian or their native tongue. So he and Viola quickly learned the native language, thus establishing early rapport.

The natives diet was very meager. It consisted mainly of wild plants, animals, insects, pumpkins and pumpkin leaves which they grew. During the wet season, elephant grass would grow to at least 10 feet tall. During the dry season, when food was scarcer, the natives would organize a huge hunt. After setting fire to vast areas of elephant grass, they would take position on the opposite side to spear animals fleeing the fire. Frequently several spears, or arrows, would land in the same animal and arguments would arise as to who administered the lethal blow. The native rule was that the man who struck closest to the heart was to be awarded the largest, choice piece. However, they wanted the meat to be tender, so they aged it until it was sometimes infested with maggots. Then it became Anton's unsavory job to help apportion the spoils to the eligible hunters. When he killed large animals such as elephants, he would sell meat to the natives for a small pittance to give him enough money to buy ammunition.

As the family became victims of malaria, they kept a generous supply,of quinine with them. Yet, after several years of suffering, it became essential to move to a moderate climate for most of a year before returning to the Congo. So they would either come back to the USA or go to South Africa.

On his second tour of duty the family settled in a village where no missionaries had been. A fierce village chief had complete control over the people until Anton's arrival. He hated my brother, but had great respect for the huge rifle that spoke thunder. The chieftain's house sat on a high hill,surrounded by a fence. On the top of each fence post was the skull of a human he had personally slain. Strangely, the chief was extremely fond of Anton's little daughter and we have pictures of her sitting on his lap. The natives were very prolific, often having about ten living children, plus many who died in early infancy. Those who had not accepted Christianity believed that a new born was possessed by evil spirits and these could be exorcised by plunging the child in the Congo River. Frequently this caused pneumonia with resultant death. While Anton was away on a hunting trip a newborn died as a result of the heathen practice. The village chief decided to show that he, not Anton, still had complete control. He held a mock trial and sentenced the whole family to death. As he was grooming his oldest son to someday take his place, he decided the son would carry out the public execution. As the son honed a huge knife, the family was lined up with short pieces of rope around their necks which the intended executioner could firmly grasp. Some of the converted natives rushed into the jungle and found Anton. Running back to the village he fortunately arrived just as the first person was about to lose their head. At a blast from his rifle over the heads, the crowd parted. Anton marched up to the sitting chief and struck him so hard in the face with the back of his hand that he dislocated a finger. Turning to the condemned family, he removed the ropes from their necks and said, "You are free, follow me" and left the scene with them trailing behind. Thus the incident ended and no executions were tried later.

In 1933 the World's Fair "Century of Progress Exposition" opened in Chicago. My brother Marvin and I avidly read in the newspapers, Popular Science and Popular Mechanics magazines about all the wondrous things that were on display. As a fifteen-year old boy I often wished I could see this marvelous display. As the Exposition closed its doors after a very successful 1933 season.they decided to continue it through the summer of 1934.

In late May, when sister Olivia arrived home from teaching at Newport School near Gills Rock, she announced that she was going to the fair and was taking me along. What a treat, when a slack time in farming occurred, we boarded brother Chris' freighter, Wisconsin, for a 9 hour overnight trip to Green Bay. Then I got my very first train ride on the Chicago and Northwestern RailRoad. Even though the coach cars were quite old and with the windows open we received a generous amount of coal cinders from the steam locomotive, I didn't mind a bit. I was too busy watching all the new sights on.the way.

Arriving in Chicago we made our way to half-sister Mary's flat on the northwest side. Again here was my first opportunity to ride streetcars. In addition to thoroughly covering the fair grounds, we also visited the Shedd Aquarium, Lincoln Park and the Zoo. Fair's Sky Ride, which we couldn't afford, carried people in suspended cars high above to and from the island which had been built out into Lake Michigan.

On Children's Isle there was a house built out of marbles and a huge figure of a boy with a coaster wagon. An Indian in war paint would leap out suddenly and frighten the children. A number of midgets were to be seen in a small-scale village. White Castle hamburgers sold for a nickel apiece. Some Good Humor bars contained "lucky sticks" making the next one free. When a cold breeze came in from the lake.the Wonder Bread Bakery building was a good place to get warm. Bakers, high above, sang,"Yoho, yoho, yoho, we are the bakers of Wonder Bread! "

Huge Sinclair dinosaurs were visible over the fence when on Outer Drive.

Among the many mechanical marvels which I had wanted to see was an exhibition of square gears that worked. I couldn't fathom how this could be accomplished, but upon seeing that the corners were rounded and they were actually meshed together and turning, I had to believe.

Marvin had built a sixteen foot skiff and was anxious to get a used outboard motor to power it. I visited a dealer on Navy Pier and found a 7 1/2 horsepower Elto motor at a price of sixty-five dollars. It looked good and had very good cylinder compression, so I took his name and address to report back to my brother.

Eventually we took the train back to Green Bay and caught a ride on the "Wisconsin" back to the Island.

Marvin took my word on the outboard motor, sent a money order to the dealer and shortly he received the motor. Years before, Ole Evinrude had sold his original company and had agreed not to go back in business with the same design. So he developed the Elto with a different ignition system using a "hot shot" 6 volt dry battery. On our first trip across Detroit Harbor it ran beautifully, then it quit and could not be restarted. So we rowed back to Pete Christianson's where we kept the boat. Pete immediately set the motor up clamped into a barrel of water and started testing. He found a broken ignition wire which he repaired and for many years thereafter the motor performed unfailingly.

For many reasons, it was a great day on the farm when the new "Wish Books" arrived. Sears Roebuck, which we nicknamed "Rears & Sawbuck" and "Monkey Ward" were welcome additions in the spring and fall. First it was wonderful to pore through the pages and dream about what we would like to have. The gamut ranged through clothing, household and kitchen appliances, kitchenware, farm implements and tools, wagons & buggies (later autos), food items and the wonderful pages of toys. Our table model, wind-up phonograph came from Sears along with our first record "The Prisoner's Song" sung by Vernon Dalhart. Later we acquired "I'm Looking Over a Four-leaf

Clover" and my sister, Sylvia, taught me to dance to that recording.

We boys gazed with wonder at the pictures of women in whalebone corsets and other undies. Of course, all my shoes, socks, overalls, shirts, “union suits" (long winter underwear), BVDs (which we called "Buttons Vay Down"), caps, mittens and jackets came from the mail order houses. Still I got lots of "hand-me-downs", especially from my cousin, Raymond Richter, who was a few years older. My school graduation suit, of which I was very proud, was a made-to-measure one from Sears. My brother took all my measurements which were carefully entered on the order blank and in a few weeks I was the possessor of my first suit.

Another reason why the new catalogs were so welcome was the use made of the old ones which were now hung on a nail in the outhouse. Before doing so, as a young lad I would cut the pictures of guns out, glue them to a wooden piece from a cigar box, cut around the edges with a coping saw and pretend they were real weapons.

Usually by the time the old catalog made its way to the outhouse, the previous one had been used way down to the shiny sheets. These stiff pages were avoided until nothing else was left. It was therefore a great relief to be able to use thinner, softer ones even though they never approached the luxury of Northern Tissue. While no one thought so at the time, we were probably the first “recyclers”. Thank goodness that the pages were of newsprint and not the heavy, slick-coated paper that is found today in modern catalogs. Is it possible that the "backhouse" spelled the doom to the mail order industry of Sears?

Service from both major mail houses was outstanding during the 20s and 30s. Very often an order which was mailed from the Island on Monday morning would arrive in Thursday's mail, certainly on Friday. In recent years I have mailed orders which have not been filled for nearly a month. While it is sad to see Sears finally abandon their catalog end of the business, I think they could have avoided having to do so if they had followed the practices used during those earlier days.

Losing the Sears "wishbook" is like losing an old friend. It provided education, recreation, inspiration and dreams. Perhaps,,most importantly, the dreams.

From the late 1800s until just before WW II hundreds of thousand homes were bought by mail order from Montgomery Ward, Sears and Roebuck and Aladdin Redi-cut Homes. The complete house kits were shipped to cities and towns in nearly every state.

Sears,alone, sold 100,000 houses in 450 styles. They offered everything from small cottages to two-story four-apartment buildings as well as barns from 1908 through 1940. There are clusters of Sears homes in Lake Geneva and Manitowoc.

The only Sears home on the Island that I know of other than Sis's is the bungalow at the intersection of Detroit Harbor and Rangeline Roads. This house was built for Andrew Cornell's family, recently it has belonged to the Willis Carpenters. In the catalog it was called "The Westley" and was offered from 1913 through 1929 at prices ranging from $926 to $2,543. To a large degree the prices varied according to what features and accessories were desired. The catalog said, "This two-story bungalow is built on a concrete block foundation and is sided with narrow, beveled clear cypress siding. All rooms on both floors are light and airy. Seven rooms and one bath. Shed dormer opening onto balcony; full width front porch supported by brick and wood piers; exposed rafter tails and knee braces; front door with beveled plate glass. Colonnaded openings off hall." In the floor plan the bedrooms are labeled "Chambers". In the early days that term was common and the "convenience receptacle" was called a "Chamber Pot."

The words "Bed Room" were used on the floor plan for Sis and Spencer's home which was offered from 1933 through 1939. This is "The Wilmore" and is described as: A five-room, bungalow-type design, probably the most popular of all American homes. Harmonious gables, batten shutters, circle-head door and attractive grouping of windows show English influence, but the interior is typically modern American. The vestibule opens into a large, pleasant living room.with windows on two sides and good wall space. Five rooms and one bath. Front terrace; batten shutters; arched front door. Arched opening between living and dining rooms. Price: $1459. "The materials included in that price were millwork, cabinetry, lath, roofing materials, flooring, siding, building paper, downspouts, doors, window sash, shutters, hardware (in a variety of patterns), nails, paint and varnish. Not included was the cost of bricks, concrete blocks, cobblestones, plaster or other masonry products, even though these were shown in the designs and listed in the specifications. Optional materials and equipment that could be obtained from Sears at extra charge were screens, storm doors, plaster board and plumbing, heating and electrical fixtures. Sears offered three categories of houses. "Honor Bilt" was the highest quality with the finest materials. The largest knots in the framing of Sis & Spen's were what is usually called "pin knots." "Standard Built" houses had studs and joists spaced further apart and were not as warm as Honor Bilt. The third category was the "Simplex Sectional Cottages." These modest one-story houses were built for summer use, were lightly framed and were not plastered on the interior. The cottages ranged in price from a three room and no bath at $210 to a four room with one lavatory at $690.

After considerable study of the models offered in Sears catalog Sis & Spen ordered their home in June 1937. As soon as this was done Sears system went into action. F.W. Martin became their service representative and confirmed the order instructions, provided a construction manual and enclosed a shipping schedule and origin sheet noting from where the materials were being shipped, along with specific instructions for plastering, electrical work and plumbing and heating. Also enclosed was a paint catalog from which the owner was to select body, trim, shingle stain and sash paint. The Certificate of Guarantee was sent either with this package or separately, stating that the Modern Homes materials would be sufficient in quality and quantity or Sears would pay all shipping costs and refund the purchase price.

The construction manuals, some as long as 75 pages, were written for both the owner and the contractor and included detailed instructions for every phase of construction. The blueprints consisted of elevations, floor plans and a foundation plan drawn to one-fourth-inch scale and framing details drawn to three-eighths-inch scale. On each blueprint was printed a list of materials required for each portion of the design. Letters on the prints corresponded to key letters on the precut lumber, the number of pieces, length of material and purpose. Every piece of framing lumber was precut to size and numbered at the factory for assembly on site. The number of separate parts, not including nails or screws, averaged about 30,000 in a house. Because of precut lumber and detailed instructions, Sears estimated the house could be built in about 583 hours, an impressive 40 percent savings in labor. Sears also offered to provide homes with the floor plan reversed, or even to put together a package to the owner's individual specifications. They said the average house package would fill two railroad box cars.

It was scheduled that the house would be shipped on August 19th from the Norwood Building Material Factory, Norwood, Ohio (a suburb of Cinncinnati). It was shipped via Chicago & Northwestern RR to Green Bay, where brother, Chris Andersen, on the "Wisconsin" brought it to the Island. It was a full boat load. Trucker George Hansen made numerous trips to deliver the materials to the building site. His flat bed Chevy truck was either one and a half, or two ton capacity.

To dig the basement for their house the Nelsons had Raymond Gunnlaugsson with his team dig it using a small metal scoop. (No bull dozers or back hoes were available then.) As this was practically all sand it was easy digging. This digging cost five dollars. Charles Johnson and Roy Cornell were hired to form and pour the full basement and their labor cost $65. 30 barrels of cement to do the whole basement cost $95. They had planned to have an Island carpenter do the construction, but when he puzzled over the blueprints and declared it was "an awful mumble-jumble" they decided they had better get men who could work from blueprints. (At that time most island carpenters were either self-taught or had learned from their father.)

(One old carpenter would get a door jamb perfectly plumb by using a level, then he would stand back and eye it and tap either the top or the bottom over a little before securing it.) The shipment, weighing 45,000 pounds, cost $37 by rail from Norwood to Green Bay. Chris brought it to the Island for $45,.George Hansen charged $35 to haul it to the building site.

Roland Johnson, Spencer's brother-in-law who lived at Gills Rock said he knew two very good Sister Bay carpenters. So they hired Ralph Seaquist and Ralph Larson to construct the house. These men declared this would be "duck soup" as all the framing, even Jack rafters, were precut to exact length and angle and the blueprints showed exactly where they should go. I recall them saying they made a mistake on just one piece.They misread where it should go and recut it so they had to go to Mann's for another piece of lumber.

While the house was being constructed a working party of family and friends was organized to stain the 24" sawn cedar shingles which would serve as siding. Sears had provided enough grey stain to first dip the shingles, coating them on all sides, and then apply a second coat to the outer surface. Enough stain was placed in an open-topped 55 gallon barrel. Sheets of galvanized metal, bent into V shape, were erected so that excess stain would drain back into the barrel. The stain had to be kept well stirred so the pigment would not settle to the bottom. Each worker would grasp several shingles between his fingers. Holding them at the thin end he would dip the shingles well into the stain, then spread them on the metal Veed sheets where the excess stain could run back into the barrel. When no more stain came off the shingles, they were carefully set aside to dry. This was done to every siding shingle and they are still in excellent condition.

Irwin Heins, who had married our cousin, Viola Hannesson, was a mason in Chicago. He agreed to come here and put up the chimney for which he charged $18 for the labor.

Joseph Vandergeeten firm from Green Bay was hired to do the interior plastering and their labor came to $115. 40 sacks of cement plaster, costing $38.60 and 22 sacks of trowel finish, costing $37.95 were used.

Brother Marvin, Spencer and I dug all the trenches for the septic tank bed.

Paint provided by Sears included enough for 3 coats on outside trim, 1 coat of shellac and two coats of varnish for all interior woodwork, wood filler and two coats of varnish for oak floors.

Electric wiring materials have been figured for the armored cable system with rigid conduit system in the basement. Three wire service and circuit panel box are included.

"In addition to the 4-in-1 strip shingles which have been figured for the roof, we have included sufficient quantity of 1 x 6 #2 yellow pine boards to be laid tight together with one layer of asphalt felt between the roof boards and the shingles.

"Because of present market conditions, we cannot guarantee the price quoted later than June 6, and it will be to your advantage to place your order prior to that date. If you cannot send us the full amount of your order within the time specified, send us a deposit of $500, and we will be glad to protect you on this low price for shipment not later than July 6, 1937. Your money is simply deposited with us until your material has been received, accepted and found satisfactory in quality, and quantity." Total cost of the house, land and well was less than $5000.

As both my sister, Sylvia, and I have been poetry lovers since childhood, when I wrote about forming corn shocks my memory flooded back to James Whitcomb Riley's "When the Frost is on the Punkin". Often when working with corn shocks the words kept running through my mind. Riley was a great "nature" poet and I hope these words will bring back to you some childhood memories.

WHEN THE FROST IS ON THE PUNKIN

When the frost is on the punkin and the fodder's in the shock,
And you hear the kyouck and gobble of the struttin' turkey-cock,
And the clackin' of the guineys, and the cluckin' of the hens,
And the rooster's hallylooyer as he tiptoes on the fence;
0, it's then's the times a feller is a-feelin' at his best,
With the risin' sun to greet him from a night of peaceful rest,
As he leaves the house, bareheaded, and goes out to feed the stock,
When the frost is on the punkin and the fodder's in the shock.

They's something kindo' harty-like about the atmusfere
When the heat of summer's over and the coolin' fall is here-
Of course we miss the flowers, and the blossums on the trees,
And the mumble of the hummingbirds and buzzin' of the bees;
But the air's so appetizin'; and the landscape through the haze
Of a crisp and sunny morning of the airly autumn days
Is a pictur' that no painter has the colorin' to mock-
When the frost is on the punkin and the fodder's in the shock.

The husky, rusty russel of the tossels of the corn,
And the raspin' of the tangled leaves, as golden as the morn;
The stubble in the furries-kindo' lonesome-like, but still
A-preachin' sermons to us of the barns they growed to fill;

The strawstack in the medder, and the reaper in the shed;
The hosses in theyr stalls below-the clover overhead!-
0, it sets my hart a-clickin' like the tickin' of a clock,
When the frost is on the punkin and the fodder's in the shock!

Then your apples all is gethered, and the ones a feller keeps
Is poured around the celler-floor in red and yeller heaps;
And your cider-makin' 's over, and your wimmern-folks is through
With their mince and apple-butter, and theyr souse and saussage, too!
I don't know how to tell it-but ef sich a thing could be
As the Angels wantin' boardin', and they'd call around on *me*-
I'd want to 'commodate 'em-all the whole-indurin' flock-
When the frost is on the punkin and the fodder's in the shock!

Dad cultivating with Dick and Flossie, “The Old Grey Mare”

FAMILY FARMING

Usually in February or early March the seed catalogs arrived. Even though the snow drifts were still piled high, it was fun to study these publications, page by page, and begin dreaming of new things that might be planted next spring. I recall that one time I planted watermelon seeds, but was quite disappointed to finally get melons that were no larger than a normal musk melon.

The box of seeds left over from the previous year was examined and a list was made of the items that needed to be ordered. The order was carefully written out. Then it was normally my job to take this to the Post Office where a Postal Mail Order was purchased to pay for the seeds and shipping costs.

Sometimes we would let a little sweet corn ripen and would gather these ears plus some field corn ears.for seed the next year. Frequently at school during the winter months the teacher would have us make "rag-doll testers" to see if the corn kernels would germinate.This device consisted of taking a large piece of cloth, usually muslin or blanket sheeting, and folding it several times so a roll about a foot wide could be made. The cloth was then laid out flat and carefully marked so we could later tell which ears the various kernels came from. A number of seeds were placed in each square,, then it was tightly rolled and thoroughly dampened with water. It was placed in a warm place, often near the wood stove, and re-dampened each day. Of course, then the anxious waiting began to see how many kernels from each cob would germinate. In about ten days we would open the “Rag Doll” and. count the sprouts. If 2/3 of the seeds had sprouted we would plan to shell that ear for seed, if not, it was shelled to use, for chicken feed.

After the garden was plowed and harrowed by our horse team, we hand raked all the soil smooth. A long string was stretched from one end to the other and a hand-held furrowing tool was pulled alongside of the string to make an opening in which to plant seeds which were placed by hand with careful spacing. The seeds were covered. Weeding began as soon as the sprouting vegetable plants could be identified, and it seemed that endless hoeing and weeding continued through the summer. In those days, with no raccoons to ravage the sweet corn, we always had a substantial crop. Much of this was sold to summer residents for about 25 cents a dozen. Before picking, each ear was tested by pulling the husk back enough to expose some kernels. Pressure with a finger nail would cause a kernel to pop. If the juice came out the consistency of fresh milk the ear was just right but if it looked like curdled milk, it was too ripe. I still use this method today when buying corn.

As garden crops matured, they were picked and much of it was canned and stored for later use. Green tomato relish and piccalili were popular side dishes with a main meal. Mother canned lots of ripe tomatoes which had been sweetened and spiced with a small cloth bag of whole cloves. This was eaten like fruit sauces. 0ccasionally, pumpkin meat was diced, sweetened, spiced, cooked and canned to be used as sauce.

Beets, carrots and parsnips were dug and stored in the cellar about when the first fall frost arrived. Some carrots were canned and some beets were pickled. Later we learned that if parsnips were left in the ground until after several frosts they were sweeter. Potatoes and other root crops were stored in bins in the cellar.

When dad was alive, he always raised huge carrots, we called them "horse carrots", and mangels that looked like tan beets.These were stored in a bin near the horse's stalls where they would not freeze. Each day some were placed in a wooden box and chopped fine with a spade. A small portion was spread on the animals' noon feeding.

When spring arrived on the farm, all the animals that had been pent up over winter were delighted to be able to spend the whole day outdoors. Frequently the calves and sometimes the cows could be seen cavorting about the pasture. Plowing ground began shortly after the frost left the ground, however, because of the coldness most crops were not planted before Memorial Day. Corn and potatoes were both planted by hand. As soon as the plants were high enough to distinguish the rows my brother and I started cultivating to kill weeds. He manipulated the one row cultivator while I led old Dick, our horse, down the middle of the row. One time my nephew, Roy, asked me to help him with cultivating and suggested I ride old "Major" rather than walk. This sounded much better to me. However, I soon found that "Major" had a very protruding backbone and in short order my rear end was getting sore. Roy got a pillow for me to use as there was no saddle available. This was an improvement until we finished our job and Roy unhitched “Major” from the cultivator and the horse headed for the barn and freedom at a full gallop. Of course, the pillow had now settled on his rump and that only made him go faster. All I could do was hold tightly to “Major's” mane and cuss like heck. The net result was two large blisters on the part of my anatomy where the sunshine seldom shone. From then on I much preferred to lead horses by the bridle. Soon the weeds very close to the plants were in need of hoeing and this was a tedious task. About the time that the potatoes blossomed, bugs would appear and feast on the leaves. So as youngsters,our job was to go down the rows, pick off the mature bugs which we dumped into a can with some kerosene in it and also smash the tiny, orange bug's eggs with our fingers. We had tried using Bordeaux Mixture, a combination of paris green and arsenic, as a spray to kill these pests, but always seemed to have to finish off with the hand process.

Many years we had bad infestations of grasshoppers and locusts. These could strip out a crop in a hurry. Also, they loved the salt from our sweaty hands,which deposited on the handles of tools. We were very careful not to leave tools in the fields over night as the grasshoppers would thoroughly etch the handles making them rough and thus causing blisters. When these infestations were extremely bad, the Town would have the road crew mix up poison with molasses and spread it on sawdust. We would then strew this by hand over the fields hoping to do away with the pests.

One year a mass of some sort of tree moths descended on the Island and their larvae was particularly fond of beech tree leaves. Many of the trees were denuded. Some of these larvae would fall from the trees producing a sound like rain. One neighbor got the bright idea that by pounding the trunk of the tree with a sledge mallet he could shake the tree enough to get rid of these pests. He was so energetic that he pounded right through the bark damaging the cambium layer with the result that he killed most of his beech trees. Still,the next winter he had lots of firewood to cut. Crows were another pest. We used a special marker to "checkerboard" the field where we would plant corn. Thus we could cultivate I crosswise as well as down the length of the field. As soon as the corn was planted we would run a "spike tooth" harrow over the field to erase the "checkerboard" pattern.

Otherwise the crows would walk down the rows to where the cross marks were and dig the seed kernels out. Later we found that a mixture of turpentine and pine tar on the seed corn made it less palatable.

Harvesting corn was done by hand using sharp, short handled hoes to cut with one hand while the stalks were held by the other hand. Then it was tied into large bundles with old fisherman's' cord and hauled into the apple orchard area where it was stacked in shocks for winter cattle feed.

We always raised about thirty chickens, so we had eggs to sell as well as use. The chicken coop was of cedar block"stovewood" construction built by Dad in the late 1800s. The remaining blocks now form the walls of my "trophy room". Each spring mother would select the fertile eggs to be placed under a "brood" hen which we called “Ole Cluck” as that seemed to be the noise she would make when calling the baby chicks to food she had found. This hen was kept for many years just for brooding purposes and she wore an identifying band on one leg so she was easily recognized. In those days, chicken stealing was quite prevalent among certain factions on the Island. We had to faithfully padlock the coop each night. This was often my task, but one evening, in a blinding snowstorm, I failed to lock up. The storm quit about 11 P.M. Next morning, when Mom went to feed the chickens she saw snowy footprints leading from the coop, right across the road. She quickly determined several birds were missing. So she followed the tracks right to the neighbor's back door. Without bothering to knock she marched into the kitchen where the lady of the house was preparing breakfast. Mom grasped the oldest teenage boy by the ear and demanded, "Where are my chickens?" His weak reply was, "They're in the barn next door." So on Mom's return home I was directed to go with gunny sacks and retrieve our chickens. We got a good laugh over the fact that "Ole Cluck" was among the stolen ones. We often wondered how long they would have needed to cook that old bird to get any tenderness from the meat. When Dad was still alive it was always traditional to kill a large rooster for Thanksgiving and Christmas dinners. Dad always stuffed the bird with prunes and to us it was a delicious treat.

My brother very much disliked killing animals, so soon it became my job to do the dispatching. At first I would hold the bird by the legs and try to get the neck onto the chopping block. Then I would use a hand hatchet. However, frequently at the last instant the bird would move and I would either miss or cut too much of the neck off. This would result in unkind comments from Mom as we always used all the neck meat. Finally I learned that by slipping a string noose over the bird's head and holding this string tight with one foot,l could rest the neck securely over the chopping block and my aim became very accurate. Besides the roosters, we tried to butcher only non-laying hens. I learned to measure not only the potential laying capacity, but also the present production of a hen by measuring the pelvic bone area. After that, it was rare that the wrong hen met with the chopping block.

Eggs from these farm hens had so much better flavor than any we buy today. Except in winter the birds spent all day in the barnyard feeding on green plants, bugs and any kitchen scraps that they found. A special chicken “smorgasbord” was the once-run-through horse's "rolled oats" as we called them. Occasionally, a hen who thought she could brood her own eggs would build a hidden nest away from the coop. One time we had one that began laying in some hay in the barn driveway. I soon discovered this cache and daily collected all the fresh eggs, leaving a dummy egg to lure her back. It so happened that we had a half-grown beagle dog that often slept in the barn. He discovered this nest and accidently broke an egg which he found was very tasty. From then on,whenever the hen would cackle when leaving the nest after depositing an egg, the dog would think,"Oh Boy! It's mealtime!" After secretly watching him break and eat the egg I decided to cure him. So, I gently opened both ends of an egg, removed the contents and filled the shell with all sorts of "goodies" like red pepper and other strong tasting ingredients. After waiting to find the hen on her nest, I chased her away. Her loud cackling quickly drew the dog to the scene while I hid in the hay mow to observe. Upon tasting my vile concoction, the dog got the most puzzled look on his face, tried to wipe the taste from his mouth with his paws and finally departed to never again go near that spot.

While today the Island Sportsman's Club obtains hundreds of day-old pheasant chicks to raise and release, as a youngster I decided to try incubating them from eggs. Wisconsin Fish and

Game Department (predecessor to DNR) offered pheasant eggs to farmers to get the population of birds started. I learned that 28 pheasant eggs could be placed under a large brooding hen, though she could handle only 21 chicken eggs. Also the brooding time was longer. Practically all the eggs hatched and I was delighted. Soon my elation turned to dismay as the young chicks began dying right and left. With Ma's help I learned that they and the brood hen had acquired bird lice, probably from the English sparrows that shared the barnyard. An easy solution to this problem was to smear lard on each bird's head just behind the comb. This was quickly accomplished and no more birds were lost. The success of this method was due to the fact that lice occasionally need moisture. Therefore they climb up to the top of the bird and then descend to the nostrils where moisture is present. When they reach the partly melted lard, it closes their breathing pores and they suffocate.

The old brood, or cluck, hen would scratch the ground looking for “goodies” to eat and then loudly call the young ones to share in the feast. To her dismay, young pheasants were ingrained with feeding quietly to avoid detection by predators. Therefore they merely looked puzzled at her performance and would not respond. This drove her into a tizzy and she would work harder than ever to no avail.

We normally had a small shed behind the house where we kept the cluck hen and youngsters at night. As dusk fell she would herd them into the shed so we could close the door for the night. As soon as the young pheasants had "sprouted" enough feathers to where they could hop up on the lower tree branches, they began choosing these and higher roosts when nightfall came. Mother hen would stand at the shed's door calling and beseeching her brood to join her in the shed. Nothing doing, they instinctively had found a safer haven for the night. Today I am sure that the insurmountable obstructions that were heaped upon that cluck hen caused her demise. She didn't last till the next spring to allow us to place regular chicken eggs under her.

Perhaps in a way she got even with me over the years. It was often my job to gather the fresh eggs from the nests in the chicken coop. Frequently I would find a hen sitting on the nest waiting to lay an egg. The usual practice was to just reach under these laying hens and remove the fresh eggs. This did not seem to bother them as they concentrated on getting rid of the egg which was giving them a "pain in the behind". Unfortunately, the old cluck hen often just sat on a nest all day hoping for some eggs to be brooded to appear. As I was cautioned by my mother to do a thorough job, frequently when I reached under old "Cluck" I was rewarded with sharp, rapid pecks on the back of the hand that drew blood. So, maybe, in the final analysis we are about even.

The pheasant birds grew to maturity. As winter came we harvested corn with not quite ripe ears. This was "shocked" near the apple orchard to be later chopped and fed to the cattle during the winter. Two cocks and six hens found this to be their favorite feeding place and they remained throughout the winter. As raccoons were then non-existent on the Island and foxes were rare, several broods of wild pheasant developed the next summer.

We practiced "crop rotation" long before this was strongly advocated by the Federal AAA that came into existence shortly after Franklin Roosevelt became President in 1933.

A field that had been pasture land for our dairy cattle for some years was selected for raising next year's corn crop. In the fall we broke and turned the sod with a single bottom plow, making a furrow about 14 inches wide, pulled by old Dick and Flossie, the grey mare. Next spring the winter's piles of horse and cow manure were hauled and spread on the field. We wore boots and using manure forks spread the fertilizer across the field by handpower. While during the winter the sod had rotted to a fair degree, when spring came we set the plow to go deeper into the ground and thus buried the old plant life to a point where it surely rotted and provided nutrients for the coming corn crop. These nutrients we called "green manure". A few Island farmers even planted buckwheat and then plowed it under before the seeds ripened to provide "green manure".

After the plowing was completed and time drew near for corn planting we "cross dragged" the plowed field to smoothen the ground and to kill any emerging weeds. This was started from one corner of the field to the opposite diagonal corner. As we kept turning only 90 degrees at the fence line we were able to cultivate in a diamond pattern and thus did a double dragging, with the spring-toothed harrow.

As the time for corn planting arrived, usually near the end of May, the ground was made smooth with a roller which dad had made out of a large log. One inch round steel axles on either end of the log fitted into the framework which was carried upward to a plank platform extending from one side to the other. An implement seat was attached in the center of' the platform, thus allowing the teamster to ride in a seated position. The whole field was rolled smooth. Next the field was marked in checkerboard fashion to show where each bunch of corn kernels should be planted to allow cultivating in either direction. This saved a lot of hours weeding with a hoe to kill the unwanted plants that always appeared. The row marker was a long timber with teeth from a spring-toothed drag fastened in a way that allowed the spring teeth to glide over the smooth ground marking four rows at each pass. After marking in one direction we then worked across the field the opposite way. Afterwards the hand-operated corn planters were filled and we marched back and forth across the ground. As we stepped close to the X-mark in the soil we pulled the handles outward. This closed the steel jaws at the bottom and drew the proper number of seeds from the hopper into the chute where they traveled down into the closed jaws. At the X-mark the jaw end was thrust into the ground, the handles were brought together and the opening jaws allowed the seed to drop into the earth. As the planter was pulled upward and we moved towards the next X, a slight scuffing over the seed hole assured that the seeds were well covered with soil.

After the planting was finished we promptly passed over the whole field with a spike-toothed drag, or harrow, to prevent the smart crows from merely digging out the corn at each X-mark. As soon as the corn was sprouted to where we could see the rows, cultivating to kill weeds commenced and continued throughout the summer until the corn was too high to move through with the horses. For many years our farm used a single-row cultivator that was a two person operation.Brother Marvin manipulated the cultivator while I, as a young boy, led old Dick down the rows while he pulled the cultivator. It was a relief when we finally purchased a two-row riding cultivator from Will Jess, who sold some farm implements. While this required two horses to operate, it needed only one person who rode in the seat. With a set of foot pedals, the cultivating teeth could be moved from side to side to avoid gouging out corn or other plants like potatoes that were being weeded.

Haying usually began in late June and this hard task lasted nearly a month. When dad was still alive most of the hay consisted of clover and timothy grass. Later alfalfa was introduced which was a boon to dairy farmers as it was a sturdy perennial that provided much more nourishment for the animals.

First the hay was cut with a horse-powered mower. If we had sunny weather, the hay usually dried in about two days. If the crop was very heavy we had to go through the fields the morning after mowing and turn it over so the sun would dry that side also. Frequently if it rained on the new mown hay, we had to perform the same operation. We always waited until heavy dew had disappeared before raking. This was done with a "dump" rake which the horses pulled. The hay was arranged in "windrows" and then stacked to further cure before hauling it into the barn.

It took at least two persons to load the hay on the wagon's hayrack. One on the ground pitching hay on the wagon and the other on the wagon spreading it properly to secure it and get the maximum load.

We had only one good-sized hay mow in the barn, so much of the work involved stuffing hay into small crannies. We used the loft above the chicken coop and the old log barn that stood in front of our main barn.

Before I was big enough to pitch hay, my job was always to tramp the hay down and help stuff it in under the sloping rafters. This I accomplished by grasping the rafters and hanging at an angle while kicking the hay in tight under the roof.

It seemed that the humidity was always high and these lofts were very hot from the sun shining on the roof. Therefore, it was a real luxury if, after a full day's work, we could grab swimming suits and head either for Detroit or West Harbor for a cooling swim.

Of course, this stored hay also naturally settled and by the end of the haying season we could add more to the places that had been filled earlier.

During the winter, when that hay in the main mow was used up, we had the extra task of carrying the hay from the other building into the main barn driveway so we could feed the cows and horses. All this handling of hay was done using a three-tined pitchfork.

The old horses, Dick and Flossie, were finally replaced with a beautiful young team, Dan and Queen, purchased from Husby in

Sister Bay. They were very spirited. One day we were hauling hay from the field across from the school. As our farm was the gathering place for the neighbor youngsters, cousin Murray Cornell was riding on the wagon with me. When I picked up the reins and said, "Giddap" to move to the next stack, I noted something was wrong. I pulled hard on the reins and hollered, "Whoa."

Evidently Dan had been bitten by a fly and rubbed against Queen somehow removing his bridle. That left no bit in his mouth to check him. He took off at full gallop "running away." We went through the nearest fence, over very rough ground, and into the woods behind our house. Fortunately, some distance later, the horses straddled a tree, the neck yoke fetched up tight. It brought the team to a halt.

Naturally there was no hay left on the wagon, the rack was all busted up. I was straddling a plank with my legs hanging down against the "wagon hound." My shins were thoroughly skinned and Murray was bawling his eyes out. However, soon other neighbor boys showed up and with hastily dried tears, Murray proudly strutted around announcing, "I was on the wagon!"

We sold Flossie to Harry Hansen, who operated a dairy with his brother Charley. While haying, two of Harry's sons loaded the wagon very heavily and Flossie decided she wanted no part of that so she "balked" and just stood there. Old remedies such as tying a string around the ear or pouring water into the balking horses's ear failed. One of them vowed they would move her so they lit a tuft of dry hay under her. This moved her just enough so the burning hay was under the wagon. They frantically beat the fire out before it could extend to the hay load.

Dad brought with him from Denmark the practice of harvesting "green oats" hay for the horses. When the oats crop had "headed out" we mowed it and treated it similar to other hay, storing it in a separate mow in the barn. Usually it had to cure longer before placing it in the mow.

One year, after placing it in the barn, we noted a suspicious odor and drove a sharpened fence-post into the oats mow. Upon removing the post and thrusting our hands into the hole, we found it was so hot that we could hardly let our hands remain there. In spite of a hot muggy day, we had to take a hay knife and cut a huge square hole in the center of the mow. This let the spontaneous heating dissipate and avoided having the barn burn down. Many barns have burned during summers from spontaneous heating of improperly cured hay.

After the mow was filled with hay we always looked forward to sleeping in it overnight with some of the neighbor boys. However, some, who looked forward eagerly to doing this, would "chicken out" after darkness settled and one could hear bats beginning their nightly prowl. Other noises also became evident. Often one or more of the party would timidly arise, gather up their bed articles and announce, "I think I'll go home."

Grain harvesting occurred in August. When Dad was alive, the grain at the edges of the field and in the corners had to be "cradled" by hand, then raked into bundles with an old wooden rake. It was then tied and stacked out of the way so that the grain binder would not mash any ripe grain down where it would be lost.

We grew a mixture of barley, oats and rye. The longer rye-stalks were pulled out of the bundle and used to form the "tie" which held the bundle together on the "cradled" grain, or on any bundles that the binder's knotter failed to tie. The bundles were stacked in shocks so the green growth present in the ripe grain could cure before hauling the crop into the barn.

Threshing was always an exciting time for a young farm boy. When Andersen Brothers sounded the steam whistle on the tractor at the nearby farm we knew it was time to make final preparations for threshing. The steam tractor pulling the grain separator, with threshing crew following, came slowly down the road and up our lane to the barn.

A heavy block and tackle was used to pull the separator into the barn with the blower pipe sticking out in front in proper position for forming the straw stack. It was always my job to tramp down the straw while the machine was blowing it all over me so I ended the day as the dirtiest person in the crew.

The steam tractor that burned wood, was placed a good distance from the barn and a long, flat belt was led to the separator's driving pulley. There was always a danger that a wood spark would ignite a nearby shingle roof or the barn contents and if an adverse wind was blowing, the spark arrestor was inserted into the tractor's stack.

Two men worked in the mow feeding grain bundles into the separator. Threshed grain passed through a counting mechanism to record the bushels obtained. The grain was gathered in two bushel canvas bags, which weighed 120 lbs. when full. If the crop was heavy, two men were needed to carry these bags to the granary bins.

Farm wives always prepared their finest meal for the crew who were always fed as soon as the threshing was completed. No one lost weight if they followed the threshers during harvest time.

When my sisters would come out to the barn to find when we would be through, Conrad Andersen would always get a kick out of turning the blower pipe on them, hitting them with straw.

One year, they decided to get even with all the crew who laughed when that happened. So I picked some bitter wormwood, which they placed in one of the coffee pots and served to all the merrymakers. However, they had another pot to serve to those who were innocent.

Martin "Saltum," who operated the steam tractor, got regular coffee but grumbled because the girls had pulled this trick. While Hans B. Hansen, who had not partaken in the merriment as he worked in the back of the hay mow, was disappointed that they did not serve him the wormwood coffee.

Modern Haymaking Doesn't Cut It!

Recently I read an article with this title and it made me compare how nephew, Martin, today harvests hay in comparison to how we did it in the 1920s and 30s. Martin's baler puts out round bales that weigh nearly as much as a small auto. There is a joke that has been well passed around that the U.S. Dept. of Agriculture is going to outlaw round bales because the cows can't get a "square" meal. Somehow I think "making hay" had more CHARACTER in the old days. Time was when a hard-handed farmer could refer to haymaking as "lostacking" A "stack" meant a temporary, small, hopefully waterproof pile of hay built to protect the hay in case of rain. Many Island farmers took as much pride in the quality of their stacks as they did in the straightness of their plow furrows.

My brother, Marvin, took pride in the construction of marvelously symmetrical stacks, which were proof against all but the most outrageous "gullywasher". Haying was not rushed in those days. It was understood that it would begin in late June and last through most of July.

This period was cut in half by the tractor-drawn baler which, with the machine's unthinking cruelty, also swept away the haystacker builders. When I returned to the Island in 1977 I helped my brother bale hay in the smaller square bales and hoist them via tractor power and barn hayfork to the ridge of the barn where they then traveled along a track. With the aid of a "tripping line" he could drop them from the fork to the part of the mow where he wanted them. No more handling the hay by hand umpteen times. Where previously we had to turn the heavy hay in the field by hand with hay forks, take the hay from the raked "windrows" with a fork to mold the hay stacks, later pitch the loose hay onto the wagon where a second person spread it to make an even load, once in the barn the hay was pitched from the wagon into the mow where another person then spread the hay into even layers followed with a sprinkling of salt to help it to "cure".

Certainly, the haymow wasn't as bouncy when filled with bales, but the special aroma of new mown hay was still there ... and the huge wasp nests in the rafters were as scary as ever.

Now, haymaking requires far less labor. A single person can mow, rake, bale and store an entire hay crop and do it in as little as a quarter of the time required 10 years ago, which was a fraction of the time required in the 20s and 30s.

The key is an oversized bale, variously called the “big bale" or “rolled bale".It seems somehow significant that farmers - a group highly noted for picturesque terminology - can produce no more evocative name for this breakthrough than "big bale".

These balers can produce 1,500 lb. bales at the rate of 10 to 12 per hour rather easily. Some are equivalent to 28 conventional rectangular bales, or a full load on brother Marvin's hay wagon. Equally important, rolled bales are essentially waterproof. Thus unlike ordinary bales which must be stored under cover as soon as possible, the big, rolled bales are individual hay stacks that may be collected virtually at leisure.

Since there is little possibility of using hand labor with a 1,500 lb. bale, gathering the rolled bales into a convenient corner of the field for winter storage is sometimes delegated to a youngster in need of practice in driving the tractor-mounted bale hauler. As efficiency is the name of the game on today's farms, and a frightening small handful of farmers must feed 97% of the population, I guess it's imperative that a teenage youngster be able to move as much hay in an easy day as our whole family did in a month.

Modern farm youngsters don't even know what they are missing. With rolled bales stored outdoors, you can't dangle your feet over the edge of the hay load as the horses pull it into the barn. Nor can you find comfort sleeping in a mow filled with soft hay, or watch the incomparable contentment of well-fed cattle in the manger far below. Playing cowboys and Indians in the barn on a rainy Saturday is gone. In my day on the farm we always had a number of neighbor children indulging in these things.

As the author of the article said, "In my humble opinion,modern big bales are positively baleful!"

Every summer the farmer's "Bull Picnic" was held. The present Farm Museum Labor Day weekend "Farmer's Picnic" follows along a similar theme. Games, food and much conviviality were and are the order of the day.

I have counted 77 places on the Island where animals were raised and land was, cultivated in the early part of the 1900s. The Island Holstein Breeders Association was an organization to which many dairy farmers belonged. Their herds were thoroughbred Holstein cattle.

To keep the strain pure and to avoid in-breeding of the young heifers, the Association bought a new bull every two years. Different Association farmers boarded the bull and received free breeding service. Other members paid a small bull service fee. I recall that, as a youngster, I took cows to be bred at these farms:

Wilfred Koyen's-now Arni Foss's;

Ole Erickson's-now Ken Koyen's;

Louie Hansen's-now Shirley and Jake Ellefson's;

Lawrence Klingenberg's-now ?

Christ Hansen's-now the "Green House";

Vernie Richter's-now Jeanine Ronning and Mary & Jon Andersen's.

Normally it took two persons to handle the cow; one leading with a rope tied around the horns and the other following with a small switch to keep the cow moving.

As the bull's young "daughters" reached their third year and were ready for first breeding the farmers did not want in-breeding by the same bull. Therefore, the old bull was "put out to pasture," so to speak and a new, young one became the breeder. The farmer who had boarded the bull was allowed to keep him. Usually the old bull was then fattened and slaughtered for meat.

Christ Hansen's bull, Blue Boy, was a tough critter. Christ had suspended a large, hard, pine stump, on a chain from a tree limb for Blue Boy to exercise with. He would back up and ram the stump, which'would swing forward and then come back, hitting him soundly on the forehead, whereupon Blue Boy would repeat the action.

Finally, when Blue Boy had been fattened, the time had come for butchering. Christ called Steve Gunnlaugsson to do the job. Steve used his 32-20 Winchester, lever-action carbine to dispense with cattle.

The two men led Blue Boy forth to the slaughtering site by luring him forward with a bucket of feed. At the chosen location, Steve chambered a live round into the rifle and sent a bullet into. Blue Boy's forehead, hoping to drop him. However, Blue Boy merely shook his head and wiggled his ears, apparently thinking that a damned fly had stung rather hard.

Quickly Steve pumped two more rounds into the animal. By that time Blue Boy was getting rather vexed.

Realizing that his 32-20 rifle was not going to do the trick and that he'd better accomplish the trick pronto, Steve remembered that Wellington Lockhart, who lived where Kermit Jorgenson now resides, had a 30.06 army rifle.

Steve jumped into his old Chevrolet 2-door and quickly sped to and fro, ending up back at the slaughtering sight where he would try another shot. This time, however, he decided to aim into the bull's head from behind the ear. One blast from the high-powered weapon felled Blue Boy.

After skinning and gutting, Steve decided to find out why his formerly very trusty 32-20 had not done the job. Using his two-handed butchering cleaver he finally split the skull open and found that Blue Boy had about three inches of bone on the forehead. The original shots had penetrated only about one and. a half inches.

Fortunately the irksome shots had not riled Blue Boy to the point where he had launched an attack.

They drive home the cows from pasture,
Up through the long, shady lane
Where the quail whistles loud in the wheat field

That is yellow with ripening grain.

Many times as a lad, I thought of this poem while bringing our milk cows home. Part of our farmland was the 20 acres from the old soccer field east to Airport Road. While several fields there were devoted to growing corn, potatoes, hay or grain, we always had some that were used for pasture.

After the morning milking it was my job to drive the cows to pasture and then bring them back home for evening milking. Usually they were fairly obedient, but sometimes when the pasture land had been nearly stripped and their bellies were not full, they would spot some succulent plants in areas where they did not belong and I would have difficulty rounding them up.

The Detroit Harbor school was on the present school site with an acre of land to the rear for a playground. We boys always played baseball at recess and noontime school breaks. Sometimes the cows would leave "doilies" in the baseball area, which were later mistaken for one of the base markers. If one of the players happened to slide into that "base" I would catch heck and sometimes have to run very swiftly.

In the early days there were about 100 places where animals were raised. In the late 1800s several farmers used spans of oxen as draft animals. In fact, we have an old photo in the Farm Museum of an ox teamed 'with a horse. In the early part of this century farmers used two-horse teams. In the late '20s tractors began to appear here. The earliest ones I remember were Fordsons. On a heavy pull the front wheels would come off the ground. Some farmers tried to remedy this by filling the front wheels with concrete. However, when pulling stumps or real heavy rocks, they would still rear-up and if not stopped would turn completely over right onto the driver. Fortunately no Island farmers lost their lives this way but throughout the state several were killed.

Some sheep were raised. Our neighbor, Charley Jensen, always had some guinea hens that were real "watchdogs." They always made a racket when anyone other than Charley or wife, Cassey, would enter the yard, and if a hawk soared overhead, they would raise a tizzy.

Almost every farm family raised chickens for meat, eggs and for sale. It was usual to raise at least enough pigs to supply the family with pork. In the '20s and '30s the Town Board did not hold a November budget meeting so the annual Town Meeting in early April was an important one and always very well attended. Students old enough to be studying "Civics," were given time off from their regular classes to attend this meeting.

By the '30s several commercial fishermen had taken down the fences in front of their homes and planted lawns. These presented a special attraction for cattle that were being driven to or from pasture. Besides their hooves leaving big divots, the "calling cards" complicated mowing. If the grass had gotten tall enough to hide these, the person doing the mowing frequently had more than grass cutting deposited on his clothes.

The subject was brought up at an annual meeting, but then was bypassed for another issue. August Koyen, who always had lots to say at town meetings, was not about to let this subject be ignored. He jumped up and loudly asked, "Well, what are we going to do about the cows?" Whereupon Jim Boyce, the local wit, responded, "Cut their tails off and let the sunshine in!" That nearly broke up the meeting.

One time one of the cows was anxious to see the bull. Even though she was consumed with this desire, she stubbornly refused to be led to Ole Erickson's, where the Association bull was quartered. As my brother, Marvin, was busy at other things, I needed a second person to follow behind and use a small switch to keep her going. Our farm was a great gathering place for all the neighborhood youngsters. Fortunately, Charley Magnusson, the ten year old son of our postmaster, arrived at the nick of time. I am sure he would have taken on the task just to observe, however I "sweetened" the proposition by offering a dime for his help.

All of our family was accustomed to seeing mating of cattle, pigs,chickens and dogs. We just considered this to be a common occurrence in nature, not so with Charley's mother. When she learned of what had happened I caught "Holy Hell".

Nowadays with much more selective breeding, especially of dairy cattle, it is rare for it to occur in the manner which nature intended. To a major degree this is accomplished by "artificial insemination". Perhaps this is why cows have such long, sober faces since they no longer experience any pleasure in breeding.

Today, semen from prize bulls, descended from record-producing cattle, brings a high price. Also, heifer calves from the union of the prize bull's semen and a high producing cow bring a handsome amount on the market. Very complete records are kept and many of today's dairy cows produce staggering amounts of milk.

In the 1920s the State of Wisconsin had started a program to wipe out tuberculosis in dairy cattle. This was a rather common malady in cows. As our Island was well isolated and had a strong Holstein Association, the state officials felt it would be a very good place to eliminate cattle TB. At a meeting of the farmers it was agreed to have everyone's cows tested and that all those that reacted positively to the TB test would be shipped to market. A State man came to the Island to conduct the test, which was done in almost the same way as on humans. A small amount of serum was injected under the skin, on the lower side of the tail close to the anus. This part of the animal's hide is very thin and any reaction would be quite apparent. After what seemed like a couple days the State man returned to each farm and felt the spots where the serum had been inserted. A raised bump meant a positive reaction and the animal went to market. As with humans, a positive test did not mean that the animal had TB, but that the germs had, at some time, entered the body. We lost two or three milking cows from our herd.

A cattle buyer, named Peter Yudin, (he insisted it be pronounced "you-deen") came to the Island and bought up all these cattle. He had hired Captain Hill's boat out of Escanaba to take the critters away for slaughtering. This Jewish man frequently visited the Island thereafter and always greeted a farmer with "Any cattle for sale". However, he spoke with a very broken accent and the first time he approached Ma she thought he asked, "Any kettle for sale". This made her wonder what type of a buyer he was.

Naturally, he never offered a good price to begin with. Much price dickering back and forth had to occur. I believed he really would have been disappointed if a farmer accepted his first bid. Like with car buying and selling, when it got down to a few bucks difference it was obvious he had gone just about as far as he would go.

In those day no trucks came to the Island to haul cattle away. They all departed via lake freighters. Usually this meant that the critters had to be led to what was then called "Johnny Young's dock", down the Washington Harbor hill from Kleinhans' place.

Another affliction that affected dairy cows was "Bangs Disease". This was to some degree contagious and resulted in "stringy" milk issuing from one or more of the four parts of the cow's udder. We referred to this milk as "gargot". Again the State was interested in eliminating this problem from Island herds. Agreements to dispose of the affected cattle were reached and tests were conducted. Many cows again left the Island for the one-way trip to the slaughterhouse. This time we lost one or two milk cows, but now had a TB and Bangs disease free herd, as did all other Island farmers.

All milking in those days was done by hand. Also all tilling of the soil was accomplished with the aid of a team of horses. Therefore it was common to remark that farmers spent much of their time either "pulling tits or hollering 'whoa'".

In the fall after the first killing frost we harvested the corn. Again, this was all done by hand. We found that a sharp garden hoe, fitted with a short handle, was the best tool for cutting the stalks from the roots. These were always cut close to the ground to give more cattle forage as well as leaving less stem that could house corn borers over winter. We were never badly infested by borers, but occasionally we would find a tall stalk that had suddenly drooped over to the ground. The corn borer larvae would begin at the ground level and work their way on up through the stalk eating out the center and causing the resultant drooping.

By grasping the stalks in a hill with one hand and striking a sharp blow with the hoe with the other hand, the corn was cut. Then we laid it together to form proper sized bundles. After finishing the cutting we bound the bundles with old cotton "meter" twine salvaged from old fishing nets which had been give to us by commercial fishermen.

During the winter,on cold days when we could not cut cordwood, we sat in the house and cut this twine away from the gill net mesh. About three-foot long cords were made with a noose on one end and a knot tied on the other to prevent raveling. With a bunch of these cords fastened to our waists, we worked across the field reaching down to pass the line under the bunch of corn, then running the end of the cord through the noose, drawing the cord tight and tying a knot. When this was finished a group of several corn bundles was stood up to form a corn shock. Here the corn dried and cured until late November or early December when we loaded it either on the hay wagon or on a sleigh pulled by horses after a snowfall. It was then re-shocked in a field close to the barn where the fencing kept the farm animals from entering. As previously mentioned we then hauled the shocks into the driveway of the barn on a man-pulled sled fitted with ski runners. This was done each time we needed more fodder for the cattle.

Normally we tried to plow under the remaining corn roots in the fall. Again in the spring the ground was worked with the sprinp-toothed drag. We then planted grain, a mixture of oats, barley and rye, to be used as feed for cattle, chickens and pigs. The grain was loaded in sacks onto a wagon and the grain drill was pulled behind to the field. The grain drill's hopper was filled with seed and the horses were hitched to the tongue end. Discs at the bottom of the grain tubes opened the soil as the grain dropped down through tubes at a regulated rate. Usually chains to the rear dragging on the ground gave assurance that the grain would be well covered.

Often we raised grain for two years in the same field. However, the second year we would plant the hay seeds for next year's crop. In early years this was mainly timothy grass and red clover, but with the learning of the advantages of alfalfa, we switched to that.

Before planting the alfalfa we obtained "inoculation" from the government agricultural agency. The innoculant came in a gelled solution in a small bottle. This was filled with warm water and the resultant solution was sprinkled over the seed in a wash tub. We thoroughly stirred with our hands to make sure that the inoculant reached every seed. Alfalfa is a legume. Legumes have the capability of drawing free nitrogen, an excellent plant fertilizer, from the air and storing it in the ground in small root nodules. The inoculant insured that the plants would successfully perform this valuable function.

A smaller hopper on the grain drill, behind the main grain hopper, was where the hay seed was placed. That year's grain crop served as a "nurse crop" for the tender, small hay plants. When the grain was harvested the sickle on the binder was always set high off the ground so that a generous amount of grain stubble would remain to catch and hold the drifting snow so the ground would not freeze deeply and kill the tender hay roots.

For many following years the hay field would produce very well. When the field no longer yielded a good hay crop, it was turned into pasture for several years. Then the crop rotation cycle started all over again with the planting of corn.

Butchering day was always looked forward to by me. If a hog was to be slaughtered it was my job to catch the blood from the stuck pig in a wash pan containing a handful of salt. Immediately I carried the pan to a snow drift and continuously stirred the blood so it would not clot. Then I took it into the house where Mom added graham flour, seasonings and chunks of fat pork. Casings for the blood sausage were made of muslin which was dampened before being dusted with flour on the inside to keep the sausage mixture from seeping through. The sausage was cooked in a copper wash boiler on the wood stove. I always thought a good breakfast consisted of a fried slice of blood sausage, fried potatoes with pork cracklings and eggs.

Steve Gunnlaugsson did the butchering for us and he always wanted to hear any new jokes I had come across since his previous visit. After the pig was shot and bled it was scalded to loosen the hairs so they and the outer layer of skin could be scraped off. Over the years Steve got very adept at checking the water temperature with a thermometer and timing how long each end of the hog sat in the hot water. If the animal was over-scalded it was a mess as the fat would ooze through the pores and the scraper would just slip over the skin. Then it was necessary to use a straight razor to remove the hairs.

Hams and shoulders were placed in a 20 gallon crock and were first thoroughly coated with a mixture of salt, brown sugar and saltpeter. After a couple days a thick solution developed which was boiled to purify, then enough water was added to this liquid to cover the pork in the crock. In later years we used a brine pump with a sharp needle to penetrate into the center of the meat and thus cure it more quickly. This was followed with at least a week of smoking in a structure that resembled a "chick sale", but I can assure you that Dad built it as a smoke house and that is the only purpose it served. Mom always sliced the side pork, then baked it in a slow oven and stored it in butter crocks with a covering of lard. As we had no refrigeration, this was stored in a small room on the north side of the house with the window open. One time I thought I could sneak the pork bellies into the ham brine and smoke them for bacon. After they had been in the brine two days, Mom gave me heck for doing that and made me remove them. However, she discovered the brining had added a delicious flavor and thereafter I was allowed to continue the practice.

Beef cattle were also butchered in mid-winter. We always selected a cow that was no longer a good milk producer. It was usual to hang one hind quarter in the wood shed where it froze solid. Then when we wanted beef the chunk was brought into the kitchen and a frozen piece was sawed off.

Eventually the Door County Agricultural agent taught the Islanders how to "cold pack" meat, vegetables and fruits. This was a godsend for us as we now could have meat the year around. About the time I entered high school I became interested in making sausage. We got a hand operated sausage stuffer and bought hog intestine casings from Sears by mail order. I smoked the sausage links and they were extremely tasty. One day I thought I would "treat" some of my school friends so I placed a pan of links on the flue pipes in the old coal-fired furnace. After a time the cooking smell invaded the upper rooms and one student commented that it smelled like pork cooking. Fortunately I rescued them in time to share with my friends.

When bull calves were born Mom would direct me to shoot and bury them. Once I decided that I would use one to learn how to butcher. So I got all the paraphenalia ready, shot the animal, stuck it to bleed it then gutted and skinned it. Mom did not want any of the meat, but I learned that a needy neighbor family had no meat so I offered it to them. They were delighted with the gift. Only years later did I learn that new-born veal is a delicacy.

During my high school years I became interested in tanning hides. Pete Christianson, Lorraine Andersen's grandfather, had tanned some to make flat belts that powered his shop machinery from a line shaft. He gave me the basic instructions on tanning, which I supplemented with books from the Wisconsin Free Library.

The hides from the cows we butchered for meat were worth very little on the market so one of these provided part of my raw material.

Also Old Dick, our faithful horse, had attained the remarkable age of 33 years. He had lost his teeth and was down to "Skin and bones." It was decided that the most merciful thing that could be done was to shoot and bury him.

Since we had no high powered rifle on the farm, we got Jack Andersen to do the job with his 45-70 Winchester. I figured that horsehide leather as well as cow hides would be useful on the farm so I skinned our old horse before burying him deep in a sand hill.

The first step in tanning was to place the hides in a 55 gallon wooden barrel with lots of wood ashes to form lye which would loosen the hair so it could be removed. After the lye had done its job, the individual hides were placed on a low saw horse with a rounded plank nailed on top. Then began the tedious task of scraping all the hair off using a drawknife turned the opposite way of normal use. As this was pulled across the hide great chunks of hair fell to the ground.

Since lye is a very strong alkali, it was essential to then thoroughly rinse as much as possible out of the hides. The barrel was then emptied and thoroughly scrubbed.

Fresh water with lots of white vinegar was placed in the barrel with the hides to neutralize the alkali.

After another thorough rinsing it was time to start the tanning process. Since there were lots of hemlock trees in the back forty of the farm, it was easy to get a good supply of hemlock bark which contains an abundance of tannic acid. Many hours were spent at the old wood chopping block reducing the bark to chips and then using a heavy hammer to pulverize the bark in order to get the maximum amount of tannic acid released into the water.

Daily the hides were moved about in the tanning solutions so that each part was exposed thus allowing the tannin to penetrate into the hide.

After many weeks I would look for a spot on the edge of the hide where it was very thick. Using a sharp knife I would cut for a distance greater than the thickness of the pelt to see how far the tannin had penetrated. It was clear how this progressed as the part in the center where the solution hadn't entered would be flesh colored while the outer sections should be deep brown.

Finally, the tanning stage was completed. The hides were removed from the barrel and laid out to begin drying. As the drying progressed it was essential that neatsfoot oil be brushed on both sides of the hides at frequent intervals. Over a long period of time the oil penetrated through the hides.

Now came the real work session. Animal hides naturally have a large amount of glue in them. In the early days of furniture making and carpentry it was very common to see "hide" glue used consistently in gluing wood together. Of course, this glue when thoroughly dried made the hides stiff as a board. To make the leather supple it was necessary to "break" the leather.

A footed stand, similar to a cobbler's one, was made using a two-by-four. It was smoothly rounded and extended above my knees about ten inches. With my feet planted firmly on the bottom board and the two-by-four wedged between my knees I began the seemingly endless job of seesawing all parts of the hide over the rounded edge to "break" the leather.

After one experience in tanning leather, I did not attempt to repeat the process but turned instead to other endeavors.

While it was a chore to crank the cream separator, this was mild compared to the job of cleaning it after each morning and evening use. Every part that the milk contacted had to be thoroughly washed and then sterilized with boiling water.

The hardest job was washing the bowl. Frequently we would begin by running clear water through while the crank was being turned. Then the bowl had to be taken apart using a special pin wrench to get the securing nut off the top. After the outer part of the bowl was removed, the discs, which were made of thin tinned metal and cone-shaped, were transferred to a holding rack that looked like a modified huge safety pin.

The slots in the center of the bowl had to be very thoroughly cleaned out. If one failed to do this, eventually dried milk left in there would form what was called "milk stone." That would require a sharp knife blade to remove.

After the discs were washed and scalded they were separated on the holding rack to allow them to freely air dry.

Another crank to turn was the one on our wet grindstone. My job was always on the crank as my brother would hold the tool to be sharpened against the grindstone and properly shape the cutting edge.

Occasionally the scythes that we used to cut fresh hay for the horses would need sharpening, as would axes, sledges, knives and other cutting tools.

With a bucket of water to keep the stone wet we would head for the barn. Often the jobs were accomplished in the cold winter so we kept the grindstone in the horse barn where the heat from the animals would keep both the water and us from freezing.

Water was placed in the wooden trough under the round stone. Then the trough was propped up to where the lower part of the stone would be continually wetted. The secret of the wet grindstone was the water constantly running over the tool's sharpening edge kept it from heating and taking the temper out of the metal. Still, resharpening an axe blade that had some nicks in it seemed to take forever. Today I continue to sharpen tools with a wet grindstone. However, fortunately this one is electrically powered.

When the time came to start haying we always removed the sickle bar from the horse-drawn mower and ground the individual blades to a sharp edge. A special grinder was provided to accomplish this unusual sharpening. The clamping device on the bottom was specially shaped so that it could be clamped securely to the top of the cast-iron mower wheel. Starting at one end, the sickle bar was also clamped into the proper position so that the grinding wheel would meet the cutting edge of the blade just right.

As the crank handle was turned, the v-shaped grinding wheel revolved and moved steadily up and down between two blades, sharpening those two edges at the same time. Then, in turn, the bar was unclamped, moved to the next position and reclamped until all blades were sharp again. This same grinder could be used for sharpening the sickle blade on grain binders.

We had another hand-cranked machine which was a real monster to operate. Dad called it a "hackels" cutter and he used it to chop up cured green oats for the horses. However, we used it to cut up corn bundles to feed to the dairy cows.

A huge rotating cast-iron flywheel was on the front of this device. Sharp, curved steel blades, about 3/8" thick were mounted on this flywheel. As it turned, the knives just cleared the steel chute through which the corn was fed. The resultant chopped corn was about 3/4" long, very similar to silage.

Rotating, grooved feed rollers kept the corn moving forward. Cranks were provided on both sides of the machine and believe me it took both of us to keep it operating with many rest periods in between.

We were grateful when we acquired Uncle Johnny's 5 HP "hit and miss" gasoline engine and this machine was fitted with a suitable pulley. This formerly tough chore then became "a breeze."

As I look back on my childhood on the farm, I spent a lot of time manipulating handles on farm equipment. Most were operated with cranks but some, like the old well pump, just had to be worked up and down. These, which today are powered by electricity, later could be operated by early "hit and miss" gasoline engines.

One tool that I remember dad using was a grain flail, for threshing grain. This was accomplished on the flat plank floor in the driveway of our barn. It was made of two pieces of round hardwood about 1 1/2 inches in diameter. The handle, which was about 4 or 5 feet long, was attached to the beater by a heavy leather strap nearly 1/2 inch thick. As I remember, very large spikes driven through the leather strap into the ends of the two parts held the device together. The beater was about 2 1/2 feet long and rotated around the end of the handle.

A fair amount of skill was required to "flail" grain. A suitable amount of ripe grain was spread on the driveway floor. Then dad began by swinging the beater over his head and striking the grain stalks in a manner so that the beater would hit flat against them. As a youngster I tried it a few times but never met with much success. It demanded more force than a skinny lad could provide.

After a few minutes of proper flailing, we would clear away the straw with a pitchfork and shovel up the residual grain.

Threshed grain, whether flailed or run through some of the early threshing machines, always had a certain amount of chaff entrained. The Bible's reference to separating the grain from the chaff certainly struck home. To accomplish the final separation we turned to a device known as the fanning mill.

This big complex wooden contraption had a large trough at the top into which a fair amount of grain could be dumped. By moving a slotted board up or down, one could control the rate of flow of the grain into the machine. Turning the handle, which was attached to the axle holding a large rotary fan, produced a blast of air to blow the chaff out of the opposite end of the mill. The cranking also powered the grain sieves that shook back and forth while the grain passed over them. It eventually ended either in a drawer on the bottom or directly onto the driveway floor.

Different sets of sieves were provided with the mill to allow for the proper fanning of various kinds of seed and grain. Usually we set the fanning mill so that the breeze blowing through the driveway would carry the chaff well away from the barn.

Another hand-cranked device was the corn sheller. This was also usually operated in the barn driveway. This was harder work and required both my brother and me to operate it. We took turns on the crank as the other person would feed the corn ears into the hopper on the top. Inside, rasping plates grated the corn off the cob and cast the shelled cobs out of the opposite end. The shelled corn poured out of a tubular opening in the bottom and landed in a bushel basket.

Of course, early morning and each evening after milking, the cream separator had to be cranked at a steady 60 revolutions per minute. The fresh milk was placed in the large container on top of the machine. With the crank being turned at the right speed and containers to receive the cream and skim milk in place, the spigot was opened to allow the milk to begin flowing at the proper rate.

The ingenious part of the separator was a well-balanced bowl spinning at a high rate of speed. The milk entered the top center of the bowl and traveled down. The great centrifugal force in the spinning bowl forced the milk outward through a series of discs. Cream, being lighter in weight than skim milk, was forced upward and discharged through a spout into the cream container. The skim milk, which did not rise as high in the bowl, was discharged through the lower spout into a milk can. The skim milk was considered somewhat of a nuisance and was either fed to the calves and cows, or soured to be given to the pigs and chickens. Little did I know that some day I would be paying $2.47 for a gallon of skim milk on the Island in 1996.

Many animals have personalities. This was especially true of our old horses. Dick, the gelding or "seedless Thompson," had been castrated as a colt and was very placid. We could do anything around him and he was never bothered by what we did. However, Flossie, the old gray mare, was very temperamental and innovative. She learned how to open nearly every gate on the farm. The one between the barn and the house she would grasp with her teeth and twist to open until my brother "foxed" her by building a wooden frame around the handle.

Some of the gates leading into hay fields were made of long, slender poles. Flossie discovered that by placing her rump firmly against the center of the gate and sashaying her behind back and forth she could force the gate and thus get into a nice field of green hay. As a teenager I decided to remedy that.

I took several 1" x 4" boards, drove sharpened nails through them, and nailed these to the gate so the nails protruded in the direction from which Flossie would mount her "rearend" attack. After releasing her from her barn stall, I hid behind a tree to observe. She attacked the gate in the usual manner, but quickly a puzzled look appeared on her face. Something was wrong! After several more attempts she gave up. However, she then exhibited her usual reaction to frustration by kicking her hind legs high in the air, loudly breaking wind and then galloping away.

I always knew that Flossie detested work but Marvin and I had a scheme to lure her into the barn so we could harness her. Next to the barn we kept a small field of hay and we would cut fresh hay to feed the horses before working them. Before cutting the hay, we always noisily honed the scythe blade with a sharpening stone. Flossie would hear this and think, "Oh, boy! I'm going to be fed," and come at a trot. In spite of her intelligence in other things, she never caught on to this ploy.

I learned of another animal with quite a personality from George Haas, Sr., who was a Pilot Island Lighthouse keeper. He lived where Jack Cornell now resides and often visited our farm for dairy products. This happened outside of Holland, MI where George had previously been stationed.

A middle-aged man wed a middle-aged lady. The morning after the wedding they arose early and he told his wife he was going out to feed the animals while she was preparing a sumptuous bridal breakfast. He pushed hay from the barn driveway through a small feed door to his stubborn ass. This animal immediately swung his head, pushing hay out of the manger trough onto the floor where he struck it with his front feet, driving it under the trough where he could not reach it. The farmer walked into the stall by the jackass to pick up the hay and place it back in the trough. Whereupon the jackass began striking at the farmer with his front feet, driving the man under the feed trough. Here he was safe from the animal's front feet, but was trapped there. Each time he tried to escape, the menacing hooves struck out driving him back into cramped safety.

In the meantime, the bountiful breakfast was ready and getting cold. Finally his wife made her way to the barn and discovered his plight. He instructed her to get into the driveway and find something to reach through the feed door hole and drive the jackass back.

After some searching she decided to unfasten the whippletree from the wagon evener and drive the animal back in the stall. Finally she succeeded to a point where her husband was able to hastily stand and dive through the feed door.

He was mighty grateful for his rescue and thought that ended the affair. However, the editor of the local weekly paper learned about this event and published a full account of what had transpired.

The newly-weds were not too happy when they saw the banner at the top of the story saying, "Bride of One Day Beats Ass Off Husband With Whippletree."

To any farm history buff the Northeastern Wisconsin antique Power Assn. Thresheree at Valmy on August 20 and 21 this year is a spectacular event. While I am departing somewhat from straight, Island history, still many of the things I have seen at this Thresheree brought back memories of early Island farm life.

The 1926 Door County rotary snowblower reminded me of the excitement when Waldemar Hanson began plowing big snowdrifts on Main Road with an Allis-Chalmers cleat-tractor fitted with a large plow on the front. When the Sturgeon Bay owner of “Grandpa Bill” , a 1916 Case 60 Horsepower Steam engine powers the grain thresher I think back to when Martin "Saltum" Andersen and threshing crew came to our farm. Crosscut saw cutting competition floods my memory of the countless hours that brother Marvin, and I spent in winter cutting and splitting our year's supply of wood fuel, all by hand. The "hit and miss" one cylinder gas engines are very similar to the old Gilson 5 HP one we acquired from Uncle Johnny Hannesson. This machine relieved us of lots of hand labor. Grain binding will be shown in the same manner as Charley Hansen or Lauritz Klingenberg did on our farm, as we did not own a binder. The sawmill operates in a manner much like Koyen's mill did when we had the hemlock and balsam trees made into lumber to build our garage in 1935. Husking, shelling and grinding corn is still done here the old-fashioned way.

Of course, the antique tractor pull on Saturday,August 20th,is something I never witnessed as a boy. These machines dating from 1955 or earlier compete in weight classes ranging from 2800 to 8500 lbs.

Any lovers of draft horses should be sure to see the "Barefoot Horse Pull" on Sunday where beautifully matched draft horses with outstandingly decorated harnesses compete in pulling a timbered sled, loaded with more and more concrete blocks until the winners emerge.

Sunday afternoon a relaxing event for spectators is watching the "Kid's Pedal Tractor Pull" followed by the "Little Farmer Contest" where the best dressed tiny farmers show off their attire.

Between scheduled events there is time to tour the grounds of the Geisel Farm to see such things as shingle and lath mills in operation; cutting, raking and loading hay; a hay press; potato digging; stone crushing of Door County limestone (similar to the way early Island road builders made crushed stone); horse and antique tractor plowing; cyclone and straw chopping; woodcarving; l/4 scale Case steam engine; miniature Case hay press and mule horsepower.

While all these are continuous displays of operating equipment, the "Ladies Tent" has ceramic "Country" souvenirs; spinning wheels; beekeeping display; miniature toy display; country pillows and quilts and caps and T-shirts.

For the admission price of only $4.00 a person receives a souvenir button good for both days. Children 12 and under FREE. Saturday evening at 5:30 P.M. a barn dance is held with music by The Whiskey River Band. This year's special attraction is a 1912 German Fair Organ. Islanders who remember Freddie Kodanko's polka music in previous years, whenever Baileys Harbor baseball team played on the Island, will be amused and entertained by his "Toe Tapping" music.

Great food and refreshments such as hamburgers, brats, beer and pop will be served by Threshermen's wives.

Unfortunately,this year the first day of the Valmy Thresheree is the same day as the Island Fair. We don't want to miss our Fair, but remember some very interesting things are scheduled for Sunday and all of the displays will be operating.

See you at Geisel's farm, just north of Valmy, well marked by signs on Sunday, August 21st.

FARMER'S UNION

As a farm boy growing up on the Island in the 20s and 30s I was intimately aware of the Holstein Breeder's Association to which our family belonged. However, until I became involved in'the Island Farm Museum and began researching the records of early Island farming, I was not aware that there had been a very active Farm Union here. This was a part of the State Farm Union. Fortunately the locals chose Jens Jacobsen as secretary who faithfully and completely recorded all their doings. Further, his penmanship was beautiful, making it very easy to read his recordings.

This appeared on page 1 of the Journal:

Pursuant to notice duly given a meeting was called at Nelson's Hall on October 28, 1908. Meeting was called to order at 8 P.M. by J.W. Simms, Deputy Organizer-American Society of Equity, who delivered a lecture and duly organized Washington Island Local Union No 5439 with the following members:

Gust Lindstrom(now Beamishes), Christ A. Hanson (now tne "Green House"), George Hanson (oppo.Sievers), John D. Johnson (Jackie Obergs), Hans B. Hanson (Potato Farm), Jens Jacobsen (Michigan & Eastside Rds.), J.W. Sims (State Organizer), Ole Hagen (Jack Hagens), Vernie Richter (Jon Andersons), Morton Jorgenson (Dr. Russe & Bill Jorgensons), Gustav Swenson (opposite Briesemeisters), August Koyen (Paul Walachs), Gust L. Boucsein (Jack Cornells), John S. Johnson (Eastside Park), Ole C. Ericson(Ken Koyens), Louis Gunnlaugson (Jane Deweys), Peter Gunnlaugson, Sr. (Nancy Kaniff), Peter Gunnlaugson, Jr. (Irvin Goodlets)

The Union then elected officers as follows:

Gust Lindstrom President, Christ A. Hanson Vice President, Jens Jacobsen Secretary, August Koyen Treasurer.

It was on motion adopted to hold the next meeting at Nelson's Hall on November 11th 1908.

Thomas Nelson agreeing to let the Union meet in his hall once each month or oftener for $20.00 pr. year.

Meeting on motion adjourned sine die. Jens Jacobsen, Secretary

In the following meeting, these members were admitted after paying dues (Dues originally were $3, later raised to $4)

Lars Bilton (Flaths Cottages), Steve Gunnlaugson (N. of Ray Hansens), Christ Jensen (Sportsmens Club), Knud Hanson (Richards-Mtn. Rd.) Chas. J. Schmidt (Alex Koyens), Sigurd Sigurdson (East of Smalls), Henry B. Olson (Jim Gages), Sophus Anderson (John Herschbergers), George Nelson(Paul Jewels), Thomas Launders (Gordon Jaegers), Peter Jensen (Kirby Fosses), Christ Jacobsen (Crowley's residence), Mads Hanson (Emily Jensens), Christopher Einarson (Richard Hansens), Olafur Einarson (Russ Gunnlaugssons), Ole Bowman (Lonnie Jorgensons), Wm. Malloch (Kincaides & Rob Gunnersons), John Aznoe (Jim Gunnlaugssons), Wilfred Koyen (Arni Fosses), Lars Anderson (Caroline Caldwells), Nels Nelson (John Gunnlaugssons), Curtis Allen (Ted Jessen, Sr.), Martin Andersen-Saltum (Jack Hagens), George Madson (Randy Sorensons), John Anderson (Ted Hansens), Marcus Peterson (Charles Jacks), Chr. Nelsen (Bernadette Claytons), Arthur Wickman (Ron Pepsniks), Robert Gunerson (oppo. Smalls), Ernest Boucsein (S. of Jack Cornells), Jake Lindal (Caroline Caldwells), Conrad Anderson(Jeff McDonalds), Jens Hansen (now "Green Acres"), Chas. Jensen (Nathan Gunnlaugssons), Theo. Gudmundson (Norbert O'Connells), Martin A. Andersen (Lorraine Andersens), Ossie Olson (Danny Hansens), Walter Launders(Gordon Jaegers), Ed Aznoe (Jim Gunnlaugssons), Andrew Swenson (Bill Schutzes), Elsie Cornell (Milt Kolars), Cpt. Peter Hansen (Airport), John Einarson (Bill Schutzes??), Henry Einarson (????), Lois Hanson (Jake Ellefsons), Carl Anderson (Richard Hill), Gus Jacobsen (Beverly Hudsons), Mack Gunnlaugson (Basquins), A. Gudmundson (Lou Small), Lawrence Klingenberg (N.E. side of Main & Townline Rds.), Thos. Johnson (Kickbushs), Soren Jensen (formerly Chuck Goodlets), Chas Sand (Randy Sorensons), Lars Lindal (oppo. Airport???)

The farmer's Washington Local Union No. 5439 originally held meetings at very frequent intervals. Often a subject for debate would be selected to be presented at the next meeting. In reviewing Jens Jacobsen's complete minutes I found many items of interest such as the following:

Dec. 10, 1908--The principal discussion for the evening was the shipping of potatoes. The members all agreeing that the present way was unsatisfactory and anyone, who would freight potatoes for the union must show'an itemized account showing selling price, freight and other charges and the net price to the farmer.

Dec. 22, 1908--The debate "Resolved that dairying is more profitable to the farmer than the growing of peas" was then called. August Koyen being the leader on the affirmative assisted by Morton Jorgenson. The negative was led by C.A. Hanson assisted by Gustav Swenson. Steve Gunnlaugson, Thomas Launders and Ole Hagen acting as judges decided the debate in favor of the affirmative.

Jan. 6, 1909--A debate-Resolved that it is profitable to raise horses was then taken up. Ole C. Erickson leading the affirmative and August Koyen the negative. Chas. Schmidt, Hans B. Hanson and George Hansen decided in favor of the affirmative.

Jan. 20, 1909--Christ A. Hanson then gave a lecture on applying manure and Ole C. Erickson a lecture on dairying.

Feb. 2, 1909--The Secretary was instructed to write for prices of clover and timothy seed. Jens Jacobsen then talked on fruit growing and Gus Lindstrom gave a lecture on potato culture.

Feb. 17, 1909--A talk on barley by Knud Hanson followed by a general discussion.

Mar. 2, 1909-Orders were then taken for clover seed and Timothy seed and the Secretary was instructed to telephone to Jeweles & Brandeis at Sturgeon Bay to find out if they would still except (sic) $6.25 pr. bu. for clover and 1.90 for Timothy. Gus Lindstrom sugested (sic) that the Union form an Animal Insurance Co. Motion made and seconded to leave the animal insurance for the next meeting (tabled for one year at next meeting).

Mar. 17,1909--The Secretary was instructed to inquire for prices of Alsike Mammoth and Alfalfa seed, also Alaska peas.

A discussion on Cherries by Jens Jacobsen then followed. The President appointed as a committee, A.V. Koyen, Henry Olson and Morton Jorgenson to write Town ticket and have same printed for the Union.

April 7,1909--Orders were taken for peas and contracts forwarded to G.O. Whitford by Secretary. Moved and seconded that A.V. Koyen and Hans B. Hanson help Mr. C..A. Hanson divide clover and timothy seed-carried.

C.A. Hanson then talked of crop rotation and discussion followed.

April 21, 1909--Motion passed to hold meetings in private homes in the future on Saturday evenings instead of Wednesdays.

May 1, 1909--Paid Thos. Nelson balance of hall rent $7.50. A lively discussion on getting a motorboat to run between Washington Harbor and Escanaba.

May 15,1909--A correspondence from Joannes Bros. of Green Bay was read and followed by a discussion on purchasing bindertwine and other necessaries.

June 5, 1909--A letter was read from Mr. Wes Tubbs wherein he expressed views of local unions buying goods together at wholesale rates. It was decided that we should send together for bindertwine.

June 19,1909--Orders were taken for bindertwine and the secretary instructed to inquire for prices of Paris Green (bug poison) and Flour.

July 3, 1909--George Mann was given a chance to supply the Union with Paris Green.

July 17, 1909--The union was supplied with Paris Green at 25 1/2 cts pr lb.

Sept. 4, 1909--Motion-passed that Union members ship their potato crop of 1909 together-agreement signed by 27 members. Motion passed to leave in the hands of the Secretary the task of securing schooners to carry the potato crop to market.

Motion passed to call a special meeting if there should be a chance to sell the potatoes here. Motion passed that Union members raise no contract peas of the wrinkled varieties for less than $1.50 for year 1910.

Sept. 18, 1909--Motion passed to correspond with Eastern firms for contracting peas.

Oct. 9, 1909--A correspondence was read from several potato schooners and the Sec. was instructed to write Sec. Tubbs if the Potato Growers Association could find sale for our crop.

Oct. 16 1909--Motion passed to hire Schooner Joses of Racine to freight a load of potatoes. The freight to be 7 cts. per bushel if sold at wholesale and 8 cts if peddled. Motion passed to hire Schooner Stevens of Sheboygan at the same rate 7 and 8 cts. Motion passed to hire Schooner Frances Miner of Manitowoc to freight a load of potatoes from Detroit Harbor, a freight of 10 cts. to be paid if peddled. (Schooners to come in the last week of October.) Motions passed to send Wm. Malloch with the Frances

Miner, Ole Ericson with the Joses, Gus Lindstrom with the Stevens. Motion passed that Jens Jacobsen look after the weighing of the potatoes at A. A. Koyens (now St. Michael's Chapel).

Oct. 30, 1909--Motion passed that Jens Jacobsen hire Schr. Loma Burton or some other Schr. to load potatoes for the Union at Washington Harbor.

Nov. 6, 1909--Voted by ballot that Mr. Morton Jorgenson go with Schooner No. 4 to sell her cargo. Motion passed that non-union potatoes bring 1 ct. less (to grower) than those of Union members, the 1 ct. to go into the Treasury of the Local Union.

Jan. 5,1910--The Union then proceeded to audit bills and make settlement with the men who had sold potatoes for the Union. The work was by the day and the wages paid $2.00 pr day and actual expenses.

March 19, 1910--The Union then proceeded to write Town Ticket and the Secretary was instructed to have the ticket printed.

July 16,1910--Owing to the small attendance it was decided not to meet regularly for some time and that the next meeting be a called meeting.

Oct. 8, 1910--(next meeting) The Union proceeded to estimate their potato crop for shipment and about 7000 bush. were signed up. Motion passed to ship potatoes to Coyne Bros. at 161 South Water'St., Chicago. Coyne Bros. asked to send a Chicago Schooner to load potatoes at Washington Harbor about Nov. 1, 1910--500 sacks from Coyne Bros. to come with schr. to be used in the hatches.

Oct. 22, 1910--A letter from Coyne Bros. stating they could get us a Chicago Schooner to freight potatoes at 6 1/2 cts. pr bushel. Motion passed for Coyne Bros. to secure Schooner for loading at Washington Harbor on Nov. 1. Jens Jacobsen to look after weighing of potatoes. Jens Jacobsen paid $9.75 for trip to Sturgeon Bay in March 1910.

Oct. 29, 1910--Jens Jacobsen reported $25.26 in the treasury available for dockage and Hans Hanson and Thos. Launders promised to advance the balance. Sacks were divided as follows: C.A. Hanson 100, Thos. Launders 100, Lars Bilton 50, Ole Hagen 50, Martin Anderson 25, Knud Hanson 30. Jens Jacobsen elected to go with Schooner.

Dec. 6, 1910--Jens Jacobsen reported that he had sold the cargo of potatoes on Schooner Geo. A. Marsh at Chicago for

$4800.00 and that he was ready to make settlement with all shippers. Motion passed that his bills be allowed in full and that he complete the settlement with checks on the Bank of Sturgeon Bay.

Jan. 21,1911--Motion passed that Special Members be admitted into the Union at 75 cts. each. The Secretary was instructed to write Door County Equity Elevator Co. to send our members their notes which they gave in security for seed peas 2 years ago and have been paid in full but were still at the Bank of Sawyer (across the bridge to south).

Sept. 16,1911--Objections were made to inferior stock, called cow potatoes, going in with the better lots in making up cargos and no business could be done.

Sept. 23, 1911--More farmers signed up potatoes and the Secretary was instructed to hire a suitable boat to freight them.

Dec. 9, 1911--The meeting was largely attended. Jens Jacobsen having announced that he was ready to settle with all farmers who had shipped potatoes on the schooner Grace. M. Filer to Chicago. The net price for this cargo was 72 cents per bushel for all good stock.

Jan. 6, 1912--It was decided to have a party at August Koyens and that the Secretary send out notes of the same in the near future.

Sept. 7, 1912--Jens Jacobsen prepared a list and those wishing to ship potatoes with him signed up an estimated amount of bushels. Mr. Morton Jorgenson offered to supply farmers with Flour, Feed and Groceries for 5 percent above the wholesale price and freight.

Sept. 28, 1912--Motion passed that money derived from the sale of potatoes from the several Schooners be made one fund and that the price to the growers be one for all good stock inspected. Also that in case of loss by shipwreck, freezing or otherwise each shipper receives a lower price per bushel to cover the loss. One price to all.

Dec. 21, 1912--Jens Jacobsen read a statement and showed all bills connected with the sale of potatoes of Schooners G.M. Filer, Belle Brown and Geo. A. Marsh. Motion passed that Jens Jacobsen be paid about 1 ct. per bushel for his services.

Sept. 20, 1913--The Secretary prepared a list where those wishing to ship potatoes could sign-up. Motion passed that each member signs his name to the list himself and if any member fails to deliver the number of bushels set opposite his name by reason of shipping elsewhere he shall pay the freight on same. Jens Jacobsen be paid for selling potatoes 1 ct. per bushel if the price paid to be 50 cts. or less and 1 1/2 cts. if the price paid be 60 cts. Motion passed that weighing be done on Geo. 0. Mann's scale, A.V. Koyen to furnish slides and shoveling boards. Schooner to load about Oct. 25.

Mar. 21, 1914--The building of a dock at West Harbor was discussed and upon motion Jens Jacobsen was asked to correspond with John Paulson for the purchase of a lot for Dock and Warehouse at West Harbor. The chair appointed Jens Jacobsen, Ole C. Ericson and George Hanson a committee to look after the shipping of potatoes next fall and to draw plans for same.

May 30, 1914--The Secretary reported having procured Clover, Timothy and other seeds for the members in the amount of $160.00. A letter from John Paulson was read wherein he stated that he would give a lot for the dock and warehouse at West Harbor. Motion passed that we start a stock company to be known as the Washington Island Dock Co. to be capitalized at $5000.00. Shares to be sold to Washington Island people only at $10.00 per share and no one to own more than 10 shares or $100.00 worth. The said company to buy, or build, own, rent and operate such dock or docks as may be needed for shipping. Also to dredge channels to and about their dock or docks as the case may be. The Washington Island Dock Co. then elected by ballot 5 directors as follows: John Paulson to hold 5 years, Jens Jacobsen 4 years, Martin Anderson 3 years, Arthur Wickman 2 years, Wm Malloch 1 year.

Sept. 12, 1914--Motion passed that Jens Jacobsen look after the shipping of potatoes and receive the same pay as last year. Motion passed that round and long potatoes be kept separate on the Schooner as much as possible. Motion passed that half of the number of signers on the list haul first day of loading and second half the second day and that no one haul more than 4 loads in one day. Motion passed that we load with baskets and that we have 4 doz. baskets and 500 sacks come up on the Schooner. Motion passed that Jens Hanson be Inspector at $2.00 per day.

A letter from James Larsen Construction Co., Marinette, WI was read, but the work at West Harbor was indefinitely postponed.

Sept. 4, 1915--Meeting called for the purpose of arranging for shipping peas . and potatoes. Motion to send for 1000 Grain Bags lost, then Motion passed for 700 Grain Bags for shipping peas or such number as might be ordered in addition. Secretary was asked to correspond with dealers and if possible induce a buyer to come where the peas were threshed.

Sept. 29, 1915--Motion passed for Jens Jacobsen to look after the shipping of Peas and that he be paid $2.50 per day for his services. Motion passed that 1 ct. per bushel be paid into the treasury on all peas and potatoes handled by the Union.

Oct. 9, 1915--Motion passed that we start shipping peas next Tuesday. Secretary to send for $2.00 worth of twine and 1 doz. needles for sewing sacks and 1000 Coyne Bros. tags. Secretary asked to write Wm. Schlosser in Milwaukee if one of his vessels would be available for a potato cargo from Washington Harbor and the conditions.

Oct, 16, 1915--Jens Jacobsen to again have charge of shipping potatoes. Again the first half of shippers as appearing on the list will haul the first day and second 1/2 to haul the second day of boat loading. Ole C. Ericson to be Inspector of cargo at $2.00 per day. Peas will be graded on Geo. Mann's mill for shipment.

Jan. 29, 1916--Motion passed that Ole Erickson look after the purchase of Seed Corn and Grasses. Motion passed that any member in good standing having shipped produce with this Union during 1915 be exempted from paying dues 1916. (last minutes by Jens Jacobsen, Art Wickman became new Secretary.)

Feb. 19, 1916--Secretary instructed to buy seed corn No.8 and Timothy from Jeweles & Brandeis, Red clover from Ed Evenson of Ellison Bay.

Aug. 26,1916--Secretary to write Holmes in regard to shipping stock. (First mention of uniting in shipping livestock.)

Sept. 17, 1916--400 pea bags were on hand as ordered and delivered to members at the price of 21 cts. and money turned over to Treasurer in the amount of $84.90. Check drawn for sacks $80.00. Check to A. Wickman for telegrams, phones and freight-$2.65.

Oct. 7, 1916--Jeweles and Brandeis offer of $4.10 for peas to be excepted(sic) by Tuesday if no better offer is received by that time. Motion to start hauling peas on Tuesday with Christ Jensen and Art Wickman in charge of weighing and financial business with pay of $2. 50 per day. A number of members refused to sign on account of their having promised to hold their peas for Jens Jacobsen. Jens read a·letter from A. Dickenson Co.in regard to peas. A number of complaints were presented and a lively discussion on unionism followed.

Oct. 21,1916--, Motion carried to allow four days pay for clerical work on peas. Left-over pea bags sold at auction to members and money turned into treasurer. No action taken on potatoes.

Dec. 7,1916--Secretary presented an offer of getting clover seed direct from the farmers across the Door at about $10 per bu. Motion carried to buy $120.00 worth at no more than $10 per bushel. Members ordered 30 bushels.

Jan. 4,1917--Motion carried that the Union intends to ship stock in the spring. Offer of Northern Potato Co.to sell us certified Rural New Yorker (seed potatoes) at $1.75 per bushel. Members ordered 30 bushels.

April 7, 1917--Motion carried to buy binder twine through the Equity.

Aug. 11, 1917---Motion carried to have Secretary send for grain bags from A. Dickenson Co. at 40 cts. Motion carried to advertise for a blacksmith and wheelright in the Door County news.

Sept. 22, 1917-Motion carried to ship stock about Oct. 1st. George Johnson to take charge and Jake Bowman to go along and help load stock on cars. Motion carried to have directors inspect Peter Hanson's scale and buy it they think it is good enough to use. Motion passed to have all Union peas fanned before shipping.

Oct. 20, 1917--Members signed up potatoes for Schooner Stafford. Motion passed that members pay 1 ct. per bu. and non-members pay 2 cts. per bu. on potatoes shipped. Art Wickman to take charge of the shipment and August Koyen to be Inspector in loading the boat. Motion passed that we charge 3 cts. per bushel on peas shipped.

Aug. 23, 1918--Motion carried that peas be graded on Geo. Mann's grader before shipment. Second hand bags were sold to highest bidder-8 bags to Art Wickman at 75 cts., 8 bags to Martin Andersen at .55, 7 bags to Lars Lindall at 30 cts. Motion passed that A. Koyen keep record of stock to be shipped. Motion passed that in case of loss of any animal after being loaded on board of boat, the loss shall be on the whole shipment according to weight. Motion that Union buy the wagon scale of L. Gislason at cost price. Motion carried to have Union tickets printed for primary (election).Motion to ship potatoes.

Sept. 6, 1918--Potato shipping and grading was discussed. Secretary was instructed to inquire of Mr. Goff as to laws governing grading and also to secure prices on graders, etc.

Oct. 2, 1918--An address by Mr. Goff on potato grading. Motion carried to order two large potato graders. Ole Erickson appointed to take charge of potato shipment.

Oct. 23, 1918--Motion carried that when about half shipment of potatoes is sold, money be placed in bank to the credit of the Union and shippers be allowed to draw same amount on the shipments. Motion carried that A. Koyen and Jens Jacobsen take care and drum up potatoes for cargo.

Jan. 8, 1919--Jens Jacobsen report of potato shipment read and adopted. Motion carried that the Board of Directors settle with Hanson Bros. for use of potato grader. Motion carried that we go ahead with Moors proposition and offer peas at $5 per bu., sacks included and Directors to use their judgement about lowering price if necessary. Binder twine orders taken. A. Koyen to be in charge of seed order.

June 3, 1919--This meeting called to consider joining the County livestock Shipping Association. After talking it over a motion was passed that we join and send ten dollars fees. Our Secretary was asked to keep posted as to shipping days and Ect.(sic) and August Koyen agreed to make arrangements with Capt. Hill in regards to rates and also about making a direct run to Sturgeon Bay with stock.

Sept. 23, 1919--Motion carried that Wilfred Koyen and Art Wickman cover the Island with potato list at once. Motion passed that Sec. write boat owners in regard to securing a potato boat. Motion passed that Union get up an order for flour and feed.

Jan. 22, 1920--Pea report by President. Potato report by Art Wickman. Equity troubles discussed by President. Motion carried that we all become full Equity members and pay up dues, fees and Ect.(sic) and hereafter nobody will be considered a member of our Union unless he become a full Equity member. Vote was by ballot with 14 in favor and 5 against.

Feb. 20, 1920 An interesting report was given by Jens Jacobsen of the doings at the County convention and a motion was passed to allow him 15 dollars for expenses. Motion carried to allow Wilfred Koyen $2.25 for making Bulletin board to be put up at creamery. Ole Erickson gave an interesting talk on creamery and cheese factory problems. Seed orders were taken for about $550.00 and Art Wickman was to take charge of same. Coffee and lunch was served by Wilfred Koyen, which we all enjoyed.

Sept. 3, 1920--Motion passed that Rob Gunnerson take charge of shipping livestock. Motion passed that we ship peas this fall with Jens Jacobsen in charge. Motion carried that we buy a potato grader with Ole Erickson to look into same. Secretary to inquire about a boat, take bag orders and buy same. Ed Aznoe to buy a bag stencil for the Union. Orders for 130 bags received.

Sept. 22, 1920-- Motion carried that Rob Gunnerson go around with potato list. Wilfred Koyen elected to take charge of (potato) graders and engines.

Mar.15,1921--Motion passed that we sell all assets and liabilities of L.U. 5439 AS of E of Detroit Harbor, Wis. to Ed Aznoe for one dollar. Motion then passed that our Local Union disband after tonight. The bunch then proceeded to organize and elect officers of the Washington Island Produce Co. After which the members of our Local Union, AS of E remaining, proceeded to elect officers for the following year, and they were as follows: Ole Erickson Pres., Jens Jacobsen Vice Pres., Art Wickman Sec. Treas., Rob Gunnerson Director, Jens Hanson Director.

All the above paid dues of $5.00 for the ensuing year.

So ended Washington Local Union No. 5439 of the American Society of Equity.

In reviewing the minutes of the AS of E Local Union over the years I could tell by sort of "reading between the lines" that a number of controversies developed. One which became quite apparent had to do with Gus Lindstrom. He had accompanied a shipment of Union potatoes to market on a schooner.

At the November 6, 1909 meeting - Motion passed that the Secretary instruct Mr. Lindstrom to place money for cargo of potatoes on (schooner) J.H. Stevens in Bank of Sturgeon Bay in the name of the Union, so the Secretary can draw checks on same.

January 5, 1910-Gus Lindstrom not being present, and his bills not corresponding no settlement could be had with him. The secretary was instructed to proceed with the settlement for potatoes and to leave out Gus Lindstrom's settlement.

January 22, 1910-A letter from Gus Lindstrom was read by Sec. Mr. Lindstrom's account on potatoes was reviewed and it showed Mr. Lindstrom indebted to the Union.

March 19, 1910--Motion passed that Secretary appoint a committee to try to make settlement with Gus Lindstrom. Wm. Malloch and Sophus Andersen were appointed as committee.

April 1, 1910--The committee appointed to settle with Gus Lindstrom then reported that they had called on Mr. Lindstrom and that he had promised to be present at this meeting. Mr. Lindstrom did not appear but sent a letter and his expense bill. The letter was read and his bill laid before the house and considered. Committee was paid $1.00 each. Motion passed that secretary make a copy of the Lindstrom bill and return the original to Mr. Lindstrom and ask him to go before a notary public and make an affidavit that every item charged is a correct and true expense of his trip. And if he shall return the bill with said affidavit by April 23, Washington Union would allow it in full.

April 23,1910-A letter from Gus Lindstrom was read and on motion tabled.

May 21, 1910-Gus Lindstrom's letter was called for and read. Motion passed that Gus Lindstrom be struck from the membership roll of Washington L. U. 5439 A. S. C. according to his own request. A settlement was had with Gus Lindstrom for selling the cargo of potatoes of Schr. Stevens in November 1909. Mr. Lindstrom's promissory note for $20.00 was accepted as payment in full.

Author's note:

Washington Island Local Union No. 5439, part of the American Society of Equity, lasted from October 28, 1908 to March 15, 1921. During those years it taught Island farmers to work cooperatively in selling their crops which were mainly potatoes and ripe peas. Also they learned that by purchasing seeds, produce and other commodities together they could save money. Other than the Lindstrom controversy, I could not find any real reason why the Union finally faded and was dissolved. In the minutes of the last meeting, as previously reported, on March 15, 1921 a group of Union members organized the "Washington Island Produce Company" and elected officers. I had never heard of this organization, but hope to learn more about it and report it to you.

HOLSTEIN BREEDER'S ASSOCIATION

The Washington Island Holstein Breeders Association(WIHBA) was organized early in 1918 with the help of Mr, Bailey, Door County Agricultural Agent. Mrs, Ted(Charlotte) Hansen kindly loaned me the Journal and other associated papers which had been kept in her father's house. Her father and grandfather, Christ A. Hansen, helped to organize the association and served very actively in it.

The Constitution and By-Laws of the WIHBA states: "The object of this Association shall be to promote the breeding and improvement of high grade and pure bred Holstein cattle in the Town of Washington, Door County, and to aid its members in buying, using and selling first class animals; also the establishment of Washington Island as a Holstein breeding center. The annual membership shall consist of farmers interested in the object of the Association and paying the required annual fee(50 cents)."

In addition to the offices of President, Secretary and "Treasurer they agreed to have four Vice Presidents, "one from each township".(Actually this amounted to having one in each of the four school districts, Detroit Harbor, Washington Harbor, Jackson Harbor and Eastside or Lucke School.)

"It shall be the duty of every member to improve his herd of cows by mating his cows exclusively with pure bred Holstein bulls and doing as much as he can to care for his herd in an up-to-date manner.

It shall also be the duty of members to co-operate so far as possible with fellow members in the use of pure bred bulls and in buying and selling animals; also to get new members and encourage them in the practice of better methods in caring for their herds.

All members in good standing shall be entitled to a vote in the business meetings of the Association. A member in arrears over one year shall cease to be a member, but may be restored by paying all arrears.

It shall be the duty of the several Vice Presidents to look after the interests of the Association in the various townships and they shall have the privilege of calling local meetings and doing all in their power to promote the general interests of the Association in such manner as the Executive Committee shall deem fit."

May 2,1918 The first meeting was called to order by County Agent D.S. Bullock who was elected chairman of the meeting. Lauritz Klingenberg, Ole C. Erickson, Arthur Wickman and Jens Hansen served on the nominating committee. Results of the election were:

President	Christ A. Hansen	21 votes
	Lauritz Klingenberg	7
Vice Pres.Dist.1	Theo. Gudmundson	16 (Washington Harbor)
	Volney E.Koyen	13
Vice Pres.Dist.2	Ole C. Erickson	15 (Detroit Harbor)
	Christian Jensen	13
Vice Pros.Dist.3	Carl Nelson	16 (Eastside)
	Christopher Einarson	11
Vice Pres.Dist.4	George Hansen	18 (Jackson Harbor)
	George Nelson	9
Secretary	George O. Mann	21
	Bo L. Andersen	7
Treasurer	Nels C. Nelson	19
	Jens Hansen	9

May 31,1992 At the annual meeting of the Washington Island Holstein Breeders Association, County Agent Bailey suggested a plan for Island farmers to buy pure bred bulls and a motion was carried for Mr. Bailey to see the Sturgeon Bay bankers about "backing the Association in Buying Pure Bred Stock."

June 6,1922 At a special meeting, Mr. Bailey reported that the bankers preferred Association notes rather than small notes from individuals. Association loan could be made at 7 per cent while individual notes would be at 8 per cent. It was suggested that the sentiment of the house, on proposition, be ascertained with the result that the following gentlemen voiced their favor:

Chas. J.Schmidt	8 cows	B.L. Andersen	2 cows
Jens Jensen	6	H.A. Gudmundson	6
Geo. Hansen	8	Carl Nelson	8
Thorwald Johnson	5	Arthur Wickman	3
A.G.Swenson	6	Ole Hagen	9
John H. Malloch	1	Geo. Madsen	6
Jens Hansen	5	Chr. A.Hansen	1
Carl Anderson	5	Nels Nelson	5
Vernie Richter	7	Wilfred Koyen	4

Knud Hansen	6	Chris Nelson	1

Making a total of 20 names and 100 cows.

"The following gentlemen volunteered to canvas the Island for additional subscribers:

Haldor Gudmundsen and Alfred Hansen in School District No. 1.

Carl Anderson and Vernie Richter in School District No. 2.

Wilfred Koyen in School District No. 3.

Jens Hansen and George Hansen in School District No. 4."

Motion passed that the bull Chr. A. Hansen is about to buy be taken over by the Association if it is organized.

June 29, 1922 Motion passed to get one bull old enough for service and a younger bull from Murphy Farms.

Motion passed that $2.00 per cow assessment be the limit for purchase of bulls.

August 15,1922 The WIHBA was incorporated with the seven directors of the association declared officers in the new incorporated association to comply with the law. The constitution and by-laws were read and adopted by those present, twenty five in number. Motion passed to authorize the directors to insure the sires at a reasonable amount. In regard to tuberculin testing, there were fifteen men present who desired a test of their herds and Mr. Bailey agreed to inquire regarding federal tester, or if not available, to find out what charge would be made by a veterinarian from Sturgeon Bay.

It was decided to have a picnic on August 29th with arrangements by Bo Andersen, Vernie Richter and Ole Hagen.

Mr. Bailey talked on cooperation in the sale of potatoes.

December 5,1922 Motion passed that the Association purchase the sire of C.A. Hansen at his cost price plus allowance for freight, keep at a rate of $125.00 per year, and other minor expenses he has been put to since date of purchase.

Plans for an entertainment and social were made to be held the latter part of January. Committee as follows:

George Madsen	Mrs. George Madsen
Charles Jensen	Mrs. Clara Boyce
Vernie Richter	

Nov. 3,1922 At the Executive Committee's meeting tentative lists were drawn up with patrons into blocks for cow's service by the nearest bull. C.A. Hansen notified the Association that his bull is for sale and he asked remuneration for purchase price, freight, feeding and care and that he be paid at the rate of $135.00 per annum. As the other keepers are paid $125.00, it was decided that we could not pay him more. Mr. Schmidt and Mr. Nelson were appointed to see him. If he accepted the terms, a canvas was to be taken of the district which his sire would serve, to see what support the farmers there would give.

June 18,1923 A meeting of the directors of the Washington Island Holstein Breeders Association was held with County Agent Bailey present. Nels Nelsen was unanimously elected president to fill the balance of the term of Bo. L. Andersen, deceased.

It was decided to insure the bull purchased from Mr. Hansen for $300.00. Motion passed that any non-member wishing to breed a cow to an Association bull might do so by paying $1.00 more than the regular fee, subject to approval of the board of directors. The members were assigned to blocks as follows:

Christ A. Hansen's Block (just north of Ted Hansens)

Nels Nelson	5 cows	H.A. Gudmundsen	7 cows
Carl Anderson	6	Gus Andersen	4
Mrs. Boyce	5	Severt Barneson	2
Chas. J. Schmidt	8	Ole Hagen	9
Chris Sorenson	7	Geo. O. Mann	1
Frank Richter	1	Alfred Hansen	5
Christ A.Hansen	1	Chas. Haglund	2
Chas. O. Hansen	8	Harry Hansen	5
Jens Jensen	5		

Non-members from Frank Richters north and Waldemar Hansens north to Fred M. Hansen--Boundary of Block l.

George Madsen Block No. 2

George Hansen	9 cows	Rob Gunnarson	6 cows
Maurice Andersen	3	George Madsen	6
Knud Hansen	5	Thorvald Johnson	5
S.K.Lunde	2	Andrew Andersen	3
Chr. Einarson	6	P.J. Gunnlaugsson	6
Jens Jepson	3	A.G. Swenson	6

Non-members from Creamery north, from Ted's Store east, all Gasoline Town and Jackson, and all from Jens Jacobsens north on east side of road.

Ole Erickson Block No. 3

Bo L. Andersen	2 cows	R. Gunnarson	6 cows
V.Richter	9	Conrad Andersen	2
Wilfred Koyen	6	John Malloch	1
Carl Nelson	8	Arthur Wickman	3
Mack Gudmundsen	4	L.Gislason	2
Ben Johnson	1	Mary Nelson	4
Nor Shellswick	1	Ole Erickson	10
August Koyen	10	H.Johnson,Sr.	1
Martin Andersen	6	Chas. Jensen	3
Peter Christianson	2	Jens Jacobsen	2

Non-members from Jens Jacobsens and all south and east, O. Einarson's to Dr. Leasum's residence to Martin Andersen and all territory in that circle included in this block.

Mr. Bailey agreed to send typed notices to the members placing them in their respective blocks.

This makes a total of 49 members with 224 cows. Lots of non-members had cows, some had approximately 10 while others might have only one cow to provide milk for their family. Most of the milk went to the creamery which was also operated as a cheese factory over the years until it burned down. Later the larger dairy farms shipped milk in cans via the ferry to Lake to Lake trucks on the Mainland. Eventually Lake to Lake refused to take any more milk from the Island.

Chuck Goodlet, who had a large herd knew this was coming so he had contracted with a mainland farmer to take his herd when the time came. That day his herd left on the ferry. Some, left stranded for a place to sell their milk, put their old cream separators into use making cream. From this some made butter while others made ice cream or used the cream in cooking. I think my brother, Marvin, milked longer than anyone. He kept one cow to provide milk for the household up until shortly before he died.

July 18,1923 A meeting of the Washington Island Holstein Breeders Association was held at Nelson's Hall. It was decided unanimously that the "bull" picnic be held on August 21st.The following committees were appointed:

Grounds: Rob Gunnarson and Jens Jacobsen

Sports: Jens Hansen

Refreshments: Carl Jensen

Evening Entertainment: Chas. Schmidt and Vernie Richter.

Mr. Bailey, County Agent, introduced Mr. Ganrovsky, who talked on the extermination of grasshoppers.(I recall summers when we had a heavy infestation of grasshoppers all over the Island. They chewed up lots of plants and we quickly learned not to leave pitchforks out in the fields over night when harvesting hay. The grasshoppers loved the salt on the handles, caused by our sweating. In the morning you would find the handles rough from grasshoppers chewing to get the salt. Eventually the town provided a mixture of sawdust, molasses and poisons, such as arsenic, for farmers to spread by hand over the fields in an attempt to control these pests. I have seen clouds of them, probably locusts, take to the air from fields.)

Mr. Hopkins spoke in regard to the future of dairying on the Island if we stick to one breed of cattle.

Mr. Donald spoke on farm accounting and sold some books.

December 11,1923 At the annual meeting it was suggested that arrangement for an entertainment be made to take place during the winter. A program committee was named as follows:

George Madsen, Mrs. Geo. Madsen, Chas. Jensen, Mrs. Boyce, Vernie Richter. A motion was passed to pay the Secretary $10.00 per annum.

It was suggested that the association cast about for a young bull, to be located centrally, for the purpose of breeding the younger cows or heifers. No vote was taken in regard to purchasing same, but it was left to the Directors to look up prices on sires of less than one year of age, to be able to report on same next spring if at that time it seemed necessary to make this purchase.

December 16,1924 At the annual meeting at Nelson's Hall it was decided to carry our own insurance. A motion was passed that the sum of $50.00 be set aside each year until $300.00 has accumulated to act as a reserve fund in place of insurance.

Motion passed that sires be changed May lst. Assuming that Jackson Harbor be Block No.l, Erickson's Block No. 2 and

Washington Harbor No.3 and that No. 1 go to No. 2 and No. 2 to No. 3 and No.3 to No. 1.

July 30,1925 A special meeting was held at Nelson's Hall to arrange for the annual picnic to be held August 25th. Mr. Bailey was asked to get some ribbons made to be awarded to cattle at the picnic. (Farmers brought their best animals to the picnic.)

August 3,1925 The directors met at the home of Chas. Hansen, Secretary, to line up picnic committees as follows:

Vernie Richter- Evening program
Carl Jensen- Sports at picnic grounds
Mrs. James Boyce- Refreshments
George Hansen- Cattle exhibit.

It was also decided that the Assn. buy a 2 burner oil stove and wash boiler. The Secretary was also asked to write Mr. Bailey and try to make some arrangement for a Speaker for the afternoon of picnic.

December 10,1925 (This is the last recorded meeting of the Washington Island Holstein Breeders Association.) A motion was passed that the Board of Directors try to settle with the bull keepers in regard to their pay for keeping bull. Settlement to be made at the rate of 5 dollars per year or on a percentage basis.

Motion passed that the association give a free time (party) some time during the winter.The Board of Directors to serve as entertainment committee.

Mr. Bailey gave a talk on the testing of heifers and their dams from the three association bulls to find if we can see any improvement in our heifers over their dams.

In reviewing the list of members I found the following:

1918-19	41 members
1922	42
1923	35
1924	34
1925	31

According to the records eleven members paid dues in 1926 and five did so in 1927. Still many farmers kept raising and breeding pure bred Holsteins. To keep the strain pure they made certain that young heifers were not bred to the bull that was their sire. During the years I was growing up on the farm the bulls we used were kept at Ole Erickson's (now Ken Koyen's), Wilfred

Koyen's (now Arni Foss'), Louis Hansen's (now Jake and Shirley Ellefson's) or Lauritz Klingenberg's (just south of Floyd Koyen's)

The only record of prices paid for bulls in the Journal is $255.51 for the one purchased from Christ Hansen. 26 farmers loaned moneys to the association for purchase of sires and they received promissory notes.There are also records of loans from Bank of Sturgeon Bay. Interestedly, the Assn. bought 26 "Pure Bull" signs at a cost of $6.50.(I guess these were for farmers to display.)

Some old bills were found in the Journal with several from: Geo. O. Mann "Fancy Groceries and Meats, Fruits and VEGETABLES, Furniture and General Merchandise Phone 4-3 Phone 20-B 2 Detroit Harbor, Wis."

Charges include:

200 heavy paper plates $1.19

2 gal oil	.44	1 can	$.50
1 dishpan	.60	2 pkg. Napkins	.20
2 doz. cups	2.40	107 lb. bananas @.07	7.63
50 wood plates	.50	1 paint brush	.35
1 paint	.65	1 pt. enamel	.85
1 brush	.10	17 yds. canvas	5.44

From TED'S CASH STORE Theo. Gudmundsen, Prop.GENERAL MERCHANDISE

Purchases for the "Bull" picnic on 8/26/26 show:

5 gal. Chocolate Ice Cream	$6.50
5 gal. Vanilla " "	6.50
5 gal. Strawberry " "	7.00
625 Ice Cream Cones	2.75

Purchases from TED'S in 1924 for picnic and parties include:

1 ham	$1.39	6 Rye Bread	$.90
6 white Bread	.90	100 paper plates	.85
12# Sugar	1.08	88# Bananas @ .10	8.80
3 doz. Oranges	1.05	28# Weiners	5.88
8# Coffee	3.60	5# Butter	2.00
6 yds.Oil Cloth	2.52	1 Ice Cake	.25

Records of the Washington Island Holstein Breeder's Assn.show the following on the bull kept by George Madsen:

Dec.1,1924	Credit Membership note	$12.00
	Cash earned by sire	166.00

	Due to Mr. Madsen for keep	145.82
	Paid to assn.by Madsen	32.18
Dec.1,1925	Total earnings of sire	139.00
	Paid Mr. Madsen for keep	125.00
	Taxes paid	2.25
	Due to Assn.	11.75
	Less service to 1 cow-Hannes Johnson	1.50
	Due to Assn.	10.25
Dec.1,1926	Total earnings of sire	148.00
	Paid Mr. Madsen for keep	130.00
	Taxes paid	2.00
	Turned in to Assn.	16.00
Mar.17,1927	Madsens left the Island for Oregon.	
	3 months keep of sire	37.90
	Turned in to Assn.by Madsen	16.00
	Paid Geo. Madsen	21.90

William Jacobsen took over the Madsen farm and bull.

Dec.14, 1927	8 1/2 months keep of sire	92.25
	Sire fees paid	67.00
	Sire fees to be collected	31.00
	Due to Assn.	5.75

Records of bull kept by Ole Erickson:

Dec.1,1923	Keep to Dec. lst	156.26
	Equipment purchased by O.E.	6.40
	Total earnings of sire	195.00
	2 breeding bills for collection	2.50
	Due to Assn.	32.34
Dec.1,1924	Total earnings of sire	180.50
	Care of bull	125.00
	Paid for taxes and bull rings	6.02
	Net earnings of sire	49.50
Dec.1, 1925	Total earnings for 5 mo.10 days	41.00
	Tax and care of bull	58.25
	Total due to Assn.	9.23

Balance of 1925 the bull was at Louis W. Hansen's.

	Total earnings 6 mo.20 days.	141.00
	Paid Hansen for keep	69.46
	61 days work on pen-$3. per day	19.50
	4 pr. of hinges	2.10

	Due to Assn.	27.94
Dec.1,1926	Total earnings of sire	231.00
	Paid for keep & expenses	130.10
	Due to Assn.	100.90
	Outstanding	16.00
	Collected from 1925	23.00
	Paid to Assn. by Hansen	107.90

Harold(Pat) Koyen kept an Assn. bull in 1927.

Dec.14,1927	Keep of bull Aug.21 to Dec.1	36.10
	Turned in to Assn. by Pat	23.50
	Due Pat Koyen for keep	12.60

The last entry made in the Journal is for Christ A. Hansen

Dec.14,1927 Keep of sire 1 year 130.00

Taxes paid 2.56

Turned in to Assn. 73.00

Due C.A. Hansen 59.56

In the early part of the 1900s most Island people were engaged in either commercial fishing or in dairy farming.Some of the fishermen and others kept only one or two cows to provide their family with dairy products.From the Breeder's records,my memory and discussions with, old-time Islanders I will attempt to identify places where dairy cows were milked.This will be principally done road by road with some deviations to the side:

MAIN ROAD-south to north (Read across to follow sequence)

Ole Christianson		
*Bo Anderson	*John Malloch	*Martin Andersen
Frank Richter	*Chas. Jensen	*John Hannesson
*Carl Anderson	*Chas. Schmidt	*George Mann
*Mrs. Clara Boyce	*L.Klingenberg	Lindstrom
*Harry Hansen	*Chas. Hansen	*Christ A.Hansen
*Jens Jensen	*Volney Koyen	*Alfred Anderson
*Chas. Haglund	Valentine Irr	*Severt Barneson
John Larson	*Theo. Gudmundsen	Henry Einarson
*Kari Bjarnarson		

AIRPORT ROAD-south to north (Read across)

Hans Mads Hansen	Waldemar Hansen	*Haldor Gudmundson

Peter Hanson	Clarence Koyen	*Fred M. Hansen
Earl Peterson		

RANGELINE ROAD-south to north (Read across)

Oddur Magnusson	*Lawrence Gislason	*Ben Johnson
*Arthur Wickman	*Chris Nelson	William Wickman
*Wilfred Koyen	*Ole Erickson	Pete Jensen
Chris Saabye	Jacob Lindahl	Farm across from Lindahl
Haldon Johnson		

EASTSIDE ROAD-south to north (Read across to follow sequence)

Mac Gudmundson	Jake Bowman	Walter Launders
Louis Gunnlaugsson	*Pete Gunnlaugson	Maurice Andersen

AZNOE ROAD-west to east (Read across)

John Aznoe	"Ezie" Cornell

DETROIT HARBOR ROAD-west to east (Read across)

"Outney" Gudmundsen		
Hans B. Hansen	Pete Christianson	Nor Shellswick

LAKEVIEW ROAD-west to east (Read across)

*Vernie Richter	Karl Koyen	John Peterson
Walter Lucke	*Carl Nelson	Ole Bowman
*Rob Gunnerson	*Hannes Johnson,Sr.	Gunnar Sigurdson

WEST HARBOR & MICHIGAN ROADS-west to east (Read across)

Lars Bilton		
*Ole Hagen	*William Arendt	Edward Peterson
*August Koyen	Berent Gunnlaugsson	*Jens Jacobsen

TOWNLINE ROAD-west to east (Read across)

*Chris Sorenson	*Nels Nelson	Albert Olson
*Christian Jensen	Conrad Andersen	*Louis Hansen
Martin Andersen	*Christopher Einarson	Olafur Einarson
Anton Andersen	*Chris Jacobsen	Steve Gunnlaugsson
Mac Gunnlaugsson	Newman???	Aussey Olson

JACKSON HARBOR ROAD-west to east (Read across)

Bert Cornell	Martin Bros.	*Jens Jepson
*George Madsen	*Henry Olson	*Jens Hansen

*Thorvald Johnson	*George Nelson	*George Hansen
Martin Johnson?	John Johnson	Pete Peterson
Christopher Peterson	L.Hahnkuper	Jacob Ellefson
Chas. McDonald	Alex Esperson	

MOUNTAIN ROAD-south to north

George Jorgenson *Knud Hansen

SWENSON ROAD-south to north (Read across)

*Andrew Anderson * S.K. Lunde *Andrew Swenson

LOBDELL'S POINT

*Walter Chambers

This adds up to 113 places where someone had to "pull teats" twice daily. Undoubtedly I have missed some and made errors on other. Please, readers, let me know so I can make corrections.

The asterisks* placed in front of the names denote members in the Washington Island Holstein Breeder's Association.It appears probable that once there were at least 400 dairy cows on the Island.

Another Journal showed the activities of "The Washington Island Cow Testing Association". Two Executive Committee meetings are recorded. At the first one on May 13,1919 at Nelson's Hall all members were present. This was associated with the Breeder's Assn, and the four Breeder's vice presidents had canvassed their districts. They found that 28 herd owners with 113 cows wished to make a yearly test. Haldor Gudmundsen agreed to act as tester. Ole Erickson and George Hansen were appointed to inspect the testing outfit, get it repaired and secure other needed equipment.

July 8,1919 at an Executive Committee meeting Ole Erickson was paid $7.60 for repairs and equipment for the testing outfit. As there was not enough cash in the testing fund to pay Mr. Erickson it was agreed to borrow a sufficient amount from the Breeders fund. Motion passed to authorize the tester to collect membership and testing fees to turn in to Secretary. It was decided to pay the tester quarterly, witholding 25 percent of the first quarter until the end of the year. An agreement was drawn up for Robert Gunnerson to present to Haldor for his signature.(Nowhere did it tell what type of testing was to be done. Perhaps it was milk butterfat content?)

During the time Haldor was the tester he was paid a total of $53.40.

A communication from Haldor at N.Pt.Light House, Lake Park, Milw., Wis. dated Dec.15,1919 shows a money order included for $46.25 for testing fees collected. He also tendered his resignation.

Tester Assn. members for 1919 were listed as follows:

George Hansen	12 cows
Conrad Andersen	6
George Madsen	16
Theo. Gudmundsen	13
Volney Koyen	9
Haldor Gudmundsen	18
Nels Nelsen	9
Fred M. Hansen	13
Peter Hansen	6
Jens Jensen	12
Chas. 0. Hansen	17
Harry Hansen	9
Christ A. Hansen	3
Ole Hagen	11
Chris Sorenson	12
Vernie Richter	6
Carl Nelson	11
Chr.Einarson	12
Knud Hansen	9
George Nelson	4
Jens Jepson	4
Jens Hansen	2
Ole Erickson	12
Ole Bowman	4
Kari Bjarnarson	6
Robert Gunnerson	6

These 27 members had 245 cows in 1919.

In the records of the Holstein Breeder's Assn. it shows:

Christ A. Hansen	Cash payment on sire "Blue Boy"	$ 53.51
	Note due 12/1/23	100.00
	Note due 12/1/24	100.00
Dec 1,1924	Total earnings of sire	125.50

	Paid Mr. Hansen for keep	125.00
	Due Association	.50
	Tax paid on sire by C.A.H.	2.88
	Two cows @ $1.00 not entered above	2.00
	Interest to C.A. H. on note	6.00
	Paid to C.A.H.	6.38
Dec.11,1925	Total earnings of sire	97.00
	Taxes paid	2.88
	Due C.A. Hansen	30.88
Dec.1,1926	Total earnings of sire	89.00
	Paid Mr. Hansen for keep	130.00
	Taxes paid	2.59
	Wire and staples	5.07
	Due C.A. Hansen	48.66

In 1930 two Hansen brothers, Harry and Charley, started daily delivery of milk products throughout the Island. These men were sons of Christ A. Hansen, who had been very active in the Farmer's Union and also in the Holstein Breeders Association.

Harry agreed to deliver to customers who lived north of Townline Road while Charley took the other half of the Island. Since Charley had more customers and fewer cows, he had to get milk from Harry who normally was milking twenty-two to twenty-three animals.

All milking was done by hand with the teat-pulling crew normally consisting of father Harry and sons, Murrel and Dean. At times mother, Catherine also helped out.

The fresh milk was aerated and then bottled. Eight-year-old sister, Ione, stood on a tipsy bench to reach up and bottle the milk. Caps bearing the Hansen Bros. name sealed the bottles.

Next the sealed bottles were placed in a large water tank filled' with cold water fresh from the well. Harry had constructed a stepped wooden platform so that quarts, pints, and half-pints containers could be submerged up to their necks.

While the evening's milking had to be stored in a cool environment overnight, the morning's milking was placed in the family's two-door Chevy and individual deliveries began.

The back seat had been removed from the car to allow placing of many crates of milk in there.

In the beginning the price of a quart of milk delivered to your kitchen was five cents. Later, inflation set in and the cost became six cents. Milk in pints was three cents.

Hansen Bros. Dairy operated from 1930 until the summer of 1936 when the brothers decided to continue operations independently. However, they still maintained the same territories. Charley's operation became "Evergreen Dairy" while Harry's bore the name of "Harry's Dairy."

Operations continued into 1940. In the later years Harry's Dairy acquired a "Lafayette" auto made by Nash. By stacking the milk racks high they were able to get 100 to 120 quarts in the vehicle.

In summer, large deliveries were made to the two Island girl's camps. Camp Pierce on the road to Little Lake is now Lehman's property; Camp Panhellenic, in Jackson Harbor stood where Lon Frye's new home is now situated.

When the huge stone barge "Cumberland" came into Washington Harbor to load stone, Captain Alexander would immediately place a big order for milk to be delivered as soon as possible. This meant that Harry's family had to bring the cows into the barn to be milked off schedule, cool the milk and get it down to Washington Harbor. Usually Alexander wanted 20 gallons. Of course, when the regular evening milking time came, the milking chore was tough.

Since the glass bottles were used over and over, it was essential that they be thoroughly washed when returned. As they had no modern means of sterilizing, Harry built a rack on the sunny side of the house where the bottles were placed for "solar sterilization."

Since Charley's wife, Clara, had relatives in Menominee, MI, they sometimes took a vacation to visit there. Their daughter, Luella, and cousin, Dean, did all the chores during her parents' absence.

Charley's barn was overrun with cats so the two young people decided to get rid of most of them. They gathered the cats in stone-weighted bags, took them down to Hannes Johnson's dock and tossed them into Washington Harbor. Did they catch heck when Charley returned!

In 1939 and 1940, when Charley was Town Chairman, Dean did all the field work with Charley's horses, "Silk" and "Satin", for one dollar a day plus food.

One Spring, George Mann had lot of potatoes that needed culling, since there were many that had rotted. Harry agreed to have the sorting done, so all the potatoes were brought to his barn. Murrel and Dean were given the unsavory task. They decided to throw the rotten ones through the windows. Of course, this resulted in most of the barn's window panes being broken with resultant severe chastisement.

Dad driving hayride party

Old "Saxty-Sax", Nels Sorenson, lived where Margaret Smith now resides. He was a carpenter who doubled as the local undertaker. In the early days he made his own caskets and "rough boxes", which which were lowered into the grave hole to receive the casket as the services ended. His nickname was earned by the amount he charged for a funeral. It was always "Saxty-Sax" dollars and "Saxty Sax" cents. When it became clear that a person was on their death bed he would always pay a visit and mentally measure them so he could construct the right-sized coffin. After death had occurred his consoling statement to the bereaved family was, "Dey were good ting he(she) died!" At the cemetery the casket was always lowered by ropes into the "roughbox". The lid was placed on this box, then the preacher intoned the last words and sprinkled the dirt. At this time old "Saxty-Sax" would nervously pull a screwdriver from the back pocket and step forward saying, "Well,everyting is over now, we can screw da lid down" and he immediately commenced doing so.

In those days, there was no embalming. If the doctor was present at the time of death, he closed the eyelids and placed pennies over them to keep the lids shut. You have undoubtedly heard of thieves who would steal "the pennies off a dead man's eyes", well, that's where the expression originated. Usually either the family or friends would wash the body and dress it before rigor mortis set in. Little or nothing was done to improve the corpse's facial appearance. Our neighbor, Charley Jensen, usually transported the casket on his Model T truck, with evergreen boughs arranged around it, to the church from the home and then on to the cemetery.

Dad died January 12, 1928 and was buried on January 14th from the original Bethel Church. Reverend James Christiansen, first fulltime Lutheran minister on the Island, conducted the services. It was customary to hold services in the home before departing for the church. The pall bearers carried the casket to the front of the church near the altar and it was kept open during the service. When the service ended the family remained in the "mourner's" seats while everyone present filed by and paid "their last respects". As a ten year old boy, this was the hardest part to have to just sit there while interminable footsteps sounded down the aisle. I then made a vow that this would never be afflicted on my family when I leave this world. In fact, I am leaving explicit orders that my body shall be cremated after any useful medical parts have been removed. My wife questioned desire, so I told her that as a retired Fire Chief this would be the last "big blaze" I would go to.

In the early days it was customary to bring food to the bereaved family's home rather than to have a gathering at the church following the service. In fact, churches in those days had no accomodations for serving food.

When Dad was still alive it was usual to hitch the horses to the buggy with the fringe on top and make the momentous trek to the cemetery, all the way to Washington Harbor, to, weed and decorate the family graves with flowers. The weeding chore was endured because we got to see a part of the Island remote from our immediate neighborhood. The original cemetery had a painted,white fence all around it and you entered only by the gate on the south side.The old well was there and we drew water from it to place around the flowers and shrubs such as "bleeding hearts" that grew over the graves.

I still recall an amusing statement made by Jim Boyce,who lived just north of Mann's store. A cantankerous old bachelor, who lived where Marian Sweeney now resides, passed away.Jim remarked, "Don't waste a coffin on that ornery old bastard. Lay him out in the sun. Stiffen him up and then take a post maul and drive him into the ground!"

The Island had not only a number of "characters," but also its share of "wits." One night in the early 1900s, an Island farmer met young Dave Kincaide on the Main Road at night carrying a lantern. The farmer asked Dave where he was going.

"Courting," Dave replied.

As it was a moonlit night, the farmer then asked Dave, "Why are you carrying a lantern? I never carried a lantern when I went courting."

Dave's quick response was, "Ya! And look what you got!"

Upon seeing the farmer's wife, it was obvious that Dave was right. Among other things, it was said that she combed her hair back so tightly that she couldn't keep her mouth shut. Much of her day was spent either on the telephone or sitting at the window with her unmarried daughter watching the people go by.

The daughter undoubtedly never had a boy friend. As she grew elderly, young Karly Jessen made the remark that this inscription should be placed on her tombstone:

"Here lies the body of

_____________ _____________

Life held for her no terrors.
Born a virgin, died a virgin;
No runs, no hits, no errors."

Maggie Richter, Arni's mother, and her brother, Mac Gudmundsen, each had delightful senses of humor. I felt quite sure that one of them made up a jingle about the Karl Koyen family, who had the property where Leroy and Marjorie Bass now reside. Koyen's three children never married and Freddie was always known to respond to nearly anything with "Yaw Haw." So this ditty became well known:

Karl Koyen sleeps in a feather bed,
Olga in the straw,
Wilfred doesn't sleep at all,
And Freddie says, "Yaw Haw."

Jim Boyce, who lived just north of Mann's store, was a very witty Irishman. I'm told that he and Tom Guinan, Karly's grandpa, fished together at one time. One day they decided to take the boat to Escanaba for a little "relaxation." However, they first had to "fortify" themselves for the trip by visiting Nelsen's Hall. Tom never liked paper money and carried "hard cash." Unfortunately, somewhere between Bowyer's Bluff and Escanaba, Tom fell overboard and had to empty his pockets in order to remain afloat till he could be rescued. Consequently, somewhere in the waters of Green Bay, there is a trove of old coins waiting to be reclaimed.

One spring, shortly after Roosevelt instituted the WPA program, hardly any Island men got calls to go sailing. Times were very hard. The Detroit Harbor Board applied for WPA assistance to make some improvements and help some of the needy families. Jim Boyce, who had short legs, and his neighbor, Nels Nelson, who was about 6' 3", both got hired and daily walked the mile from home to work. One day Jim arrived out of breath and remarked, "I can't keep up with that Nels, he's split clean up to the shoulders."

Once, during the early winters when no roads were plowed, Jim decided to walk to the post office. On his way back home, facing a strong sub-zero wind, he neared a large bread box with two small holes cut in it heading his way. As the box drew near, he raised it up to find a small boy from a needy family using the box for shelter while on his way to school. Jim remarked that the boy didn't have enough clothes on to "flag a handcar."

Shortly after my sister, Sylvia, married, a spinster neighbor came to visit and was extremely upset. I seems that she had written to someone who repeatedly vacationed in the Jackson Harbor area. The lady had mentioned that she had been having some health problems, to which the man responded by letter that as one grows older their anatomy changes. Huffily, the woman said to Sis, "He dared to talk about my 'Anna Tomy!'"

During prohibition, other things than "moonshine," home brew and wine were consumed to "get a jag on," as many Islanders described it. Of course "druggist" Tom Nelson dispensed lots of bitters for "stomach problems." Lots of vanilla extract, with about 50% alcohol, was consumed. Pete Andersen, who carried the mail and passengers from Ellison Bay for many years, drank so much tonic called "Peruna" that he was nicknamed "Peruna Pete."

Interestingly, many Women's Christian Temperance Union members, like Carrie Nation, fought a stern battle against saloons and even chopped some up with axes. Still they could not survive without Lydia E. Pinkham's Vegetable Compound that contained 13 1/2% Ethyl alcohol (used solely as a solvent and preservative). By the way, this calculated to be 27 Proof. Right now I am looking at a full bottle which says "For relieving hot flashes and certain other symptoms associated with 'change of life' (menopause) and cramps and other distress of monthly periods (menstruation) ... not due to organic disease. Acts as a uterine sedative." Recommended dosage was one tablespoon 4 times a day. However, some ladies took a much more generous "shot."

Bootlegging did not entirely cease after the 18th Amendment was repealed in the early 1930s. One Islander later got caught by the "Feds." Fortunately Jake Fessler, an excellent criminal lawyer who vacationed in the "Jensenville" area of the Island, agreed to handle his case. Jake got several influential summer resorters to testify to this man's "good character" and got him a very light sentence.

Wilson Trueblood recounted that at the trial as the bailiff announced, "The United States Government versus--- ---," the defendant sank deep into his chair.

Benny and Nels Jensen, who lived in the house where John Adams resided on Gentry Farm, made some of the finest cherry wine any connoisseur could wish for. I never sampled any of their wine but I can attest that Russell Nelson's cherry wine was superb. The firms who today are making wines in NE Wisconsin could have taken lessons from him. Of course, Mads and Andrew Swenson were also fine vintners.

During the depths of the Depression, my cousin's husband was laid-off in Green Bay. He brought the family to the Island and lived where Lonnie Jorgenson now resides. He made and sold lots of home brew before the repeal came about.

Matt Waller, who lived just south of Sister Bay, was one of Door County's "outlaws." In those days there was no open season on deer, but he poached regularly. He also made lots of "white lightning." "Revenoors" frequently raided his place. He drove a big Chandler touring car and always approached his house from the south on Highway 57. If the two kitchen shades were uneven, his wife was signalling, "Matt, don't come home." He would continue on the road.

One day, while he was busy in the fields, a carload of "Feds" drove in and immediately scattered in all directions to search for booze. One entered the kitchen where Mrs. Waller was about to wash the noonday dishes. The only booze on the premises was in a crock on the stove.

Calmly, Mrs. Waller took the dinner plates, walked to the stove, covered the crock with them and then walked to the sink and turned on the the water. With her back to the "Fed" she poured the booze down the drain. The "raiders" could never figure why they came away empty-handed. Matt had passed away before I taught school in the Sister Bay area, but I had his young daughter as a pupil and that story was often related.

Probably the "bootlegger" who was active for the longest time on the Island was Pete Peterson. Even though nearly everyone on the Island knew this still was in operation during Prohibition the "Revenoors" never caught Pete, because a brother-in-law in Sturgeon Bay warned him when the Feds arrived there before coming here. In the late 1800s steamers often stopped at Furlong's dock in Washington Harbor to get cordwood for their boilers, well, in the earlier part of this century steamers stopped there so the men could re-fuel their systems with good "moonshine". Just plain farming was a poor way to earn a living. With much frugality a family could barely "keep the wolf from the door". Thus it was appealing to turn to making home brew, wine or to distill "white lightning" for sale.

However, some made beer or wine only for their own family consumption. The famous "Kap" Anderson told me that his dad made "home brew" for that reason. Not having a hydrometer to assure that he bottled it at exactly the right moment, he merely used his good judgment. Frequently, some time after capping he would have the pressure build to where the bottles burst in the cellar. Usually when the bottles were uncapped most of the beer gushed out and was lost. Kap got his dad to open the bottles under an inverted water bucket held over a wash tub. Thus they could recover all the contents, but it took on a metallic flavor as a result. One day Kap's dad announced he had solved the problem. He popped the cap and immediately thrust the bottle neck into his mouth. His dad was wearing a loose fitting vest at the time and Kap said "I watched Dad's vest fill out fully!" Consequently that system was abandoned post haste.

Frank Richter, who lived right across the road from our farm, ran a still for some time. He kept the fermenting mash in the barn hay mow. (This was common practice as the barn and silo odors would mask the alcoholic smell making it unlikely that any "furriner" could detect what was going on.) One day, while Frank and Ivy were visiting friends their cow got into the hay mow, discovered the mash and ate most of it. Upon returning home they discovered their very intoxicated cow cavorting gaily through the pasture. With a few phone calls to friends they soon had a large audience observing her antics.

One day Plum Island Coast Guard station was alerted that a "rum runner" from Canada would be coming around the Island heading for Green Bay. They were ordered to intercept and take the boat and crew into custody. So, armed with Springfields and sub-machine guns, they boarded the Bull (which now lies at our Maritime Museum) and waited in readiness off the west side. As the "rum runner" captain saw the Bull he thought it looked like another fishing vessel and ignored it until the Coast Guard crew ran up the flag and ordered them to stop. The boat and its cargo was brought into Johnny Young's dock. The arrested crew was taken to jail. Meanwhile, before the cargo was inventoried, many loads of good Canadian "stuff' disappeared. In fact, our neighbor, Charley Jensen, who ran a draying business with his Model T truck was hired to haul several loads away. Finally it was decided that enough illicit liquor must remain aboard so that a conviction could be obtained in court.

My nephew, Roy Andersen, told me that when he was sailing with his Dad and brother on regular trips to Green Bay they frequently would see this same "rum runner" anchored by Bay Beach, where at night smaller vessels would come alongside and relieve them of their cargo.

Many Island old-timers remember that local "moonshine" was available all during Prohibition at about a dollar a pint.

While it was common knowledge who the "bootleggers" were, very few ever actually saw the stills.

Now, Pete Petersen's grandson, Phillip, has loaned Pete's still to the Farm Museum and I have set it up in a case upstairs in the red "Gallery" barn.

A recipe for "Johnson Club Whiskey" is displayed so you can see one method of whiskey making.

After the mash had finished working, the liquor was drawn off and placed in the copper distilling vessel. Heat was applied and when the liquor began to boil the contained alcohol began boiling off first as its boiling point is 180° F. These vapors passed upward into the "chimney" part of the still and on into the copper tubing of the large, galvanized condenser. This condenser was filled with cold water and efficiently changed the “moonshine” steam back into liquid which then ran into the "little brown jug."

Many have asked what the "proof" of the whiskey would be. That depends on the sugar content of the ingredients, how effectively the mash was fermented and the care in distilling the liquor.

This was, by no means the only still operating here during Prohibition, but it was undoubtedly the largest and produced much more than any other one.

During the 1920s and early 1930s Federal "revenuers" made lots of raids on illicit operations, but did not catch any Islanders. An effective "grapevine" system operated by friends in Sturgeon

Bay would pass the word that the revenuers were in the county and the Island stills would be transported to safe hiding places.

I don't know how many years this still was used but ever since the first colonists arrived in America there were efforts to outlaw intoxicating beverages. In 1917, Congress passed a law prohibiting the manufacture of liquors other than beer or wine. January 21, 1918, by proclamation, President Wilson reduced the alcoholic content of beer to 2 3/4 % by weight.

January 16, 1920, the 18th Amendment, commonly called the "Volstead Act," went into effect banning the manufacture, sale, transportation or consumption of alcoholic beverages.

By 1933, it was obvious, that the 18th Amendment was a flop. Postmaster General Jim Farley estimated that the Federal government's annual loss of taxes and import duties was a billion dollars. States, counties and municipalities were losing about $500,000,000 annually in levies that could have been imposed if liquor had been legalized. Costs from having Federal men and the U.S. Coast Guard trying to enforce the existing laws reached a staggering amount.

In February 1933, Congress raised the alcoholic content of beer to 3.2%.

December 5, 1933, the 21st Amendment revoked the 18th, and "booze" once more flowed freely.

No. 26

The "White House", first frame building in Door County, stood on the hill above Furlong's dock in Washington Harbor. It was close to where the Main Road pavement now ends. This two story building served as a boarding house well into this century. The last person to operate it was Annie Einarson. Several Washington Harbor school teachers stayed there, including Ray Krause, who in later years became our first electrical co-op manager and acquired the affectionate name of "Mr. REA".

Other early places where boarders and resorters stayed were Englesons (now Sunset), Sorenson's West Harbor Resort (now Gibson's), Idabo Inn, Shellswick's, Aznoe's, and Hotel Washington.

Bo and Ida Anderson started the Idabo Inn and Bo also had a store in the building that is now Holiday Two. After Bo and Ida died, the inn was vacant for a number of years and was owned by Nor Shellswick, a relative. Then Annie Einarson purchased it and operated it as a year-round boarding and resort place. She frequently walked to our farm to purchase dairy items.

After the 18th Amendment was repealed, Bill Jepson's son-in-law, Ralph Wade, came to the Island and opened a tavern in what is now Holiday Two. During my high school years we played basketball and roller skated on the second floor. I was told an interesting story of something that happened while Bo was running the store. An Island man, who had been imbibing too freely of his own moonshine, had become very belligerent in the store. It so happened that Benny and Nels Jensen, who lived in the house where John Adams resided while working for Gentry, were in the store. These two brothers had sailed for many years in salt water sailing vessels and had undoubtedly seen their share of barroom brawls. Nels, a quiet man with flowing handlebar white mustache, just happened to have a set of brass knuckles in his pocket. He slipped these on and walked up to where the drunken man stood by the counter. Without bringing the brass into view he rapped heavily on the counter placing dents in the wood,then quickly pocketed the brass while loudly saying, "Shut up and behave!". The drunk felt the dents in the counter. Thinking Nels had done this with bare knuckles, he turned pale and left the premises.

Ben Johnson, who was known as "Hotel Ben", started the Hotel Washington, later owned by Menafees. His wife was a Gislason and between the two of them they turned out sumptuous meals. Quickly this place became a favorite of summer resorters. Many of these people later purchased homes in "Jensenville".

According to Ben's son, Johnny the musician, an interesting event occurred at the hotel. One of the boarders was a young man who had a pension for fondling young boys. This had come to the attention of some of the fathers. They were engaged in a heated discussion in the backyard of the hotel when Ben happened to overhear Judge Herbert remark, "We'll hang the son-of-a-bitch in the morning!" Knowing Herbert to be a stern judge from Tennessee, Ben figured he had better do something immediately. So he went across the road to Ignatius Kiss and asked him if he would take a passenger in his gasoline launch after dark to the mainland for $25. Kiss agreed to do so. Thereupon Ben went to the young man's room and told him he was in big trouble and if he wanted to save his neck he would give Ben $25 for which a boat would be waiting for him at the end of Gislason's dock (now Munao's). He was to pack his bags and be at the dock at 9:00 P.M. This he did and was never again seen on the Island. The aftermath, however, was that henceforth the judge was known as "Hanging Judge" Herbert.

Automobiles were a fascination to me. The oldest auto I remember is a one cylinder Stearns which was discovered covered with hay in the old Lindstrom barn on Main Road when Pete Petersen bought the farm. This place was later owned by the Beamishs. It was in a very worn condition so Bill Smith, who started the garage where Jack's Service now is, agreed to put it in good condition. It had hard, white rubber tires and the radiator was copper tubing with cooling fins added. The hood resembled that of a very early Mack truck. The next oldest car I saw belonged to Ole Erickson, who had the farm now owned by Kenny Koyen. This was an Oakland touring with right hand drive and leather straps extending to the front of the fenders to help hold the top in place. We children called it the "potato car" as we learned that Ole got enough money from a cash crop to buy the car new. I recall the town crew's Riker truck which had been an Army one during WW I. This had been fitted with a hydraulically operated dump box for spreading gravel. Occasionally the hydraulic mechanism would malfunction and the box would suddenly drop. Waldemar Hanson, road boss, repeatedly warned his crew to never reach under the extended box. Unfortunately, one day, in haste, Walter Launders did just that and died from a crushed skull. Many times I sat by our gate and watched the town crew smooth the Main Road with a small grader pulled by this truck.

Chris Saabye, Ruth Cornell's step father, was one of the early car purchasers. His place was approximately where Del & Marion Garmon live. On his first attempt to put the car in a shed instead of applying the brake he pulled back on the steering wheel and shouted, "Whoa, whoa, if I had reins I could drive you better". Meanwhile the car took the back wall right out.

Carl Jorgenson, Walt's uncle, had purchased a new Model T. I am told that he struck a tree with it while heading home and never drove it again.

Many of the early commercial fishermen "cross-chained" the steering on their boats. Thus,whichever way they turned the wheel the compass card would respond that way. However, turning the wheel to the right made the boat go to the left. My cousin, Leon Cornell, told me about an interesting experience. John Cornell, Mary Richter's father, had just bought his first car and was proudly going to take several fishermen for a ride. They were traveling up Main Road when John decided to head toward West Harbor so he turned the wheel to the right and entered Michigan Road. Leon, in the back seat, said "John, you weren't planning on going that way!". The quick response was, "Like hell I wasn't!"

In the late 20s Moeller's Garage, Sturgeon Bay, was selling Hudsons and Essexs. Art and his dad brought six new vehicles to the Island and sold them all, several to commercial fishermen. John Cornell bought one of them. Consequently we got John's Model T sedan, which was the first car on our farm. I remember applying a blowtorch to the engine pan in winter to warm the oil so we could crank the engine. Hessler shock absorbers, which were essentially large coil springs, had been added to the rear axle to give a smoother ride. I am told that Hessler, the inventor, was found dead in an outdoor toilet on Rock Island.

The next farm auto was a new 1930 Model A Ford which cost exactly $600 including the license. This was the one I learned to drive in and I would not be surprised if it is still being driven by someone somewhere. Actually I wish I still had it.

Detroit Harbor had a lot of summer residents who owned cottages along the waterfront. The common Island title for them was"summer resorter," however, we called them "summer snorters." Most of them lived on the east shore of the harbor in the area still known as "Jensenville."

Charlie Jensen's father built a number of those cottages. His widow, "Grandma" Jensen lived with Charlie and Cassie in an old house just north of the present "Rec" Center. We nicknamed her "Dumma Dunton" and frequently would see her walk past school to visit Jensenville resorters. She had the nasty habit of chewing tobacco and we discovered that she would pick up discarded cigarette butts along the road to chew. So, when we would see her leave Charlie's house we would sneak out and deposit cigarette “snipes” then scoot back into school to watch her pick them up, remove the paper and start chewing.

Ernie Boucsein told us that one time she arrived at a Jensenville cottage as the lady of the house was hosting several neighbors for tea. She graciously invited Dumma to join them but Dumma refused, saying, "You'll have to inscuse me. I only drinks tea when I am constipated and den I drinks Rocky Mountain tea. "

Some of the earliest resorters I remember are Herschbergers in Jensenville and Kokens who had two cottages where Arni Richter now lives. Both families bought farm products from us. Bunny Herschberger and wife, Nita, summered at the south end of Detroit Island and traveled to Lobdell's Point in a motor boat. He is the first person I knew of who swam across Death's Door.

Kokens, who owned the Koken Barber Chair Company in St. Louis, frequently came to our farm in an old air-cooled black Franklin sedan. It had a narrow, square body. Their large, racing sailboat, "Scapa," was always anchored between Snake Island and the bayou.

Occasionally Charlie Jensen would be hired to race the Scapa in the Ephraim Regatta. Charlie refused to use her silk sails when racing because the boat did not perform as well as when she was carrying cotton sails. He was also leery over the large amount of lead ballast and fearful that if she shipped any large amount of water she would immediately leave him floundering in the water.

Kokens had the east side of the bayou dredged and it became a very good fishing ground.

Ma and Ann churn butter

Clifford Fay had owned the place where his grandmother spent many summers. She always bought our freshly churned butter. I recall placing a crock of butter in a cloth bag tied over my shoulder and biking to her house to deliver it. My usual reward was an oatmeal cookie.

Markels, who owned a box-making plant in St. Louis, had a Jensenville cottage. They not only bought our butter in the summer, but also supplied us with waxed, one-pound cartons and corrugated shipping boxes so that in winter we could mail butter to them.

Bessie and Louise Thrall, who owned the place, were teachers in La Jolla, California. As a youngster I thought this must be just about at the ends of the earth. They always walked to our farm for dairy products. At their first visit each season they had to see how much the "little one" had grown so I had to come forth to be displayed. One year I decided there had been enough of this so I hid under the porch until they left. Ma never did find out where I had been.

In the early days Detroit Harbor had a lot of boat activity. Originally, the early ferry Wisconsin, owned by Bill Jepson, landed at Gislason's dock, now Munao's. Even after Bill had the first real ferry boat built, (the *Welcome*), he still landed at Gislason's. Later a dock was built on Nor Shellswick's property at Lobdell's Point, now Will Kruger's. This shortened the trip by about two miles. After Richters acquired the ferry line the facilities were eventually moved to the present location.

Jack Anderson operated the "hooker" *Diana*, which was earlier owned and operated as a freighter by Al Shellswick. After the *Welcome* was placed in service, my brother, Chris, bought the "Wisconsin" and hauled freight to and from many ports in NE Wisconsin and Upper Michigan. Regularly three trips a week were made to Green Bay. One week Chris would make one trip and Jack would make two, while the next week the opposite occurred.

Fishermen knew which days the boats would be going to Green Bay. They would lift their nets or set hooks on that day. Charley Jensen or George Hansen would truck the boxes of iced fish to Cornell's dock where they would be loaded on the boat late in the day. Then, with a deck-load of empty oil barrels, the boat would leave and sail throughout the night, arriving at Green Bay early in the morning.

Usually the first stop was at Standard Oil to drop off the empty steel drums, then on to the wholesale fish company docks to deliver fish.

There were about six fish companies and fish were delivered to whichever one the Island fisherman was dealing with. Today it is hard to imagine that these boats would traverse all the way up the East River to beyond Main Street bridge to Johnson's Fish Company. As this was just past the Main Street bridge it was a delicate place to maneuver out of.

Before leaving Johnson's dock, the boat would blow the signal to the bridgetender to open the bridge. Since the river normally had a swift current running, this had to be timed just right.

The old *Diana*, which had originally been a yacht, had a long bow sticking out in front. One day Jack decided to try a different way to leave Johnson's dock. Unfortunately, when he made the turn the *Diana*'s bow struck a chicken-butchering plant across the river. Soon the air was filled with flying chickens.

After delivering fish, the boat would proceed to the foot of Pine Street on the Fox River, right by Prange's power house. The skipper would call Joannes Bros. wholesale grocery, Morley Murphy wholesale hardware, freight terminals and other places that might have freight for the Island. Then the day was spent loading the boat's hold. Light freight was passed hand to hand, while heavy stuff was hoisted by a small gas engine located near the mast. A single boom from the mast was swung by hand into the proper position and a rope fed through pulleys extended down, with hooks on the end to grasp the freight or oil barrels. Often there was enough free time to go uptown and take in a ten cent movie.

Late in the day the load of barrels of gasoline, fuel oil and lubricating oil would be picked up at Standard Oil's dock, then the boat would depart and arrive at Lobdell's Point the following morning.

In those days there was no thought given to air or water pollution. As the boat neared Green Bay, especially during the Great Depression, it was comforting to see black coal smoke issuing from the paper mill and other stacks as we knew that men were working. Window curtains quickly turned grimy. Stinky sulphur-water poured into the Fox River from paper mills. Dead hogs and other creatures floated down the East River. In fact, one time at Johnson's dock the propeller was kept turning to counter the strong current and the men came out to yell because they could not stand the smell from the churned-up water.

As a boy, it was fun to row around Detroit Harbor and see all the activity. Freight boats would even dock at Bo Anderson's--now Holiday Inn--also at Nor Shellswick's, Gislason's, Richter's on Detroit Island, and Cornell's and Chamber's at Lobdell's Point.

Captain Hill's boat from Escanaba, would occasionally land at Detroit Island as well as at Young's dock in Washington Harbor. In the summer, there were as many as six commercial fishing rigs operating from Detroit Island. The "hookers" would stop there to pick up fish before going on the Green Bay.

It was fun to go on board Chester Pederson's yacht, "As You Like It" and dream of someday owning such a boat. Cap Pederson had a log house at the head of Pederson's Bay where the family lived for many years before residing in Detroit Harbor on the Island east of Holiday Inn. My mother told me that for a short time her family lived in that Detroit Island house.

The Morton Jorgensons had a house quite a distance down the east shore of Detroit Island. They also owned the building which is now the Observer office. A small store was operated by "Mamma Morton" in that building. Known as "The Fair Store," it offered "junk" jewelry and ornaments which she called "Twinkets." A stick of licorice with a brass ring attached sold for a penny. The ring soon turned your finger green. Small wax “goodies” filled with fruit-flavored syrup were available in the candy counter. You bit into these to release the syrup and then chewed the wax-like chewing gum. Sewing items, like thread, pins, needles, bias-tape and rick-rack were offered. Later the front addition was added where her daughter, Anna Gunnlaugsson, had an ice cream parlor.

Other dwellings on Detroit Island included "Bunny" Herschberger's on the very south end and a cottage just up from Richter's dock, where Ida Richter lived in summer while her husband, Fred, and two sons, Earl and Roy, fished.

At Lobdell's Point, Cornell's dock, now Island Outpost's, was always a beehive of activity. Besides several fish tugs operating from there, the *Wisconsin* and *Diana*, hauled freight in and out. Fishing was very good commercially.

Once when we were fishing in the Harbor and the tug, "*Bub*," was nearing the dock I heard Bill Cornell, who had a voice like a foghorn, yell from the dock, "How much did you get?" We could not hear the response, but then clearly Bill exclaimed, "Sixty hundred!"

Often the men did not finish cleaning the catch before they arrived at the dock. Consequently, they often dumped the fish guts next to the dock. This created a bountiful supply of such game fish as perch, rock bass and black bass. In fact, my nephew, Roy, told me that they would frequently bring coal for Cornell's to heat the shed where they overhauled nets and hooks. To get closer to the coal shed, they turned the *Wisconsin* around and backed up to the head of the dock. So many perch were struck and dazed by the propeller that Bill Cornell got in a skiff and scooped them out with a net. He recovered enough to ship a whole box of perch to market. After that they would walk the boat back with hand lines to avoid killing so many fish.

Chambers dock, now Voights, was also busy in summer. Few people today know that once within sailboat distance of Detroit Harbor there was a woman who was very accommodating with sexual favors. One old sailor would frequently hoist the sail and pay her a visit. His neighbor began to think he should also avail himself of the opportunity so he bought enough canvas for the sails which he started making. Meanwhile his wife became aware of his scheme. She said, "I cried more tears than I could hold in my hand to think what that man was going to do." Later she reported, "But I fixed him. I took the scissors to that sail, cut it up and made a 'madras' (mattress) out of it."

Uncle Jens Andersen was one of the founders of the Lutheran Church on the Island. While it was said that he did not leave deep tracks in the Danish church, he was known by many of the old ministers from Marinette and New Denmark who visited the Island to perform religious rituals.

Jens was born in 1848 in Aale township, 3 miles west of Horsens, Denmark.

When he was 9 years old he set out to work for his food and clothes. The man he worked for was supposed to keep him in school in the winter, but it was far from steady.

Because of his learning ability (despite the problems) he managed to be the second best student. The school was not the best, for in the first half of his school time he had a 70 year old teacher who used his temper as a means of education. Because of this situation it was said "The one who can go through Aale school unpunished can go through hell without being burned". Later they had a teacher named Dahl,who was much admired and loved.

When he was 14 years old Uncle Jens became an apprentice to a blacksmith. He learned the trade exceptionally well and gave it careful attention, working faithfully so his youth passed with no unusual upheavals.

When he finished his blacksmith internship he was called to war service in the Danish military. After a service trip to the West Indies, he travelled, with his young bride, to America and settled on Washington Island where he lived for 22 years and where his 12 children were born.

The Island at that time was not productive, soil was sandy with many stones so farming was a very poor livelihood. There was much hard work to clear away stumps and stones to prepare the land for plowing.

Therefore it was through his blacksmith skills he was able to feed his big family.

At that time Island people lived much as a large family. Uncle Jens' home was a gathering place for them, just anyone who had something on their mind or heart. There was a large reading group (society) and they decided to send a call to minister Laust Jensen who accepted and came to the Island. His wife, Kari Jensen, told much about living here.

Later came the following ministers: Rasmus Nielsen, a minister Kolding, S.H. Madsen, C.N. Pedersen, Aaberg and perhaps others.

In the 22 years Uncle Jens lived on the Island he worked so skillfully and created such good products that many of his plows, harrows, discs and spike-tooth drags may still be found despite many years of use. Some were called Swedish harrows and were especially necessary to scratch out the stones. He also made the same harrows after he moved to Withee where they were especially useful for digging out quack grass. Uncle Jens moved to Withee just as the settlement was developing and lived there till his death on February 28, 1927, one year before my dad, his brother, died.

A relative said of Uncle Jens, "His life may not have set up deep roots, but he has had many friends and no known enemies."

He had a friendly nature which was already shown in his childhood when he tended sheep on the farm. Then he became friends not alone with sheep and lambs, but also with the birds. He could entice and call the birds till they came and sat on his head. He could take the lark in his hand and pet it. It was this friendly side of his character which gave him so many friends and therefore his grandchildren gathered around him and he was like a father to them. Because of this it is natural for his daughter-in-law to be kind and loving to him till the last. The day he died he asked me to sing the well known verse of Brorson:

"Let not the world lead us astray
That we our Christian faith betray
But grant that our longings be
O Lord, forever of thee."

His huge forge bellows, which he brought with him from Denmark and used on the Island, have been permanently mounted in the Museum's blacksmith shop. They have been completely restored and provide lots of air to the forge. Some of the tools in the blacksmith shop and many still on our old farm were made by Jens.

Mac Gudmundson, Arni Richter's uncle, had a delightful sense of humor. He lived where Lou Small now resides. In the late 1920s my sister, Olivia, was teaching at the Lucke School and if the weather was bad she would stay at Mac's house rather than walking home. We visited there many times and it was always a delight to listen to Mac's stories and poems that he made up about his neighbors. For many years he was relief rural mail carrier and he always made the route much faster than John Malloch. A big reason for this was he had a horse that had formerly been involved in many races and that steed really wanted to travel fast.

Sometime around World War I Mac decided to publish a newspaper which he entitled "The Washington Island Glab." I often wondered what "Glab" meant. Finally, several years ago when my cousin from Iceland, Kolbein Thorsleifsson, was visiting here I asked if it was an Icelandic word. His immediate response was, "Oh, yes!." He had some difficulty in translating this into English, but finally wrote, "A common word meaning the negative sense of staring, sticking one's nose into another's business." "How true," I remarked and I think you will agree when you read what Mac wrote. I feel that this is certainly a part of Island living "Through the Years" so it will be reproduced here in these issues. If any descendant of anyone mentioned in the "Glab" takes offense to what is said therein, please bear in mind that I am not responsible for any slurs or insults. When someday you arrive in the "hereafter" take the issue up with Mac, not with me. This is a reproduction of Mac's paper.

THE WASHINGTON ISLAND GLAB

Magnus Gudmundson, Editor-in-Chief, Price 3 Cents Per Copy, 2nd Edition

Announcement

In the first issue of the "Glab" we stated that it was both the first and last issue, fully expecting that the long-suffering and indignant public of Washington Island would suppress the publication of a second issue of a paper that was bold enough to tell the truth.

On the contrary we have received so many appeals for more items of personal mention, so many demands for advertising space, etc., that we decided to extend ourselves once more and grant the public this request.

Owing to the enormous expense we are under for reporters, especially war correspondents, it has been necessary to raise the price of this issue to three cents, which will include your good will. And be it further understood, good people, that whatever political prejudice or personal indignation this paper may cause, do not arise and smite the editor, but kick yourself in the shins because it was you, the people, and not we, the editors, who demanded this publication.

Editorial

It cannot be truthfully stated that the fishermens convention at Sturgeon Bay, at which the Island was so well represented, was without results. Speaking, alcoholicly, there have been more successful parties given on the Island since the return of the representatives than there have been since the holidays.

We were pleased to see such a large audience here this evening in spite of the fact that officers of the church at their last gathering refused to announce this concert. In view of the fact that this band has given the church the proceeds of several previous concerts, and is still willing to help a good cause along, the members cannot help feeling that the church is "out to beat the band." If they exert as much in trying to beat hell as they evidently are in trying to beat the band, we feel sure they will have a prosperous year.

Things are fairly buzzing around Koyen's store these days since the first kiss of spring has livened up the blue tailed flies.

(To be continued)

Charlie Hagen has returned from the Windy city where he has been taking a look at the sky scrapers. He managed to bring back safely his hand bag which was the envy of all eyes, even at the N.W. depot. He was particularly impressed by the benevolence of a Chicago policeman who told him where his relatives lived.

Charlie Betts is rapidly recovering from an attack of paralysis that rendered him speechless. Bert says that Uncle Charley is getting so fat and greasy they have to put ashes in his bed to keep him from slipping out.

A valuable addition was made to the already large number of gas carts on the Island recently when Clarence Dana delivered a brand new automobile to Hans Hanson. The car is of the latest model and is certainly a beauty. No doubt you are interested in knowing the make of this car, as was Martin Engleson who is a crank, not only on his own, but on all automobiles. Before the car arrived Martin asked Hans what kind of car he was buying. Hans who is not familiar with cars, said after a long hesitation, "Why - it's a Vomit car". "No", Martin says, "you must be mistaken.There is no such car made". But Hans was sure it was a Vomit car until the happy thought struck him that it was not a Vomit, but a Buick. (However-Hans called it a ~Puick)

PERSONAL-MENTION

Walter Launders spent a very enjoyable week at Ellison Bay visiting his intended spouse. During the visit the young people decided to take a sight seeing trip to Sister Bay. It happened that the stage was crowded and Walter asked his pretty Jennie if she thought they could squeeze in there. "Better wait until we get to our hotel" was the unexpected reply.

Jake Bowman who has always been careful of his health, the more so since many batchelors have been taken sick, is known to cut loose once in a while just the same. Here is what he confided to a very intimate friend the other day. "The papers say there are microbes in kisses, but I like the little devils".

Earl Malloch, latest son of Wm. Malloch, East Side, has been making a brief visit with his folks the last two months.

Ted Thorarinson came very near bleeding to death the other night and he can be thankful his good and faithful wife was at his side at the time for it was she who rendered first aid and put in this call for the doctor who immediately responded. "Doctor, Ted has had a nose bleed all night and is now lying at death's door. For pity sake get a move on and help us pull him through". Ted is still among us, you will notice, although minus his mustache and a few pounds of blood.

Gibbie Goodlet, the well known sky pilot, who acted as janitor on John Christiansons boat last summer has been the guest of his wife this winter.

Abe Jessen and frau spent a very pleasant outing last Monday while angling for trout in Green Bay. They must have had a good catch for they both fished out of the same hole that Hans Mads had fished in every winter since he came to the Island.

Young August Sigurdson, son of old man Sigurdson, will no doubt be a great help to his mother when he grows up.

Nels Friis, vendor of and noted authority on nonalcoholic liquors recently declared that all whiskies are good, but some are better than others.

Al Goodman invested in a new comb the other day. He claims he loaned his old one to Bill Engleson who broke all the teeth out of it combing his curly hair. (Note- Bill was nearly bald.)

Now, what has become of that notorious Oconto dentist who used to fill your mouth with cotton and then ask you about your relatives.

Nels Sorenson, our local undertaker, says he is the only man on the Island who could box Jack Johnson and do it up right.

The other day Sever Severtson upon seeing himself in an uptown mirror while out on one of his good natured trips, decided he needed to consult a tonsorial artist. He at once made tracks for John Malloch's barber shop and plunked himself down in the chair. John very properly asked "Do you want a hair cut?" "I want them all cut" says Sever there-by proving himself a sport. The other day while out soliciting subscribers, I stopped at

George Moe's and wanted to sell him a year's subscription to the "Glab". He said it would not be necessary for him to take the paper as he had just joined the Ladies Aid.

Bess Helgason said he never had his heart in his mouth but he has had many of them up his sleeve. Oh you blackleg.

I asked Jonnie Barnes the other day what he would do if a man called him a l iar. "How big is the man?" asked John.

Owing to the shortness of Frank Olsen's pants, the natives of Jensenville have spent a very pleasant winter playing checkers on his sox. Arnold Sodderburg Sundayed at the home of Mrs. Bennie Andersen last week. The following day Alton Jess met Eleanor on he road."I passed your place yesterday Eleanor" says Alton "Thank you" says she.

John Malloch our local tonsorial artist, states that he will not shave a customer on Sunday but he will trim him on Monday.

Mrs. Nor Shellswick says that during these long winters she has to make a little go a long ways in feeding her husband.

Buy Rob Knudson's second-hand Saxon car and you will never live to regret it.

John Christianson says the hardest things for him to dodge are the grippe and Jackson Harbor wire fences. John didn't sweat half as much cranking his Buick car last summer as he did trying to get his first linen collar on. There's a woman in that case, though.

UNCLASSIFIED ADS

Mr. Bo Andersen wishes to announce that although he is not a drinking man and is strongly opposed to liquor, he will guarantee anyone a skate on at his rink on Wednesdays and Saturday nights of everyweek.

Beginning next Monday morning there will be a sale at the Gislason Mercantile Co's store. Raisins, prunes, currants dried apples, dried peaches, etc., will be sold at cost. The sale starts at 9 A.M.

Remember that the early bird catches the worm.

Bilton Bros. Offer all kinds of fresh, smoked, and salt fish and herring for sale.

SOCIETY

Mr and Mrs Lawrence Gislason entertained a few friends at a pretty little party at their home the other evening. Music was the feature of the evenings entertainment. Besides there was a mandolin solo by the host.

The last meeting of the Farmers Union which was held at the home of August Koyen, was well attended by both officers and members.

The vice-president Jens Hanson,read an interesting article on the subject of "Proper feeding of hogs", after which the hostess appropriately laid troughs for those present. Every morsel of food was eaten thereby proving the success of the subject under discussion.

Surely a successful meeting without a grunt of disapproval.

We have noticed with some satisfaction the progress our young people are making in learning the new dances. Willie Cornell seems to be the most promising in this field.He would be able to dance the tango very gracefully if it were not for two things - his feet.

(This is the-end of the ~"Glab"-Second Edition)

During the 20s and 30s all the commercial fishermen at Lobdell's Point knew who the 'Harmony Twins" were. These two brothers fished together for a lifetime and constantly fought and argued. Once I heard one brother remark, "One of these days there is going to be two of us going out on the lake and only one coming back."

Once, in the middle of a big argument, they brought the fish tug into the dock and were so engrossed in their differences that they failed to tie the boat to the dock. Next morning when they arrived ready for another day on the lake, to their dismay they saw the boat had drifted across the west channel. It was grounded on Detroit Island. They had to get another fisherman to pull their tug back into the channel.

My cousin, also a fisherman -- and a teller of tall tales -- once told us that these brothers got caught fishing in Michigan waters with net mesh that was too small to be legal. They were allowed one phone call which was placed to my cousin on the Island. According to him he got a sprayer and a generous amount of sulfuric acid then ran across the lake during the night. In the darkness he sneaked up to where the nets were boxed and waiting to be presented as evidence in the court next day. He liberally doused them with acid causing them to fall apart, leaving no concrete evidence for the Michigan warden to present. So the brothers were released.

The brothers bought a Model A truck right after Ford first began making them and used it for many years. Usually they finished their work at the dock about 4 p.m. and got in the truck for the ride home. However, when they arrived at the corner where Jack's Garage now is, the brother who always drove would look down the road to see if his wife was standing out in front of their house awaiting his arrival. If he did not see her, the truck turned left and they headed for Nelsen's Hall for a "few refreshments." But if she was in sight he would obediently turn right and head for home.

His wife was always on the lookout for bottles of booze which he hid in such places as stone fences. Once, she discovered a whole cache of moonshine and jumped on him with both feet. He, being a quick thinker responded, "My gosh, I hope you didn't smash the bottles," which I she normally did.

She wanted to know why she should not destroy this booty. He said, "They aren't mine! They belong to Leslie Cornell (a neighbor) and Emma (Leslie's wife) won't allow booze in the house."

She immediately hot-footed it to Leslie's house to inform Emma that Leslie had a secret cache of booze on their property.

Emma quickly informed her that no way would this belong to Leslie as he could have liquor in the house any time he wished.

With greater fire in. her eye the wife made tracks for home to get this issue settled once and for all.

Well, the husband, knowing what the eventual outcome would be, had hastily emptied the booze into a large container which he hid in a better place. Then he refilled the original bottles with a hasty brew of tea, leaving them in the same locations where his wife had placed them.

On her return, she triumphantly smashed every bottle and figured that she had performed a true "Carrie Nation" act.

In the dead of winter, when the fishermen did not venture forth he spent the whole day at home but would be dead drunk by nightfall. She racked her brain trying to figure out where he was getting the booze. He never left the house but occasionally went into the basement to stoke the furnace. She never learned where the hiding place was.

A concrete cistern to catch rain water from the roof for washing clothes was built into one corner of the basement. Its upper rim was a few inches below the floor joists in the basement ceiling. Ingeniously, he had figured that he could tie a string around the neck of the whiskey bottle and lower it into the cistern where it would be well hidden. Every time before and after stoking the furnace, he would take a big swig. As the day wore on, it seemed the furnace needed stoking more often.

Summer had faded away. The trees were bare and gusts of wind whipped the fallen leaves about the house. The haunting cry of migrating geese no longer filled the skies. Hoar frost instead of morning dew told us that Jack Frost had begun his nightly visits. The breath of winter was in the air.

October 31st, the time of Halloween was at hand. A spooky aura prevailed as darkness fell for this was the night when ghosts, goblins and things that go bump would be abroad and up to no good. Sometimes rain and a strong wind thundering through the trees behind our house sounded like the cries of lost souls. As a small boy it was comforting to remain within the shelter of the farm house with the protection of other family members. Of course, as I grew older the urge was strong to get out and engage in the tricks that were popular. During my youth there was no approaching a house and requesting "trick or treat". Slinky and nasty tricks were the vogue of the day especially if there was no moon to give some illumination. Still, even with a full, harvest moon the pranksters were afoot and were not deterred to any great degree.

One of the most popular Halloween tricks was to overturn the "Chick Sale" outhouses that graced the grounds of every Island home. On one occasion the home owner decided to sit in the back house to catch the evil doers. After waiting a considerable time he lapsed into the "arms of Morpheus". Probably the tricksters were aware of his intention as they made a quick rush from the rear and toppled the toilet forward onto its door.The rudely awakened occupant found himself trapped within and was forced to raise up the toilet seat board and clamber out the bottom in a most undignified manner. On another Halloween, one of the young men was wearing a new suit as he was planning to attend a party later in the evening. However, his plan of party attendance came to an abrupt halt while participating in an overturning. As the back house tipped over he lost his balance and fell into the pit. This resulted in an immediate ostrasizing by his companions and the ruination of what he had hoped would be a delightful night. As some of his descendants still reside on the Island I will not reveal his identity.

In my later high school years I was able to sneak out of the house and join a group of Detroit Harbor boys to do some deviltry. Behind Abe Jessen's barn was a very large "three-holer". This was the only "comfort station" in the vicinity of the ball park so it found heavy usage by both sexes whenever the Island team played at home. Abe had repeatedly bragged that no one could tip over this large structure. On Halloween when Karly was with us he remarked about his father's bragging and strongly suggested that we make a concerted effort to prove his dad wrong. We promptly applied ourselves to the task. There was room enough between the toilet and the barn for persons to walk in between. So,pooling our brain power we decided that one of the other taller boys and I would place our feet against the toilet wall, our backs against the barn wall and in a crouched position walk upward until we were close to the toilet eaves. Our positions were close to the outer edges of the toilet walls. The next two boys would travel upward in the same manner, but keep near the center to avoid having us descend upon them if and when the structure tumbled. The rest of the gang would apply force at ground level. We, at the top, agreed to jump outward to avoid clobbering one of our pals. With Karly softly counting out our rhythm we began rocking the building. Finally, with a mighty heave from all of us, over it went. However it did not stop there. As it was perched on a hill it began rolling northward toward West Harbor Road. With each revolution it disintegrated more until when it came to rest any salvage was out of the question. Shortly thereafter Karly entered his home and found his parents sound asleep. After waiting for some time, dressed in his pajamas he went into his folk's room, shook his dad awake and said, "Hey,dad. I just heard some noise outside, I wonder what it was." Together they conducted a search and saw what had happened. Of course, Abe never suspected that son, Karly, had been a party to the deviltry.(Jessen's home is now Nerenhausen's.)

Youngsters who were physically too small to engage in toilet tipping did find other ways to indulge in "Tricks" on Halloween. Big, yellow bars of Fels Naphtha soap were most useful in soaping windows. These markings varied from circles and Xs to nasty words. A popular noise maker consisted of a large, coat button through which strong string had been threaded and tied in a loop. The operator held either end of the loop in each hand and with slack in the string he or she spun the button to wind it up. Then by alternately pulling tight and slacking off, the button twirled forward and back at a high rate of speed. When the spinning button's edge was applied against a window pane it made a frightful sound. Another favorite trick was to fasten a long string to the screen door of a house then hide behind a tree or bush and pull the door open and let the spring pull it back closed with a loud bang. These last two tricks were sure to promptly lure the home owner outside in hopes they would hurl angry epithets into the air or attempt to chase and catch the culprit.

Certain persons, who were known to react strenuously, always became targets on Halloween. One favorite was Bill Arndt. Any trickery about his place would lead to his swift pursuit of anyone perpetrating a misdemeanor about his premises. One Halloween Ludlow Richter, one of the Detroit Harbor group, was in a bunch being chased by Bill. Ludlow, who thought he had successfully eluded Bill, felt a sudden urge of nature. Slipping behind a stone fence he had hardly dropped his trousers to his ankles when Bill came over the fence. Fortunately, with rapid, deft maneuvering Ludlow avoided his pursuant's clutches.

One of the nastiest tricks I ever heard of was pulled many years before I was born. Just before Halloween Ed Aznoe had readied a huge wagon load of grain to take to the grist mill the following day. The loaded wagon sitting in the barn yard was too great a temptation for a notorious gang of Island hell raisers. Imagine the labor they put forth that night, first in unloading the sacks of grain from the wagon. Then taking the wagon apart so that, piece by piece, it could be hoisted to the peak of the barn where it was reassembled. Following this they laboriously carried the sacks of grain up and reloaded them into the wagon where it posed in early morning looking just the same as when Ed had left it the night before, except now it was in a very lofty position.

After arising, Ed soon discovered his wagon was missing and his first thought was that somebody had towed it away out of his yard. After a diligent search of the neighborhood without success, he returned home. Finally he peered upward and to his amazement found his wagon. With a generous mixture of consternation and anger he mounted the roof with an ill-advised plan to get the grain and wagon, back down to earth. A straw stack right next to the barn seemed to afford a soft, safe landing place for the full bags of grain so he began sliding them down the shingled roof. Unfortunately, projecting shingle nails tore many of the sacks open causing the grain to be generously scattered about the premises. Undoubtedly this made the chickens in his flock and the wild birds very happy, but lent nothing to Ed's "good humor". According to my cousin, Leslie Cornell, Ed never learned who had done the dastardly deed. Perhaps this is fortunate as mayhem and murder may have resulted if he had ever caught up with the culprits.

Depending on how cold the weather had been, ice harvesting usually was carried on between January and early March.

Commercial fishermen had their own ice houses in close proximity to where they docked their boats and packed the fish. These places included Lobdell's Point, Gasoline Town, Johnnie Young's in Washington Harbor, Nelson's,-Hanson's and Johnny Christianson's as well as McDonald's in Jackson Harbor. Richter's had a large ice house on Detroit Island. On the west side, ice was harvested for Engleson's and the tugs from West Harbor.

Additionally some of the hotels also stored ice. Mann's, Ted's and Gislason's store kept cake ice for sale. It was delivered by truck, along with grocery orders, to those customers who had the luxury of a kitchen icebox.

The remaining ice house behind the Jackson Harbor Maritime Museum is a representative example of how these building were constructed. The studs remain bare to the outside with the sheathing nailed inside to form a smooth wall. This allowed freer movement of air and kept the interior cooler in the summer.

An exception to this is John Christianson's ice-house of concrete block - which still stands across from the Maritime Museum. Traditionally an opening was left in the wall facing the waterfront to allow both placing ice in the shed and taking it out.

When the ice was the right thickness to make good cakes, the harvesting began.

I remember that George Hansen, Eleanor Rohling's father, had an icecutting saw. It was mounted on a sled with a gas engine to power the blade. With the blade to one side of the sled he could move along on solid ice and make the cuts nearly through the surface. Once a small pond was opened the workers using long chisel bars could break off the cakes. These were then floated to a ramp leading into the ice house In later years some of the ramps were mechanized.

Generous amounts of sawdust (for insulation) was spread between the cakes and between each layer. These cakes were stacked neatly in place.As the height of the ice storage grew, loose planks were placed across the front opening to keep them from sliding back out. After harvesting was finished it was easy to see how much ice was in the house just by observing how high the opening had been planked.

A few private residents had small ice-houses for their own supply for summer months.

As a school boy I was always excited by the ice harvest. Horses pulling large heavily loaded sleighs would pass our school at regular intervals. Besides, I sometimes got the rare opportunity to go down to Detroit Harbor and watch the sawing and loading which continued from dawn to dark. In later years, trucks replaced the horses and sleighs, notably Charlie Jensen's Model "T" and George Hansen's Chevy.

Ole Christianson, who built and lived in the house now owned by Carol Lemon, (at the foot of Main Road) had his own small ice-house. Perhaps because the harvesting was being done off the shore of his land he thought he should have priority of getting ice. One time he "muscled in" on Charlie Jensen, who was trucking to Mann's store. Charlie quipped, "I've heard a lot of people call you 'Ole Hog' and now I know it is true!"

In the late '60s, while on vacation from California, I needed ice for my camper. Even though the Nelsons had not harvested ice in many years, Spencer suggested that I dig down into the sawdust in their ice house. To my amazement I found enough ice to serve our needs while visiting the Island.

Nelson's Hall offered first rate movies every Wednesday when I was a teenager. George O. Mann, the store owner, always sat not too far back from the screen. Several of us high school boys had learned to convert fountain pen barrels into pea shooters. We would place ourselves in the back row of the hall where we could stand and not interfere with anyone being able to see the movie screen. From these positions we would take aim at George's bald dome and begin firing peas. Over the weeks George moved further away from us, but this only provided temporary relief as several of us had now become pea sharpshooters. He finally discovered that the best relief was to wear his sheepskin jacket, raise the big collar up and scrunch down so that no part of his "ivory dome" was exposed. For defense he wore the sheepskin even on hot summer nights.

When I say we got first-rate movies, that is absolutely true. We would get them while they were also playing in Green Bay. The poster advertising the following week's showing was always tacked to the wall right next to where Charley Schmidt sat to collect the price of admission. Another poster was at the west end of the bar. Frequently people would call during the week to learn what to expect the following Wednesday. Tom Nelson was always irked when he had to walk from one end of the bar to the other to read the poster and pass the information along on the telephone. In those days the movie stars were always listed with their last name first--Crosby, Bing would be an example. One busy day, Tom was interrupted from his card game by an inquiry as to the name of next week's feature. He said,"Gest a minute", laid the phone receiver down and walked to the poster then reported back to the caller the title of the movie. However,they were not satisfied with just learning the title and asked who was playing in the movie. This further irked Tom and he responded,"Goddam, gest a minute". Again he traversed the length of the bar and upon return announced into the phone, "Tracy, Spencer and some other son-of-a-bitch!"

The projection room was a very small area just on the other side of the west wall of the main hall. Here Ray Krause always ran the projector. It was a great day when “talkies” replaced the silent films. About the first talking picture I remember seeing was "The Jazz Singer" starring Al Jolson. As Tom had only one projector there was always a waiting period when a reel ended and another had to be placed in the machine. If a person had a little "loose change" in their pocket there was always ample time to go into the barroom part to buy candy, gum,or Tom's home-made ice cream or soda pop.

He had a good sized structure behind the hall with a small steam boiler and one cylinder steam engine (now in the Maritime Museum) which was used to power the ice cream making machine. He bought the soda pop syrups in various flavors, added these to well water, filled the bottles and then capped them. Once in a while boys would sneak into his bottling area, mix their own soda and enjoy the results.

When Tom learned that I was entering the U.S. Merchant Marine Academy in the summer of 1941, he pleaded with me to get him a grass skirt to hang over the bar, only he called it a "gwass skut". Upon my first arrival in Hawaii I purchased one and shipped it back to Tom along with a "wild" story that I had chased a brown-skinned maiden down Waikiki beach and finally divested her of this piece of apparel. I believe the "skut" hung over the bar until after Tom died.

While the Island today still has some unusual individuals residing there, the number of "characters" as they used to be called, is an insignificant number compared to when I was growing up and even before my time.

I suspect that very few today would remember some of the earlier nicknames, sayings, and incidents that were common knowledge. I hope no living relatives take offense. Try to match the following persons in these scrambled columns:

1. Whispering Hope	1. Sigurd Sigurdsson(E.side-Bjarnarson'sRental)
2. Stone John	2. Ole Christianson (Carol Lemmon's)
3. Black John	3. Tom Nelson (Nelson's Hall)
4. Big Chris	4. Mrs. Jack Andersen (oppo. Butch Jess)
5. Pete Crab	5. Andy Cornell (NW corner Det. Hbr.& Rangeline)
6. Snow Snake	6. Phil Carlson (Plum Is. second-in-command)
7. Speaker Louder	7. Harry Hansen (Carrol Koyen's place)
8. Comin' on the Next Boat	8. Rodney Cornell (Townline Rd.)
9. Up There	9. Bill Cornell (Det. Hbr. Rd.-Greenfeldts)
10. Little Boy	10. Paul Jorgenson (Walt Jorgenson's son)
11. Pirate	11. John Peterson(SE corner-Lakeview & Rangeline)
12. Captain Blunt	12. James Sorenson (West Harbor Hotel)
13. Lefty	13. Vernie Richter (Jon Anderson's)
14. Ha-By-Goss	14. Art Wickman (Ron Pepsnik's)
15. Youncey	15. John Johnsson (Percy Johnson's grandfather)

16. Mary Pete	16. Roger Gunnerson (Big milk drinker)
17. Peruna Pete	17. Andrew Nelson (Jackson Hbr.)
18. Laura Pete	18. Margaret Weidemann (Lee Engstrom's)
19. Mary George	19. Elizabeth Peterson (Thor Williamson's)
20. Saltum Brother	20. Alex Koyen (Caroline Koyen's)
21. Sievert	21. Frank Olson (SE of Aznoe & Rangeline Rds.)
22. The Holy Rollers	22. Louie Engelson (Sunset Resort)
23. Bible Back	23. Kate Koyen (Washington Hbr.)
24. Hawkshaw	24. Tom Koyen (Alex Koyen's son)
25. The Harmony Twins	25. Maynard Olson (Detective in a school play)
26. Long Balsam	26. Mrs. Pete Peterson (Beamish's-Main Rd.)
27. Annie Jack	27. Mrs. Pete Andersen (later Mrs. John Christianson.)
28. Gentleman James	28. Nels Sorenson(Margaret Smith's)
29. Ole Hawg	29. Hannes Johnsson,Sr.(Gasoline Town fisherman)
30. Satchel-Ass	30. John Christianson(Jackson Hbr. Fish Cottage)
31. Uncle Vernie	31. Ben Johnson (Rangeline Rd.-Wash. Hbr.)
32. Drainwater Chris	32. Pete Jensen (Kirby Foss)
33. Goss Dang-it	33. Ben Johnson (Hotel Washington)
34. Poop-A-Looper	34. Pete Peterson (Beamish's-Main Rd.)
35. Chickadee	35. Lawrence Gislason (Comment when out of stock)
36. Harry Dairy	36. Earl & Roy Richter (Fished from Detroit Is.)
37. Double Daisy	37. Sigurd Sigurdsson (E.side-Bjarnarson's rental)
38. Number One	38. Mrs. Geo. Hansen (Across from Sievers)
39. Lodge Pole	39. Angus Swenson (Expression often used by him)
40. Ole	40. Steve Gunnlaugsson (Self-taught vet)
41. Big Wootsie	41. Charley Schmidt (Spoke in loud whisper)
42. Bowser	42. Harold Johnson (Island's outstanding pitcher)
43. Saxty-Sax	43. Religious sect meeting in homes
44. Fineshot Art	44. Frank Richter(Name hung on him by Jim Boyce)
45. Little Ben	45. Chris Jensen (Bachelor-E. part of Main Rd.)
46. Sterilizer Elizabeth	46. Chris Sorenson (Don Green's)
47. Milk Belly	47. Conrad Andersen (Jeff McDonald's)
48. Hotel Ben	48. John Johnsson (Hannes Johnson's son)
49. The Animal Doctor	49. Sigurd Sigurdsson(E.side Bjarnarson's rental)
50. Pete Duffy	50. Clara Garrett (Deafer than a post)
	51.Pete Andersen(Early Mail carrier)
	52.Martin Andersen(Townline E.of Airport Rd.)

Try your hand at matching the right names together. In the next issue I will give you the solution. Anyone getting over one-half right must be an old timer in the Island.

Here are the solutions to the nicknames and incidents in the last article. As I said,if you got over half right you must be an Island "old timer". If any of you made a list of numbers and attempted to match the left and right hand columns in my previous article, note the numbers to the left of the nicknames above. For example: No. 1 "Whispering Hope" matches No. 41 "Charley Schmidt".

1-41	Whispering Hope--Charley Schmidt.
2-11	Stone John--John Peterson.
3-15	Black John--John Johnsson [Percy's grandfather]
4-45	Big Chris--Chris Jensen
5-32	Pete Crab--Pete Jensen
6-21	Snow Snake--Frank Olson
7-50	Speak Louder--Clara Garret
8-35	Comin' on the next boat--Lawrence Gislason
9-39	Up There--Angus Swenson
10-17	Little Boy--Andrew Nelson
11-30	Pirate--John Christianson
12-25	Captain Blunt--Maynard Olson
13-42	Lefty--Harold Johnson
14-29	Ha-By-Goss--Hannes Johnsson,Sr.
15-48	Youncey--John Johnsson[Hannes Sr's son]
16-27	Mary Pete--Mrs. Pete Andersen
17-51	Peruna Pete--Pete Andersen
18-26	Laura Pete--Mrs. Pete Peterson
19-38	Mary George--Mrs. George Hansen
20-47 & 52	A Saltum Brother--Conrad & Martin Andersen
21-49	Sievert--Sigurd Sigurdsson
22-43	The Holy Rollers--Religious sect meeting in homes
23-5	Bible Back--Andy Cornell
24-9	Hawkshaw--Bill Cornell
25-36	The Harmony Twins--Earl & Roy Richter
26-49	Long Balsam--Sigurd Sigurdsson
27-4	Annie Jack--Mrs. Jack Andersen
28-12	Gentleman James--James Sorenson
29-2	Ole Hawg--Ole Christianson
30-44	Satchel-ass--Frank Richter
31-13	Uncle Vernie--Vernie Richter
32-46	Drainwater Chris--Chris Sorenson
33-3	Goss Dang-it--Tom Nelson
34-22	Poop-a-Looper--Louie Engelson

35-18	Chickadee--Margaret Weideman
36-7	Harry Dairy--Harry Hansen
37-23	Double Daisy--Kate Koyen
38-6	Number One--Phil Carlson
39-10	Lodge Pole--Paul Jorgenson
40-8	Ole--Rodney Cornell
41-24	Big Wootsie--Tom Koyen
42-20	Bowser--Alex Koyen
43-28	Saxty-Sax--Nels Sorenson
44-14	Fineshot Art--Art Wickman
45-31	Little Ben--Ben Johnson [Washington Harbor]
46-19	Sterilizer Elizabeth--Elizabeth Peterson
47-16	Milk Belly--Roger Gunnerson
48-33	Hotel Ben--Ben Johnson [Hotel Washington]
49-40	The Animal Doctor--Steve Gunnlaugsson
50-34	Pete Duffy--Pete Peterson

Now that the nicknames are matched with the Islander's names let me tell you some interesting things about these people.

Charley Schmidt had something happen to his voice box to where he spoke like a loud whisper, maybe some of the early Island "moonshine" had something to do with it. Anyhow, Charles "Buzz" Gislason could mock him to perfection. Many years after Schmidt died we were at a party at Gislason's home in California and Buzz sneaked up behind me and imitated Schmidt. My reaction was, "My gosh. Old Charley has come back from the grave."

Old "Stone John" Peterson was always suspicious that local grocers were out to cheat him when he sold farm products to them. One day he arrived at Mann's store with a large basket of eggs to sell. When asked by George Mann how many dozen were in the basket he claimed he did not know. After George laboriously counted them and announced he found eleven dozen Stone John responded, "Accurat".[sic]

"Big Chris" Jensen, who lived in a small shack near the east end of Townline Road, would hire out to do manual labor. One year, as haying season grew nigh, Rob Gunnerson asked Chris if he would help in harvesting the hay. Chris said he might. Rob then asked what wages he wanted per day. Chris responded, "If I work for a man I get a dollar a day, but if I work for a 'son-of-a-bitch' I get two dollars a day." Haying season arrived and Rob sought out Chris to see if he would work for him. Chris agreed to do so, but when Rob asked what wages he wanted he promptly responded, "Two dollars a day!" This was a story that Rob's son, Roger, loved to tell.

I don't know exactly were Pete "Crab" Jensen got that nickname, but I remember well hitching the horses to the farm wagon and taking grain to Pete's to have it ground into meal for the cattle. Pete and Hattie had almost enough sons to have their own baseball team. I remember how strong Myron was. He was a little younger than me, but while still in grade school he would take a two-bushel sack of grain under each arm and carry it into the grist mill. The grain in each sack weighed 120 lbs. The Jensens lived nearly two miles from the Detroit Harbor school and I felt sorry for the boys walking that distance on nasty winter days, while I lived just across the road from the school.

Frank "Snow Snake" Olson was given his nickname by Dave Kincaid and this has been covered in an earlier story. However, there is another story that some old timers still tell about him. According to one man well in his 80s, Frank used to run a small fish boat. Normally two men would man a fish tug, one would steer while the other one worked the engine and answered the signal bells from the skipper when docking and undocking. As Frank was the only man aboard he had to perform both tasks. Yet, before stepping down to maneuver the engine he would always sound the proper signal bell, then hurry below to answer the bell.

Clara "Speaker Louder" Garret was given that nickname by Ernie Boucsein, our rural mail carrier. He frequently encountered her while delivering mail and often was beseeched to "Speak louder". Frank Richter, our neighbor once told us that he and his wife, Ivy, Abe and Grace Jessen and Clara Garret were playing cards one night at Jim and Clara Boyce's home. Someone in the party loudly broke wind, which created a gale of laughter. Of course "Speaker Louder" had heard nothing so she quizzed, “What's that? What's that?” This prompted witty Jim Boyce to remark, “She would not know if that happened to her unless she felt the jar on her !”

"Comin' on the next boat" was the expression used by Lawrence Gislason whenever a customer in his store asked for an item not found on the shelves. Like Mann's and Ted's store,

Gislason's delivered groceries, some hardware items and ice to your door, actually to your kitchen. How many today remember the Vilas Brothers paint sold by Lawrence, or the Patek's paint found at Mann's store? The ice sold by Gislasons in summer had come from just off Gislason's beach the previous winter.

The expression "Up There" was readily identified with Angus Swenson who frequently used this to refer to "Up Town" or more specifically to Nelson's Hall. Some Jackson Harbor fellows about Angus' age said he loved peanuts. He would place the whole nut in one side of his mouth and the shells would come out the other side. Angus was an excellent wine maker and, of course, he consumed quite a bit of his own product.

Andrew "Little Boy" Nelson from Jackson Harbor was a good buddy of John Christianson. Often John would transport Little Boy to and from Nelson's Hall in his Chevy coupe that had a small pick-up box installed in the trunk with the trunk's lid removed. One night after an enjoyable sojourn at Tom's, John offered rides home to some other neighbors. Little Boy had to ride in the pick-up box. To John's amazement upon arriving in Jackson Harbor he found that Little Boy was missing. "My God!" he said, "I've lost Little Boy". Retracing his steps he found Little Boy not much the "worse for wear".

John Christianson probably acquired the nickname"Pirate" from the name of his fish tug. He built and lived in the "fisherman's" concrete block cottage opposite the Maritime Museum. His small, concrete block ice house still stands on the shore. After many years of bachelorhood, he married Pete Andersen's widow and was an excellent father for her sons. Often they spent the summers in the Jackson Harbor cottage and the winters in wife Mary's Detroit Harbor home where she and Pete had lived. He built the log cabin that still stands on this property plus the one across the road from Jim Cornell's. Here he and Mary spent their final days. One day in the late 30s I was sitting next to John at Nelson's bar when a lady vacationer sitting on the other side of John observed the tattoos on his arm. First she asked if that hurt to which he said, "Naw". Then she asked if she could feel them. With this John remarked. "You aint seen nothin' yet." Whereupon he bared his chest revealing a full-rigged sailing vessel tattooed thereon. This dumbfounded her. As John rebuttoned his shirt he poked me with his elbow and remarked,

"Ya, Ve are tough fellers. Ve don't have any hair on our chest, but ve never vash it."

During our high school years we always produced a play which was presented at Nelson's Hall. One year a mystery was selected which involved a ghost. Maynard Olson was chosen to play the part of the ace detective, Captain Blunt, who solved the murder. Frank Olson's son, Maynard, was short of stature so the name fit very well and stuck from that day on. Our English classes would sometimes indulge in formal debates. One subject was "The World Is Flat". Our teacher, Clara Jessen, chose Maynard and I to prove this was so. We argued so convincingly that we won the debate. Many years later while visiting on the Island I ran into Maynard who still proudly remembered that we had done what was apparently considered impossible.

Harold "Lefty" Johnson, grandson of Hannes Johnsson,Sr., was undoubtedly the finest pitcher the Island team ever had. His curve and drop ball was baffling to batters. For several years he occupied the mound dressed in blue dungarees, now called jeans, and a sport shirt. Finally he was convinced that he should don the team's shirt, but never did give up the dungarees. One summer a Milwaukee baseball scout observed his performance and he was invited to their camp to try out for a pitching position. During try-outs the pitching coach instructed him to throw straight balls. The batters hit them very regularly and this upset Lefty, so he resorted to his special pitches. After being instructed by the coach to resume throwing straight balls, which he refused to do, he was told to go home. For many years he led our team to victory after victory. Lloyd Young, a fine player, usually was the catcher, sometimes grabbing the difficult balls with his bare hand. In those days other players included Harold "Dutz"Cornell, Leonard Jorgenson, Russell Nelson, Art Young, Harvey Cornell, Irvin Goodlet, Cliff Vogel [played shortstop and had a sneaky hidden ball trick], "Bub" Cornell [played right field and often delivered a fly ball back to the catcher at home right across the plate]. Levere Cody played for years and then became home plate umpire. From his gestures and loud voice, spectators always knew what the call was. Harvey Cornell had a very effective fast ball as pitcher. Carl Haglund played outfield for a long time. John Coppersmith, a former Chicago bootlegger, had purchased the place across from Dave's Garage, where my mother had grown up. John, who had been a fine ball player, began showing up at nearly every evening's ball practice. He was an excellent batting coach and the team's batting record vastly improved under his guidance.

Hannes "Ha-By-Goss" Johnsson was a very successful commercial fisherman. His sons, Hannes and Youncey, worked with him over the years. Later grandsons Stanley & Harold also became fishermen. My earliest remembrance of Hannes was when Wally Aronson flew an old two-seater biplane to the Island and "barnstormed" from Charley Schmidt's field, where the bank now stands. As a poor farm kid the price of a ride was to me astronomical. Therefore I was amazed when old Hannes treated all his grand children to airplane hops around the Island. Hannes always had a big dog that usually hung around Gasoline Town dock. Uncle Johnny Hannesson and Howard Foss were fishing for Matt Foss. When they would bring the carriers full of fish out of the tug onto the dock, Hannes' dog would run up and put his nose in the fish. This irked both guys so they decided to discourage the dog from hanging around. One day they arrived armed with a corn cob and a bottle of turpentine. One lured the dog to him and held it while the other rubbed his behind with the corn cob and generously applied the turpentine. As the smarting began, the howling dog took off up the hill, then slid down again on his behind on the gravel roadway. Soon it discovered a pile of shaved ice and sat down on this to find relief. Old Hannes was very upset and remarked, "Ha-by-goss! Dey turpentined mine dog!" From then on the dog seemed to stick pretty close to Hannes' dock which was further up Washington Harbor where Bibs Rusing lived for years.

Mary Pete and Pete Andersen had five boys - Gerald, Jim, Ned, Willis and Philip. Quite some time after Pete died she married John Christianson, who taught her how to drive. She always drove slowly and cautiously. One day she and Jim came to our farm to buy dairy products. As she was leaving Sis decided to go to the Post Office. Mary offered her a ride in the little Chevy coupe. As there was not room for three in the front seat she told Jim he should ride in the pick-up box in the back. To exit our yard she had to back and turn.She went too far and hit the clothes line post. When this happened she remarked to Sis, "Oofa! I hope Jim pulled his legs in".

"Peruna" Pete Andersen got the nickname from drinking Peruna tonic which contained a large percentage of alcohol. For many years he carried the mail from Ellison Bay to the Island. Stories about Pete were legion in those days. In summer he had a gasoline powered boat, one of which was the "Navarre". This vessel was large enough to carry an automobile across the deck. Pete never seemed to have an over-abundance of gas in the tank. Plum Island Coast Guard station maintained a 24 hour watch in the lookout tower. Whenever Pete ran out of fuel he would signal the Coast Guard and the tower lookout would yell down, "Pete's out of gas again", whereupon the USCG would fill a can with gas and the crew would deliver it to him.

In winter, after the ice bridge had solidly formed between the Island and the mainland, Pete and his horse, old Maude, would make the trip daily, Monday through Saturday, weather permitting. Maude pulled a small freight sleigh which always had three planks fastened to the side. Sometimes they would encounter expansion cracks in the solid ice where a person could look down into open water perhaps twenty fathoms deep. One-eyed Maude would stop, Pete would get off and lay the planks across the crack in a manner so that one was directly in front of Maude and the other two furnished support for the sleigh runners. Maude would cock her head sideways so she could see the plank with her one good eye and trustingly she would safely get to the other side. [After Pete died my brother, Chris, acquired old Maude. As youngsters we used to have fun placing an old board across a mud puddle, then leading old Maude up to it and watching her carefully traverse the puddle on the board.] Sometimes, in early spring, with a northwest wind blowing, a large ice floe would break loose and begin traveling out into the lake with Pete, Maude and sleigh on it. Upon discovering Pete's plight, the Coast Guard would man the "Bull", make their way to the floe and push it back to solid ice where, by using the planks, Pete and Maude could once again return to safety. Mary Pete's dad, Nels Jepson, sometimes remarked, "If it wasn't for the Coast Guard Pete Andersen would have been in Hell long ago". When Pete first took the exam for mail carrier he was asked if he was a bigamist. Old Nels said, "The silly son-of-a-bitch didn't know what a bigamist was." One of Pete's downfalls was that Mike Anderson, owner of the old Hillside Hotel in Ellison Bay, had what was then called a "blind pig". During Prohibition he sold pints of "moonshine" for a dollar. Often Pete would find a passenger waiting at Ellison Bay dock for transportation to the Island. He would immediately collect the "convenient" fare of one dollar and head up the hill to Mike's for his pint of "hooch".[Mike Anderson's nickname was "Lord Dee", an expression he commonly used.) After loading the mail and any freight aboard, Pete would start the engine, untie the boat and get it past Door Bluff. Then he would ask the passenger if he had ever steered a boat. Usually the response was,"No". So Pete would give him a quick lesson and tell him what point to steer for with an admonition to wake Pete upon arrival at the bell buoy outside the West Channel. Pete would then disappear with the pint which became a "dead soldier" before arrival at the bell buoy. Everyone expected Pete to die "with his boots on", but he finally succumbed to pneumonia in his own bed.

In the days when I was growing up it was quite common to give married women a nickname of their first name and the husband's first name. A little of that still exists today.

Laura Pete, wife of Pete Peterson,was from the Schlise family in Sturgeon Bay. My mother often cut her hair. Once she told Mom this, "My mother was a true Christian and she never swore, but when I prepared to move to the Island after marrying Pete she advised me 'Don't let those Island people crap on you and then rub it in.'"

Laura's sister was married to George DesEnfant, owner of Roxana Hotel in Sturgeon Bay. Some Island boys stayed and worked at the Roxana while attending Sturgeon Bay High School. Percy Johnson was one who did this. Once when Laura and Pete were visiting the Roxana, she became very upset as she could not find her purse. Percy asked George what was so important about that purse. George replied, "Don't you know. She has all their money from bootlegging in it. They don't dare put all that in the bank."

The Saltum Brothers were Martin, Maurice, Conrad, Anton and Chris, while Steve Gunnlaugsson's wife, Bertha, was a sister. I am told that the reason particularly Martin was called "Martin Saltum" was because there was another Martin Andersen, my dad, living on the Island. Dad had migrated from the Horsens region of Denmark while the other Andersens had come from the Saltum area. I remember Martin Saltum always wore a "handlebar" mustache. He was the engineer who ran the steam engine that pulled and powered the threshing machine. Chris and Conrad operated the blacksmith shop where the Jeff McDonalds now live. When the steel rims on our farm wagon would loosen due to repeated pounding on stones and gravel roads we would hitch the team to the wagon and go to the blacksmith shop where one of the men would remove the rim, heat it red hot in the forge, then place it back on the wheel and plunge it into cold water. This would shrink and tighten the rim firmly in place.

If our horses were going to be worked on gravel roads a lot, we would also have them shod. As a small boy I always was fascinated by the preparation for horseshoeing. First a curved-bladed knife was used to thoroughly trim out the center of the hoof while the horse's leg was held firmly between the smith's knees. The outer nail part of the hoof was then trimmed and flattened with a rasp so the shoe would fit properly. Each shoe was then heated red hot and shaped on the anvil to conform to the horse's foot. After plunging in cold water to cool it, the shoe was nailed to the hoof. These special nails were hammered through the outer hoof and the part that stuck through was nipped off with sharp pincers. As a small boy I always winced when this operation was performed as I thought it must be painful to the animal although it was obvious that it did not hurt for the horse never complained. I subsequently learned that this part of the horse's foot had no more feeling in it than the outer end of our finger and toe nails do.

It was fascinating to watch blacksmith work being done. I was always reminded of Longfellow's poem, The Village Blacksmith. "Under the spreading chestnut tree the village smithy stands. The smith a mighty man is he with a large and sinewy hands And the muscles of his brawny arms are strong as iron bands."

How "Sievert" or "Long Balsam" got to the Island is somewhat of an enigma. Sigurd Sigurdsson, a bachelor, had chosen Winnepeg, Canada as his destination when he contracted with the agency to migrate from Iceland. Among the Icelandic immigrants on the same vessel was the widow of an Eyrarbakki fisherman, Gunnar Bjarnarsson [that is believed to have been his last name]. He had drowned when a large fishing boat propelled by oars had capsized when attempting to return to port in a storm.

Possibly her brother, Hannes Johnsson,Sr. may have assisted her financially in getting to America with her two tiny children. Upon her arrival at New York the U.S. immigration officials were fearful that she might not be able to support her family,so they coerced her into marrying "Sievert".

According to her great-grand-daughters it was certainly "not a marriage of love". Sievert was a sort of "revolving son-of-a-bitch" which is one no matter what angle they are viewed from. Anyhow they settled on our Eastside off Lakeview Road [the house now belongs to and is being rented by Robert Bjarnarson.] Since Sievert wore a long, black, pointed beard and was quite tall he somehow acquired the nickname of "Long Balsam". He raised some milk cattle and a substantial herd of sheep. The little boy from Iceland, Reinbaldt, later adopted the Americanized name of Robert Gunnerson and ran the farm just west of Lou Small's place. Over the years other children were born, one of which was postmaster in Sister Bay while I was teaching grade school at Appleport a few miles to the east. It was customary for Sievert to transport the neighbor's milk to the cheese factory in the mornings. He rode in an open buggy pulled by one horse. Frequently the neighbors would ask him to pick up butter and cheese from the factory for them. One hot, summer day Sievert had become quite thirsty so he decided to detour via Tom Nelson's before returning home. After considerable thirst slaking he headed for home but presently fell sound asleep. His horse, feeling no direction from the slack reins decided to fill his belly. Spotting some nice green grass just opposite Vernie Richter's house the horse wandered into the ditch which resulted in the buggy taking a severe slant downward. Slumbering Sievert slumped over in the seat with his face landing in the neighbor's butter and cheese. After some time had passed, Vernie happened see the horse and buggy in the ditch with Sievert in an awkward position. Fearing something dire had happened he quickly ran over to the buggy and shouted and shook "Long Balsam" who finally raised his head to reveal what Vernie described as a very unappetizing sight. Sievert's black beard and face had melted cheese and butter all over it. Besides that he gave forth with a loud, "Hah!" and a whiskey loaded belch that nearly floored Vernie.

I am sure that Sievert probably never took a bath and wore the same suit of underwear the whole winter long. He gave us two lambs that had been abandoned by their mothers. Both ewes had given birth to twins and would only accept one of the twins to nurse. So we raised them on bottles with nipples for babies attached. Unfortunately the ewe died, but the ram grew to maturity. Each spring Mom would get Sievert to shear our pet sheep. Usually he would arrive on a hot, spring day about the end of May still wearing his winter underwear. By the time he had finished the hand shearing he would be sweating profusely and I would really endeavor to keep on the up-wind side of him.

The "Holy Rollers" were a religious group who met in various member's homes. Old Chris Nelson said that they practiced "Home Made" religion. One Sunday they were meeting in a Jackson Harbor home not too far from where Elmer Anderson lived [his place is now Sylvia Nelson's cottage.]. Bachelor Elmer had a certain amount of deviltry in him and it came to the fore that Sunday. On this warm, summer day he sneaked up to the open windows and generously sprinkled red pepper across the window sill. Then he quietly blew the pepper into the meeting room causing a tremendous outburst of sneezing. Of course having Elmer demonstrate how how he pursed his lips and blew through his white, handbarred mustache lent more emphasis to the story.

I suspect that one of the Lobdell's Point commercial fishermen hung the name "Bible Back" on Andy Cornell. He and his wife, Selma, were very active in the Lutheran Church. Still one of his favorite expressions was "Be Jesus Christ" which may have prompted someone to coin his nickname.

Bill "Hawkshaw" Cornell always did the shore work at Cornell's fishery on the Point, undoubtedly because any time he stepped on a boat he immediately got seasick. At that time there was a comic strip in the daily newspaper featuring an inquisitive detective named "Hawkshaw". Bill also had an inquisitive mind so probably this is where the nickname originated.

"The Harmony Twins", Earl and Roy Richter, who fought constantly were covered in a previous story. At that time, however, I did not reveal their names. In the early years their parents, Fred and Pearl Richter, started what came to be one of the most successful fishing operations on the Island. In fact, they had a large dock and beautiful fishing buildings near the tip of "Richter Point" on Detroit Island. In summer mother Pearl lived in the frame cottage close to the sheds and dock. She also operated a small fishing boat named "Pearl".

Annie "Jack" Andersen and family lived in the tall, frame house across from Nelson's Hall. Many girls and boys were born in this household. Their son,Elliot, was in the same school grade as I was. When he was a preschooler few people could understand what he said. As they lived just a few doors from Mann's store his mother would often send him to get an item she needed to finish the family meal. One day at the store he told Fred Mann, "Ma wants some tawntart!" Fred queried him several times seeking a clearer pronunciation to no avail. Finally Fred said, "Elliot I can't understand you. Go home and have your mother write on a piece of paper what she wants and bring it back to me." Upon reaching the door Elliot turned back towards Fred and in a loud voice said, "Tit my at! You undertand dat?" Elliot had been sent for cornstarch.

"Gentleman" James Sorenson and wife, Martha,owned and operated the West Harbor Resort for many years. He had a very erect, military posture which may have helped to give him his nickname. I remember him driving a large Chandler touring car that had two folding "jump" seats behind the front seat. Frequently he could be found on the roads chauffering hotel guests about the Island. Many of their early vacationeers later became homeowners in or near West Harbor. Martha had an excellent reputation for providing outstanding meals.

Ole "Hawg" Chirstianson had his new home built in the late 20s [it now belongs to Carol Lemmon]. They formerly lived in an old house just south of the present one. After moving into new house, he rented the old one to our high school teachers for some years before tearing it down. Ole came from Norway and he told my mother that when he first landed on the New York streets he was hungry. He spied a fruit stand where he saw tomatoes which he thought looked delicious although he'd never seen one before. He bought one, but was very disappointed when he tasted it. His wife was a wonderful Norwegian cook. Often she would call our farm to get some rich cream for baking. She spoke only Norwegian and talked very fast on the phone. If my sisters happened to answer they would immediately drop the crank telephone receiver and yell, "Hey,Ma. It's Mrs. Ole." Then Ole would drive in his little Oldsmobile club coupe to pick up the farm products she wanted. One day when leaving the farm he forgot to release the hand brake. As he traveled down the Main Road we could see smoke billowing from under his car. Soon he discovered that the car was on fire, so he got out and had to use the only available liquid to extinguish the fire. This happened to be the container of milk which he had just bought at the farm. As Ole was noted for his frugality, we knew he was reluctant to have to use the milk for this purpose. He skippered many vessels on the Lakes, first using sailing schooners, one of which was the "Madonna" whose model is displayed in our Lutheran Church. The "bones" of the old Madonna are buried in the mud in Detroit Harbor, just south of the end of Main Road. Ole's last freighter, "Flotilla", was later fitted with an engine and propeller to power it. Some of the Jensenville boys bought her from Ole and had her placed on the reef off Gislason's dock to use as a club house, however, ice and seas led to the vessel's demise and very little still remains. I understand the boys who bought her included Gene Gislason, Johnny Johnson and Louie Kiss.

Frank "Satchel-ass" Richter lived right across the road from our farm. He fished on the "Ione Estelle" from sheds on Detroit Island south of Earl & Roy Richter's sheds. Frank, who walked with his rear end sticking out prominently, received the nickname courtesy of Jim Boyce. He often came to our house to buy dairy products. If Ma had just taken freshly baked pumpernickel bread from the oven he would beg her until she sold him a loaf to take home. His plea often included, "You know, Gertie, eating that storebought bread is just like eating fog."

"Uncle" Vernie Richter farmed NE of Lakeview & Airport Rds. While he was a real uncle to many Island children, we all called him "Uncle Vernie", a very kind and generous man who loved children. He never married, but was a great cook and baker. I always liked to hire out to him because he was jolly, witty and served delicious food.

"Drainwater" Chris Sorenson lived where Don Green now resides. His nickname came from the fact that if he was having trouble hearing what someone was saying he would tilt his head to such an extreme position that one day somebody remarked that it looked like he was trying to drain water out of his ear. Thus the nickname was coined and it stuck.

"Goss Dang-it" Tom Nelson opened Nelson's Hall before the turn of the century. Of course, it is well known that when the

18th Amendment went into effect he was aware that Angostura Bitters had 45% alcohol, or 90 proof. So Tom got a druggist's license and began dispensing shots of bitters to cure "health" problems that seemed to plague former drinkers more and more. Today there are vast numbers of "Bitters Club" members. The distinction being attained by drinking a full shot of bitters, followed by a chaser of one's selection, at Nelson's Hall. The bartender authenticates the Bitters card by wetting his/her thumb in the remaining drop in the shot glass and thus placing their fingerprint on the card. I am sure that most of these members have never read what is printed on the bottle. To prove Tom's soundness in dispensing this "drug" it says in part, "It has long been known as a pleasant and dependable stomachic". Having never heard of this word before I turned to Webster for assistance and found that"Stomachic" means "a digestive tonic". "Goss dang-it. Dat's what I said it was," I'm sure Tom would have said had he been asked. The label goes on to state, "As a stimulant for the appetite, one to four teaspoons before meals is suggested; for flatulence, one to four teaspoonfuls after meals. Because of its delightful flavor and aroma it has become popular for use in soft drinks, cocktails and other alcoholic beverages and it imparts an exquisite flavour to soups, cereals, salads, vegetables, gravies, fish, grapefruit, fresh, stewed or preserved fruits, jellies, sherbets, ice cream, many sauces, puddings, mince pies, apple sauce and all similar desserts, regulating the quantity according to taste".

I have followed some of their recommendations "For Cooking and Table Use" and find it vastly improves many dishes. They suggest: FRUITS:2-3 dashes Angostura--or flavor to taste.

SALADS: Blend 2-3 dashes with each cup of mayonnaise, French or other dressing.

PIES: 4-5 dashes per cup of mince meat or pumpkin filling. 1-2 dashes to apple or other fruit.

SOUPS: 1-2 dashes to each serving of canned soups, fish chowder, bisques and chicken soups. Stir in at last minute."

Tom never married,but he was fond of women. While he found some Island ladies to his liking, his favorite was one from Milwaukee named "Esther", however, Tom pronounced it "Esta". His philosophy on marriage was simple and really covered the issue when he remarked, "Why buy the cow when you can get the milk for free?"

His place was a favorite gathering spot for many reasons. Usually, after the fishermen's work was done for the day, you could find the same group of Island men deep in poker playing. Sometimes these seasoned players would permit a fledgling "sucker" to join them. For a long time there were slot machines in his bar, mostly nickel ones. Even so, when hourly wages were thirty-five cents an hour, or less, it did not take long to lose one's daily pay at the "one-armed bandits".

Tom was very kind to children. My first "exposure" to Tom's Hall occurred when a professional group came to our Detroit Harbor school and got the parents and teachers to agree to their production of a "Tom Thumb Wedding". This involved most of us and I played the role of the preacher performing the ceremony. The group furnished our costumes and it was very well attended. [In a later story I will cover this event and include the wedding picture, plus who was in the party]. Tom always graciously let our High School produce our plays in his hall. He never asked for any money but just figured that the business he would get in the barroom was adequate pay.

Louie"Poop-A-Looper" Engelson achieved that nickname since one of his common comments to a fellow youngster was "You're nothin' but a Poop-A-Looper". In his later years most of his day was spent at the Island ferry dock greeting everyone who came off the incoming boats. He wore a nautical type cap with a fouled anchor insignia. Undoubtedly,many newcomers thought he was an official greeter in the employ of the Ferry Line.

Margaret"Chickadee" Weideman was discussed in an earlier story. "Harry Dairy" Hansen also was covered previously.

When Kate and Volney Koyen were living in Jackson Harbor near Nelson's fishing sheds, she would sometimes visit the sheds to get some fish. As she was a large woman, one of the fisherman nicknamed her"Double Daisy". Traditionally, the Island has held Memorial Day services each year, at least ever since WW I. Kate was very instrumental in seeing that these programs were conducted successfully. For a long time a wooden, white gazebo was situated between the original Bethel Church and the "soldier's" monument as we youngsters called it. In good weather the festivities were held here. I have been told that Bo Anderson once composed and presented either a very appropriate song or poem for one Memorial Day.

Philip Carlson, who for years was second-in-command at Plum Island Coast Guard station was fond of saying, "I'm Number one", so soon many were calling him that. Later, during prohibition, he was transferred to the Detroit area. One of the Coast Guard's many tasks was to be alert for "rumrunners" and nab them as they were illegally sneaking loads of booze into this country. While some Coast Guardsmen did not take this part of their duties very seriously, this was not true for Philip. If he was assigned a job he always carried it out to the letter of the law. Thus he was instrumental in the arrests of many boat skippers. Windsor, Ontario was just across the river from Detroit and the bootlegging traffic was heavy. The rumrunners decided to eliminate Philip and thus solve some of their problems. Consequently, one day when he manned the patrol boat and pressed the starter, a bomb planted therein blew up destroying the boat and sending Phil to the hospital for a long time. He emerged with a permanent brace on his leg and a pronounced limp for the rest of his life, but he continued to serve his country until retirement. He and wife, Ella, returned to the Island upon retirement, lived at Lobdell's Point, and he spent many years as a successful sport fisherman in and near Detroit Harbor. In fact, he used to anchor a sort of houseboat in that harbor.

I picked up the terms "Lodgepole" and "Ole" when I first hunted with a group of young men for the Island in western Wyoming. Paul Jorgenson, Walt & Mary's son, was quite tall and slim and this "handle" he had earned before I met him. Rodney Cornell's name of "Ole" is still somewhat of a mystery to me, but I am told that at one time he gave his name as "Ole Oleson". On this same hunting trip I learned that Tom Koyen also went by the name of "Big Wootsie". Of course, we never called Tom's dad by his name Alex, but as "Bowser".

Nels"Saxty-Sax" Sorenson, the local undetaker, always walked in a bent over position. We had heard that people who worked hard "kept their nose close to the grindstone". From looking at "Saxty-Sax" we youngsters were sure that his nose was never far from the grindstone. Carl Christianson,"Ole Hawg's" son, carried the mail to the Island for many years after Pete Andersen. He and wife Hattie,and family lived where John Hanlin now resides. Sister Sylvia often visited their home in the evenings. Carl,a real jokester, would sometimes get the children to go with him as they sneaked over to Nels's house in the dark.

Nels and wife, Maria, spent their evenings seated at the kitchen table with a kerosene lamp for illumination. As she knitted, Nels would read the newspaper. Carl would be equipped with a child's balloon which he would blow up, then place it close to the kitchen window, stretch the balloon neck and let the air slowly escape while making noises like a distressed chicken. Maria, upon hearing this would say, "Nels,I tink someone is stealing the kikens." Whereupon he would respond,"Nah, Maria, dey were only da wind." So Carl would re-inflate the balloon and make the sounds louder which would then make Maria insist that "someone was stealing the kikens". To please her, Nels would light the kerosene lantern to go out and investigate. At this point Carl would tell the children, "We'd better get to heck out of here!"

"Fineshot" Art Wickman lived NE of Rangeline & Detroit Harbor Roads.. The nickname was acquired one night right after he married Blanche, when they were both close to middle-aged. Over the years it had been customary to "shivaree" any newly married couple. Usually this event took place after dark, often after the newlyweds had retired for the night. Friends and neighbors gathered with whatever items could be used to produce a loud racket which did not cease until the couple appeared at the door and invited the revelers into the house for some hospitality. In this case, however, it was not a gathering of friends and neighbors, but a group of "rowdies" who had spent the evening at Nelson' Hall imbibing "Dutch Courage". At someone's suggestion that they conduct a "shivaree" for Art & Blanche, they piled in their cars and made a beeline for that house. When the racket they were making did not bring the couple forth, someone noticed smoke coming from the fireplace chimney so it was decided that a sure way to get the couple out of the house was to "smoke them out". One of the revelers climbed onto the roof and blocked the fireplace flue. In short order the house filled with smoke making the interior quite untenable. However, to the crowd's amazement the couple did not appear at the door. Only Art came forth and lo in his hands was a shotgun fully loaded with fine shot whereupon he began blasting at the Rogues. As "Broken Nose" Hank Peterson from Washington Harbor turned to flee he got a full charge in his backside. One of my relatives, whose name I will not divulge, took off at full speed only to find "Dutz" Cornell going by him like he was standing still. Dr.

Farmer was employed for most of the balance of the night in removing fine shot from "Broken Nose" Hank's and other's posteriors.

In the early days,it was not customary to have nice wedding receptions like those held nowadays at Karly's. The couple usually expected to be "shivareed" and had prepared food and drink in anticipation. Noisemakers often consisted of large kitchen pans, washtubs and the like. By the early thirties our mailcarrier, Ernie Boucsein, had refined upon this. He began placing a tire chain on one rear wheel of his Chevy mail truck and sneaking up to the newlyweds residence accompanied by an appropriate throng, he jacked up the rear wheel, started the engine, placed the truck in high gear, donned leather gloves and ear muffs. He then placed an empty 55 gallon steel barrel firmly against the revolving wheel.The resulting racket could be heard about a mile away.

I think the last "shivaree" of that type was held when my niece, Ann Andersen, married John Schroeder. Ann's young brother, Peter, and I connived to follow in Ernie Boucsein's footsteps.[We were vacationing on the Island at the time.] Peter and I equipped brother Marvin's Dodge sedan with a tire chain and quietly drove the vehicle behind the Bethel Church hall. Right after the wedding ceremony the reception was ready to begin in the hall. The two of us sneaked outside, fired up the Dodge and I laid the empty barrel against the spinning rear wheel. It is possible that the resultant din caused some of the Island ancestors in the nearby cemetery to move about in their final resting places. I still remember the astonished look on Howard Foss's face when he came out the door exclaiming, "What in the Hell is going on!"

An amusing side light I remember being told was that after my cousin married Chris Nelson [where Havegard used to be] a “shivaree” was held and Chris emerged in his night shirt and politely remarked, "Would you folks please go away. Mary and I want a little peace."

"Little Ben" Johnson, son of Tommy and Eva, had many talents. He fished for most of his career, sometimes ran a "still" and did very well playing the harmonica; not a bad poker player either. Probably his nickname came to distinguish him from his relative "Hotel Ben" who operated the Hotel Washington for many years and also sometimes sailed as a cook on Great Lakes ore vessels. Both Bens could really "swing a mean leg" around the dance floor and had a great love for music. Of course, Hotel Ben's son, Johnny, became a professional musician and played for years and years with big name bands. After he retired to the Island I was told that he still received royalty checks for big band recordings made while he was a band member.

"Sterilizer" Elizabeth Peterson was the wife of Chris Peterson, a shoe cobbler, and they lived where Mae Williamson now resides. Elizabeth was a nurse and very particular about cleanliness from which she acquired the nickname.

Steve Gunnlaugsson, The Animal Doctor, was self taught and had an excellent understanding of animal's ailments and how to treat them. As long as I can remember his standard price for either treating a sick animal or butchering was one dollar. Of course, in those days a dollar went a long ways. It was always a day that was looked forward to in great anticipation by me when a cow or pig was to be slaughtered. Ahead of time implements were moved out of the shed and a block and tackle was securely fastened to the overhead rafter for hoisting the carcass so it could be skinned and gutted. After this was accomplished, Steve would use a two handled meat saw to split the carcass right down through the spine. Afterwards the meat was left hanging for at least a day to thoroughly cool. Then the big job of cutting up the meat followed by canning, brining or smoking. Lard was rendered and placed in crocks for use in cooking or baking. Pork "cracklings" were saved to be later added to fried potatoes giving them a delicious flavor. Hog's heads were cooked in the wash boiler, then all the meat was stripped off, ground, seasoned and packed in crocks as "head cheese" which made a very tasty sandwich.

Steve Gunnlaugsson always wanted to hear my latest jokes and would laugh heartily at any Mae West joke. He always dreamed about someday making a trip to Florida for a nice long rest but never made it. He was one of the first members of the Island Lion's Club when it organized in the mid-thirties. Meetings were usually held at James and Martha Sorenson's West Harbor resort where a delicious meal could always be expected. In those days the Lions demanded more participation at meetings by all members. One asignment for the next meeting was to make up a poem about the member sitting to your right. This was to be presented at the next meeting. It so happened that Steve was sitting on brother Marvin's right. Marvin tried desperately to create a suitable poem about Steve. Finally,with my assistance, this was accomplished.

"Pete Duffy" Peterson, Laura Pete's husband, was one of our most successful "moonshiners". An earlier story was devoted to this type of enterprise.

Shortly after the ice had left Detroit Harbor brother Marvin and I would put the boat in the water and tie it either to Ole Christianson's old dock at the foot of Main Road, or at Koken's dock which was in what is now Arni's Bayou. From then on during the spring and summer when we got the rare chances to get away from farm work, we would go fishing.

Old Tom Einarson worked as handyman for the Kokens who owned Koken Barber Chair Company in St. Louis. The family would spend the whole summer at their Island place. During May, Tom would prepare the vegetable garden. About that time of year the snapping turtles would emerge from their winter stay in the Bayou mud and the large females would head for likely spots where warm sun would assure that the eggs they deposited in the ground would hatch. Koken's garden was a favorite place. One day as we were heading for a fishing trip, Tom called us over to the garden to the largest turtle we had ever seen. As she as she slowly journeyed towards her favorite spot we noted that, unlike the smaller mud turtles, she did not slide along on the bottom of her shell. The bottom of her shell cleared the ground by about two inches. While the upper portion of her shell was massive, the undershell, when we turned her over, was so skimpy that it seemed barely adequate for the purposes of decency. The general proportions of a snapping turtle are all wrong. They have none of the symetrical dimensions of mud turtles, nor the pretty shells. They cannot withdraw into their shells when threatened, but are quite adept at stretching their neck out and snapping at whatever is within reach. If you decide to pick up one of these creatures, do not grasp them by the shell as you would a mud turtle, but pick them up by the tail. Thus the head cannot reach far enough to neatly remove one of your fingers or other part of your hand. Also hold it well out from the rest of your body. With its large, wartlike tail, long claws and wickedly hooked beak, it looks like a scaled-down stegosaurus. While a mud turtle which has been turned over on its back is helpless, the snapper with a thrust and twist of its mighty neck uprights itself and is prepared for mayhem. Its very bad temper is evident, for as you approach it opens its mouth and hisses. If you draw closer, it lurches at you with such vehemence that it lifts itself off the ground and its jaws snap savagely at empty air. It is said that an adult can strike with the speed and power of a large rattlesnake. Its pale mouth gapes open like a water moccasin's and its aggressiveness involves an exaggerated and theatrical posturing.

Old Tom held a broomstick in front of this female that weighed at least twenty pounds. It took considerable goading before she seized it, but when she did it was held, crushed and pulped like a piece of chewed sugarcane. At this, Tom remarked, "Those goldam turtles, you could drag them from here to Washington Harbor and they wouldn't let go of that stick".

We noted the shell and skin was a muddy gray and the eye also was of a murky mud color with a black pupil shaped like a star or spoked wheel. A strange, yellowish glint in the eye reminded us of looking down into turbid waters and seeing light from a smoldering fire.

Snappers feed on about anything, dead or alive: fish, flesh or fowl. The fish they catch by luring them into range with their veriform tongues. Interestingly, I have since learned they can be lured into traps baited with bananas. They are death on ducks as they rise from the oozy bottom and grasp the unsuspecting bird's leg, then sink back down where they maul, mutilate and eat the bird right down to the toenails. Unlike other freshwater turtles, they never emerge to bask on rocks or logs. In late spring they emerge, often with a clump of wet mud still on their backs, to find sandy soil in which to lay their eggs, close to the boggy, miry waters they inhabit. However, they may cross large areas of suitable terrain before finally deciding on a spot to dig. We observed her thrusting her anterior into the sandy soil as first one hind leg and then the other scooped out the ground to form a hole in which to deposit her eggs. Once she began this operation she seemed completely oblivious to our presence. This was a wonderous thing of nature we had the privilege to observe.

Early Island Fire Fighting (This was prepared by me and presented at an Archives program in 1994.)

In early days, before green lawns became popular and garden hoses came into use, small fire fighting in the home was often done with a drinking dipper and water bucket. Outside fires were attacked either with a wet sack to beat the flames out, or a garden sprinkling can. Later garden hoses and nozzles came into play.

About the very early 1930s the Washington Island Mutual Fire Insurance Company purchased 2 1/2 gallon soda and acid extinguishers. The large part of the brass container had a mixture of water and baking soda in it, while the smaller, lightly stoppered, glass bottle contained sulfuric acid. The extinguisher could be safely stored and carried in an upright position, but when inverted the acid freely flowed out and mixed with the soda water creating a pressure of about 125 pounds per square inch. This forced the wet solution out through the short hose and nozzle to have the stream played, hopefully, on the base of the incipient fire. Later the Island Insurance Company bought foam extinguishers of the 2 1/2 gallon size which were designed to extinguish not only Class A fires, but also Class B fires in burning petroleum products, oils and greases. The trade name of these was "Phomene". The inner cylinder contained an aluminum sulphate solution, while the outer shell held bicarbonate of soda solution to which was added a foam stabilizing agent. When inverted, as in the case of the soda-acid extinguisher, the two solutions mixed creating a pressure to force the developing foam out through the nozzle. A 2 1/2 gallon unit would produce about 18 gallons of foam which was lighter than water and very cohesive. It floated across the burning liquid, ultimately covering the entire surface and snuffing out the fire by denying it the oxygen required to sustain combustion. The foam bubbles were in essence carbon dioxide bubbles that had been given stability through the foam stabilizing agent.

These extinguishers were placed in the homes of Island residents who carried insurance with the local company. When the fire alarm was sounded, responding persons were expected to bring their extinguisher to the fire scene. Upon receipt of the word that a fire existed and the location, the Washington Island Telephone Switchboard Operator would begin by transmitting the fire signal over the nearest trunk lines to the fire first. Later this same message would be repeated to those living further away from the fire scene. Upon hearing ten short rings or more on the old crank telephones, residents would simply pick up the receiver to learn from the operator where the fire was located. Then there was a mad scramble in private autos to the scene, taking your extinguisher with you, which by then proved to be a rather futile exercise.

I recall when Shellswick's Hotel burned in February 1932 on a below-zero day. On receipt of the alarm Marvin and I manned our Model A Tudor Ford with him driving and me securely holding the extinguisher between my knees in the front seat. As there was less snow and it was shorter and easier to drive across Detroit Harbor, we avoided using the road and were one of the first to arrive at the scene. A small opening in the chimney masonry in the attic had allowed the flames from a chimney fire to ignite the nearby wood. George Haas, Pilot Island Lighthouse Keeper, arrived just before us and reported that if he had with him a pitcher of water, he could have put out the incipient fire, but by the time we got to the attic area it had spread to where our feeble efforts were in vain. The resultant fire reduced this structure to ashes and rubble.

Aurora Shellswick had beautiful house plants in the hotel. Annie Einarson, who was operating the Idabo Inn which later became Holiday Inn, offered to accept the house plants to keep them from freezing. However, she superstitiously believed that to bring an oleander plant into a house foreboded bad luck so she refused to accept this plant. Consequently the beautiful, huge plant froze.

Jake and Lars Bilton had a two story home similar to the present one at Flath's Resort, which was originally their property. Several Island homes had built-in Coleman gasoline lighting systems. A central, pressurized tank contained white gasoline with an air bank above it. Small piping led from there to individual lighting fixtures usually fastened to the ceilings in the centers of the rooms. To ignite these mantel-equipped lights it was only necessary to place a strike-anywhere match next to the generator and turn the valve on. While these were much more convenient than the portable Coleman lights and lanterns, sometimes a hidden hazard developed. Such was the case at Biltons when a leak in the piping developed between the first floor ceiling and the second floor. Unknown to them, they proceeded to light a ceiling fixture which immediately ignited the pent-up gasoline fumes in the hidden ceiling space. Another pile of ashes and rubble resulted. One of the few homes with a serious fire, that was saved, was Fred (Mads) Hansen's where Bob Young now lives. This fire, which occurred later, was extinguished and the house was repaired.

In 1931, or early 1932, as a freshman in High School, I found our studies excitedly interrupted when brother Marvin opened the door and yelled, "Mann's Store is on fire." Emory Hansen, who was seated the farthest from the door was nearly out of the room before our old teacher, Mr. Hill, could place his hands on Emory's chest and say, "Be Careful!" With that we were out the door, piled into cars and sped to the scene. The fire, which developed in the north section where the lumber was stored and where the light plant was situated, was already traveling rapidly in the attic space above the ornamental metal ceiling. However, it gave us time to carry a lot of the merchandise out and into Harry Hansen's hall across the road. Until the new store was built, Harry allowed George Mann to conduct his store at that dance hall.

The building, which was originally the parsonage for the Baptist Church, was where George's son, Fred, and wife, Lettie, were living. It was a very threatened fire exposure. For fear that it too would be destroyed, all furnishings were removed to a place of safekeeping. Interestedly, I observed one Island man carefully carry a mattress from this home and gently place it on the grass. Whereupon he returned to the upstairs and pitched a mirror out the window.

With practically every household using wood for cooking and heating the home, it was quite common for chimney fires to occur, especially if people burned wood that had not been cut at least two years before and properly handled. Even though we burned only well-seasoned hardwood, usually once or twice a winter a fire would occur in the south chimney of our farm house. Several times I saw flames standing about four feet out of the crest of the chimney. This was a very frightening thing, especially for a small boy to observe. Neither chimney in our farm home had tiled liners, thus it was much easier for creosote to pocket on the rough interior as the flue gases cooled while traveling the height of the chimney. To compound the problem, the south chimney was severly corbeled over to the east so that it emerged through the roof right at the peak. This left many horizontal brick ledges where a greater amount of creosote could gather.

Of course, as soon as a chimney fire was discovered, the first thing to do was to close all dampers at the stove to deny the fire as much oxygen as possible. An "old-wives" treatment was to throw handfuls of salt onto the stove fire. Later, Lorraine Andersen's grandfather, Pete Christianson, sold a black block of material called "Imp" which was supposed to subdue chimney fires if thrown into the stove. I don't recall any of our fires that it successfully put out.

On vessels the Coast Guard required a certain number of Pyrene extinguishers. These one quart, hand-pumped units contained a solution which had at least 25% carbon tetrachloride. It was intended to extinguish fires in petroleum products, electrical fires and small Class A fires. However, carbon tetrachloride emits a very toxic fume which results in great damage to one's kidneys and liver. Fortunately, over the years other better and safer agents developed and smarter people not only eliminated the Pyrene type extinguisher, but also outlawed their use. Salesmen used to sell glass "fire bombs" containing about a pint of carbon tetrachloride and the user was instructed to fling them with force at the base of the fire. One glib salesman convinced a large grain elevator owner that all he needed for absolute fire safety were these magical "fire bombs". The owner could never be convinced that a smart move would be to sprinkler his elevator. The salesman swore that if a fire occurred and reached a "fire bomb" the thin glass would break and the carbon tetrachloride would extinguish the fire. In the 1950s I was back on the Island on vacation while serving as a Lieutenant in the Oakland, CA Fire Department. While at Sis and Spen's the party fire alarm sounded with a report of "fire at Harbor Grocery." I took off in Sis's car and on arrival found considerable smoke erupting from the storage shed just east of the store. After seeing there was no attempt to hit the fire at its seat, I asked Gordy Jepson, Fire Chief, if I could borrow one of the 1 1/2 inch lines from the front of the tanker and one of his men.He agreed,so I grabbed Irvin Smith and told him to adjust the nozzle to about a 30 degree spray. When I said we're going inside and knock the fire out", Irvin responded, "You've got to be kidding!" However, after assuring him that I would be right in back of him he got as far as the door and opened the nozzle. I directed him to whip the stream around like he was "beating snakes". Which he did, but it was clear he had no intention of preceding any further into the building. At this point, with his heels solidly skidding in the dirt I pushed him and accompanied him into the burning structure where we quickly completely extinguished the fire. After reaching clear air outside and spitting out smoke he turned to me and remarked, "Boy! Did I learn something. I didn't know you could do that." I assured him that was the normal way we attacked fire in Oakland.

How many Islanders know that school children helped to choose "The Star Spangled Banner" as the National Anthem? Surely many of the "old-timers" who were in grade school at the time will recall this.

"Current Events", a very popular weekly magazine printed on newspaper, was circulated to schools with an accompanying guide for the teacher.This factual publication accurately chronicled what was happening around the World. It was an excellent teaching tool, recommended by the State Superintendent, and widely used. In 1931 an organization proposed having The Star Spangled Banner as the national anthem conducted a student poll across the country. There was opposition to the songs "militant" words and a feeling that the high notes were very difficult to sing. "Current Events" was used to reach the students and the choices were"The Star Spangled Banner", "America" and "America The Beautiful". As an eighth grader in Conrad Andersen's class in the Detroit Harbor School, I recall heated discussions before a secret vote was taken. Unfortunately I do not recall the outcome at our school, but when the results were in, students across the nation had voted 2-to-1 for our present national anthem.They felt it was most representative of American patriotism.

When Congress learned of the results of the student poll, they passed a 15-year.old bill favoring "The Star Spangled Banner." With President Hoover's signature it became the national anthem on March 3,1931.

Often at the beginning of the school day we would stand and recite the Pledge of Allegiance. Then the students would sing patriotic or other songs from "The Golden Book." Usually one of the girls, who.was taking lessons from Gladys Chistianson, would play the piano. As I couldn't carry a note, I merely mouthed the words.

Most students had learned that Francis Scott Key had penned the words to the anthem on the back of an old letter during the War of 1812. He had boarded the British ship "Minden" under a flag of truce to arrange the release of a friend who was held prisoner. The ship was docked outside Fort McHenry in Chesapeake Bay and the British commander agreed to free Key and his friend only after British troops attacked the fort. On the deck of the Minden, Key kept a hopeful eye on the American flag, for as long as it waved he knew the Americans had not surrendered. With the flag still there he knew his comrades had survived the "bombs bursting in air". Soon the British retreated and the war ended a few months later. Shortly thereafter Key took his poem to a musician friend, who felt the words fit well with a popular drinking tune of the day, "To Anacreon in Heaven".

First called "The Defense of Fort McHenry", it became popular with regiments in Baltimore and Washington as well as people throughout the country. During the Mexican-American and Civil Wars, it touched a patriotic nerve and was played during drills. It was finally recognized ae the national anthem by President Woodrow Wilson in 1916.

However,Wilson's proclamation in 1916 wasn't made law until 15 years later when school children assured Congress that the militaristic words weren't offensive to their young ears. A California reader said,"I think voting for the national anthem remains so memorable because it was the patriotic thing to do. I'm glad I lived in an innocent time when schoolchildren were asked their opinion and their votes really counted!"

The 1920s saw people starting to use electricity in the homes and other places. This installing of independent lighting systems grew until about 1945 when Island Electric Co-op began functioning.

Many of the early plants were 32 volt direct current. To provide the electricity 16 two-volt large glass battery cells were placed either in the basement or in a nearby shed. A single-cylinder gasoline powered generator was placed next to these cells. The building was wired and lights and outlets were installed. When the batteries needed charging, the generator was hand started and run till the cells were fully charged. Of course all light bulbs and appliances had to be for 32 volt DC. These plants were also installed on such Island vessels as the "Diana" and "Wisconsin". Tom Goodman, who lived next to the airport, later erected a 32 volt windcharger. I am told that when his son, Paul, returned from serving in WWII he proudly brought his mother a 32 volt clothes iron only to find that the REA was now operating.

Kohler 110 volt electric plants were also quite popular. I recall when one was installed in the Detroit Harbor School. Ray Krause, Washington Harbor School teacher, sold the plant and did the installation and wiring. While this was being done I was over there whenever I was free and often helped Ray pull wires through the walls. He used BX cable throughout.

Several 6 volt auto batteries were connected to the generator for starting the four-cylinder gasoline engine. Whenever a switch was turned on or an appliance plugged in, a solenoid would close and provide electricity from the batteries to energize the starter winding in the generator. This would then crank the engine to get it started. The choke and accelerator were automatically operated. When the engine reached running speed another solenoid closed and electrical current began flowing throughout the wiring system. A gasoline storage tank was buried outside with a supply pipe running to the engine.

Ray Krause sold many electric plants and did nearly all of the original wiring of homes and other buildings. He was very instrumental in getting the federal REA loan so that the first generating plant and electric power lines could become a reality here. As the need for more generating power on the Island came to pass, he oversaw the purchase and installation of large Diesel generators. In the early '70s it was decided to buy a new Enterprise Diesel generator.These were manufactured in Oakland, Ca. where I was then a Battalion Fire Chief. I had the privilege of taking Ray Krause to the large plant and accompanying him throughout the plant tour.

After I retired here and became active in the Rescue Squad I transported Ray in the Island ambulance “across the Door” on his final trip to the hospital. The Door County Ambulance met us at Gills Rock and we prepared to make the transfer to their unit. A small female County EMT was getting ready to place his gurney in the ambulance. Ray looked at this small woman and said, "Do you think you can lift me?" She responded, "If I couldn't lift you

I would not be wearing this uniform". Ray was a very outstanding citizen of the Island.

Sister Sylvia and I developed an early love of poetry. To brighten your feelings in the dead of winter I thought you would enjoy *The Old Backhouse* by James Whitcomb Riley:

"When memory keeps me company and moves to smiles or
tears,
A weather-beaten object looms through the mist of years.
Behind the house and barn it stood, a hundred yards or more,
And hurrying feet a path had made, straight to its swinging
door.

Its architecture was a form of simple classic art,
But in the tragedy of life it played a leading part.
And oft the passing traveler drove slow, and heaved a sigh,
To see the modest hired girl slip out with glances shy.

We had our posey garden that women loved so well,
I loved it too, but better still I loved the stronger smell,
That filled the evening breezes so full of homely cheer,
And told the night-o'ertaken tramp that human life was near.

On lazy August afternoons, it made a little bower,
Delightful where my grandsire sat and whiled away an hour.
For there the morning-glory its very eaves entwined,
And berry bushes reddened in the steaming soil behind.

All day fat spiders spun their webs to catch the buzzing flies,
That flitted to and from the house where Ma was baking pies.
And once a swarm of hornets bold, had built a palace there,
And stung my unsuspecting aunt -- I must not tell you where.

Then Father took a flaming pole -- that was a happy day --
He nearly burned the building up, but the hornets left to stay.
When summer blooms began to fade and winter to carouse,
We banked the little building with a heap of hemlock boughs.

But when the crust was on the snow and the sullen skies were
gray,
In sooth the building was no place where one would wish to

stay.
We did our duties promptly, there one purpose swayed the mind;
We tarried not, nor lingered long on what we left behind.

The torture of that icy seat would make a Spartan sob,
For needs must scrape the goose flesh with a lacerating cob,
That from a frost-encrusted nail was suspended by a string --
My father was a frugal man and wasted not a thing.

When Grandpa had to "go out back" and make his morning call,
We'd bundle up the dear old man with a muffler and a shawl.
I knew the hole on which he sat twas padded all around,
And once I dared to sit there - twas all too wide, I found.

My loins were all too little and I jack-knifed there to stay.
They had to come and cut me out or I'd have passed away.
Then Father said ambition was a thing that boys should shun,
And I must use the children's hole'till childhood days were done.

And still I marvel at the craft that cut those holes so true,
The baby hole, and slender hole that fitted sister Sue.
That dear old country landmark; I've tramped around a bit,
And in the lap of luxury my lot has been to sit.

But ere I die I'll eat the fruit of trees I've robbed of yore,
Then seek the shanty where my name is carved upon the door.
I ween the old familiar smell will sooth my jaded soul,
I'm now a man but none the less, I'll try the children's hole."

* * *

During my Island childhood, all farms and nearly all other residences had "Chick Sales." In a future issue I will tell you what misfortunes befell them and Halloween pranksters who made them their targets.

A number of people have asked me to have my stories published in book form. I have felt that when I neared the 100 article mark it might be time to consider doing that. So far my writings have been largely confined to farming, characters and nicknames. When I grew up on the Island the two main ways of existing were either farming or commercial fishing. At one time there were over forty independent fishing rigs operating here during the summer.

Last year I obtained a large collection of USCG Captain Gene Gislason's papers from his widow, Elayne. These will become part of the Archives records. One of his binders contains official documented statistics on vessels associated with the Island. A number of them were built here either in Detroit, Washington or Jackson Harbor. I hope to add this information to my book when published. Hopefully, I will be able to get pictures of these vessels to display along with the information from Gene's records.

Vessel	Owner
+Agnes H.	John (Jack) Andersen
American Girl	" "
Arbutus	Charles McDonald
As You Like It	Chester Pederson
Bessie Louise	Niels Jepson
Big Peder	Thomas Goodman
Bub	John Cornell
Cecelia M.	Carl Jorgenson
Charlotte C.	Carl Christianson
+ Clara C.	John Cornell
Darline	Arthur Hanson
Dawn	Leslie Cornell
+Diana	John Andersen
Dora	Engelsons
Dorothy R.	Lars Bilton
Eddie	J.S. Smith, Sawyer
Edna	Verner Greenfeldt
Elizabeth Wilhelm	Walter Wilhelm, Oconto**
F. Hunter	Matt Foss**
Fred	Fred Richter
Gertrude	Niels Jepson, builder
Gladys	Berend Anderson
Gloria	Arthur Hanson
H.W. Davis	Jacob Weber, Sturgeon Bay
Hazel Jeanette	Hannes Johnson & Sons
Helen C.	Elsworth Cornell

Iona Estelle	Frank Richter
Irma Janette	Matt Foss
+ J.W. Cornell	John Cornell
Jane	George Nelson (later Randy Sorenson, then Jeff McDonald)
Jane Elizabeth	Anker Greenfeldt
Joffre	John Paulson
Johanna W.	Frank Cabot, Sturgeon Bay
Jeannie W.	Charles Jensen
Josephine A.	Ernest Ellefson
K.E.M. Jacob	Jacob Ellefson
Lakme	Wilson Trueblood
Laura	Matt Foss (lst gasoline boat)
Leona	Niels Jepson -builder
Lettie May	Lars & Jake Bilton*
Liberty	Berend Anderson
Lillian	Alfred & Newell Cornell*
Little Georgia	Andrew Irr*
Lucille	Wm. Jepson & Carl Christianson
Majestic	Harry Hagen
Marion	Carl Hansen
Maritana	Charles McDonald
Marold II	Anthony Wons (Hill Family)
Martha E.	----------
Mascot	Swara Hagen
Minnie S.	Wm. Jepson, then Lars Bilton
Mishap	Niels Jepson-builder
Myrtle	Carly & Wally Jorgenson
Navarre	Pete Anderson
Nor	Fred M. Young
North Shore	W.I. Ferry Line
Pathfinder	Minor Dagneau,Sturgeon Bay
Pearl	Fred and Ida Richter- Niels Jepson-Builder
Pirate	JohnChristianson- Rasmus Hansen-Builder
R.E. Helen	Albert Goodmander & Haldon Johnson
Ragna	John Ellefson *
Rainbow	John B. Young-

	Niels Jepson built.
Ramona	Maurice Martin
Razor Back	Pete Andersen-Niels Jepson built.
Regina	S.M. Klary,Marinette
Rosie L.	Wm. Jess-Amundsen built.
Rosemary	Fred M. Hanson
Sea Bird	Hannes Johnson-Amundsen built.
Sea Queen	Pete Christianson-Amundsen built.
Service	Hannes Johnson,Sr.
Shine On	Carl G. Richter- reported built on Plum Island
Sofie Fournica	Robert Knudsen (later "Oil Queen")
Sunrise	John Cornell
Try	John Cornell-Amundsen built.
Two Brothers	Fred S. Richter
Una	Ben Johnson,Jr.
Velox	Leon Cornell
Volunteer	Pete Andersen
Water Lily	James Johnson
Welcome	Art Hanson- Rasmus Hanson built.
Welcome(ferry)	Wm. Jepson
White Swan	Oriental Mills Transit, Manitowoc
Wisconsin	Wm. Jepson (His first regular ferry)
4590	Armour and Dave Kincaide(later Pete Andersen's in mail service.)

* Vessels built by Alfred Cornell in Washington Harbor.
** Some vessels built by John Amundsen in Jackson Harbor. According to Ray McDonald, his nickname was "Paint & Putty".

In the 1800s sailing vessels transported iron ore from Escanaba and other Lake ports to steel mills. Island men served on some of these. As a small boy, I remember Uncle Anton

Jessen singing about "The Red Iron Ore". The vessels needed steam tugs to pull them in and out of harbor, but once they were clear they used sails and spread lots of canvas to the wind.

THE RED IRON ORE

Come all you bold sailors that follow the lakes
On an iron-ore vessel your living to make.
I shipped in Chicago,bid adieu to the shore,
Bound away to Escanaba for the red iron ore.

In the month of September, the seventeenth day,
Two dollars and a quarter was all they would pay,
And on Monday morning the BRIDGEPORT did take
The E.C. ROBERTS out into the lake.

The wind from the south'ard sprang up a fresh breeze
And soon we encountered some fast rising seas,
And away through Lake Michigan the ROBERTS did roar,
And on Friday morning we passed through Death's Door.

This packet she howled cross the mouth of Green Bay.
And before her cut waters she dashed the white spray.
We rounded the Sand Point, our anchor let go,
We furled in our canvas and the watch went below.

Next morning we hove alongside the exile,
And soon was made fast to an iron ore pile.
They lowered the chutes and like thunder did roar,
They spouted into us the red iron-ore.

Some sailors took shovels.while others got spades,
And some took wheelbarrows--each man to his trade.
We looked like red devils,our fingers got sore,
We cursed Escanaba and the damned iron-ore.

The tug ESCANABA had towed out the MINCH.
The ROBERTS she thought she had left in a pinch,
And as she passed by us she bid us good-by,
Saying "We'll meet you in Cleveland next Fourth of July".

Through Louse Island it blew a fresh breeze;
We made past the Foxes, the Beavers, Skillagees.
We flew by the MINCH for to show her the way,

And she ne'er hove in sight till we're off Thunder Bay.

Across Saginaw Bay the ROBERTS did ride
With dark and deep water rolling over her side,
And now for Port Huron the ROBERTS must go
Where the good tug KATE WILLIAMS took us in tow.

We went through North Passage--O Lord, how it blew!
And all round the Dummy a large fleet there came to.
The night was so dark that Old Nick it would scare.
We hove up next morning and for Cleveland did steer.

Now the ROBERTS in Cleveland made fast stem and stern,
And over the bottle we'll spin quite a yarn.
But Captain Harvey Shannon had ought to stand treat,
For getting to Cleveland ahead of the fleet.

Now my song is ended and I hope you won't laugh.
Our dunnage is packed and all hands are paid off.
Here's health to the ROBERTS, she's staunch, strong and true;
Not forgotten the bold boys who comprised her crew.

ROCK ISLAND

This series of articles about Rock Island contains information gleaned from the Washington Island Archives files. Many thanks to Barbara Ellefson, Archivist and Goodwin Berquist for their assistance.

Rock Island has been known as Menominee, Pottawatomi and Louse Island. While I have no knowledge of how it came to be Rock Island, the moniker "Louse Island" apparently stemmed from the fact that when viewed from well out in Lake Michigan its profile resembled that of a louse.

Professor Ronald Mason, his wife and about ten Lawrence University students in the summers of 1969 and 1971 unearthed a treasure of Indian, French traders' and early white settlers' relics. Mason put together an archeological record of Rock Island dating back to the Second Century, A.D., when occupied by aboriginals in the Middle Woodland period. Mason found materials proving innabitation here at least 3000 years ago. Later Pottawatomi, Ottawa, Chippewa, Huron, Iroquois and Menominee Indians left debris. However, there were many periods when no one lived on Rock Island. For well over 1000 years Indians went to live on Rock during the spring, summer and fall, but vacated in the winter. Pottery and stone tools from the Huron-Peton tribe was unearthed. It appeared that the Hurons arrived about 1650. Not too much later, Iroquois from New York, whose beavers had been depleted, moved to Rock Island for beaver trade. As they "muscled in" the Hurons:moved down the Mississippi Valley to avoid attacks. Pottawatomis and Fox Indians came several years later..

Tons of relics were found in the archeological digging site inland from the southeast sand shore. Rocks and boulders believed to have been used as a foundation for a palisade were found. It appeared that one palisade enclosed about 45,000 square feet of land. There was evidence also of smaller forts. Mason said there was enough relics here to "keep 50 students busy for 10 years." Fox and Pottawatomi did a lot of trading with the French who in 1678 wanted beaver pelts. 300 year old Jesuit rings and many trinkets were dug up. Indians who were converted to Christianity were presented with jewelry bearing a cross.

Buttons from French officer's coats were found that dated back to the French and Indian War period - 1750 to 1760 era. Also there were clay pipes marked "Robert Tippett III" which had been used in trading with the Indians. As the Indians found that British goods were of higher quality, they switched their alliances from French to British.

About 1634 Jean Nicolet traveled through these waters and probably stopped at Rock Island. Not until 1658-59 did fighting among rival Indian nations calm enough for more foreign exploration and the ultimate onslaught of white traders, soldiers and missionaries. The next 175 years saw continuous exploration and invasion of these lands by French, British and Americans, along with various greedily made alliances, clearing the trail for the burgeoning fur trade. Well known figures such as Joliet, Father Marquette, LaSalle, Friar Hennepin, Charlevoix, Pontiac and Jonathan Carver all looked or wandered on this rocky outpost.

LaSalle and his men dug deep V or U-shaped trenches in which to stand the tall timbers for building or palisade walls. Building floors were dirt and the log walls were pegged or chinked with mud. Very few nails were used. Roofs were made of saplings covered with bark or skin. A scattering of gifts shows that perhaps a fight took place. When given brass sewing thimbles, the Indians bored small holes so they could hang these as ornaments from their buckskin clothing.

LaSalle's first store on Rock Island was in the palisaded Pottawatomi village. He needed a sailing vessel to successfully conduct his fur trade with the Indians so he had the "Griffon" built on the shore of Lake Erie. This galleon was about 70 feet long with three masts. It was the first Lake ship to deal with the Indians. She was nearly wrecked on Long Point, Lake Erie, then almost foundered in a storm on Lake Huron. Her tired, 30 man crew rested at Mackinac Village before entering Lake Michigan and reaching Rock Island. She probably carried jewelry, brightly colored glass beads, brass kettles, iron knives and other European goods to trade for furs. (Materials and shipbuilders from Europe had been imported to build the Griffon. Some moneys at 40% interest were borrowed.)

The Griffon left Rock Island with a load of furs on September 18, 1679 with a skeleton crew and vanished, never to be heard from again, thus she gained the distinction of being the first to sail the lakes and the first to succumb. Conflicting stories say she sailed from Detroit Harbor, not Rock Island. Some believe the ship sank in a storm, while others think the skeleton crew stole the fur cargo and scuttled the vessel as they were secretly in the pay of LaSalle's enemies.

LaSalle and the rest of his party journeyed south on Lake Michigan by canoe the day after the Griffon departed. That evening a storm forced them to camp on the Door County shore for four days before they could continue. LaSalle's plan to colonize all along the Mississippi River depended largely on having the Griffon as his supply barque. He had come to Canada in 1666, age twenty-two and was murdered by his own men in 1687 near the Trinity River in what is now Texas. MacLean in his book *The Fate of the Griffon*, said that LaSalle ordered his pilot, a 7 foot Dane, to take the Griffon back to Niagara Falls with a crew of only five men. Even though the pilot protested this was too small a crew he was told, "You will do as I command." MacLean said the vessel sailed from Detroit Harbor.

In 1955 MacLean and a lifetime commercial fisherman in Georgian Bay are certain that they recovered remains of the Griffon in an inner cove of Russell Island. The entire keel, bow, stern 13 ribs and quite a bit of the port planking are still there. The fisherman said that his family had known about the wreck for more than 120 years.

In all probability, Rock Island was the first place to be visited by white men. By 1816 Fort Howard (Green Bay) had been established as a fur trading post. By 1819 there were steam powered vessels on Lake Michigan. By 1824 schooners delivered mail. In 1832 commercial fishing was important on Rock Island. Fish were cleaned, salted and packed in barrels to be shipped to Chicago or Buffalo where they were sold for $6.50 per barrel. Cordwood was cut and shipped. T.T. Miner had a thriving grocery and dry goods business. He received such supplies from Chicago as flour, salt, soda, calico, fowling pieces (guns) and bits of brocade.

A traveling preacher was to marry two Norwegian couples in double rites. Being unfamiliar with the Norse language he mistakenly married the two grooms to each other. When he started to join the brides, the interpreter stepped in and got the whole thing corrected.

By 1855 the Town of Washington composed of Washington, Rock, Detroit and Plum Islands, was the most populous in Door County with 318 souls living there.

April 20, 1836, Wisconsin's territorial government was established and the lighthouse site on the northwest tip of Rock Island was cleared for the construction of the first lighthouse on Lake Michigan. At first the lightkeeper was the only white settler between Mackinaw and Green Bay.

In 1837, the first structures were one for the light and a small keeper's residence. Dave Corbin served there for 16 years and is buried there. Fortunately the Archives has a copy of the blueprints made by the Corps of Engineers for the old, masonry lighthouse that still stands there. It is the oldest remaining building in Door County and was built in 1858. The prints show: Kind of Light--Coast Order of Light--4th Characteristic of Light--Fixed White. Site reserved by President of U.S. on June 8, 1840. Area of Reservation to Mid High Water Line--153,7 acres. Base of Tower above water level--121 feet.

The building had a basement-cellar. On the first floor (Keeper's Quarters) there was a kitchen with a gas refrigerator, pantry, living room, bedroom, entrance and hallway with stairs to the second floor. On the second floor (Asst. Keeper's Quarters) was a kitchen with gas refrigerator, pantry, living room, two bedrooms, hallway and office.

Some of the lightkeepers who served there included William Betts, Jesse Miner, Charles Boshka, John Fitzgerald, Earl Malloch, Sr. and Ernest Lockhart.

As a very young farm boy I remember William Betts coming to our farm for dairy products. The family lived just east of the condominiums near Holiday Inn. He was tall, stood very erect, had a well-trimmed white beard, wore a black, broad-rimmed hat and chewed tobacco. In fact he cured people's warts by spitting tobacco juice on them. I held him in awe for, my gosh, this man had been a soldier in the Civil War.

The Archives has excerpts from William Betts' Lighthouse Log, Pottawatomi Light, Rock Island. I found them to be interesting so am chronicling them here:

June 26,1873 Since the twenty-first of this month there has been the worst weather that I can remember seeing. Not much wind but fog and rain. A steamer on her way to Green Bay lay for 30 hours without hearing of this light house and could not get through. She got through the door(sic). A brig got on the reef off St. Martins but got off without damage. The Bark Vanderbelt touched the NE point of Washington Island there was so little wind and they hove her off without trouble or damage.

July 2,1874 Last night at ten o'clock I noticed a comet north and a little west about fifteen degrees above the horizon tail pointing SE apparently.

December 9,1876 Last night Dec 8th at 5 o'clock a gale commenced here that will be remembered a long time.It was a hurrycane(sic). It last till after midnight when it began to die away,the weather was very cold about zero I would think. All over this island trees are torn out by their roots.In one place today I saw where a tree top had been broken off and carried six rods (nearly 100 ft.) before it came to the ground.It would weight(sic) I judge about half a ton. About one mile from the lighthouse on the west side of the island there were two fish sheds one of them had stood there ten years. They were thought to be far enough from the water to be perfectly safe, but last night they were both crushed almost in an instant. I was afraid for some of the time that the tower would be carried off from the light house. There is no light to be seen tonight at Poverty Island or Point Peninsula. The direction of the wind was NW to N.W. by N.

December 14, 1876 No light at Point Peninsula to night it is something like election returns. One day we hear that old Reb Tilden is elected and the next we are positively assured that Gov. Hayes is the happy man, now we do not know who will be our next President or what is the trouble with the Light Houses at Point Peninsula and Poverty Island.

July 10,1877 The captain of a small trading schooner informed me today that he fell in with a water spout two days ago in the bay south of here. He said the spout came directly towards his vessel and he thought it would crush him but it changed its course and passed to one side making a loud moaning noise.

July 3, 1878 Dry not much wind from any quarter warm and pleasant.

July 4,1878 The glorious fourth has passed again. We stayed at home quietly did not even hear a cannon.

June 19,1879 The supply steamer Dahlia made her annual visit at four o clock P.M. Inspector Miller is not well pleased in regard to the way the Engineer treats the repair reports from this station. The stairs up the bluff are in very dangerous condition and have been for some years. The Engineer treats my reports with dignified but silent contempt.

June 27,1880 A shocking occurence took place at Port du Mort Light Station (Pilot Island) on Sunday the 20th of this month. The second assistant John Boyce cut his throat with a razor and was found dead in half an hour from the time he was last seen alive. No cause for the deed is known and unless he was pretty deranged there was no apparent cause. He was a noble hearted man, kind to all and had many friends in this vacinity (sic). May God for give him. Grace to his ashes.

July 3,1882 The U.S. Supply Steamer Dahlia made her annual visit today and delivered supplies. House and grounds inspected by Commander Watson and all things found satisfactory.

July 3,1883 The most thunder and lightning that I remember and a good deal of rain not much wind, fog at night.

July 4,1883 The glorious fourth has passed quietly here day dry and warm. We could hear cannons at Escanaba.

June 6, 1884 Owing to defect in the cistern and no rain there is no water here now.

June 30, 1884 Our cistern is still dry and water has to be carried up one hundred and fifty-four steps.

July 3, 1884 Wind northeast fresh in the afternoon. It rained but did not rain as much as I wish it had.

July 31, 1884 If the men who pretend to keep up repairs at the light stations do not provide for a water supply here before long, I shall quit this business. They make wells at other stations where water is handy without wells but neglect this place almost entirely.

July 3, 1885 Dry and hot not much wind some smoke at night but fine weather.

May 11, 1886 The Dahlia passed this A.M. and I received a letter from Jesse Miner that he has been tranferred from Port du Mort (Pilot Island) to this light. I am glad to be away from here for I am as tired of this business as I can be.

May 14, 1886 New keeper moved in. Moderately west wind in the morning south in the evening.

In 1835 fifty fishermen brought their families to Rock Island and built a village. With them was Dave Kennison who was born in 1736. He had been a member of the Boston Tea Party, fought in the Revolutionary War and War of 1812. After moving to the Chicago area he had survived the Fort Dearborn massacre and retired at age 80. During his lifetime a falling tree had fractured his skull, a cannon discharge at a military review had broken both legs, a frisky horse had kicked him in the forehead and all but one of his 22 children (by four wives) had deserted him. At 100 years of age he moved to Rock Island to repair nets and clean fish. The son, who had come with him, deserted him and he was forced to move back to Chicago to collect his government pension. He died there in 1852 at 116 years of age and was destined to be buried in a potter's field. However, a patriotic society intervened and had him interred in Lincoln Park where a huge, bronze tablet commemorates a doughty old warrior whose death saved the government Eight dollars monthly pension payments.

Excellent fishing in the nearby waters lured more whites to settle on Rock Island. It is not known what the maximum white population was, but Archives records show at one time there were 160 residents. In 1863 the first public scnool opened with Miss Rosalia Rice as teacher. Boons, Miners, Wrights, Curtises, Grahams, McMillens, Amos Lovejoy, Andrew Oliver, Dave Corben and others lived and died here,or eventually left. One report says that in the late 1860s Indians and whites abandoned Rock Island.

Former Sergeant Amos Lovejoy fished with Chief Silver Band and other Indians. Lovejoy was a ventriloquist and when a large trout was caught he would make it sound like the fish was talking to the Indians in perfect (not too flattering) Ojibwa dialect. As a result the Indians named him "Demon Man". Many people today think that Indian languages were very similar, but it was noted that Menominee and Winnebago tongues were as different as English is from Chinese.

While Lovejoy got along well with the Indians, it took John Boon's diplomacy to avoid a major massacre of whites. Widow Oliver had set her son to peeling potatoes while she attended a sick neighbor. Indian boys passing by began calling Andrew "Squawman". He threw a potato which shattered a window pane and the glass blinded one of Silver Band's son's eyes. An Indian War Council was called and they planned to get Indian reinforcements from Pottawatomi (Washington) Island to annihilate the white "Illinois Colony". When Lovejoy's efforts for peace failed, Boon's diplomacy and Widow Oliver's abject apology saved the day.

Records show there are three white cemeteries on Rock Island. The one a few hundred yards southeast of the lighthouse has twelve graves in regular rows each marked by a piece of field stone. Dave Corbin and friend, Jack Arnold, both 1812 veterans tended the light. Corbin died in 1852, and is buried here.

Seven graves hold the remains of shipwrecked strangers whose bodies washed ashore. Newman Curtis and family rest in four graves. Newman came in the late 1840s and a son died of scarlet fever in the spring of 1853.In a few months, Newman, wife and daughter, Jerusha, and a new baby went to St. Martin's Island for the summer where Newman would fish. In the fall he rented an old schooner to return with the family to Rock Island. Two young men, W.W. Shipman, a nephew, and Volney Garrett were taken on as crew.During the passage a storm arose and the old vessel became waterlogged and unmanageable. It was dashed onto the rocky shore. Curtis and Garrett were able to launch the yawl while Shipman was sent to fetch the baby who was asleep below decks. A heavy sea washed Jerusha overboard and the next wave tore the yawl loose and pinned Curtis under it. He drowned and when his wife saw this happen she stretched out her arms and was washed overboard. Garrett, Shipman and the baby, made it ashore. Next day the three Curtis bodies were found on the shore. The baby was placed in an aunt's care near Joliet,Illinois and when nine years old was playing with a toy sailboat in a nearby canal and drowned.

Along the eastern bluff is a small cemetery containing the graves of two children of Tom and Frances Miner. They came in 1843 to fish for the season, but in 1849 they settled there and Tom opened a small store and cobbler shop. Rosalinda, about 4 1/2 years old, died of scarlet fever in April, 1853. Cecelia, less than four months old, died a few weeks later. Skillfully carved stones from Green Bay were brought that summer. Within a year the family moved to central Wisconsin, but the markers remain. Rosalinda's is inscribed:

"Precious treasure thou hast left us
Here to mourn thy loss in vain

But in heaven we hope to meet thee
Where we ne'r shall part again."

The principal cemetery is near the southeast shore where sand makes the digging easy. Here was the original Indian burial ground. Some records state that Mrs.Louis LaButte who died in childbirth in 1843 was the first white buried there. Louis was listed in the 1835 U.S. Census which was taken to confirm Wisconsin's eligibility to become a state. The discouraged LaButte left, but while working in an Illinois lumber camp in the winter of 1843-44 he "sold" five young farmers on the merits of fishing Rock Island waters. They arrived the next spring and became some of the most solid citizens. Jack Arnold, who helped David Corbin care for the lighthouse, died in 1846 and was carried the full length of the island for burial in this southerly site. Apparently later a designated burial ground near the lighthouse was deemed a necessity. John Boon came for seasonal fishing, but became a permanent settler probably in 1836. He was a quiet,soft-spoken man and a pillar of the community.

When the town government was established in 1850 he was the Justice of the Peace. When a church was organized on Washington Island he became a deacon. He understood Indians, spoke their language and helped to smooth over rough encounters. He died in March 1866 at 51 years of age. There is no hard evidence to show that he was related to Daniel Boone(e). He was buried beside his only son Francis, who died of cholera in 1847, age 5. After his death, his widow moved to Traverse City, Michigan. Boon's grave marker says "And ye now have sorrow, but I will see you again and your heart shall rejoice and your joy no more be taken from you."

In the Island library is the book *VESTURFARASKRA 1870-1914* by Junius H. Kristinsson. This is a record of Icelanders who emigrated from Iceland to America during those years. In 1873 Hjortur (Chester) Thordarsson, 6 years old, left Reykjavik on the vessel PERA with the rest of his family. This included the father, Thordur Arnason, Bondi (farmer); mother, Gudrun Grimsdottir; two sisters, Gudrun Thordardottir, 22 years old and Ingiborg Hjalmrun Thordardottir, 13 years old; two brothers, Grimur Thordarsson, age 19 and Arni Thordarsson, age 4.

At an early age, Hjortur took a great interest in electricity. He also studied the mysteries of the "Northern Lights." I recall reading an article in American Magazine about his achievements and this fascination with the "Northern Lights." He knew that Iceland's glacial streams and underground steam offered a great potential for generating electricity. He hoped to someday perfect a means of transporting electrical power through the air from a generating station to a remote receiving station. This would have given Iceland a very valuable export. Some people theorize that he built the stone water tower, which still stands on the east side of Rock Island, as a possible receiving station for electricity arriving through the air. Even in Hjortur's early years when he was earning four dollars a week, he had a great thirst for knowledge and spent one-fourth of his pay for books. Early employment included winding armatures, At age 27, with the princely bankroll of $75, he went into business. His wife, Juliana, had an exclusive dress shop in Chicago and sold to Mrs. Marshall Field and the Palmer House family. This income helped greatly during the struggling years. In 1904, in 28 days, his shop built the first one million volt transformer which was put on display that year at the St. Louis World's Fair. He was credited with over 100 inventions, including radio transformers that eliminated the need for "B" and "C" dry cell batteries on early home sets. His firm made the ignition coils for Ford Model T autos. There were four in each auto's coil box, one for each spark plug. They were encased in beautiful wooden cases with the corners dovetailed together. He acquired a thorough knowledge of botany and in 1929 the University of Wisconsin awarded him an honorary MA degree. In 1915 he received an award for transmitting high voltages for long distances.

In the early 1900s he became very interested in Rock Island and in 1910 he purchased 775 acres, of the approximate 900 total acres on the island, for $5735. He originally planned to build on the Lake Michigan side, but lake storms tore out his pier so he moved to the southwest part of the island. In 1913 the first building, a log house, was erected. Hjortur and Chicago architect, Frederick Dinkelberg, developed the plans for the "Great Hall". The 40' by 81' Hall was patterned after the Althing at Thingvellir, Iceland, their Parliament building. The boat house and Great Hall was started in 1925 and it took 20 masons three years to complete it. It is reported that at one time a total of 35 masons were at work on Rock Island. The 3 foot thick walls are of concrete, not stone mortar. The beach-washed limestone rocks were carefully matched in size as the structure arose. Thordarsson boasted of having the largest fireplace in the world in the Great Hall. He claimed the next largest was in Mussolini's Alpine retreat. Four men could sit inside the fireplace and dine there. A whole ox could be roasted there. The construction of the Great Hall and boat house in the 1920s cost $250,000. The beamed ceiling of the hall is all of Douglas fir brought in from the western USA.

On the southwest side of Rock Island, eventually thirty acres was cleared and fourteen buildings were erected. Thordarsson preferred having limestone walls, steep pitched red tile roofs with deep eaves and tall, narrow windows. The general architecture was similar to buildings found in Iceland. A summer home with birch log walls was especially built for his good drinking partner, "Big Bill" Thompson who was mayor of Chicago from 1915 to 1930. The two of them often boarded Thompson's steam yacht, "Doris" and sailed around the lakes. As they imbibed freely, they often did not know what port they were in or where they had been. Most of the building materials were shipped by rail to Escanaba where my brother, Chris, and two sons on the "Wisconsin" would sometimes pick up three boat loads a week and bring these supplies to Rock Island. If Hjortur was here he always wanted to accompany them to Escanaba. Naturally he always brought a supply of "booze" along and every passing boat, buoy or interesting thing encountered on the trip had to be generously saluted with a big swig from the bottle. Often, when they got back he had to be helped or carried ashore. Both he and his wife loved plants so an elaborate greenhouse was constructed and filled with exotic plants. All through the winter season this was heated by a large boiler using hardwood. Most of this cordwood came from dead trees and it took many full cords, (4 ft. by 4 ft. by 8ft.) weekly to accomplish the heating. There were several guest houses and a dormitory for the construction men and masons who were kept busy into the late 1920s.

Attorney Clarence Darrow and author Earle Stanley Gardner were among the visitors. The 50' high water tower had a fireplace in the lower level intended to heat water. It was said that his retreat, if finished, might have rivaled Hearst's San Simeon. An eight foot high fence surrounding the built-up area did not successfully keep the deer out. Thordarsson had enough political "pull" to get the Wisconsin Fish and Game Department to have a mass deer drive conducted to chase the animals across the waters of the "Cut" to Washington Island. 75 men and boys drove about 25 deer to Carlin's Point on Washington Island. Hjortur then - brought a few pair of purchased deer to Rock Island and the State agreed that any deer on Rock belonged to him as a private herd and could be harvested anytime he desired venison. Of course, probably most of the animals that had been driven away returned very quickly to their normal habitat.

Thordarsson died in 1945 and his remains were cremated. A gravestone has been placed in the southeast cemetery and one of the newsclippings in the Archives says the "sandbeach is an appropriate repository for Thordarsson s ashes". This is not so. His son, Trygvie, told my nephew.Roy Andersen, that he kept the ashes in the trunk of his car for a long time. Finally,one day while traveling on the Island ferry he decided to deposit them in Death's Door.

After his death, the library he had amassed during his lifetime reposed in the "Great Hall". In 1946 the University of Wisconsin regents voted $275,000, plus $30,000 brokerage fee, to buy "the most important collection the University had ever purchased".

In 1941 there were 11,000 volumes and by his death many more had been added. It was reported to be the largest collection of Icelandic literature in the world. Other books included the “Cloverdale Bible” and “Audubon’s Elephant Folio.”

Thordarsson’s Rock Island property was left to sons Dewey and Trygvie. After Trygvie's death his widow, Julie Louise, and daughter, Julie, became co-owners along with Dewey and his wife, Helen. Dewey and Helen planned to live there and care for the property. Julie Thordarsson lived there the first seventeen summers and some winters of her life. She was a teenager before she learned that every little girl did not have her own private island. Deer came to her picnics. She said, "I wish the State would make it a park, then all little girls would have a chance to enjoy happy days like those I had on the island".

For many years the property sat idle and the elements began taking their toll on the more vulnerable structures. Then an interest developed in having the State of Wisconsin acquire the land and make it into a primitive park. Various cost figures were discussed ranging from $170,000 to $200,000.

The Advocate said that in June 1964 the State approved buying the 900 acre island for $170,000. Elsewhere $175,000 is cited.

And again I found that the Conservation Commission of Wisconsin made the purchase in April 1965. At first it appeared that many of the buildings would be restored. Unfortunately this was not to be and now the only remaining structures are the substantial ones made of masonry.

Roen from Sturgeon Bay constructed the dock for the State Park System. A well replaced Thordarsson's elaborate system of using “pure” Lake water.

The beautifully carved pieces of furniture that now grace Great Hall are part of what originally included two tables with twenty chairs, a desk and chair set, a settee and a dictionary stand. Each carving depicts scenes from Norse mythology. These carvings were made by Icelander Sigurd Einarsson who is also credited with the limestone carvings on the low bluffs on the southern shore. (When the large group of Islanders visited Iceland in 1987 many of us saw a whole, large room in the Selfoss museum filled with his carvings.)

The "King's Chair" has a verse on the back from the “Poetic Edda” carved in runes. This chair is now privately owned. The "Queen’s Chair" in Viking (Great) Hall bears a regal female figure representing the spirit of Iceland.The legs are each decorated with a legendary animal and the back is carved with a non-mythological scene, the meaning of which was probably known only to Thordarsson. Four dwarfs, known in Norse mythology to hold up the sky, occupy the corner posts of the desk. "Austri" (representing east) holds a drinking horn, "Nordi" (north) carries a blacksmith hammer and tongs, "Vestri" (west) holds Treasure bags and "Sudri" (south) eats an apple.

The desk's front panel features five scenes of human occupation during the Viking Age: sheepherding, weaving, scribing, smithing, and haying. Below these is carved the ocean and some of the animal life it supports. Connecting all these scenes is the central figure of "Yggdrasil", the World Tree. Look closely at the central leg of the desk, which represents Ygggdrasil's deepest root. The dragon, “Nidhögg” can be seen gnawing at the root.

MEDICAL SERVICES

In the papers from Charlotte Hansen I found a 1924 edition of "Pierce's Memorandum and Account Book designed for Farmers, Mechanics and all people. A present from the World's Dispensary Medical Association". On the back was a picture of his huge, six story building in Buffalo, NY, where "Within its walls is prepared a series of remedies of such exceeding merit that they have acquired a world-wide reputation and sale."

As a boy I remember peddlers going door to door selling these types of products promising to cure anything that ailed any human being. Over 50 years prior to 1924 Dr. Pierce "became famous for his success in the curing of disease and placed his 'Golden Medical Discovery' in drug stores of the United States". This alterative and vegetable, non-alcoholic, tonic was to be taken "when you feel run-down, out of sorts, blue and despondent." As with most of his other medicines, prices were: small tablets-65 cents, large tablets or liquid $1.35. His FAVORITE PRESCRIPTION" is an herbal tonic for the chronic weaknesses of women." The ANURIC TABLETS were "a new remedy for Kidney, Bladder and Uric-Acid Troubles". His IRONTIC(Iron-tonic) TABLETS "make Redder Blood". His PLEASANT PELLETS were "for Stomach, Liver and Bowels". The COUGH SYRUP was "for Coughs, Colds, Hoarseness, Bronchial Coughs and Non-diptheric Sore Throat." His HEALING SALVE "is a superior dressing for open, running or supporating sores or ulcers. (We used this type which contained carbolic acid successfully on animal wounds as well as our own.) His ANODYNE PILE OINTMENT "is a soothing, cooling, healing, antiseptic ointment for Piles". His AMMONIO-CAMPHORATED LINIMENT "is for relief of pains associated with sprains, bruises and muscular stiffness". Dr. Pierce's MENTHA-SOOTHALINE "is especially recommended for Sunburn, Chilblains, tired, burning, aching feet, chapped skin. Applied after shaving it is very cooling and healing."

He also sold "at actual cost" a 1008 page and profusely illustrated book entitled "The People's Common Sense Medical Adviser, in Plain English, or Medicine Simplified". Originally 680,000 copies of this book had sold at a regular price of $1.50. Afterwards two and a half million copies sold for one dollar to cover cost of paper, printing, wrapping and mailing. Now he has a new, up-to-date revised edition at total cost of one dollar. Better send NOW before all are gone, he cautioned.

In 1923 nearly a million bottles of his GOLDEN MEDICAL DISCOVERY were sold. A lady's testimony said, "Through the help I got, this and his FAVORITE PRESCRIPTION I was able to do all my own work without the slightest inconvenience during the expectant periods of my five children. Its effect upon me was to quiet my nerves and strengthen my body. When my son returned from France he came home with a heavy cold and a case of 'flu'; he was in a bad way. I gave him Dr. Pierce's Golden Medical Discovery and within fifteen days the fever had gone and the cold was broken up." Another said, "When I was about fourteen years of age I had an operation for appendicitis and the doctor said it would retard development until I was 18 or 19 years of age, but I heard how good Dr. Pierce's Favorite Prescription was for young girls so I took four bottles of it and came into womanhood within one year. Then I started getting healthy and strong. Before I took Dr. Pierce's medicines I weighed only 72 pounds-now I weigh 107. Later I took a breaking out on my face. I wrote to Dr. Pierce and he advised me to take the 'golden Medical Discovery.' I took two bottles of it and my skin is as smooth as I could wish for."

The Dr. Pierce's products which were sold door-to-door on the Island were mainly extracts of roots and herbs "which will cure the diseases that afflict mankind." He said that animals know by instinct what is good for them and will search until they find some plant that they need for correcting indigestion or constipation, etc. While in active, general practice Dr. Pierce "found that a combination of certain roots and herbs made into an alternative extract without the use of alcohol, would always put the stomach in a healthy condition, nourish the tissues, feed the blood and nerves and put healthy tone into the whole system.

In 1924 he had a very large, four story hospital in Buffalo called the "Invalid Hotel." The head doctor at Massachusetts General Hospital wrote on "Better Doctoring for Less Money." He said, "A new era has come in the practice of medicine. We are emerging from the stage where the doctor was a peddler, selling goods house to house, into the more advanced era where he stays at his place of business and the people come to him. Dr. Pierce had associated with him a dozen physicians and specialists, as well as four chemists. They offered X-ray examinations and chemical tests such as very few experts were capable of making. Included were experts on the eye, the ear and the throat. Every invalid is treated by a specialist - one who devotes his undivided attention to the particular class of disease to which the case belongs.

At the Invalid's Hotel was a "Cage for High-Frequency Treatment to defer old age." The patient was placed on a bench with a full-length wire cage surrounding them. "The treatment has to be skillfully administered with strict attention to the individual's strength. The elimination of poisons is greatly increased. If the organs are weak it is necessary to measure up their abilities by the usual physical tests known to the skillful physician, and to administer, at first,.a mild current, to increase the activity of the cells of the organs which carry away poisonous matter; as these cells gain in strength, the dose is increased until a reasonable full activity, of the vital powers is obtained. Patients of seventy years of age after a course of treatment, express themselves as feeling from ten to twenty years younger than when they began the treatment, and their general appearance certainly bears out the truth of their statements. They touted that the practice of chemical analysis and microscopical examination of the urine became famous many years earlier. They treated "Inflammation of the Bladder, Gravel, Retention of Urine, and Stones. No matter how large, the stone was crushed, pulverized, washed out and perfectly removed by our Surgeons, without any cutting."

"Large numbers of Tumors, not favorable for reduction and cure by electrolysis, are annually removed by our Surgeons, without any cutting."

"Many diseases can be treated by us when at a distance about as well as if they were here in person. Since our experience has enabled us to judge of the nature and extent of the disease from a written description of the symptoms, and from answers to questions which we ask, we can, therefore, adapt remedies to suit each individual case. All communications are regarded as 'sacredly confidential' and great precaution is always taken by us to send all letters and medicines in plain packages so that no one can even suspect the contents, or by whom sent. If you have a problem, don't hesitate to write giving a full statement. A medical specialist will advise you, frankly and confidentially, at no charge whatsoever -- simply enclose a stamp for reply."

The next series of articles will be on medical services here.

I remember my mother talking about the terrible flu epidemic of 1923. Fortunately, the archives has the *Advocate* article, "Perilous Journey Over the Ice Brought Back Sick Boys to the Hospital."

"A short time ago, television viewers throughout the nation had an opportunity to see Door County's flying doctor, Dr. Dan Dorchester as he made plane flights to help patients on remote Washington Island. The advent of the airplane and the fact that the Island usually has a resident doctor temper the difficulties Washington Islanders have always had in securing medical attention. But many Islanders no doubt recall the troubles they had years ago.

"Particularly vivid in the memories of Islanders should be January and February of 1923 when a flu epidemic almost prostrated many Door County communities, striking particularly hard on Washington Island.

"One of the most heroic episodes in Door County history took place in that epidemic, an episode that points out vividly the difficulties faced by the Islanders back in the days when hospital facilities were half a day's journey away.

"Taken from the pages of the Feb. 2, 1923 issue of the *Advocate*, the story of that perilous journey across Death's Door to save two youths needs no rewriting to recapture the drama, the *Advocate* reported: -

'Rivaling ancient myths of the Norse land is the most unbelievable story of the adventure and daring of a little party of Washington Islanders who crossed the treacherous ice of Death's Door last week with two lads whose lives were threatening to flicker out unless immediate surgical care could be given at the nearest hospital 68 miles away.

'The boys were Charles Jensen Jr. and Oliver Bjarnarson, both 19 years of age. They had been ill for four weeks with the flu, which threatened for some time to bring death to many residents of the Island township, when Dr. (Charles) Leasum, the boys' physician, saw evidence of pus forming in their lungs and said that a surgical operation would be their only salvation.

'The boys were operated on by Dr. G.R. Egeland and Dr. Leasum the morning after the arrival of the heroic party last Thursday evening. The surgeons reported both boys out of danger a few days ago.

'All Wednesday members of the Plum Island Coast Guards, under the direction of Captain George Moe, tested the ice and waited for the freeze which would make possible the perilous passage. 'If the wind stays in the north and it's cold, we take to the ice' Moe hopefully informed the anxious parents of the dying lads. 'One shift to the south will mean disaster. '

'While hope for the journey ran high with later weather predictions, a party of men was formed to prepare the lads for transportation. The only comfortable covered sleigh on the Island was liberally donated to the cause by Jens Hanson. 'Take it to hell if you want to,' said the generous owner, knowing well that at any time during the passage across the Door his fine outfit might be lost in the treacherous water along with the lives of his friends.

About 8 o'clock Thursday morning the long journey was begun. A sleigh handled by the mail carriers, Pete Anderson and Carl Christianson, preceded by two Coast Guards headed the procession, while the covered sleigh, carrying the two sick lads on stretchers and followed by two other Coast Guards brought up the rear. Other Coast Guards watched the party from the shore, ready to bring assistance in case of a mishap.

'It was 13 miles from Lobdel's Point to the mainland at Gills Rock. The ice, frozen only a few inches thick bridging in places larger expanses of black open water, was filled with windrows which blocked the route and had to be chopped away. Many times the weak ice nearly sank under the strain of the heavy sleigh, but the Coast Guards felt their way and took chances only when there was no other way to pass.

'It took three hours to cover the route to the Rock. The party had to run northwest of the island and then turn south to get across the death passage.

'A team of horses awaited the party on the peninsula and after a quick change the sleigh was driven at top speed breaking the road and plowing through heavy snowdrifts, stopping only at Ellison Bay to call the hospital and arrange for another team to meet them. Relieved again at Egg Harbor, 18 miles away from the city, the speed was kept up and the two lads, bearing up strongly under the great strain of the journey, were placed in Egeland Hospital a few minutes after 10 o'clock by a staff of anxious nurses and the two doctors, doing their utmost to assist the party in the heroic undertaking. '"

This hazardous journey across the Door was one of the last for Pete Anderson, Island mail carrier, who had gained fame during his 18 years of braving wind and weather. Just a few weeks later he caught the flu and died on March 16, 1923.

* * *

As I was less than six years old at this time I do not remember Pete, but the stories of his adventures and close shaves are legion and the Coast Guard went to his rescue on numerous occasions. In fact, his father-in-law, Nels Jepson, commented, "If it wasn't for the Coast Guard, Pete Anderson would have been in Hell long ago."

Carl Christianson became the Island mail carrier for many years using horse and sleigh across the ice in deep winter and his vessel, *Charlotte C.,* named for his youngest daughter, whenever possible during the rest of the year. He lived where the John Hanlin family now reside. Captain Ole Christianson, his father, lived just south of Carl. I remember Carl well. Charlotte was in my class at Detroit Harbor school.

Oliver Bjarnarson, who spent a lifetime as an Island commercial fisherman, had a keen sense of humor. When asked by visitors what summer was like on the Island his response would be, "six weeks of poor sledding."

Charles (Toddy) Jensen, Jr. lived with Charley & Cassie Jensen in a house later owned by Nathan Gunnlaugsson, near where the Recreation Center now stands. He left the Island, but returned for a while. I recall hunting rabbits with him. He had sawed about 12" off the double barreled shotgun and could hit nothing with it.

According to Archives records, the first doctor in this area was William Ellis who came to Rock Island in about 1848. Until 1869 people living on Washington Island had to call Ellis, from Rock Island. In the winter of 1851-52 two-year old, Jesse Miner was very ill with small pox. Dr. Ellis mixed cream of tartar, rhubarb extract and cold water, which he dosed Jesse with. Also a jug of hot water was placed at the patient's feet. This treatment was said to have cured one thousand people in England of small pox. After a few bad days, little Jesse recovered. In April, 1863 Dr. Ellis replaced John Boon as Justice of the Peace as Boon was too busy fishing and the price of fish was very good. In early March, 1866 Boon got wet and chilled. He contracted pneumonia and died March 16th, with Dr. Ellis in attendance.

January, 1872, Martin Bowman made a perilous, wet trip on the ice across the Door. His feet were severely frost-bitten. He eventually was brought to Sturgeon Bay where Drs. Young and McFacham amputated one foot. They expected to also to have to remove the other foot. In 1882 a sixteen year old lad had a bony tumor on his lower jaw. Dr. Soper operated, but found this to be very complicated. With the assistance of Dr. Hendricks they found bone decay from the chin to the ear joint. This was the most complicated operation ever performed in this part of the state. There is no record on the lad's recovery.

In May, 1884 a dentist, Dr. W.D. Corey, supplied music for a party at Joseph Cornell's.

Dr. Thordur Gudmundson, at the urging of his brother Arni, arrived from Iceland in 1885. The September 3, 1885 *Advocate* shows that he had set a broken arm. The 1886 *Polk's Medical and Surgical Directory* shows: "Washington Harbor population 625.

Gudmundum Thomas(sic)

Sturgeon Bay pop. 1800 - six doctors.

(County towns with doctors.)

Baileys Harbor pop. 300

Brussels pop. 30

Namur pop.. 675

Rowley pop. 200."

The Island was probably listed as "Washington Harbor" because the post office was there.

In 1888 there was an epidemic of mumps, said to have been brought from Newport.

In January 1889 Dr. Gudmundson was called away to Ellison Bay to treat a number of diphtheria cases. In February 1891 diphtheria had been stamped out, but whooping cough was prevalent. In June of that.year, every house was full of sick folks with la grippe. In August 1893 a Louis Reichel had stocked drugs and medicine for sale on the Island.

In December 1894 a doctor (no name) was attending a fishing employee of Joseph Cornell for lung congestion.

In October 1897 Dr. Wilcox, dentist of Menominee, was doing lots of work preparing Islanders for "winter masticating."

In April 1900 the influenza was raging and much "patient medicine" was being bought. In June of that year Dr. Wilson left the Island to practice medicine in Chicago.

Dr. Thordur Gudmundson, who had served the Island for 12 years, died in January 1899. His records showed 224 births and 63 deaths during this time. He attributed two deaths to hepatitis or "Hobnail Livers," as many Islanders were hard drinkers. His books at the Archives show that many of his charges for medicine were 10 cents and the very maximum was one dollar. In November 1880 he bought 4 lbs. of butter for $1.12 from Koyen's Store (now St. Michael's Chapel). From Miner he got 26 lbs. beef at 6 cents a lb., 8 Whitefish cost him forty cents, 50¢ a bushel for carrots and beets and 1 1/2 bushels of potatoes for 60¢. He paid Oddur Magnusson $1.13 for a day's work sawing wood.

After Dr. Wilson, who had served one year left, the Washington Island Medical Assn. was formed in July 1900 at a meeting at Jessen and Schmidt's Hall. Elected officers were William Jess, President, Bo L. Anderson, Secretary, and John P. Anderson, Treasurer. Dr. Frank Forman, Gladstone, MI was contracted to become the Island's physician. He had served in the Civil War, was captured by the South and served time in Libby Prison at Richmond, VA. One-third of the amount he required was raised by those present at the meeting and they were confident the balance would be forthcoming.

It appears that Dr. Forman served just a short time as in May 1901 Chicago Dr. Gustave Boucsein came to the Island, bought a house and farm and settled in where the Jack Cornells now live.

In mid July 1905 a Chicago dentist, Dr. O.J. Olafsson, was visiting the Island and doing work.

In 1905 there were so many cases of diphtheria that Chairman William Jess summoned Dr. H.A. Norden, Door County Health Officer to consult in regard to checking the disease spread. All cases were under the care of Dr. Boucsein who had served the Island a number of years and was a competent physician. Captain Peter Hansen lost three children. Oct.1 they lost six year-old Myrtle, 4 days later 10 year-old son Harold died and on the 14th they lost Alma, 12 years old. Mr. & Mrs. Cornell lost a daughter on October 2nd. There were several cases in the William Jess family, 2 in the Judin Garrett family and cases in several other families. Washington Harbor school has been closed,. also the churches were quarantined. The disease was confined to the Washington Harbor area and it was thought it would not spread to other areas. Still, in November 1905 the Ed. Cornells lost their youngest, an 8 month old girl, to diphtheria. In March 1906 M. Hansen and C. Anderson were quarantined with the same disease. In April Dr. Boucsein was kept busy with cases in the Jackson Harbor area, fortunately there were no fatalities. In May and June 1906 about half the Islanders were ill with "Russian Grip."

The first *Advocate* record of dentist, Dr. Egan, coming here was in October 1906 when he spent several days working.

In March 1908 a log rolled onto Frank Olson's leg fracturing the femur. He was transported to Ephraim where Dr. Egeland cared for him.

In 1908 Dr. Smith of Sister Bay was doing business here.

In April 1908 the Washington Island Benefit Assn. was formed at a meeting at Bo Anderson's Hall (now Holiday Two). John Malloch was elected president, Ben :Johnson, Secretary, and John Gislason, Treasurer. Also one person from each school district was chosen. They subscribed a $500 retainer to obtain a new doctor. Heads of families would pay $6 per annum and single adults $3.

With the advent of immunization, many of the early, deadly diseases no longer caused epidemics, some have even been wiped off the earth. Further, modern miracle drugs have greatly lessened the impact for sick persons today.

In the early days isolation was a common method of preventing disease spread. This was controlled by the town Health Officer. Upon learning of a case of communicable or contagious disease he immediately "placarded" the home where the sick person was quartered. For "communicable" cases, such as mumps or whooping cough, the ill person was restricted to the house for at least two weeks. Others could come and go, but a prominent placard warned any who entered that a certain disease existed there.

For "contagious" diseases, such as diphtheria or small pox, the whole family was "quarantined" and thus were restricted to the premises. Only medical persons were allowed to enter and the quarantine lasted for a longer period. It was not necessary for the Health Officer to be medically trained, as his job was to post the notices on the house, see that they were kept well displayed and to remove them after the problem was over. Archives records show the following Health officers from 1915 through 1962:

1915-16 Olafur Hannesson (my grandfather)

1917-18 Louis Hansen

1919-20 Henry Olson

1921 Haldor Gudmundsson

1922 Dr. Charles Leasum

1923-25 Dr. C.W. Colebaugh

1926 Maurice Andersen

1927 Dr. Colebaugh

1928 Dr. M.C. Crane

1929 William Jess

1930-31 Dr. M.C. Crane

1932-33 William Jess

1933 Dr. E. C. Farmer

1934 Wm. Jess & Dr. Farmer (Chicken Pox and Flu)

1935 Wm. Jess & Dr. Farmer (Chicken Pox, Measles, T.B.)

1936-38 Dr. M.C. Crane

1939-48 Robt. W. Gunnersson (1941-annual salary $100)

1949-55 Roger Gunnersson (1953 Town dump opened.)
(1954 School closed for one week-flu.)

1956-57 Dr. E. C. Farmer

1958-60 Dr. James Pinney

1961-62 Dr. Paul Rutledge

(Since there are no Health Officers shown following 1962, a person wonders if this office came to an end. I suspect the above record was in error in listing Dr. Crane for 1936-38, as I know Dr. Farmer was the Island doctor during those years. In May, 1938 as I graduated from Platteville State Teacher's College I came down with measles. Mother, Marvin and Allen Cornell had come to the graduation ceremony and so our Model A car was placarded and I returned to our Island farm house where I remained isolated until I was cured. I vividly remember when John Greenfeldt suddenly died of what was called "black diphtheria", but was actually "epiglotitis". He was Lester's brother and was in my primary class in Detroit Harbor school.)

January 1910 some enterprising Islanders wanted to build and equip a sanitarium. This thought was quickly followed by some action as reported in the February 10th issue of the *Advocate*:

"The event of the season was the great carnival held in Anderson's hall the first three evenings of this month. Let it be said right here that the affair was a complete success, both socially and financially, the proceeds being in the neighborhood of $400.00. Dr. Robb opened the meeting each time by a few well-chosen words, stating that the object of the fair was to get together money for the purpose of purchasing an x-ray and possibly other apparatus which are badly needed on this isolated place, the same to be the property of the town, but by no means his nor any other physician that may succeed him. The predominating feature of the gathering was vocal and instrumental music rendered by some home talent, very well received and applauded. Those taking part in the same were Mr. and Mrs. Linstrom, Dr. and Miss Robb, Mr. and Mrs. Andersen, Miss Breiting, Wallace Stoneman, Verner Richter and others. The African race was ably represented by Verner Richter, Henry Koyen, Chas. Gislason and Paul and Magnus Gudmundson. There were side shows, a Gypsie (sic) tent, guessing contest of seed in a squash, candy, kitchen, lunch and ice-cream counters and a department where articles of every description donated to the fair were sold. The sales ladies were Misses Bertha Arneson, Sarah Johnson and Carrie Jacobson and their goods went like traditional hot cakes. A raffle on a wooden toy horse with saddle and bridle, artificially cut out and presented to the fair by Mr. Tucker, assistant keeper of Pilot Island light, brought in the sum of $24.00. A voting contest for the ugliest man on the Island took place, also one for the most popular lady. Capt. Ole Christianson winning out on the first proposition by a safe majority, his opponent being Peter Anderson, who put up a stiff fight for the honor. We leave it to our genial skipper whether they think he did or did not deserve the distinction conferred on him. But the hottest fight took place for the winning of the prize offered for the handsomest lady, which was a diamond ring. The competitors were Miss Sarah Hansen Johnson and Miss Sarah Magnis (sic) Johnson both of the same name and nationality. Not less than 33,000 votes were cast for these ladies, the first name winning out. The contest occurred at the last hour of the fair, which closed at midnight, and a feature that was by all odds the most popular and brought in the greatest revenue. The first evening several of the ladies brought fancy baskets, which were sold at auction to the highest bidder for cash. The second evening a pie auction took place, and the only trouble was there were not enough of them, there being a small attendance on account of unfavorable weather and other untoward conditions.The last night supper was served downstairs in one side of the store, two tables being set almost the length of the apartment, but how many tickets were sold it has been impossible to ascertain. Another feature that proved very much of an attraction was the costumes worn by some of the ladies. There were Danish, Norwegian and Swedish national dresses and several wearing the Icelandic so-called 'peysufoit,' and Miss Gertrude Johnson. was arrayed in the gala of church-dress of Iceland, the garment being rich with decorations and most beautiful and winning much admiration. In conclusion let us say that the promoters of the carnival as well as the many that extended a helping hand are to be congratulated on the phenomenal success achieved. It will go far towards relieving an otherwise long and irksome winter as it affords no end of friendly as well as cheerful talk to the people of the Island."

The 4/30, 1908 *Advocate* reported that two Island children died of whooping cough.

In November 1908 Dr. Fuller, who had been here for 3-4 months, left for New Mexico where he has a sheep ranch.

In March 1909 Dr. Myron Sherper, Minneapolis, 28 yrs. old, was the new doctor making his quarters at Bo Anderson's "Ida-Bo Inn." (Now Holiday Inn.)

In July 1909 Dr. Sherper treated Rolland Koyen for injuries sustained when 3-4 bunches of firecrackers exploded in his pants pocket. In October 1909 Dr. Sherper turned his practice over to Dr. Robb.

November 1909 the John Hannesson home was quarantined due to scarlet fever. (House across from Dave's Garage.)

March 1910, there were several cases of scarlet fever and the homes of Christopher Einarson and Chris Jacobsen were quarantined. Jacobsens lost six year-old Laura on February 20. The third district school was closed to await developments.

May 1911, Dr. Egeland met John Hannesson and his 18 month-old son in Ellison Bay. The infant had appendicitis and was transported to the Sturgeon Bay sanitarium where Dr. Sibree performed the operation. In the same month, Dr. Sherper, Oculist, saw patients here. He was the brother of a doctor who summered here two years previous.

June 1911 Captain Robinson, Plum Island Coast Guard, fell with resulting internal injuries which grew worse. Dr. Egeland took him to Sturgeon Bay where a badly bruised and inflamed appendix was removed. This quickly could have been fatal.

August 1911 Dr. Egeland performed a tonsillectomy on Ruth Haglund on the Island.

On June 1911 Mrs. Lars Anderson, 71 years-old, was milking a cow that had been partially paralyzed by lightning a year previous. The cow fell on the old lady forcing her under the next cow who kicked or stepped on her destroying one eye. Doctors Egeland and Norden removed the eye to prevent more serious consequences.

August 1911 Christian Saabye suffered a broken arm while oiling his threshing machine. Dr. Boucsein, along with Dr. Detlefson who was outing at West Harbor, set the fracture.

In October 1911 Dr. Sherper, Oculist, was doing a thriving business while dentists Egan and Smith had all the work they could attend to. June 1912 many men suffered from "felons."

A.G. LeGrove had his right index finger amputated, John Malloch was nursing a sore right thumb and Henry Bilton and Will Engelson had fully developed cases. There were others with symptoms. (Webster says a felon is "a painful, pus-producing infection at the end of a finger or toe, near the nail.")

The 10/31/1912 *Advocate* said that Dr. Smith, dentist, came here on October 3 and had so much work to do that he was still busy in his 4th week on the Island.

October 1913 there was so much whooping cough that the schools were closed. It was said that nearly all the Detroit Harbor children were "whooping."

June 1914 Dr. Bynton, dentist, spent a week working here. Also Dr. Schuyler worked here for a week. Dr. Egan, dentist, was busy later in the month.

February 1915 dentist Egan and optician N.N. Strand were busy here for over a week.

In April 1915 many were ill with the "grippe" and some had pneumonia. School attendance was way down, in fact there were only ten children attending Jackson Harbor School. In September 1915 mumps was declared "an unwelcome visitor being especially audacious on Plum Island." For many years married Coast Guardsmen had cottages west of the Coast Guard Station, where their families spent the summer and other periods there. The government allowed "squatting" on its property, but the cottages belonged to individual Coast Guardsmen who bought and sold them as they were transferred on and off Plum Island.

In early November 1915 Dr. Alcorn, Sister Bay, and Drs. Hilton and Robb, Sturgeon Bay, were making calls here.

In late November 1915 Hahn's Undertaking Parlor of Sturgeon Bay handled the funeral of Mrs. Augusta Gislason, John's widow. A measles epidemic blossomed on October 1916 and it was feared that the schools would have to close. This extended over a long time and some who had had them one, two or three times before had them again.

March 1917, Dr. Boucseim was recovering slowly from.pneumonia and "weakness of the heart."

August 1918 Dr. Winward, eye specialist from Milwaukee, spent two weeks here seeing patients.

In October 1918 the deadly WWI flu struck hard. Schools were closed to comply with State Board of Health directive. No meetings, dances or church services were allowed. Usually local fishermen would move temporarily to Green Bay to catch the heavy, fall herring run, but that year they did not because that area was full of flu cases. Flu raged through military camps, and many "dough boys" succumbed to it.

Dr. Egan, dentist, spent a few days here, then traveled to Algoma on board the freighter "Diana" in December 1919.

In May 1920 little Alma Christianson became ill with what was thought to be chicken pox, but was really small pox, so the home was quarantined. There was no pox vaccine on the Island so some was obtained from Sturgeon Bay and Madison.

In April 1921 Dr. Lilly, Ephraim, called on Knut Hanson. It was also learned that both Dr. Leasums would be coming to.the Island. Chas. Leasum, M.D. and Will Leasum, dentist, later built a small office building across from Mann's Store. In August of that year Dr. Charles was busy with flu and diphtheria cases. Chris Jacobsen's house was quarantined as their youngest daughter had scarlet fever. While there was no quarantine for the flu, many thought there should be as it was quite contagious.

In September 1922 a doctor's meeting was held at Nelson's Hall. Here the people voted to keep Dr. Chas. Leasum for another year and they pledged another $5000 retainer.

In April 1923 Dr. Chas Colebaugh replaced Dr. Chas. Leasum. In April 1925 Chiropractor John Stark from Algoma opened an office at Detroit Harbor. In June of that year most of the Islanders were vaccinated for small pox. (An interesting sidelight is that persons who worked around cattle normally did not react positively to the vaccine. The vaccine had been developed from cow pox, a very mild, related disease. At age four I was scratched on the arm with a needle by Boucsein, who then applied the vaccine. A large, ugly sore developed which left a permanent scar. As I recall this immunization was good for seven years. Before I was due for the next vaccination, I was working daily around our cattle, so I never had another positive reaction until I was away from the farm for several years.)

As the island well water was short on iodine, several people had developed prominent goiters. Dr. Colebaugh,working with a drug manufacturer, instituted a treatment program for school children to receive free medication to prevent this problem.

I remember taking these chocolate flavored pills in school. They were given each day for two weeks twice a year and they contained 11 grams of sodium iodide. At this time families started also using iodized table salt.

In December 1925 Dr. Colebaugh was away taking a medical course and Dr. Getler, Chicago, was filling in for him. In March 1926 Door County no longer had a Health Nurse who used to give physical exams to school children. This problem was discussed between parents and the doctor. Colebaugh agreed to take over this work for a nominal $200.

By late 1926 it was observed that some children who had previously started getting thick necks no longer had this pre-goiter problem, thanks to the free goiter pills. Early Oct. 1927 Dr. Colebaugh took a week off. During his time away several serious illnesses developed and Dr. Leasum was called up here from Sturgeon Bay. In the meantime a contract soliciting Colebaugh to stay until May lst was circulated. It was reported he would likely stay until that date.

11/11/27 a mass meeting was held at Nelson's Hall to meet Dr. Ingersol, Madison, a prospective candidate to replace Colebaugh, whose contract would expire 4/15/28. Ingersol had 30 years of hospital, sanitarium and surgery experience. His proposal was that for $5000 guarantee per annum he would do the medical work and take care of all surgical work. It was moved to adjourn for 5 months to consider the offer. However, there was strong sentiment to make preparations and an effort towards an amicable agreement.

The *Advocate* correspondent in March 1928 reported:"Mumps have been on a rampage here for a long time, but is subsiding lately, probably because of lack of new material, just as a fire stops burning when there is no more fuel".

In August 1928 Islanders were very pleased with the results of the tuberculin tests on cattle as there was not one "reactor". Results of the first test given were about 30 “reactors” among about 800 cattle on the Island. The second test had about a dozen and the third test showed three, but there was some doubt as to them having a positive reaction. All positive reactors were slaughtered. I remember observing the tester at work on our cows. He injected a small amount of 'toxin' through the tender skin on the underside of the base of the animal's tail. In a few days the results were "read". If a raised lump had developed this meant that at some time TB germs had entered the beast's body. Tuberculosis may not have developed, but no chances were taken and the animal went to the butcher block. On the first test we lost at least two animals. I think Peter Yudin, cattle buyer, bought all the animals which were hand-led to Young's dock in Washington Harbor and loaded on a freighter from Escanaba. Yudin usually made a buying trip here at least once during the summer and bought enough to warrant having a freighter hired to transport the beasts. I don't know if John Larson's wild cow was in the first TB shipment, but nephew Roy told me that the cow was so wild it had to be blindfolded. After the cow was placed on the boat and the blind was removed, she jumped overboard, causing great excitement. The elimination of TB in cows was a great benefit and satisfaction as the Island became one of the first towns in the state to have all cattle tested.

On the heels of Dr. Colebaugh's departure a special town meeting was held to consider hiring a doctor by contract, or on paid retainer, or on salary as the health officer and to be allowed to earn what he can besides.

In May 1930 Dr. M.C. Crane, former Army doctor, had recently come here.

In June 1930 at a special town meeting, a doctor's committee was formed with a representative from each of the four school districts.

In October 1930 Dr. Crane gave diphtheria vaccinations to all school children. This consisted of three treatments, each a week apart.

Until March 1931, the doctor's annual guarantee had been settled once a year, but now this is to be done quarterly. The doctor kept strict accounts of all his work and any deficit between his income and the agreed guarantee was corrected quarterly. Dr. Crane had been so busy that there was no assessment at the end of the third quarter on March lst. If there had been a shortage it would have been covered by each subscriber paying their share. In March 1931 a widow, with two children, was very ill with a mastoid infection. This abscess of the ear had broken under the skin and was being absorbed by the body, consequently she developed a 106 degree fever. Her condition and the weather prevented her removal to a hospital, so Dr. Crane treated her at home. As her income was only a mother's pension of $20 per month, any donations to help were earnestly solicited. A pie and basket social was held at Nelson's Hall to raise funds. These socials brought about spirited bidding as the winner got to eat the food with the lady who had prepared it. Of course, everyone knew who was dating who, so all would bid against the lady's boyfriend really driving the price up.

In January 1930 the County board made appropriations for goiter treatment in all county schools. Originally this program was started on the Island by Dr. Colebaugh and was administered free for several years, then the PTA took over the costs, but now this organization is inactive. Cases were noted where unmistakable symptoms began to develop, but then disappeared after treatment.

In May 1930 there was concern that, with the declining island population, there would be a heavy financial burden on the subscribers to the doctor's guarantee. It was found that the State of Michigan was underwriting the doctor guarantees for Beaver Island and the Manitous. It was hoped that our Assemblyman Goff could present this to our legislature.

June 1930, Dr. Colebaugh is leaving as he wants more surgical and hospital work. During his five years here his contract was for a guaranteed $5000 annually. He charged the same to treat a person at the remotest site as he would to his next door neighbor. He never made subsequent calls unless strictly necessary. He never charged for advice via the phone. Non-subscribers were charged a higher rate as set with agreement between the doctor and the subscribers. (Colebaugh performed some difficult surgeries on the Island. One was when he completely repaired a young man's shoulder that had been badly torn by a close shotgun blast. His hours of surgical work paid off as the man later enlisted in the U.S. Coast Guard and served there for a full career.)

Unfortunately an *Advocate* article is not dated, but it has a picture of a number of Island people at Gills Rock to receive free chest X-rays conducted by the Wisconsin Antituberculosis Assn. It was reported that 101 persons were Xrayed at Gills Rock and a total of 921 Door County people took advantage of this test.

The antique dentist chair at Jacobsen Museum was donated by Bessie Nelsen, Nelsen's Hall. For many years this chair was kept upstairs at Nelsen's where many itinerant dentists used it.

Advocate articles tell of Dr. T. A. Egan, Sturgeon Bay, coming here in 1916 through 1919, but I am quite sure he is the dentist who extracted all of mother's remaining teeth and fitted her with dentures. This was sometime in the 1920s and I remember him having her lie on the kitchen table where he anesthetized her with either chloroform or ether and then proceeded to pull all the teeth. The denture fit was not good as often Ma would use a sharp knife to pare off high spots on them.

In 1933 B.P. Tillotson was the Island doctor. A bill dated 4/14/33 to Aussey Olson, single man, shows:

Subscriber retainer charges for
3/4 year ----------- $9.00
House call --------- $3.00
Medicine ----------- $0.15

Dr. E.C. Farmer, whose initial training was as an osteopath, served the Island for many years during the 30s, 40s and 50s. After having spent a number of years here, he moved his practice to Sturgeon Bay. Later he returned to the Island. June 1, 1957 he moved his practice to Sister Bay, but still his faithful patients traveled there to be seen by him. His knowledge of the human skeletal system was outstanding. He set a youngster's broken jaw, caused by an auto accident. It was a complicated fracture so he took the patient to Sturgeon Bay for X-rays to insure that it had been properly set. When Dr. Dorchester, Sturgeon Bay, read the X-ray he commented that if he ever had a fracture he would certainly want Farmer to set it in place. For a short time in the late 1930s Dr. Little, was the medical person here. He lived in a house on Lobdell's Point.

Farmer was followed by J.C. Pinney who served until December 15, 1960 when Rutledge replaced him and began his service in 1/l/61. In early years it was common for "midwives" to either deliver babies or assist the doctor. I remember Mrs. C.O. (Captain) Pederson and Mrs. Chris Peterson being midwives. Mrs. Carl (Pearl) Haglund had an early ability to care for the sick. She went to school in Evanston and in 1942 graduated as a trained, practical nurse. Then she opened her home as "Pearl's Baby Center" (1st house on north side of MacDonald Road). The place was efficiently equipped with Dr. Farmer's approval. Her mother, Mrs. James Boyce, and sister, Mrs. Elsie Holm, were both gifted nurses. An incubator, which was donated by the Red Cross, was used once.

Mrs. Orville (Esther) Wylie, who had worked at "Pearl's Baby Center," later took over in her home. Shirley (Atkins) Ellefson similarly worked with Esther, later for six years babies were delivered in her home with Dr. Rutledge in attendance.

In 1954 two rooms upstairs in the Detroit Harbor Ladies Aid cottage were equipped as the Island dental office. Under Chairman Roger Gunnerson's leadership over $300 was donated to buy a used chair, drill, lamp, sterilizer and tool cabinet. A dentist was booked for a solid week. It was hoped that dentists would come for several days at a timeto tend to local people's dental needs. One dentist suggested working with the teachers and PTA towards children's preventive dentistry. Some years later, Sarah Magnusson reported in the *Advocate* that a faster drill was needed as people again were leaving the.Island for treatment on the mainland.

When the Island bought the former Ole Christianson home, north of Arni Richter's driveway, for the medical doctor's home and office,'the dental office was moved to that basement. On a visit to the Island, many years ago, I developed a toothache. Since the regular visiting dentist was due here the next morning I headed for his office. He had arrived, but unfortunately there was water on the basement floor so he did not dare to operate his electrical equipment. Consequently I had to travel to Sturgeon Bay to get treatment.

Dr. J.C. Pinney is probably the first to inhabit the newly acquired Island Doctor's home. Apparently his contract extended from 7/15/59 to 12/15/60. Subscribers were still guaranteeing a minimum income to the doctor. When Pinney's books were closed all bills had been paid and the balance was $1297.15. Twenty-four families had prepaid for the first half of 1961, also 5 single persons had done so. Therefore families received a refund of $10 and singles got $5. At this time there was a total of 106 families signers, 27 single and 57 part-time signers. As there was more money in the subscriber's fund than had been needed to meet the doctor's guarantee, it was decided to give $5 refunds to family signers and $2 to singles. This left a balance of $434.65 to be used towards the new contract with Dr. Rutledge. From a public meeting circa 1940 the Doctor's Committee was made up of the clerks of the four school districts and they chose a 5th member to be bookkeeper and treasurer. Any vacancies were to be filled by an appointment from the district where the vacancy occurred. Pinney was not paid for the time last winter when he was in the hospital, but two nurses, Mrs. Hansen and Mrs. Blackmer, who provided services during that time, were paid $175.

In 1961 the four school districts were consolidated into one Island district and the old "Board of Health" was discontinued. About this time Dr. Buresh, Dentist, offered to check all school students teeth for free and Dr. Rutledge would medically examine all school children for free. The Medical Memorial Fund was preparing to buy a faster dentist's drill, but needed donations in order to accomplish this. A large number of cavities were found in the youngsters and it was obvious they needed vitamins with fluoride. Mrs. Burgoon contacted a laboratory in north Chicago to make a controlled study. Dr. Albertie from the lab and Dr. Rutledge made preparations. Mrs. Rutledge transported 6 children at at time, with parent's approval. There was nearly a 100 percent cooperation from grades l-12. Each was registered, weighed, measured, given a blood test and dental exam and the general physique was examined. There were 2 lot numbers of free pills with 57 pupils in each group and an equal number of boys and girls. Pills were of different strength and composition. One pill daily for 8 months, then free renewals. All illnesses were recorded and after 8 months parents and teachers evaluated children's health and appetite. Half of the pills contained fluoride. The cost to the lab was circa $3000.

Paul Rutledge, M.D. graduated from St. Louis University in 1927. He had vacationed here since 1936. Over the years he had developed a large practice in the St. Louis area and came highly recommended. He announced to the committee that he planned to attend four clinical conferences annually to keep abreast of new developments. Committee members at this time were Chairman Roger Gunnerson, William Jacobsen, Beatrice Bjarnarson, Marvin Andersen, Victor Cornell and Violet Llewellyn, Treasurer. The Treasurer was paid $10 per month, while the members got $2 each. Rutledge's first contract for two years included $3000 annual retainer which was paid in 12 monthly payments. This was listed as "over and above what he earns."

Subscribers paid in advance $20 yearly or $5 per quarter for families and $10 annually for single members. Summertime residents could sign up for a minimum of one quarter. It was agreed that there must be at least 150 paid-up signers at all times or the contract would be void.

Rutledge agreed to provide a substitute doctor for any of his extended absences at no extra expense to the committee.

His regular fees were:

Paid member

House Call - $4.00

Office Call - $2.50

Non-paid member

House Call - $8.00

Office Call - $5.00

A non-paid member was to pay $5 into the Doctor Guarantee Fund in addition to Rutledge's professional fee for maternity, surgery, and other situations where a set fee was charged.

Office hours: Monday, Tuesday, Thursday, Friday: 9-11 a.m. and 4-6 p.m.; Saturday, 9-12 noon. No office hours on Wednesday, Sunday or holidays, emergencies only. If possible, house calls were to be arranged before 10 a.m.

An article in the January 23, 1964, *Milwaukee Sentinel* reported on Dr. Rutledge's observations on longevity. He said that Island men definitely outlive women in contrast to the national trend. Three years ago he left one of the largest medical practices in St. Louis County, where he had patients such as August Busch, Sr. and two other Busch generations. On the Island he found ten times the number of people over 80, at least 30 and mostly men. However, the men over 80 walk, chop wood, milk cows, clean barns and work on fishing nets.

In 1967 Rutledge's annual pay was still $3000 plus what he could earn and office visits were still $2.50 and house calls $4. In 1970 the pay had been raised to $4200. In 1973 pay was still $4200, but office visits were $3 and house calls $5 with night calls $7.

In 1976 Rutledge announced that he planned to retire, but on 1/l/77 he signed a contract for one year or until a new doctor could be engaged. Pay had risen to $8400 per year. Office calls were still $3 and house calls daytime were $5, but nights, Sundays and holidays had risen to $10. When he retired on

September 1, 1977 he donated medical equipment which was appraised at $2507.70 to the Island.

Sometime during his tenure it became obvious that the subscribers alone could not meet the payment to insure keeping a doctor here. Assemblyman Swoboda was approached to see if a law could be passed so the doctor's subsidy could be taken from the Town tax funds. Consequently, under "Town Board Powers" 60.29 item (35) was added. This reads "Resident Physicians - The town board of any town comprised entirely of one or more islands may annually appropriate such sums as the board determines, to pay as a retainer, for the purpose of maintaining a physician as a resident within the town."

At the Archives I found a 1910 souvenir Booklet (postcard size) with pictures and many ads. This full page ad appeared there:

"E.H. Robb
Physician and Surgeon
Detroit Harbor
Wis.

Experienced in Sanitarium work and with Electrical, Vibratory Massage, Compressed Air and other Equipments for the treatment of those resorting on the Island for health. Patients referred by other physicians will receive every consideration."

Robb was here when the big carnival was held at Bo Anderson's to raise money for x-ray and other equipment.

In 1974 the Island Memorial Medical Fund was established to administer the legacy of Fred and Olga Koyen. This fund was started through the efforts of Dr. Rutledge assisted by many other Islanders. Its purpose was to distribute free vitamins and to buy x-ray and dental equipment. Over the years it has purchased many items for our medical and dental clinics. It is always in need of money to further improve our facilities. Any donations are greatly appreciated.

In February 1976, Dr. Rutledge announced plans to retire and the Committee agreed that any applicants should be interviewed by the Town Board. They asked Rutledge for help in making a list of requirements for a new doctor. Dr. Henry Russe (summer resident) suggested making a brochure of needs, requirements and pictures of the medical office and Island-owned doctor's home. Dr. Brown, whose father had a summer home here, expressed interest, but later decided to stay in "inner-core" practice in Cleveland.

March 22, 1976, John Turk, Door County Medical Center, met with the Committee and announced they were applying for a HEW grant and were planning to place a family doctor at Sister Bay. If the Island supported their HEW application and a grant was awarded, they would provide a Physician's Assistant to the Island if a doctor was not located by our Committee. Monies for medical and dental equipment needed here would also be asked for. He said that a telephone link-up of an Island EKG to Sturgeon Bay would cost $60 per month, while video equipment would be about $80 per month. This would allow doctors in Sturgeon Bay to direct the person with a patient in our clinic. He said a Physician's Assistant or Nurse Clinician (Practitioner) would have a Master's Degree in diagnostic work and could dispense drugs and do suturings.

In May 1976 John Mosling, Oshkosh Truck Foundation, presented a fine ambulance to the Island. Norbert and Richard Jensen were certified Emergency Medical Technicians and they now responded to rescue calls in this well-equipped vehicle.

In September 1976 the Committee continued their search for a doctor while considering the offer from Door County Medical Center. Nurse Clinician Mike Flood from Sister Bay reported that he handled 90% of the cases coming to their office. He did emergency deliveries, blood pressures and count, suturing, minor fractures, urinalysis and physical exams with doctor's approval.

1/29/76 Dr. Fogel was referred by Turk. He had camped on Rock Island and was a GP and radiologist. This 45 year old widower, with 6 children, was asking $60,000 per year through town subsidy or guarantee.

The Doctor's Committee diligently continued their search for a General Practitioner. Door County Medical Center had now received their HEW grant and was prepared to offer ser*vice to* the Island. So the Committee wanted the Islander's feelings on the situation.

A postcard ballot was prepared and sent out on November 5 with a return deadline of November 15. It read a follows:

1. Please check the alternative you prefer the Doctor's Committee to pursue. (Mark only one.)

☐ Alternative A: Recruit a Physician, recognizing that this will mean an increase of as much as 7% in our taxes.

☐ Alternative B: Recommend a Nurse Clinician.

2. If a Nurse Clinician is hired, would you be willing to utilize the services of this person for your medical care?

☐ Yes ☐ No

3. Comments:____________

The Committee reported that most doctors expected to receive $40,000 to $50,000 per year. They expected to provide $50,000 with part of this generated through medical calls, drugs, lab and Xrays. These services might generate $20,000, meaning that the current subsidy of $4800 would increase to about $30,000.

3/30/77 A "Letter of Intent" for a Nurse Clinician through Door County Medical Center was signed. This provided a $10,000 subsidy. Initial office calls would cost $7, while follow-up calls would be $6.

4/25/77 A one year contract with Kay Joseph, Nurse Clinician, as a DCMC employee, was signed. She had worked for the U.S. Public Health Service in Alaska and presently had been at Winona, Missouri. She did not recommend planned baby deliveries, but would handle emergency ones.

6/1/78 A three year contract was negotiated with Door County Medical Center with these provisions:

1. DCMC would provide supportive staff in Kay Joseph's absence (perhaps three days).

2. All grant fund equipment belongs to the Island.

3. DCMC doctors will make regular visits to see patients.

4. All office visits remain at $7 initial and $6 follow-up.

5. The subsidy remains at $9600 per year.

At the end of this three year contract, Kay Joseph had decided to return to Missouri. This left the Island without professional medical assistance. However, fortunately in the late 1970's over twenty Islanders has attended EMT classes here, conducted by NWTC instructors. All students passed and became Nationally Certified Emergency Medical Technicians. They handled all initial emergency care and supervision while patients were being transported via ferry to the mainland, where Door County ambulance crews would take over.

The Medical Committee, now made up of several new members, again began a search for a doctor. Ads were placed in several publications and a vast number of government and other medical agencies were contacted. During this time Dr. Joan Traver, Sister Bay, made a number of visits to the Island and also saw Islanders at her Sister Bay facility.

The Island Medical Committee, which served under the auspices of the Town Board, was composed of representatives from the Legion, Lions, Women's Club, Lutheran and Bethel Churches, and the CAP office. I served as Chairman of this group from 1981 to 1989.

Before Kay Joseph left, we learned of a possibility of Federal grants for medically disadvantaged communities. With her help we applied, but were not successful in getting any funds. A diligent search was mounted to find a doctor and I was told by several that we would never get one. My response to them was that somewhere in this world there was a medical person, like our dentist Tom Wilson, who would love the Island. All we had to do was find that person. As the Town Board had not budgeted any funds to cover this search, we had a severe limit on what could be spent in this search. We did place ads in the *New England Journal of Medicine* and the *Lutheran Magazine*. As a life member of the Retired Officers of the United States I was able to place a free communication in their magazine for a doctor.

I received an early response from a former military doctor, whose wife had seen the ad in the *Lutheran Magazine*. He was practicing in Mississippi, but was interested in independent, family practice. We invited them to spend a weekend on the Island. They accepted and the family of four stayed at our home. They met with the Committee and we were very hopeful that he would accept our offer. That Saturday night we took them to Orion and Jill Mann's wedding dance. They met lots of Islanders and thoroughly enjoyed the evening. The one "fly in the ointment" was that the doctor had a teenage son, from a former marriage, who was having a drug problem. He explored what assistance Door County could offer and decided this isolated community would not be best for this lad, so he declined our offer.

A few responses to the Medical Journal ad came from doctors in this country. In fact, one came up here and was so taken with the clear air that he bought a piece of property where he could view the heavens. In spite of this purchase he never showed any further interest in becoming our family doctor. When that issue of the *Medical Journal* arrived in India, I began getting lots of applications from that part of the world. While some of these were submitted with excellent English and content, others were very amateurish. The Committee scanned these without favorable response.

In the meantime, Dr. Joan Travers was seeking either a Nurse Practitioner or Physician's Assistant for the Island Clinic. Dick Hecher, P.A., was found by her and brought to the Island where he was interviewed by the Committee. They found him very acceptable, under Dr. Travers supervision. The Committee recommended that the Town Board accept an agreement with Dr. Travers, which they did late in 1983. In the meantime the state law had to be amended to allow our town to provide medical subsidy for "Physician's Assistant."

This is a copy of the contract between Dr. Traver, Sister Bay, and the Town of Washington:

An agreement between Dr. Joan Traver (I) and the Town of Washington (you).

1. I will provide medical service to Washington Island for one year. I will employ and supervise a physician's assistant. You will provide suitable space and $10,000 per year.

2. We will jointly interview and approve any medical provider for Washington Island prior to hiring.

3. When the physician's assistant is absent for a length of time greater than one week, I will make every attempt to provide medical service during that time by either coming myself or sending my nurse practitioner. This pre-supposes people waiting for appointments and weather permitting.

4. The $10,000 provided by you will be paid in nine (9) monthly installments between October and June. $1,000 will be available for medical insurance, continuing education or vacation pay. In addition, the physician's assistant will receive from me 40% of gross income generated by direct service.

5. This contract shall be in effect from October 1, 1983 through September 30, 1984.

6. Termination of this agreement may be by either of the parties involved with a minimum of three months notice in writing.

7. Expendable items will be supplied by me and I will leave an equal amount at the end of our agreement.

8. Equipment at a cost of $50 or more will be paid for by you, as well as repair of existing equipment.

9. Office operations will be my responsibility, but you will provide a receptionist.

10. I will attempt to be present on Washington Island to provide continuing supervision and to see patients as needed.

11. I will provide malpractice insurance to cover myself and my physician's assistant. Malpractice insurance is not needed for Washington Island board as they do not practice medicine.

12. All medical records generated on Washington Island will remain on the Island.

Signed,
Joan Traver, M.D.
Hannes M. Andersen, Chairman
Town of Washington
December 8,1983,

For a great many years, our American Legion and Auxiliary has worked closely with the American Red Cross in the annual blood donor drive.. During the month of May, on schedule, the ARC truck arrives at the Community Center. Legion men off-load the equipment and place it properly in the gymnasium. Years ago the lady truck driver thoroughly bossed each movement and positioning of everything in the building. If I remember correctly, Bob Overly and I privately hung the nickname "Sergeant Major" on her. Legion Auxiliary ladies provided assistance and goodies for donors after they had given blood and rested the required time. Island people have always generously donated to this drive. An article in the June 6, 1980 *Advocate* stated that the ARC quota for the Island was 50 units, but 64 persons showed up and 61 units were drawn. Many gave in the name of Kelly Jess, a lad with severe medical problems. Two units of badly needed type 0 blood were received and used by pediatric facilities at St. Vincent's and Theda Clark Hospitals the same day.

The April 9, 1990 *Advocate* reported that the Island Lions Club gave $1000 to the Island Medical Fund towards the purchase of a portable EKG machine. Total cost would be about $2600. This unit would weigh about the same as Dr. Bass' purse. A telephone could be placed on it to send messages to specialists. It was reported that it separated one reading into categories that formerly needed to be hand written.

A history of Sturgeon Bay hospitals was covered in the *Advocate*. The first was a large, two-story frame building that had once been the home of Frank Long, *Advocate* editor. This was operated by Dr. G.R. Egeland for many years. The Egeland Hospital, now part of Dorchester Nursing Center, was built in 1921.

With our clinic back in operation in late 1983, the pressing need to find a doctor for the Island lessened. However, the Medical Committee knew that the people wanted an M.D. here so the search continued. It was learned that the National Health Service Corps had a program that would loan qualified students money so they could attend medical schools. When they became M.D.s they were to be assigned to communities that were medically deprived and were then obligated to eventually repay the loans.

We began working with Fred Moscol, Madison, first to qualify as a medically deprived community and then to obtain one of the new doctors. Permanent population count was a major consideration in qualifying. Ours was way too low, but when we pointed out the heavy summer influx and the Island isolation problems in wintertime, we were in a more favorable position.

In the final analysis National Health determined that between the Island and northern Door County there was a shortage of one M.D. Through Fred we learned that a lady doctor in the Madison group was interested in the Island.

Soon the Bass family came here for an interview with the committee and to look the clinic and Island over. Rev. Bass, Dr. Bass, Marvin and Valerie all met with our committee. I told them they would be like every other person who made their first visit here; they would either fall in love with the Island or they wouldn't care if they ever saw it again. (I think it's now obvious how they felt.)

Everything seemed to be going along fine. I wrote a thank you letter to the head of the National Health Service Corps and included information on the Island, its isolation from a hospital and winter and weather problems in transporting patients.

A short time later we learned that Dr. Meyer, Sister Bay, had gone through a medical office friend in Madison and hired another lady doctor for his practice. This filled the vacancy for northern Door County and the Island. I immediately called Fred and asked him what medical service the Island could expect from Meyer's office. He said, "That's a darned good question and I'll get the answer for you."

Later in the day, after talking to Meyer, Fred called me back and said if there were 10-12 Island patients waiting to be seen on the Island, a doctor would be sent to see them at our clinic. If there were only a few, and the doctor could see more patients during that day in Sister Bay, the M.D. would not come to the Island.

I responded, "We have just been had and rolled in the snow!"

Fred agreed and we both knew it was time to "call in the Big guns." I immediately contacted the head of the National Health office and was assured that they had selected Dr. Bass for the Island and were not about to change. When Meyer discovered this he made an appeal through the *Advocate* for County residents to apply pressure for him to keep the doctor he had recruited. Fortunately he lost.

Dr. Marjorie Bass opened our clinic on August 1, 1985. We are very fortunate to have her and hope she continues to practice here for many more years.

[An interesting sidelight is that earlier in our recruiting efforts, Fred Moscol had explained that his office was not fully funded to assist in the placement of doctors. He was very willing to work with us, but if we agreed to have them do so they needed a monetary commitment from us. If they got us an M.D. and that person served the Island for at least one year, the Town would pay them $1000. As he was leaving late that day, I contacted the two supervisors, Lonnie Jorgenson and Herbert Gibson. We agreed to this and, as chairman I signed the contract. However, we were never billed.]

LEGION

Prior to the formation of the Island Legion Post, I understand that five or six WWI veterans belonged to the Archie Lankershire Post in Sturgeon Bay. From the Legion records at the Island Archives I found the following (copied verbatim):

"Minutes of meeting for organization
Held Tuesday April 9,1936.
Meeting called to order by Magnus Magnusson.
Magnus Magnusson elected temporary chairman.
Ernie Boucsein elected temporary Sect.
Post to be named Charles Gislason Post.
Officers elected for office.
Commander---------Magnus Magnusson
Vice Commander----Raymond Krause
Post Adjutant-----Leon Cornell
Sergeant At Arms--George Cornell
Finance Officer---Conrad Anderson
Historian---------L.E. Cody
Committee of Membership
Chairman----------Raymond Krause
Clifford Vogel
Charles Johnson
Meeting adjourned."

"Mac" Magnusson, as everyone called him, was our Postmaster. He lived in the house right across from the present post office, now owned by Phillip Andersen. He had purchased a building which was moved into the front of the home and became the second P.O. that I knew as a boy.

Raymond Krause taught grades 5 through 8 in the Washington Harbor school, now the front room of the Art and Nature Center.

Leon Cornell fished commercially, first with brother Leslie, then with his own boat from Johnny Cornell's dock. This dock has now become Jim Anderson's on the harbor side of Island Outpost.

George Cornell fished with his dad, Johnny, from the same dock where Leon fished. His home is now Walt and Mary Jorgenson's.

Conrad Anderson farmed and did blacksmith work where Jeff McDonald and family now live.

L.E. Cody worked for commercial fishermen at Johnny Cornell's dock and for a number of years lived where Kahlscheuers now reside.

Levere was an excellent catcher on our ball team and later put in many years as plate umpire.

Clifford Vogel worked for commercial fishermen at Johnny Cornell's dock. Later he built and ran a bakery where the Rupipers now live.

Charles Johnson lived in Jackson Harbor where the Fred Youngs now live. He began work with his father, Johnny Johnson, as a carpenter and continued in this occupation through his life.

It appears that these six former servicemen were the first members of Washington Island Legion Post 402. This series of articles will recap some of the more interesting actions at Legion meetings through the years as well as chronicling many of the community's activities in which they played a very active part. For the benefit of Legionaire's descendants I will point out when they joined as well as some of their activities with Post 402.

September 10, 1936 the Women's Auxiliary was formed with a large number of women participating.

Dec. 31, 1937- Legion members and Ladies Auxiliary held the first New Year's Eve dance sponsored by the Post.

In May of 1937, they had already begun looking for hall and considered trying to buy the "Little Brown Church" which was built many years previously, as a Methodist church. It was later occupied as a church for a few years by Baptist preacher, Mrs. Wm. Wickman. Originally the building was painted white but Wickmans painted the exterior brown, hence its new name. Jimmy Phelps'home at Lakeview and Airport Roads stands on the original foundation. No progress was made by the Legion in acquiring this property.

In May, 1938, the early American Legion members considered buying Arnold's Tavern for a meeting place. This was the former Gislason General Store that later became the first Community Center.

On July 28, 1938, they agreed to accept the flag that had been draped over Charles Gislason's coffin. He was killed in battle on the Western Front. His heroic performance on the battlefield resulted in posthumous awards from the U.S., as well as the

French Croix de Guerre, which is now displayed in our Legion Hall. Clarence Anderson made a table on which the above mentioned flag was displayed in the Hall for many years.

It seems that they did not readily give up on buying Arnold's Tavern, for at the August 11, 1938 meeting two members were appointed to contact George Mann and Nor Shellswick with an offer of $600 for the building. (I wonder if these two men held a mortgage on the property.)

On September 28, 1938, plans were made for an Armistice (now Veteran's) Day program with a program speaker and school participation. On October 6 a free dance was held honoring Armistice Day.

At the October 20 meeting a motion was passed to donate $50 to help the Lions pay for the scout cabin. The Island Insurance Company held the mortgage.

On November of that year a vote was passed to buy Christmas candy for all school children as thanks for their help in Legion programs. At this meeting a suggestion was made to start school safety patrols and to get some safety movies to show.

December 1, 1938, an order was placed for rifles to be used by the firing squad.

December 15, 1938, plans were made to order up to $15 worth of trimmings and noise-makers for the New Year's Dance. At this time Tom Nelson was providing the Post with a meeting room so they decided to scrub and paint that room.

On December 31 1938, there was a small crowd at the New Year's Eve dance, but the put-and-take board sold out. One jug, one flashlight and two tackle boxes were prizes on the punch cards. Each card netted $1.50 (probably at five cents a punch.) Noisemakers sold out but hats didn't go over so hot. We have nearly enough for next year. $24 was taken in at the door; $15 paid to the orchestra. A total of $43 was grossed for the evening. Miss Audrey Cornell and Ray Krause did not want any payment for playing in the orchestra. At the next meeting it was agreed that after all the expenses were paid, the Legion would give the remaining money to the Auxiliary.

On January 27, 1939, it was suggested that the Legion work for a larger and better Coast Guard boat for ice breaking. Also, a motion was passed to write a letter of comandation [sic] to the Coast Guard Commander at the District Office at Green Bay for the wonderful service rendered by the Plum Island crew in getting Ralph Goodlet to the Hospital. Dr. Crane and Clarence Anderson were assigned to compose a letter to the above office for comandation [sic] and for boats.

January 26, 1939, members to buy Legion caps at $2.40 and perhaps Legion shirts at $2.75 and neckties at 60 cents.

On February 9, 1939, The Post hosted a dinner for Tom Nelson on his birthday. A very enjoyable party resulted when the ladies brought many delicious dishes and Tom, in turn, provided liquid refreshments.

At the March 9, 1939 meeting, military record cards were given to each member to be filled out and returned. (As present Post Historian, I have been collecting this type of information from all Post members and would certainly like to find the records from the Island WWI servicemen.) An article was read concerning the German Bund. (I recall that at this time there was an active Bund in Milwaukee where many people of German heritage lived. The *Milwaukee Journal* carried stories regarding the strong support of Hitler and the Nazis. After WWII broke out in September 1939, the FBI began close surveillance of Bund activities.)

March 23, 1939, Post to buy two .30 caliber rifles and slings at a cost of $15.45 each plus express charges.(This may have been the start of the firing squad.) Ladies will sell poppies and Legion stickers are for sale at five cents each.

April 6, 1939, Bandstand to be painted. (This was a gazebo type structure that stood between Bethel Church and the Veteran's Monument. In fair weather, the Memorial Day program was conducted at this location.) Further comments regarding the German Bund. The headstone for Charles Gislason's grave was delivered to Adjutant Clarence Anderson.

May 4, 1939, Two ministers will act as Chaplains at this year's Memorial Day exercises. Auxiliary members are invited to a special night about May 25 to make wreaths for Memorial Day.

May 18, 1939, it was decided to have Legionaires leave Tom's Hall at 1 pm and March to the Monument. Services to be at 1:30 pm.

On May 25,1939, it was decided to march from Haglund's corner (Main and McDonald Roads), not from Tom's. A picnic supper was planned to be held at the Monument.

June 1, 1939, Legion will help financially on the $100 to be spent for the July 4th fireworks.

June 29, 1939, Tom Nelson agreed to let Legion use the South room upstairs for storing Legion supplies. (The Post had been meeting there for a long time.) Trimmings were ordered for the July 4th local dance. Mrs. Levere Cody will run the hot dog stand. The local insurance company will only insure Tom's up to $3,000. Legion will look elsewhere for insurance on their effects stored at Tom's.

August 3, 1939, A large Legion supper was held at Hotel Washington for members, Auxiliary and three State officials who were present, also several out-of-town Legionaires and Island ex-servicemen were invited. An excellent meal with refreshments after supper cost 75 cents a plate.

August 10, 1939, It was suggested that a skating rink pond be prepared on Henry Hagen's property back of the log cabin. Ray Krause agreed that he would install a light plant in Ernie Boucsein's shed (now Dave Johnson's) to provide lighting for night skating. The Bethel Church piano was tuned at a cost of $4 and paid for by the Legion. August 24th is the deadline for members to have their pictures for the records at Post expense.

September 7, 1939, the Monument is in bad shape and needs repair before winter.

October 19, 1939, The Town has offered to provide the machinery for leveling and grading of the Skating pond. With the help of Town Chairman Charles Hansen, the area will be staked out.

November 29, 1939, it was decided to plank around the Skating rink. Leon Cornell and Clifford Vogel will do it tomorrow.

December 14, 1939, Folding chairs were purchased at a cost of $1.12 each. Trucks and tanks will haul water to the skating rink. 25 gallons of gas purchased to be used to light the community Christmas tree. New Year's Eve dance admission will be 20 and 30 cents. A secret vote was taken on buying the Brown Church for a Legion Hall - results 10 No -- 0 Yes.

January 11, 1940, Leon Cornell, Earl Malloch, and Clarence Anderson hauled water in Leon's truck; also, two days of pumping were spent to flood the rink, however, the hose froze.

New member Morten Jorgenson. Cody suggested having an oyster and chili supper on January 25. Leon will get the oysters, Clarence will make coffee, Cliff Vogel will make the chili.

Clarence will make grave markers similar to those in France.

January 25, 1940, Ray Krause suggested buying a stretcher for the sick. 30 members were present at the oyster supper.

February 8, 1940, Many problems developed at the skating rink. It was suggested to possibly use Chris Sorenson's frog pond next year. (It was near Bill Jorgenson's on Townline Road.) Color Guard and firing squad to practice at each meeting for Memorial Day observance.

February 22, 1940, Legion will contact Dr. Little regarding possibly getting a hospital and X-ray equipment on the Island. Ernie Boucsein suggested scraping off snow at Detroit Harbor and flooding to get a smooth skating rink.

March 7, 1940, Dr. Little suggested that the Legion and Lions might sponsor a program for a house large enough to use as an emergency hospital and for the doctor to live in. Later a fluoroscope and an X-ray could be acquired. The Town would charge the Doctor rent. Perhaps a federal loan would be possible. The present Doctor was forced to live in the Scout Cabin when he first came here as there were no houses to rent. Perhaps for about $6,000 a suitable building with electric lights, water and furnace could be obtained. Little said a good fluoroscope and X-ray would cost about $800. John Cornell's and Bill Jepson's houses are available. Ray Krause, Cliff Vogel, Levere Cody, and Clarence Anderson to do firing squad practice with 30-40 Sharps rifles.

3/28/40: A special meeting was held to ask the Town at the annual meeting to acquire a house large enough to have two extra bedrooms, for emergency operations. Stretcher and crutches were ordered. Hildegard Anderson and Ella Carlson served lunch at Clarence Anderson's after the meeting.

4/4/40: At the annual Town meeting it was decided to have one member from each of the four School Boards or Districts work with the Town Board on acquiring a Doctor's house. The Post Commander, Ernie Boucsein and Cliff Vogel will keep contact on this. At the Town meeting Dr. Dorchester offered an old Xray machine and up to one dozen hospital beds.

4/18/40: Town Chairman Charles Hansen wishes to get housing for the Doctor and hospital facilities. The project should be pushed and finished before the Doctor's one year contract is up. At the meeting Ray Krause read extracts from Hitler's speeches. Clarence Anderson remarked, "If the average intelligence would only look back and consider what a liar this person is, then his following would be very small."

5/2/40: Mrs. Charles Johnson will make eight wreaths and the Girl Scouts will make one for the Marine dead. Adjutant will contact Mrs. C. Koyen regarding buying her wheel chair.

5/16/40: Twelve American flags ordered to be used as veterans grave markers on Memorial Day.

6/13/40: Debt on the Scout Cabin is $175. Legion voted to give $25 towards retiring this debt. Island band will play at July 4th dance-25¢ admission. As Tom's Hall is considered to be the Post headquarters, a flag staff will be erected there before July 4th.

It was suggested that the Legion, sponsor the, baseball team next year. Ralph Jacobsen collected $46.15 to help pay the cost of July 4th fireworks.

7/11/40: Financial report on July 4th Legion activities:

Receipts	
Stand and Bingo	$115.40
Dance	$ 30.40
	$145.80
Expenditures	
Orchestra	$ 15.00
Premiums	$ 33.65
Freight	$ 2.67
	$ 51.32

9/19/40: Three Legionaries will go to the west side of the Island to paint over one more Nazi signs. Samples of red paint and pictures, will be sent to the FBI.

10/3/40: The question of aliens on the Island was brought up. "Is John and Gertrude Barnson aliens" was asked at the meeting.

10/17/40: Pictures of Swastika painted on west side have been sent to the Un-American Activities Commission.

10/31/40: Members went to Earl Malloch's house [now Jack Cornell's] for lunch and rare wine.

11/28/40: Ministers will receive three dollars each for Armistice Day service. Bill Engelson, Jr. will be paid one dollar for bugling.

12/12/40: The Postal Inspector will be coming next week to register aliens. The Post will pay Tom Nelson $10.00 for gasoline used to light the community Christmas tree and for heating the rooms used by the Legion. A free dance will be held at Tom's Hall on December 31st. No band is available to provide the music so the Legion is appropriating $5.00 towards the nickels needed for "Ortifonic Music" from Tom's juke box. [This may have been the first one I remember being there. It was about six feet wide and over six feet tall. A piano, marimba and banjo played the music numbers.] They purchased $9.00 worth of hats and noise makers to be sold at the dance. A motion was passed to give each.school pupil a bar of candy on or about Washington's birthday as thanks for participation on Legion programs.

All members went to Mac Magnusson's house for lunch after the meeting

1/23/41: All post members were directed to ask Island aliens if they wished to become citizens. Oyster and chili supper planned for February 6th.

2/6/41: The Legion considered buying the Trueblood estate for a municipal bathing beach. They agreed to send Ray Andersen, draftee, a carton of cigarettes when his address was known.

5/1/41: The Adjutant reported, "Received a letter from Reibolt Studios of a picture of our prettiest Island girl as a sort of contest. This matter has been put aside, because all our girls are pretty and we would have to send them all." [Reibolts was a photo studio in Sturgeon Bay and quite a number of high school graduation pictures were done by them.]

The finance officer reported contacting Art Wickman regarding the Trueblood property. It is available for $6.00 per foot for the first 100 feet of shoreline and $7.00 per foot for for additional shoreline. This had been reported to be stony, so that is out.

Krause spoke about school consolidation.

6/12/41: The Legion will buy two nickel slot machines at not over $40.00 each and charge 50% of the proceeds for the use of the machines. It was decided to have a parade float on July 4th.

7/10/41: A motion was.passed to pay Mrs. Grace Jessen, ten dollars this year for use of the baseball field. At the July.4th baseball game $26.00 was collected by passing the hat and $20.75 was paid out. The pitcher received four dollars.

Dr. Dorchester has an oxygen regulator he will sell cheaply. The Service Officer will contact Dr. Farmer regarding this.

7/24/41: The Lions and Legion will each pay $7.50 to buy the oxygen regulator from Dr. Dorchester.

Haldor Gudmundson talked about collecting aluminum and funds for the USO.

8/7/41: The Federal Rural Electric Administration allotted $91,000 to electrify the Island. The contract to be let in late August and work to start early in October. No mechanical diggers will be used if local labor is available. It is planned to spend $25,000 to $40,000 of the allotment for local labor and expenses. The project calls for 60 miles of wire, 500 imported power poles and 75 to 100 kilowatt generating power. 200 homes will be wired or re-wired, if they presently have Delco or Kohler lighting plants. [It was noted that no local poles would be used, as some of them were hollow.]

8/21/41: It was suggested that conscientious objectors who were forced into the Army should not be entitled to receive cigarettes given by the Legion, but a carton would be sent to each draftee or volunteer. The Scout cabin will soon be paid for and plans were made for a mortgage burning celebration. Need for a bathing beach with a dressing house was discussed.

10/2/41: A bathing beach was discussed with Al Shellswick and he is thinking of donating a 100' wide strip reaching from the south side of Detroit Harbor Road to the beach where Stelters home now stands. Claude Cornell asked the Legion to help with labor or funds to construct a ski jump.

10/31/41: Ralph Jacobsen reported that the last Civil War veteran in Wisconsin has died. This will be mentioned in his Armistice Day program.

11/3/41: The slot machines are to be returned as soon as possible. Roy Richter will get the address of the person from whom they were purchased.

11/27/41: The Lions have suggested that the Town procure at least one tank of oxygen. There is about $200 of money in the Sturgeon Bay Red Cross chapter for buying oxygen masks-costing about $5 each. It has been common through the years to buy fruit or other appropriate gifts for the sick.

11/27/41: A letter was read regarding getting U.S. Marine Corps recruits.

1/2/42: List of Island service men we could think of:

Edwin Johnson, David Kincaide, Harold Saabye, George Jorgenson, Ray Andersen, Maynard Olson, Roger Peterson, Vernon Knutson, Harold Flath, Charles Gislason

1/22/42: Decision was made to disregard trying to get a skating rink for the time being. Legion will hold the President's Ball at Tom's Hall on Jan. 31st. Admission-25¢.

Ray Andersen, Stuart Sorenson, and Alvin Cornell attended the meeting and they will be leaving for camp in a few days.

2/19/42: A good discussion on Civilian Defense was held.

3/4/42: As there were no expenses, $39 profit was made at the President's Ball. Bingo will be held on March 14th to help pay expense for those persons called away for Civilian Defense instruction. The Legion will survey the Island for rifles, ammunition and field glasses. An article concerning this will be placed in the "*Islander*" paper.

4/16/42: Arnold Klingenberg was appointed Fire Chief and he plans to organize a volunteer Fire Department soon. A vote was passed to allow veterans of WWII to join Legion Post 402.

5/7/42: The Color Guards will be Ralph Jacobsen and Ray Krause. Color Bearers will be Conrad Andersen and Delbert Klingenberg. Ethel Hankuper will make the wreaths and be paid to do so. It was suggested that the large Island Coffee Pot be moved as it is a traffic hazard. [Where was it located?]

7/2/42: A letter was received from August Gislason offering the Croix de Guerre which was posthumously awarded to Charles Gislason who was killed in battle in WW I. The Post agreed to accept and display it with no responsibilty for fire or theft.

The Adjutant will write to Dr Driscoll for help in getting a dentist for the Island.

7/16/42 They learned that, if contacted, Dr. Johns, Sister Bay, may come to the Island to do dental work.

8/20/42 The Post is heading up the collection of old phonograph records. Town trucks will haul scrap paper from the schools to the boats.

10/1/42 Schools will be asked to participate in the Armistice Day program. Patriotic songs will be printed.

10/15/42 There are 22 paid-up Legion members at $1. each.

12/3/42 It is suggested that all members go to church on the afternoon of January 1, 1943 to observe a day of prayer for Armed Forces men, as requested by the U.S. President.

12/17/42 The venison supper grossed $63.33 with $25 expenses.

3/12/42 A letter was sent to the Senior Coast Guard officer, 9th Naval District, Chicago, requesting consideration for a listening amplifier for aircraft detection at Plum Island. This is considered to be an ideal spot for aircraft detection to warn Sturgeon Bay Canal, shipyards and points south.

6/3/42 Ernie Boucsein was appointed National Defense Chairman for our Post.

2/17/42 Ray Krause was appointed Air Raid Warden. The County Commander had requested that a Legionaire accept this post.

The following letter was sent:

James P. Christensen,Pastor
Trinity Lutheran Church
Washington Island,Wisconsin
The President of the United States
Washington,D.C.

Mr. President:

We, citizens and residents of Washington Island, Door County, Wisconsin, assembled January 1, 1942 pledge our undivided loyalty and support to our country and to our government.

We are determined that every ounce of toil and sacrifice required to push this war to a victorious close shall be put forth.

(signed) James P. Christensen

1/7/42 Post Naval Recruiting Committee--Chairman Clarence Anderson, Mac Magnusson, William Jacobsen, & Charles Johnson.

1/25/42 Private Alec Koyen attended the meeting and told of some interesting experiences.

2/4/43 Leon Cornell's funeral planned. Pallbearers--Charles Johnson, William Jacobsen, Roy Richter, George Cornell, Chester Pederson & Levere Cody. Aber Jessen, who had been in the Casablanca invasion, gave and interesting talk.(Aber was wounded during WW II. It might have occurred there,anyhow he later remarked that the wound occurred in the highest part of his anatomy which happened to be exposed while he was crouching in a foxhole.)

2/18/43 The headstone for Leon Cornell's grave was received.

4/18/43 Legion dues are now $3. per year.

11/4/43 Seventy-two Island men are in the U.S. Armed Forces out of a total Island population of 700 persons.

3/4/43 Motion to co-operate with the Lions for a movie show at Tom's Hall on March 19th-admission 20¢ and 10¢ for children. Proceeds will go to the Red Cross. The show raised $19.24 for the Red Cross. Ralph Jacobsen will be discharged from the Armed Forces so he can do farm work.

4/1/43 Members of Legion Post 402 who are on active military duty are: Ralph Jacobsen, Earl Malloch, Philip Carlson, Otto Lovig and Algot Johnson. The Adjutant will contact the Town Chairman regarding graves registration.

4/15/43 The Soldier's Monument needs repair. Conrad Andersen will see Herman Magnusson about having this done.

For Memorial Day the Legion will have cards printed and sent to all Island boys in the Armed Services.

4/21/43 Plans made for a Father-Son lunch and entertainment with all the Boy Scouts invited. Oysters and weiners will be served. Gordon and Milton Anderson gave interesting talks about their experiences.

5/6/43 It was decided to have printed in the "Islander" paper the correct way to give the Flag Pledge.

5/21/43 A delicious lunch was served by Fern Hansen, Ruth Goodlet and Ethel Hahnkuper.

6/17/43 Legion will get 75 copies of "AT HOME" books for families of Island servicemen. Conrad Andersen to see about cutting the grass at the baseball field.

7/1/43 Members are asked to bring their pictures to hang in our room at Tom's Hall.

7/15/43 Members appointed to serve on the phono record collection committee: Clarence Anderson, Mac Magnusson, Ernie

Boucsein, Conrad Andersen, William Jacobsen, Lawrence Hahnkuper, Delbert Klingenberg and Roland Koyen.

8/4/43 Nearly 300 lbs. of records have been collected. Allen Cornell became the first Post member from WW II. Ralph Jacobsen has been released from the service to do farm work.

9/2/43 The bill for re-roofing the grandstand for Memorial Day services was paid. Wallace Landin, USCG, gave an interesting talk on South Pacific operations.

9/16/43 A tin can and scrap paper drive is planned for September 19th.

9/18/43 A letter was sent to the USCG Commander, Chicago,regarding getting permission to collect scrap metal on Plum Island and other nearby government facilities.

10/6/43 The scrap iron collection will take place on Oct.10th. Lieut. Merrill Cornell who is home on furlough was a guest.

10/21/43 A deer hunt is being organized.

11/4/43 Venison is being prepared at West Harbor Resort for a dinner.

12/2/43 Clifford Young, home on leave, talked on his experiences.

5/4/45 $15 was appropriated towards a roadside Honor Roll of Island men in the service.

5/18/43 The Plum Island Coast Guard was invited to march with Legionaires on Memorial Day.

6/15/44 William Jacobsen, Mac Magnusson, Conrad Andersen and Clarence Anderson will help the Boy Scouts in hauling scrap paper to the boat. Ernie Boucsein's and Lawrence Hahnkuper's trucks will be used.

7/6/44 It was decided to buy lumber to build a Bingo stand.

7/20/44 The Legion will buy a hospital bed and run Bingo to pay for it.

8/3/44 Both Bingo and a Wheel will be used at the ball park on Sunday,August 6th.

9/7/44 Milton Schmitt sent a check for $25. to help pay for the hospital bed. Floyd Koyen joined the Post.

9/21/44 Ray Krause will contact the Abe Jessen home heirs regarding the possibility of purchasing this property. Captain Hans Baasch attended the meeting.

10/5/44 Captain Baasch,just back from England, gave a talk on the economy and discussed the need for an Island Community Center.

10/16/44 Ernie Boucsein reported on the cost of slot machines and it was decided the prices were too high.

10/20/44 It was decided to send the Legion magazine to all Island servicemen who are overseas.

12/7/44 Clarence Anderson is to contact Nor Shellswick regarding buying his large store (Presently Holiday Two). Lorman Greenfeldt, home on leave, was present and joined the Legion. Roy Cornell, Navy Seabees, made a "short and peppy call".

2/l/45 A social meeting was planned, smoked fish to be served, and the Auxiliary was invited.

3/l/45 The Island doctor will order an operating lamp and bill our Legion. 100 "An Open Letter to G.I. Joe" pamphlets were ordered to explain the G.I. bill and Home Loan Provisions for all returning servicemen.

3/26/45 A special meeting was called to arrange for a military funeral for the late Legion Commander Ernie Boucsein who died unexpectedly on March 26. Clarence Anderson to be in charge. Color Bearers - Conrad Andersen and Delbert Klingenberg. Color guards- Floyd Koyen and Glen Sorenson.

Pall bearers - Mac Magnusson, Charles Johnson, Ray Krause, Rolland Koyen, William Jacobsen and Roy Richter.

Honorary pallbearers - All Lions members as he belonged to that club. Chester Pederson and Mac Magnusson to handle the flag over the casket. Bugler - Bill Engelson, Jr. who will be paid. When the meeting adjourned, all members went to the Boucsein home to pay their respects.

4/5/45 The surgical lamp for the doctor cost $72. Legion paid.

4/19/45 Bingo on April 14th grossed $66.45. Sgt. Roland Koyen was a guest at the meeting. He is with the U.S. Weather Forecasting Department and expects to be sent overseas soon.

5/17/45 Staff Sgt. Everett Ellefson, Air Force, was a guest. He is flying over the Western Front from England.

6/7/45 The Red Cross was requested to provide a bank of plasma for the Island. Moneys collected on Memorial Day will be used to purchase shutters and doors for the Speakers Stand near the Soldiers Monument.

7/5/45 The Legion will pay for a wheel chair which the doctor will order. Robert Gunnerson donated lumber for the improvements planned for the Speakers Stand.

8/16/45 Bob Johnson, U.S.Army, and Lloyd Ohrman, Merchant Marine were guests at the meeting.

9/20/45 There are now 15 WW II veterans in our Post: Theresa Gudmundson, Robert Johnson, Philip Peterson, Charles Gislason, Gilbert Falk, Harley Hanson, Donovan Sorenson, Hans Baasch, Roland A. Koyen, Roger Peterson, Allen Cornell, Charles Magnusson, David Kincaide, C.Paul Anderson and Hector F. Koyen.

9/6/45 The Legion ordered another hospital bed.

10/4/45 Harley Hanson invited the members to his home after the meeting to see Don Olson's war collection and to have lunch. Don was a guest for the evening. Cliff Vogel offered to let the Post store the hospital equipment in his bakery(now Rupipers).

10/18/45 The Legion offered to pay not over $10 towards wiring the library. (This was the first public library on the Island and was offered by the Detroit Harbor Ladies Aid who still own the building just east of Don Lockhart's on Detroit Harbor Road.)

11/1/45 Jacob Gunnlaugsson will be asked if he will sell the northwest corner of the former John Cornell property (Main & Michigan Rds.) to the Legion for a hall site.

11/15/45 New members--Alex Koyen, Lenard Ellerbrock and Klemmet Ellefson. Mrs. Jacob Gunnlaugsson said they will sell 10 acres for $1000. Legion will contact Mr. Schmidt with an offer of not over $75. per acre for the 10 acre lot opposite Gunnlaugssons.(Site of the present Baylake Bank.)

11/26/45 A report was given on the action of the Lions Club in obtaining a community hall for the Island. A Legion "straw vote" was taken regarding the Lions plan for raising money for a community center and over $800. was unofficially subscribed. Legion members present agreed only if it was to be a Legion hall as they figured the community hall project would never pan out as not much had been done. The Lions suggested that the Legion drop their hall plan and come in on the community center project. Interested organizations such as Ladies Aid, Ladies Auxiliary, Women's Club, American Legion, Lions Club, Garden Club, etc.are to appoint one or more persons to act on the Community Committee. According to Mrs. Wally Jorgenson, Secretary, there is now $1000 in the community hall treasury. Edward Anderson and William Engelson have offered locations.

12/6/45 We were honored by having Legionaire Mrs. Gene Gislason attend her first meeting with us. It is planned to give "little tots" candy at the community Christmas tree on Christmas Eve - Gene Gislason will be chairman of this event. A few years ago Conrad Anderson offered a lot for the Legion Hall - he has now withdrawn the offer, but was thanked for his original generosity.

1/3/46 A request has been made to change the name to Gislason-Richter Post No. 402. Discussion on acquiring a Legion hall centered around either the old Baptist Church or Jackson Harbor school. Philip Peterson was chosen as chairman on this project and he will appoint his own committee.

1/17/46 A Legion sign will be posted at the ferry dock.

2/7/46 A wheel chair was ordered, Bingo will help to pay for it. Motion passed to get 10 rifles for the firing squad. There was a discussion on getting oxygen masks for the Island. Hospitality cards were sent to draftees William Engelson, Jr.and Walter Jorgenson.

2/21/46 The Adjutant will write to the Baptist Convention to get a set price on the old Baptist Church. Gordon Jepson and Ernie Lockhart joined.

3/7/46 The following committee will examine the Baptist Church property: C. Paul Andersen, Chairman, Ray Krause, Gordon Jepson and Conrad Andersen. Apparently the land extends to about 10' north of Mann's garage according to George Mann.

3/9/46 Bingo grossed $77.35 and every article was sold.

3/16/46 A special meeting was held to discuss the purchase of the old Baptist Church. Four different appraisal prices were offered ranging from $1500 to $2000.A vote was taken and the price agreed upon by the majority was sent to the Baptist Convention, 709 N. llth Street, Milwaukee. On April 13,1946 the following response was received:

WISCONSIN BAPTIST STATE CONVENTION

April 13, 1946

Clarence J. Anderson
Post Adjutant
Charles Gislason Post No. 402
Washington Island, Wisconsin

Dear Sir:

Your letter of April 10th just received. I wish I had had it a few days earlier.

I wrote you under April llth in regard to this matter, but as long as your intention was that your bid.of $1500.00 was for the property as it stands, including the bench seats, bell, stove, building, and lot, we shall accept the $1500.00 as per your understanding. The matter is too small to hold up the deal as far as we can see it. If there should be any articles belonging to individuals, their rights, of course, will be respected.

Trusting everything will be clear, I am
Sincerely yours

T. Knudsen

3/16/46(Cont'd) A social meeting was set for April 4th with the Auxiliary and all ex-service men invited. The meal will be served at Idabo Inn with tickets costing $1.

A progressive card party is planned at Tom's Hall with cash prizes and a 50¢ admission charge.

4/6/46 It was recommended that we pay $100 per year principal plus interest, "or as we can pay". Post members to have the first chance to loan the amount for the property before seeking other sources. Membership fees raised to $4. next year to help pay the taxes.

4/18/46 Arnold Goodlet and Merrill Cornell joined. If the Legion acquires the Baptist Church, Trinity Lutheran Church would like to buy the bell for their reconstructed church. It was suggested that the Post donate the bell as a jesture of goodwill.

4/18/46 The following were selected as color bearers: Ray Krause and Conrad Anderson. Firing squad members are: Cdr. Elmer Mossak, Merrill Cornell, Philip Peterson, Ray Andersen, Gene Gislason, Moy Hansen, Stuart Sorenson, Alex Koyen, Gilbert Falk, Orin Engelson and Len Ellerbrock.

A motion was passed to borrow $2000 for purchase of old Baptist Church and for improvements. It was suggested that each member loan the Post $30 and with 54 Legionaires this would bring in $1620. The Commander and Adjutant were authorized to sign the papers for the property.

Rifles were received with about 1" of grease on them. Adjutant Clarence Anderson cleaned the rifles. Also received was 200 rounds of ammunition at a cost of $18. including shipping.

5/2/46 The Town Assessor believes that the property won't come under taxation. Legion has first chance to buy 5 acres south of the church, extending to Jack Anderson's, for $500, but it must be bought imediately.

Dan Lindahl offered a $50 gift towards the Legion Hall. Others also wish to donate.

5/17/46 Motion passed to buy the 5 acres south of the church from Jim Boyce for a ballpark. The committee to collect donations to pay for the land includes Theresa Gudmundson, Elayne Gislason, Harley Hansen, Clarence Anderson and Moy Hansen. The commander asked Minnie Richter about having a memorial service for her son, Ludlow, on Memorial Day. He was killed in a plane crash in the Orient at the close of WWII. It was suggested that he be interred next to Charles Gislason. She agreed and the Gislason family gave permission to do so. Color bearers were Elayne Gislason and Theresa Gudmundson. Orin Engelson was the bugler. It was reported that the ceremony was one of the finest.

Donations received for buying the 5 acres for the ball park: Al Shellswick-$10; Curt Johnson-$l; Hansen Bros-$50; Mr. Gentry$10; Carlie Jessen- $10; Tom Nelson-$10; Dan Lindahl-$35; Ray Ransome-$35. Pledge; McDonalds-$50.

Charles McDonald became a new member.

5/6/46 Carlie Jessen offered the hall and half the orchestra cost for the July 4th dance.

Discussion as to whether the 5 acres is big enough for a ball field. Moy Hansen and Gordy Jepson are to look into this.

6/20/46 The 5 acres is not large enough for a ball park. Added land may have to be bought, or other acreage such as the 10 acres west of Trinity Lutheran Church. Jim Hansen was selected to chair this project. Moy Hansen and Roland A. Koyen will assist him.

A supper is planned on July 13th for about 100 persons. Guests will be arriving with the State Commander.

7/2/46 At a special meeting a motion was passed stating that when the Legion owns the church property they will sell to George Mann a half acre of the garage land for $150 with the understanding "that 1/2 interest belongs to the post as for the well". (This continued for many years as a shared well until the Island Insurance Co. offered to have the Post tie into their much newer well.)

7/2/46 Motion passed to buy one acre south of the church for $100. Motion to buy the 10 acre field west of Trinity Lutheran Church for $1000 for future baseball field.(Rescinded.) Popular opinion was negative on this site. Jack Hagen seems to want to offer the Legion whatever land they need--give,sell or lease. Ray Andersen to take over this project. The four remaining acres south of the church will be bought by Conrad Schmidt. The July 4th dance grossed $224.40 with expenses for the Two Rivers Orchestra at $110.Carlie paid the Post $25. towards the cost of the orchestra. The wheel stand at the ball park took in $96.24 and $102.20. Soda pop stand cleared $14.63 with the pop costing $6. Milton Smith gave the Legion $50 and a gas stove.

7/18/46 Ray Andersen will get a lease from Arnold Klingenburg for the ball park.

Reverend Svendsen reported on plans for a Memorial Service for Ludlow Richter at Trinity Lutheran Church on July 21st. Members are to attend in uniform and assist with the service.

8/2/46 The Hall is now transferred over to the Post and Atty. Minor of Sturgeon Bay did the legal work for free. A request was made not to sell any land to George Mann, but this was later rescinded. Ray Andersen reported that Klingenburg will give a five year lease for the ball park. Clarence Anderson will begin wiring our hall on August 5th. It was agreed he should be paid for his work. Clarence volunteered to get a flag pole erected.

8/15/46 Clarence won't accept pay for his work, so the Post gave him and son, Paul, two cartons of cigarettes. Ray Krause will get insurance for the Post building. A motion was passed to get a larger Jungers heater for the hall. Rev. Svendsen will take care of the obsolete books that were in the hall when purchased. Clyde Koyen welded the flag pole together. Clarence Anderson and Percy Young put it up. There was a discussion about having basketball court in Nor's store. (Formerly Wade's Tavern, now Holiday Two.)

9/5/46 Donations of $187.50 were turned in. Rev. Svendsen knows of a Clinton, Wis. church that needs a bell. A motion was made to sell it for $25 and they would have to come and get it. Milton Anderson joined the Post.

9/19/46 The Committee inspected Anchor Inn for possible use as a Community Hall. Arnold Klingenburg's price is $5000 including the buildings, 1 3 acres and 187' of waterfront. (North of Red Barn)

Clarence Anderson reported that Pete Peterson wants the mortgage on the hall changed from 20 years to 5 years. Our attorney will make the change. Milton Anderson donated a carved wooden ship model. We can now get emergency oxygen systems's parts from the War Assets Board. The Post has a standing order at Ted Gudmundson's store for $2. for funeral flowers. The Post gave $5. to the Island Tourist Bureau. Elmer Sorenson and Charles Worthington were visitors at the meeting. Elmer joined the Post.

Paul Anderson reported on tree hazards at the airport that needed removal. He will chair this committee with the assistance of Conrad Andersen and William Jacobsen.

10/3/46 Paul Goodman and Everett (Steve) Ellefson were welcomed as new members. Roland Koyen suggested a "Teen-ager" program using our hall for movies and dances and to get a youth orchestra started. The Community Center Committee is going ahead with buying the Anchor Inn, formerly Gislason's store, but plan to use our building for the present. Lions donated $50 to the Legion towards paying for the building.

10/12/46 Conrad Andersen has given $10.for the Legion building. The deed to the hall has been placed in the REA safe. Members discussed adding a building wing for more room at meetings. George Cornell offered a $1000 mortgage at 3% interest. Mac Magnusson suggested that members buy interest bearing bonds to cover the mortgage.

It was suggested that a WWII plaque be added to the Veteran's Monument near our present high school (now Art & Nature Center.)

11/7/46 New members are Harvey Jensen, Milton Dulong, Kenneth Gunnlaugsson, Marlyn Jepson, Len Atkins, Eldon & Doris Ettinger. Motion passed to make Clarence Anderson a life member. A discussion on enlarging the upstairs for a meeting room. Motion passed to extend the balcony (this existed in the old church)-Lawrence Hahnkuper will be in charge of construction. Hall donations: Chris Andersen-$10, Ray Andersen-$10, Phil Carlson-$10, William Jacobsen-$4.

11/21/46 Adele Cornell donated her piano to the Post.

Lawrence Hahnkuper has the lumber for the balcony extension and members are to work in the evenings to finish this. A discussion on having the Community Hall as a WWII Memorial. The Legion approved this with the consideration of a plaque to be brought up later. Legion Hall donations: Clyde Barber-$10, Kenneth Gunnlaugsson-$10, Fred M. Hanson-$2.

12/19/46 Eldon Hettinger will paint the new balcony addition. Discussed donating uniforms to the baseball team. Motion passed to give Stuart Sorenson his 1947 membership as a Christmas gift along with $1.50 worth of fruit. Elmer Mossak will present the gift.

1/2/47 Karl Jessen donated $10 to the Post. $36.70 was collected at the New Year's Eve dance from selling hats, horns,etc. There are enough supplies still on hand for another dance.

We need action in getting a government headstone for Ernie Boucsein's grave. Motion passed to give Lawrence Hahnkuper an old Army rifle for his fine work at the Post. Plans made for Schafskof (card) Tournament and Bunco Party by the Auxiliary on January llth.

1/16/47 Ray Andersen reported that the baseball field lease with Arnold Klingenburg will be signed when he gets a clear property title.

2/6/47 Eldon Hettinger reported on Schafskof Tournament. Profits--lst week-$28.40, 2nd week-$31.50, total net profit is expected to be $150. It was suggested that on the last night of the tournament a party be held with music and entertainment. Clarence Anderson suggested that the Legion sponsor a school police patrol. Eldon suggested creating a library at the Post with books regarding members' Divisions or service history.

2/20/47; 35 teenagers attended the Valentine's Day party; bingo, cards and dancing provided the entertainment. George Miller will give a prize for the children each night we sponsor a party. Next week Jacob Ellefson and Tom Cook will assist Clarence Anderson in giving the party.

Committee assigned to help the Lions re-organize the Boy Scouts is Roger Hagen, Charles Magnusson and Paul Goodman. Rev. Svendsen thanked the Legion for the use of the hall as a church while the new Lutheran Church was being constructed. Also a letter of thanks was received from the congregation.

3/6/47 Ernie Lockhart and Duane Jacobsen joined. Donations from George Nelson (Spencer's father) -$50., Angus Swenson-$10.

4/3/47 Legion donated $25. to the baseball team for equipment. Total profit from Schapskopf tournament was $133.75. Donations from George Johnson, Sr.-$20, Rev. Svendsen-$10.

4/17/47 George Mann donated cedar posts for repairs to ball field bleachers. Motion passed to pay up to $50 for a juke box from Bill Johnson.

6/5/47 Rev. Lundberg was given permission to use one of our flags at Bethel Church during the summer.

6/19/47 The Legion will have a roulette wheel and bingo at the ball park on July 4th. There is $1623.54 in the checking account after paying Pete Peterson $100 principal and $15. interest on the mortgage.

7/17/47 $1500 on the principal and $100 interest was paid on the mortgage to Pete Peterson, who then gave a $5. donation to the Post. Gordon Jepson is chairman of the committee to raffle the wooden sailboat model made by Milton Anderson. A $5.gift with a get-well card was sent to Milton at the U.S. Marine Hospital, Chicago.

8/7/47 Charles Gislason contacted an Escanaba orchestra for $130. to play at the Labor Day dance. Ray Krause will make the tickets.

9/4/47 The model boat raffle netted $136.--winner- George Johnson,Sr.

10/18/47 The Post will sponsor a basketball team. Committee for this will be Orin Engelson, Leonard Ellerbrock and Eldon Hettinger. Schafskopf tournament will be held every Monday night from Nov. 17 through Dec. 15. Toilets are to be built on the property before the tournament. Marvin Jepson joined.

11/6/47 Harley Hansen represented the Legion at an airport meeting in Sturgeon Bay to discuss the main things needed at our airport with a figure of $19,500 for improvements. Post now has $171.41 in the bank.

11/20/47 The school safety program is under way with Franklin Hansen and Donald Lockhart sworn into the safety patrol. West Harbor Resort can serve 100 people a ham dinner at $1.50 for the upcoming banquet. Post will charge $1.75 with 25 cents going into the Legion treasury.

Plans made to close off the balcony to the roof to help with heating. Ivan McHenry joined the Post and he and Mickey Jepson will help with the wall construction.

12/4/47 Jack Hanson joined the Post.

12/18/47 Gordon Jepson, Len Atkins, Ray Andersen and Charles Magnusson volunteered to dig the toilet hole next Monday.

1/15/48 The cost of the toilet was about $40, instead of the $58. estimate.

3/4/48 Present insurance is for $1600, but Ray Krause will have it adjusted to insure to the fullest. Post considered the possibility of sending a boy to Boy's State.

4/15/48 Wayne Boshka was selected to go to Boy's State (now Badger State).(Since then the Post has sent boys and girls regularly to these annual events where they practice running mock governments.) Motion passed to assist the Lions in erecting and painting a new scoreboard at the Ball park.

11/4/48 Victor Cornell is chairman of the committee to repair the roof on our hall.

1/9/49 The New Years Eve dance netted $92. Harley Hansen and Karly Jessen donated the hall.

1/20/49 Trina Richter offered to sell a large oil stove to the Post for $100. Unfortunately it was not considered large enough to heat the hall.

Charter Members of Charles Gislason Auxiliary No. 402 as signed and posted in the Legion Hall were:

Cecelia L. Magnusson (lived across from present Post Office),

Camilla C. Cornell (Now Walter Jorgensons)

Alice N. Cornell

Fern A.Cody (Now Kahlscheuers)

Hildegard A. Anderson (Now Viking Village)

Ruth M. Vogel (Home on Rangeline Rd. south of Williamsons)

A.Martha Malloch (Now Jack Cornells)

Violet C. Hanson (She and Bill started Cedar Lodge)

Kathryn Richter (Home south of Viking Village)

Julia A. Pederson (Home east of new condos-Detroit Harbor)

Emma A. Johnson (Now Fred Youngs, Jackson Harbor)

Dorothy M. Lovig (Now Bob Youngs)

Elizabeth V. Peterson (Now Thor Williamsons)

Ruby F. Boucsein (Now Dave Johnsons)

Adele C. Cornell (Camilla's daughter)

Marilyn Magnusson (Cecilia's daughter)

Esther W. Krause (Now Rob Carrs)

Ethel I. Hahnkuper (Now Brian McDonalds)

Mary Koyen (Now Mildred Goodman Jacobsens)

Christine Stenna Gunnlaugsson

(The Auxiliary organized shortly after the Island Legion Post and is still very active.)

2/3/49 Clarence Anderson gave the Post $25 under the condition that Roger Hagen, 2nd Vice Cdr., act as commander for this meeting. The Post will contact Wayne Boshka, last year's Boys State selectee, for his opinion on sending a boy this year.

3/3/49 Excess stone from Trinity Lutheran Church is available if the Post wants it. Should we sell the land north of the Hall to be used by the town for a fire house? Possible use of the bell at the Lutheran Church is to be referred to a future meeting.

4/7/49 It was decided to postpone sending anyone to Boys State this year. Only one was eligible and he plans to go sailing. The bell was removed by Clarence Anderson and Haldor Gudmundson and given to the Lutheran Church. Clean up of the grounds was started and free lunch and refreshments was served at Gordy's as his guest. A suitable shooting gallery was planned with Clarence Anderson in charge.

4/21/49 The shooting gallery is near completion. The Post donated $25 to the Community House Association with the balance to follow when funds permit. It was decided to let the Coast Guard Auxiliary use the rifle range and hall when they meet. They will return the keys to Gordy's immediately after their meetings. A get-together party with the Sister Bay post is planned with Phil Carlson in charge.

5/5/49 Meeting was immediately adjourned due to the cheese factory fire.

5/12/49 The shooting gallery is finished. Post has offered to sell land to the town for a fire truck building. Len Atkins is to be allowed to buy the first 20' of the NW corner frontage. The town will be offered the next 50' to the full depth of the lot with the Legion retaining the use of the well.

5/19/49 Sister Bay Post #527 will visit us on June 18th. Phil Carlson and Steve Ellefson will make arrangements for accomodations. A fish boil and dance are planned. (This is the first mention in the minutes of the Legion holding a fish boil. In later years it was quite common to hold at least two boils each year to raise money for the Post. Ray Hansen says that our Legion was the first in Door County to have fish boils for the public.) About 50 guests are expected and Milton Anderson has offered to take them back to the mainland on his boat.

6/9/49 $25 was donated to the ball team to help pay costs of their changing the date to have a July 4th game.

6/16/49 Arrangements are being made for a military funeral for Edward Peterson. 20 Legionaires will participate with Rev. Lundberg officiating.

7/7/49 About $500 profit was realized from Post activities at the July 4th celebration. Motion passed to allow the ball team to run the beer and soda concession. If we want the left-over stones from the building of the Lutheran Church we need to get them at once--will be done on 7/15.

7/15/49 There was a nice turn-out of workers for stone hauling, laying in front of hall and leveling of dirt. The mortgage is paid,so the hall is now our own!.

7/21/49 Sturgeon Bay Post desires to join us, possibly on Labor Day, when we burn our mortgage. Maybe we'll have a fish boil and dance.

8/4/49 Donations-Lizzie Hansen for wheel chair use and Pete Peterson gave $5. to the Post. There is $300 in the treasury. Centennial Committee report--The Legion will charge for all concession stands at the ballpark during the celebration with the right to approve, or not, any application. An electric range was hauled and installed by Clarence Anderson and Gordy Jepson. The pantry has been re-modeled with new lumber bought from George Mann.

8/18/49 Ship model tickets are again on sale for the Labor Day Dance.

9/1/49 It *was* decided to heat with oil again this winter. Phil Carlson is in charge of installing an oil barrel outside the back shed wall. Again we will use his oil burning unit. The Auxiliary will have a pancake supper for the public on 9/15. Araold Klingenberg was paid $50 for rent on the ball park. Eldon Hettinger will print a sign to post in front of the hall showing meeting nights.

9/15/49 The Labor Day Dance committee reported spending $15 for lodging the orchestra at West Harbor Resort, $8.40 to Lindsays for meals, net profit was $73.60. A committee was assigned to work with the Lions on rag weed control. Mr Gow, DeKalb, Ill.,will give $100 towards this project. Willis Andersen and Sherman Caple became members. Abstract, Deeds and Satisfaction of Mortgage were received from Atty. Herman J. Leasum with a bill for $20.75 which was marked paid as a donation.

11/3/49 Record show 190 cases of beer bought by the Post this year. Legion used 110, ball club bought 66, Orville Jess sold 5 to Hotel Washington and 7 were unaccounted for--probably used by the stone working party. A request was received to use the hall for square dance practice, this was approved provided they furnish tneir own fuel.

11/17/49 An oyster supper is planned for 11/20 with Roger Hagen in charge and Phil Peterson cooking. Eldon Hettinger will also cook chili. Invitees will be Lawrence and Ruth Gislason, Tom Nelson,Minnie Richter and Karly Jessen. Oysters not used will be sold for $1.75 a quart. They cost $5.20 per gallon. Women's Club requested use of the hall. Also Bethel Ladies Aid wants to conduct a bake sale at our hall. Approved provided they pay for the fuel. Motion passed to present Caroline Erickson with a five dollar bill and nylon hose for her beautiful work in drawing up our Legion charter. Ray Krause to measure for size and present gift. The Post paid Roy Smith $508. for the beer purchased for this season. Captain Milton Anderson gave another ship model to be raffled next summer.

12/1/49 Howard Jacobsen brought a Christmas tree to the hall. Elmer Mossak, Harley Hansen, Gordy Jepson, Len Atkins and Clarence Anderson put it up. 75 light bulbs were purchased from Roger Gunnerson.

1/19/50 Post paid Gordy $2.50 for a case of beer.

2/2/50 A public stag party is planned for 2/23. Movies will be shown,card played and free lunch will be provided with donations accepted for beer. Entrance fee will be 75 cents and door prizes will be awarded.

2/16/50 There will be three reels of stag movies and lunch will consist of rye bread, cheese, sausage, pickles and coffee. Cartons of cigarettes were sent to Phil Carlson who is laid up with a bad leg and Milton Dulong who is in the Marine Hospital.

3/2/50 A request was received for a donation for drilling a well at the Library. Finances for 1949-receipts $1866.89, expenditures-$1692.05. It was suggested that the Legion buy the ball park. The Legion will work with the Lions to get Schoolhouse Beach as Town property.

4/5/50 Arnold Klingenberg asked that no beer sales be made on his property (ball park) except on July 4th. A motion was passed to have no beer sales this summer. Women's Club asked about hall rent prices and was told a charge of $5 for hall and electricity with an added $3 to the Auxiliary if the kitchen was used.

4/20/50 Ship model raffle tickets were reduced to 25 cents, or 5 for $1.

5/4/50 Phil Carlson is chairman of re-naming -on the WW II bronze plaque on the Veterans Monument.(This involves Islanders who had been omitted. Note the names at the bottom of the plaque.) The Lions asked if the Legion would take over the July 4th fireworks. It was recommended that the Lions keep doing this and we will help as in the past. Milton Anderson will contact John Coppersmith (across from Dave's Garage) as a coach for one Junior ball team. (John had played baseball professionally.) Eldon Hettinger has the second team. Motion passed to donate 2 lawn benches to the Fire Oepartment.

5/18/50 Rev. Gordon, who was planning to speak on Memorial Day, is ill. Rev. Paulson will take his place. The Hahnkuper family made 15 wreaths at a cost of $10. The Legion will have the Bethel Church piano tuned as thanks for its use on Memorial Day. The baseball club will take over the ball park and pay the rent. Gordy Jepson painted the Legion flag pole and Milton Anderson furnished a new halyard. Bethel Church wants to fly a flag on Sundays, so we loaned them one.

6/1/50 A party here with the Sister Bay post is planned for June 24th. They will provide cheese, crackers and beer, we will have fish smoked by Roger Hagen.

7/6/50 It was reported that Lindahl and Ellefson donated the fish for the Sister Bay Party. Post commander Orin Engelson, who played with "The Stardusters" at the July 4th Dance, donated his $12 fee to the Post.

9/5/50 Funeral arrangements with color guard and firing squad are being made for Legionaire George Cornell.

9/11/50 The Bingo game scheduled for the last ball game was a flop due to the cold weather. Going away gift to each serviceman (Korean conflict) will be a $2 bill. Building Committee reports the roof must be taken care of as soon as possible.

10/18/50 A special meeting was held to plan H.O. Eione's funeral. There was also a discussion on either repairing our present building or getting a complete new building.

1/2/51 The heart campaign was organized.

1/18/51 The New Year's Eve dance took in $20 at the door; noise makers and favors provided $25.25. The orchestra did not charge, so we made $45.25 profit. A box of cigars was sent to Howard Jacobsen while he was hospitalized with a broken arm.

5/3/51 The 13 members attending voted unanimously to work for a new building. A motion was made to have Clarence Anderson look into selling our building and land. Jake Fessler is to be the Memorial Day speaker. Ray Krause will get flags for the veterans' graves.

6/7/51 The Polka Dots, Algoma, will play at the July 4th dance for $105,which includes their expenses.

7/19/51 A book was sent to Mac Magnusson who is ill. A letter from the Town Chairman requesting money for Dental Equipment was tabled for more information. The Legion will buy a new home plate for the ball field. Also they will donate a prize for the Firemen's Ball.

8/3/51 The Post paid Arnold Klingenberg $50. for rent of the ball field.

8/16/51 Six boxes of clothing were gathered and sent to Kickapoo Valley which was devastated by a flood. A motion was made to "catalogue" the cemetery--no action taken.

9/6/51 Prizes for the fish pond at the upcoming Junior Fair were ordered. Contact Orville Jess or Gunnar Nelson for a popcorn stand.

9/20/51 $10 and a letter of thanks was received from the Catholic Church for use of the hall during the summer. The Boscobel Post sent a thank you letter for the clothing sent during the flood. Hospitality cards will be sent to all servicemen from the Island.

10/4/51 Motion passed to offer the hall for sale for $3000. New building plans to be reviewed at next meeting. Wm.Kincaide transferred from Michigan to our Post.

10/18/51 The Adjutant will write to department headquarters for a plan book for the new Legion hall.

12/6/51 The Legion will donate $10 to the Crusade for Freedom. A Legion bowling tournament was discussed.

1/17/52 The Post was approached to give $50 for dental equipment, with a decision to give $25. $5 was given to the March of Dimes. A card and bingo party will be held on 1/26/52 with another one on 3/8/52.

3/6/52 The Post was asked to provide pallbearers for Kate Koyen's funeral.

4/3/52 $20 was given to the baseball club for new uniforms.

7/3/52 Wellington Lockhart was given a Life Membership.

8/7/52 Clarence Anderson has an offer of $2000 for the Legion building and property. A motion was passed unanimously to sell for $2000.

8/7/52 A fishboil is planned for after the August 31 baseball game. Ellefsons and Lindahl will donate the fish.

11/6/52 It was decided to meet once a month during the winter on the first Thursday with a social event of some kind.

2/5/53 After including the funds from the turkey raffle,it was found that the Christmas party for children cost the Post $3.56. There was much discussion on remodeling the hall.

4/16/53 The main discussion was on the type of roof.

5/7/53 It was decided to borrow $1000 from the Island Insurance Company. The plan was to lower the level of the present building with Milton Anderson as Chairman.

5/21/53 A motion was passed to raise the main room ceiling to 10 feet or more.

7/16/53 A fish boil will be held on August 8 at a cost of $1.25 for all you can eat.

8/6/53 It was decided to use blue colored, good grade asphalt shingles on the roof of the hall.

8/20/53 Admission for Labor Day dance will be 75 cents.

9/17/53 Several members worked on the hall roof. It was agreed that the tower part of the roof would be flat.

11/5/53 The supports for the roof were put up.

4/1/54 As the Department Commander is planning to visit, everyone is asked to catch and freeze perch for a French-fried dinner when he arrives.

5/6/54 Building work nights are Thursday, Friday and Sunday P.M.

7/15/54 A fishboil will be held on Saturday, August 8.

8/19/54 A fried perch supper will be held on Sunday, Sept. 5. Adults- $1.50, children- $1.

9/16/54 Ceiling blocks, 16" x 32", will be installed.

1/6/55 The lower room walls will be covered with celotex boards laid horizontally.

5/5/55 The Post will buy flags for veteran's graves and will get markers to sell at cost to relatives.

6/16/55 Admission at the July 4 dance will be $1. A $5 door prize will be given.

8/15/55 The Post will have a perch fry on Aug.28 from 5 to 7 P.M. at $1.25 per plate. A letter was received from Chaplain Roy Mumm asking that there be no beer drinking during meetings. A resolution was passed that drinking or serving intoxicating drinks be discontinued until after meetings are adjourned.

9/1/55 As Legion regulations are to take down flags from veteran's graves shortly after Memorial Day this should be promptly done. Ray Hansen volunteered to do so.

10/6/55 It was decided to hire a few men to finish the outside of the hall.

11/3/55 It was agreed to insulate the walls of the building.

3/1/56 A controversy has developed between the Legion and the University of Wisconsin regarding the use of the UW Campus by subversive groups.

5/3/56 It was agreed to give Clarence Anderson some of the old pews from the Baptist Church if he fixes the rest for our hall.

6/7/56 $150 worth of fireworks were ordered. Two men will collect donations from businesses and five men will collect at the ball park on the evening of the fireworks.

(It seems that misunderstandings and school problems occurred at this time. I found this in the Legion records.)

"The American Legion, through no fault of its own, seems to have become involved in the school controversy. It has been severely criticized, and we feel that some of you at least would like to know the facts.

We are not out to get a large handout as some of you say and we had nothing to do with this controversy. The school board asked us on June 7, 1956 if our building would be available for school use in case of emergency.

Let me quote from our Minutes of June 7, 1956 'A motion was made and seconded that our American Legion Hall be made available, (FREE) for school use in case of emergency. A vote was taken by ballot as follows: For the Motion-14 votes; Against the motion-None.'

Our past record should be enough to correct some of these crazy rumors.

1.When the Lutheran Church burned, we allowed the congregation to use it until the new church was finished,FREE.

2. We let the Catholics use it several years, FREE.

3.We let other organizations use it on numerous occasions, all FREE, such as, Bethel Ladies Aid, Women's Club, Bake Sales, etc."

(Note on bottom) Mr. Chairman, I would like this letter to be kept for future reference if necessary.

7/5/56 We will plant trees in front and lay a concrete sidewalk. A fish boil will be held on July 22 with the Auxiliary getting 25% of the profits.

8/2/56 Another fish boil will be held on Aug. 12 from 4 to 7 P.M.

8/16/56 Ray Krause, Harley Hansen and Len Atkins will serve as a committee regarding our hall use for school purposes.

8/28/56 The Lions want to use our hall for a fish boil for 40 persons from Checked Dairy Products. The Legion will receive 50% of the net and four Legionaires will assist.

10/4/56 New members are C.V. Shepherd and Ben Walden.

3/7/57 In a discussion on the fair to be held in August the Post decided to operate the shooting gallery.

5/2/57 The hall can be used for Catholic services this summer.

6/20/57 Two dances will be held over Independence weekend on July 4th and 6th-admission $1. At Clarence Anderson's request the motion was rescinded to make him an Honorary and paid-up member. (Several times before the Post had tried to make him a Life Member, but he would not accept it although he had certainly earned it for all the volunteer work he had done over the years.)

6/18/57 At the shooting gallery at the Fair - 4 shots will cost 25 cents--3 shots in the black will win $1.

9/5/57 From now on instead of giving flowers when a Legionaire dies, the Post will provide the grave marker from which an American flag will be flown on Memorial Day. Markers will also be on sale for $4.

10/3/57 22 squares of material are needed to cover the outside of the hall. This will be done instead of painting.

2/6/58 The Legion will make the same contribution towards the baseball team as the Lions.

9/4/58 A motion was passed to give $25 towards Xray equipment.

11/6/58 The Town Chairman explained the proposed non-profit organization on Medical Matters. Mac Magnusson will represent the Post.

12/4/58 Plywood was purchased to cover the upstairs floor.

4/2/59 The Post stood in silence in memory of Clarence Anderson.

9/17/59 Plans were made to install running water in the hall with Ray Krause in charge.

10/1/59 Motion passed to spend not over $160 for water works and drainage.

2/4/60 Milton Anderson will finish kitchen cupboards and install sink.

3/3/60 A stag party will be held on March 17th with rye bread and cheese served. Commander Marvin Jepson volunteered to make a sign for the hall.

7/7/60 It was decided to write a letter to Hildegard Anderson telling her that the ground improvements, stone wall and concrete were being dedicated to the memory of Clarence.

7/21/60 Ray Krause wil l make one basket and order two more buckets for fish boils.

8/4/60 Ray Krause will make two more fish boil baskets.

4/6/61 $10 was given to the Bethel Building Fund.

5/4/61 This year's first fish boil will be held on the Sunday before July 4th.

5/18/61 $25 was pledged to Little League baseball.

6/l/61 It was decided to publish Estelle Richter's essay. (This was apparently presented at the Memorial Day program.)

9/7/61 Plans were made for adding washrooms and storage on the back of the Legion hall.

9/21/61 Jack Hagen talked on the proposed Rock Island State Park.

8/9/62 Motion passed to pay Berns Bros. $125 less 2% for added building materials, with some to be returned. It was decided to have the time of Catholic service changed to accomodate the Legion fish boils.

1/10/63 The Legion will explore showing movies at the hall.

4/4/63 The Town requested that the Legion nominate 3 members with one being selected by the Town to serve on a Park Committee. Mac Magnusson, Harley Hansen and Walter Miller were nominated.

5/16/63 Fish boils will be held on July 4, August 4 and September 1.

9/19/63 Ray Krause wil contact Okie 0'Connell regarding the installation of a heating plant in the hall.

11/7/63 Building insurance will be increased to $8000.

FOREST PRODUCTS

This series will be about forest products that were marketed from the Island. Most of the information is from the Archives' copies of the Advocate from the 1860s and on. Earlier info is from Conan Eaton's notes at the Archives. "Tusen takke" (thousand thanks) to Barbara Ellefson and Goodwin Berquist for their assistance at the Archives.

1679 - The Lawrence University group who dug artifacts on Rock Island found cedar poles and planks, shaped with adzes, as remains of early buildings; dating back to that year.

1832 - Fishermen were living in a log shanty on Detroit Island.

1835 - Government surveyors ran "subdivisions and meander lines of Washington Island and Rock Island." Two chainmen and an axe man worked under Deputy Surveyor Sylvester Sibley. He also entered "a brief appraisal of both land and timber." He mentioned sugar (maple) led with 36, then beech - 33, hemlock - 27, aspen - 26, spruce - 25, ironwood - 18, cedar - 17, birch - 15, and pine - 12. One statement referred to "some scattering on pine." [While the count of pine trees was small, many were four feet or larger in diameter at the base and these trees accounted for a vast amount of the lumber taken from the Island. I wonder if what he labeled as "spruce" we called "balsam." Further, the species count could vary a great deal depending on what part of the Island it was taken on. Differences in soil composition and terrain influenced what trees would grow.]

1840s - A "wooding station" on the north end of Rock Island furnished cordwood for the boilers on steamers going from Mackinac to Green Bay. There was no dock, but the wood was slid down to the water then boats or rafts were used to transport it to the steamer lying offshore. The wood cutters did not own the land, but merely "helped themselves" to the trees.

1852 - James and William Crawl bought the Washington Harbor west shore and land. They set up a sawmill above the dock (near present Kleinhans home).

1852-53 - That winter Joseph Cornell cut wood and sawed logs for Crawl. After serving in the Civil War, he cut wood for Bert Ranney. Next spring he built a house of planks and left his early log home.

1863 - The Island produced 5800 pounds of maple sugar. Almost every day vessels would leave Washington Harbor with lumber, shingles, bolts, cedar posts, telegraph poles, cordwood, fish, etc.

1865 - The assessor valued fish barrel staves at $6 per thousand and good hardwood, on the bank (ready to be shipped) at $1.50 per cord.

By 1870 - 189 acres had been cleared on the Island and agriculture began. In 1870 William Wickman (the Dane who brought the first Icelanders here) and four Icelanders paid Fuller $400 for a 61 acre homestead with 1500 ft. of Detroit Harbor frontage and some fish nets (this was near the present Shipyard Marina). They caught all the fish they could eat in the east channel, but they were short of cash to buy other food and supplies. They decided to cut cordwood for sale. Since there were no trees of any size in their native country, the Icelanders had to be taught how to fell trees and make cordwood. Wickman got McDonald's men from Jackson Harbor to come and teach them. When they had a boat load of cordwood at the shore they got a Milwaukee captain to bring a scow near the beach. The skipper was hesitant to try to navigate Detroit Harbor, so Wickman piloted him across.

The Icelanders made a raft of pine logs on which they loaded the cordwood and poled the raft out to the scow lying in deeper water. When fully loaded the skipper decided to pilot his own vessel across Detroit Harbor, but he ran aground. Using their raft, the Icelanders off-loaded the cordwood onto the nearest beach. This freed the lightened scow which was moved to deeper water and then the laborious task of reloading it took place. [I suspect the Icelanders really earned what they were paid for the wood.] Wickman and the four men got badly needed cash.

1872 An Icelander worked for farmer Koyen peeling bark off cedar logs for telegraph poles. He got 5 cents per log but was planning to shift to cutting trees down, which paid 10 cents each. That year prices per thousand were: lumber-$12, lath & shingles-$3, pickets-$12, and cedar posts-10 cents each. Pine trees five feet in diameter were being cut.

1873 John Furlong bought Ranney's land and mill on the west side of Washington Harbor. Ranney reported that in 1872 shipments from his dock were: 2700 cords of hardwood, 3500 telegraph poles, 25,000 cedar posts and 15,000 packages of fish.

1876 In April 15-20 farmers had previously banded together and they started building a new Washington Harbor dock on Furlong's shore. The town had agreed to make a road to the dock. Several dock cribs and hundreds of logs were piled on the ice. This dock was intended to be for public use and to provide an outlet for the sale of wood. Furlong was shipping his own wood over his dock and was not inclined to let competition use that pier. The farmers had paid shares of $25 each in labor or money.

May 25, 1876 The county sheriff arrived and arrested seven men on a warrant sworn by Furlong, restraining the building of a dock on property claimed by him. Bail was set at $500 each.

June 2,1876 As the Town Board had laid out a road through Furlongs to the shore where the dock was being built, both town road and dock workers were jailed for default of bonds. They complained that Furlong would neither buy their wood or ship it over his dock and now he seeks to prevent their building a dock.

June 22, 1876 The law entitled Furlong to the monopoly. Taxes had been paid for years on "a large tract of very worthless land." (Today's property owners in the Mount Misery, Boyer's Bluff area might take issue with that statement.) "He (Furlong) ships much of his own wood. It might be well for these farmers to turn their efforts to improving the land they have cut over (cleared)," was stated.

May 11, 1876 A full-rigged, split-keel schooner awaited a favorable wind to load white fish and splitbarrel staves.

In the late 1870s John Gislason, with a ship's carpenter and William Bradshaw, were cutting cordwood on a very cold day. Bradshaw was working without a coat on when Gislason mentioned it had been 40° below zero that morning. Bradshaw stopped, donned his coat and said, "I'm not going to work when it's 40 below," and he went home.

1878 Dennis McDonald built a dock on his west side property (Denny's Bluff area) to carry on his wood business. Also Hagan and English purchased pine land and standing timber and were busy getting logs out. Captain J.J. Lobdil (sic) was supervising operations. Wood was selling for 50 cents a cord. (This was a volume of 4' x 4' x 8'.)

1878 Freyberg, Sheboygan, purchased nearly all the pine on the Island for about $2000 on the stump. A. A. Koyen had lots of cordwood ready for shipment.

March, 1879 - John Larson, Town Treasurer, reported that 3000 cords of hardwood had been cut, but there was more attention now to agriculture which was becoming more profitable.

(This part will leave the chronological history to tell the story of Freyberg's mill, West Harbor, as reported through the years by the *Advocate* and *Independent*.)

May 1879 - Freyberg's mill will be situated here, not on St. Martin's Island. It will arrive from Sheboygan as soon as navigation opens up.

July 1879 - Freyberg machinery is here and the mill is going up. There is one large circular saw and a gang edger which will be able to cut 50,000 board feet of lumber daily. Plans were to get most of the logs from the west shore and some from Ellison Bay, via log rafts.

March 1880 - Freyberg had logs piled in West Harbor. By July they had the mill running and were adding lath and shingle mills which were also ready that month. However, a shortage of knot sawyers and packers curtailed their operations. They now had a store at the mill selling to both their workers and the general public. Eight cargoes of lumber had gone to market. They planned to build a good dock. In September, four shingle sawyers and packers arrived from Sheboygan and it was reported they turned out cedar shingles second to none in Door County. In late November a Sheboygan mason was working on Freyberg's new buildings. The mill shut down for the season and the men began working felling trees.

February 1881 - Freybergs broke logging camp in Washington Harbor and all men were employed at the mill. This same year Jens Jacobsen, age 14, came to the Island. He said the Main Road was a trail between pine stumps for hauling cordwood to the Washington Harbor dock for steamer fuel or shipment. Jens was soon hired at Freybergs to pack shingles at 70¢ per thousand and worked there for five seasons. In an 11 hour day the mill cut 30,000 board feet of lumber, 60,000 shingles and several thousand laths. The products, mostly white pine, were shipped via sailing vessel to their Sheboygan yard.

August 1881 - They were busy, but said the log supply was getting short.

January 1883 - Freyberg and Bros. placed the stock of merchandise in the boarding house until spring when a store larger than the one that burned will be built.

March 1883 - They broke logging camp in Washington Harbor, but will haul logs to the mill until sleighing gives out.

February 7, 1883 - The mill roof collapsed causing $500 damage. The boiler stack was warped and tottering, but was soon braced. They had quarters for men to log 300,000 board feet of logs in Washington Harbor. Many more logs were cut at Point aux Barque, Michigan. In June log rafts were towed from Michigan to the mill. That winter 400,000 board feet of pine logs were banked, plus lots of oak and basswood (basswood was largely used for laths). Later the steam barge Burroughs made two trips here with flour, feed, etc. for Freyberg's and Corrigan's stores.

July 1883 - Steamer Julia brought a raft of 200,000 board feet of logs from Point aux Barque to the mill.

January 1884 - Freyberg Bros. planned to remove the saw and shingle mill elsewhere as their supply was nearly exhausted here, still they had cut lots of cordwood.

March 1884 - Freyberg's crew was camping on Andrew Irr's land (east of Foss Road) taking the last mill timber. They then planned to move elsewhere.

May 1884 - Freybergs prepared to operate their mill, but were delayed because of needed boiler repairs. They shipped cedar bolts to Menominee to be sawed into shingles.

Oct. 1884 (This probably occurred on Halloween night.) A ghost appeared at Freyberg's mill in orthodox white, with phosphorus and sulphurous accompaniments. It rang the bell and blew the whistle to the terror and disgust of the watchman.

April 1885 Freybergs have 100,000 board feet of logs at their West Harbor mill and 50,000 board feet at Jackson Harbor. This will probably be their last cutting here, then they'll move elsewhere.

Oct. 1885 Freyberg Bros. shut down their mill.All employees were discharged. They still had several cargoes of lumber on the pier to be shipped.

Nov. 1885 Freybergs were again logging and would continue through at least part of the season. They bought all the pine and hardwood that was available. They established a logging camp and restocked their store. They also cut 16" long stove wood at little more cost than making cordwood. All of the tree could thus be used, not just the 4' sections. The schooner *Industry* hauled hardwood slabs to Sheboygan where they were sawed into stove wood length and commanded a good price. Jan.1886 Freyberg Bros. camp on east side of Island had lots of logs which they hauled by sleigh to the mill.

May, 1887 Ice carried away About 20' of the pier decking, rebuilt this week.

Aug. 1886 Freybergs shut their mill down, but may continue operations if logs become available.

Feb. 1887 Freyberg Bros were rapidly banking logs.

June 1887 Freyberg's mill started again and was doing good work. They had enough stock on hand for nearly the full season.

Aug. 1887 Freybergs closed for the season in late August.

Sept. C.B. Freyberg and Bros. plan to remove their mill either this fall or early spring.They cut no more logs.Their store was still running to collect accounts.

Nov.1887 Freyberg's store was well stocked and the firm was buying all available cedar bolts for their Sheboygan shingle mill.

Dec. 1887 A vast amount of saw logs, piles, ties, posts, cordwood and shingle bolts, both pine and cedar, were being cut. Freyborgs were buying all the logs and bolts they could get. Nels Freis had six men working. Volney Garrett and Ed Peterson had several men cutting shingle bolts and cordwood. Tim Coffey had a large force cutting and hauling cedar. Betts in Jackson Harbor had a crew cutting lots of wood. Freybergs now had a dozen men working and were seeking 20 more. They already had 200 cords of hardwood cut and were hoping to increase to ten times that amount.

April 1888 Freybergs had 1000 cords of hardwood and 250 cords of shingle bolts ready to ship. They were quarrying 50 cords of limestone for their new Sheboygan mill

Feb. 1889 Peter Hansen cut lots of cedar bolts for Freyberg's new Sheboygan shingle-mill.

March 1889 Freybergs teams were hauling cedar for Tim Coffey,Sr. They were about to put a force to work to repair their pier into Green Bay, which was destroyed by an ice shove last spring. A new crib row was to be built outside the old site.

April 1889 Freybergs had 2000 cords of hardwood on the bank in Washington Harbor. Their West Harbor pier was being extended.

Nov, 1889 Herman Freyberg moved the store stock into the boarding house making it easier to tend to customers.

1900 John Paulson bought Freyberg's property and converted the boarding house into a hotel.(It later was owned and operated by James and Martha Sorenson, then passed on to the Gibson family who celebrated their 50th anniversary this summer-1997.)

(This is the story of the Corrigan and Gislason enterprises extending from the present Shipyard Marina to the east and north. Records do not show if Johnson & Son or Corrigan started the Pole Road, also called Tram or Tote Road to haul wood products to their dock. Later John Gislason owned and ran the set-up.)

Nov. 1880 Johnson & Son sold out to Corrigan who carried on the wood business. Arni Gudmundsson was hired as store clerk. Corrigan acquired large tracts of timbered lands and employed many men to cut cordwood which was shipped by sailing vessels to his fuel yard in Milwaukee.

Oct, 1881 Corrigan's Pole Road extended from his Detroit Harbor pier about a mile into the backwoods where he had 30 men at work. Cordwood was cut and banked along the Pole Road tracks until spring when it was hauled on cars to the dock. Each car could carry 3 cords of hardwood. The road rails on which the cars rode were from smaller hardwood tree logs partly sunken into the ground. They formed a continuous track to support the heavy cars off the ground. These 16 to 20' long pieces were notched on the ends and pinned together with dowels.

Axles were 2 1/2" diameter solid steel, 95" long overall with a center to center tread of about 70 1/2".(One of these axles stands in the SE corner of the west section of the log barn at the farm museum.) Lawrence Gislason said the cast iron wheels had concave rims about 12" wide and the wheel diameter was about the size of an old-fashioned washtub. As a boy, Jesse Koyen said he and Lawrence Gislason couldn't budge the cars on the rails. As each car carried three cords of wood, this would be 384 cubic feet of wood.

1883 Corrigan started a new industry here with the construction of 7 charcoal pits. With these going full blast he was prepared to convert 1200 cords of wood into charcoal that season.Charcoal was shipped to his Milwaukee yard where it sold for 14 to 18 cents a bushel. (These pits were located just west of the present home of Harold and Arbutus Greenfeldt on the north side of Aznoe Road. Obviously it was very close to Corrigan's Pole Road making it convenient to transport the finished product to his Detroit Harbor dock for shipment via sailing vessels.)

1884 Corrigans hauled at least 1800 cords of wood via the Pole Road. By August he he had sent 1500 cords to Milwaukee and had lots left here. Schooners Iris, Monitor and Madonna were steadily employed by Corrigan. Agnes Berman and Quickstep also took some loads. The Madonna made a round trip in 4 1/2 days, the fastest ever by sailing craft to Milwaukee and back.

1885 John Gislason bought J.C. Corrigan and Co. store, pier and other property for $2000. Corrigans still owned 2000 acres of timbered property, but it was idle.

(Led by Dane, William Wickman, John Gislason and 3 other men were the first Iceland immigrants to this part of the country in 1870.)

Dec. 1885 John Gislason planned to harvest 2500 cords of Hardwood, plus many RR ties and posts during that winter. He bought eleven 40 acre parcels from Corrigan and then sold five of those 40s to Peter Hansen for $900.

Jan. 1887 Lots of cedar, cordwood and saw logs had already been cut. The heaviest operators were John Gislason and Peter Hansen with several men employed in woods near Jackson Harbor. Hansen already had 500-600 cords banked.

1890 John Gislason banked 2000 cords of wood for shipment.

1891 Gislason harvested 2000 cords, plus many RR ties and posts in the Detroit Harbor region.

It appears that nearly four miles of pole road were constructed here. Its heyday probably lasted for at least ten years. (John Gislason harvested and sold a variety of forest products throughout the years before his son, Lawrence, took over the business. When I was growing up in the 1920s and 30s, we had four grocery and general merchandise stores: Koyen's (now St. Michel's Chapel), Gislason's (now a vacant lot across from

Gislason's Beach), Ted's (now Vagabond) and Mann's (Still at the same location.)

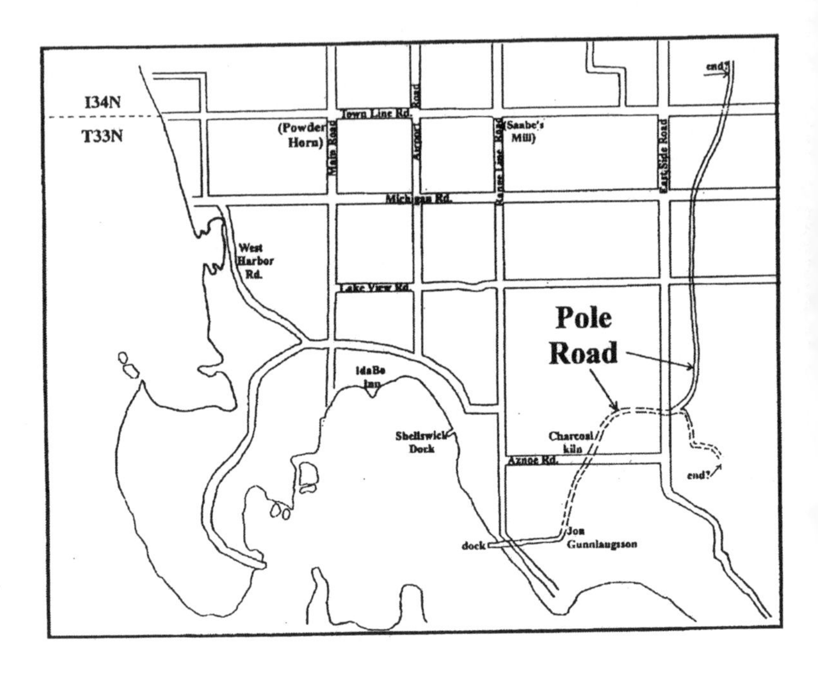

(Conan Eaton obtained this information through our library and UW library back in 1971.)

Under "Forest Railroads" subhead "Pole Roads" - they were used by lumbermen because the material for construction could be secured on.the operation at no expense except for labor and stumpage, but they are primitive in character and now seldom used (1913) except on an occasional small operation where sawed wooden rails or steel rails cannot be secured at a reasonable cost. Animals are used as draft power, although on down grades the cars may descend by gravity under control of a brakeman. Pole roads are seldom built for distances greater than from 2 to 2 1/2 miles.

A 25-foot right-of-way is required from which all brush must be removed and stumps grubbed out or cut level with the ground. Turnouts for returning teams at intervals of 1/4 to 1/3 of a mile. Maximum grade for loaded cars drawn by two animals is 1.5 per cent. Where eight horses were used (not here), trams with up to

15 per cent ascending grades on route to the woods and 3 per cent ascending grades for loaded cars on route to the mill have been used successfully.

Rails are long, straight poles from 9 to 12" diameter, with as little taper as can be secured. Poles hewn on the inner face to reduce friction on the wheel flange. Laid with butts all in one direction, top of one lap joint to butt of following one. Where joints are not the same size,they're hewn down until the wheels can pass over readily. They're braced at frequent intervals by stakes driven close to the poles on the outside. At curves, where track is liable to spread, braces are placed between the rails, and also between the outer rail and trees or stumps. Cross-skids, used only on soft ground, are spaced 6 to 8' apart. They are short, round blocks under the rails, but do not extend across the track as this would interfere with the footholds of draft animals. Poles are held together at lap joints and fastened to skids by wooden tree nails 1 1/2 to 2" diameter, driven through the poles and into the ground. The crew for building a pole road comprises six men and one team. When rails are available along the way, the crew will cut and peel the necessary poles and build 500' of straight track daily, curves are 1/3 more labor. In Idaho the construction cost on 9 miles of rolling ground was $500 per mile, while on the Pacific Coast it would run as high as $1000 per mile.

Maintenance was low, with occasional pole replacement, removing splinters from the rails usually with a spade and greasing the rails. One man can care for 2 miles of track on half time. Cars were built with a heavy framework of sawed timbers mounted on 4 wheels, each about 42" diameter with a slightly concave face, 2" flange on outer side and 4" on inner. Axles allowed side play of 6" so wheels could adjust to inequalities of the rails and uneven gauge. Bunks are 10' long and 10 to 12" apart. A reach passes through the body of the car & projects 2"2' beyond the bunks to serve as point of attachment for draft power. Two-horse cars of this character will carry 1400' log scale load. Teams will haul cars from 8 to 10 miles daily. On one Idaho road, the cost to haul 1 1/2 miles was about 85¢ per 1000 feet. Light, geared locomotives were used to a limited extent, but they were not adapted to this type of rail.

(Back to the chronological account of timbering here.)

Oct. 1881 Wood here sold for $3.75 to 4.00 per cord which was the highest price in years.

Feb. 1882 Captain C.0. Peterson, Detroit Harbor logged timber for his new scow to freight to and from the Island and elsewhere.

Aug, 1882 Shipments of cordwood and cedar from here were "quite lively."

June 1883 Prices here for maple were $2.50 per cord. Beech was $1.75 which was not yet the lowest price. At Milwaukee it sold for $5.00 per cord.

Jan.1884 Lots of cordwood was being cut by A.A. Koyen.

May 1884 The schooners Beerman, Lucy Graham and Laurel hauled lots of cordwood.

June 1884 H.O. Saabye shipped chopped wood on the schooner Laurel, but did not get enough cash to pay for the freight. He brought back a load of bricks, $9.00 per thousand, for a house he planned to build.

Feb. 1885 Olson cut a road to Jackson Harbor to enable him to bank cordwood there. As there was no pier in that harbor, wood was rafted to anchored vessels.

March 1885 So far 2000 cords, cut mostly by farmers, was banked in Detroit Harbor.

April 1885 The Scow Berman loaded with wood and RR ties was ready to sail as soon as the ice would leave.

Oct. 1885 L.P. Ottosen contracted with two men to clear 10 acres for farming for $70 and the wood they cut. He hauled the wood to the banking ground for them for 70 cents a cord. Wood then sold for $3.25 a cord on the pier.

Oct. 1885 Captain W.C. Betts (Civil War veteran) sold between 300,000 and 400,000 board feet of pine to a Sturgeon Bay firm.

Nov. 1885 Schooner Lucy Graham bought a big load of supplies for Betts' lumber camp.

Feb. 1887 Large quantities of timber were being harvested mainly by John Gislason, Peter Hansen and Mads Hansen.

Mar. 1887 Volney Garrett did a large business in cedar. Nearly 10,000 pieces were banked at Furlong's old pier on the east shore of Washington Harbor. This included the finest RR ties ever cut here. There were more forest products in Detroit Harbor than for several years. Captain Bennet was here buying

RR ties and posts for a Milwaukee firms. Ties here brought 23 cents each.

June 1887 All the logs cut by W.C. Betts and Joseph Cornell were rafted to Sturgeon Bay by the tug Lawrence. A larger amount of cedar was shipped than ever before.

H.O. Saabye was building a 70' windmill to grind grist and flour, via a turbine mill. The mill would also pump water. This would give farmers a convenience long needed. No longer would wheat have to be shipped to Sister Bay to be made into flour. (The Bonifaces presently live here on Rangeline Road.)

Aug. 9,1887 H.O. Saabye fell 53' off the mill roof onto rocks and timbers killing him instantly. Son Chris also fell, but managed to catch the scaffolding. H.O. came here in 1868. By Feb. 1889 H.O.s adopted son had completed the mill.

Oct. 1889 There was a lively shipping of wood. Vessels were scarce and freight to Milwaukee was $2.75 to 3.00 per cord.

1887 The Advocate said that "Genuine Islanders" were busy harvesting trees. Wm. Betts and Joseph Cornell were sending log rafts to Sturgeon Bay, via tug. John Gislason was shipping lots of cedar and cordwood. Rasmus Hanson was cutting & Ole Christianson had bartered away his wrecked scow Quickstep for 20 cords of wood. (In Oct. 1878 500 bushels of winter wheat was loaded on the Quickstep to be made into flour at a Sister Bay mill. Before sailing the vessel dragged anchor, was beached, wrecked and the wheat was ruined. Over 5000 bushels of grain were harvested here that year. Winter wheat produced as much as 35 bushels to the acre. In 1885 F.M. Hansen had reaped 600 bu. wheat, 300bu. oats and 100 bu. buckwheat.)

May 1888 The schooner Lucy Graham's hold was filled with cordwood in Jackson Harbor, but the water was so low that she had to move to Washington Harbor to take on a deck load. The Laurel took basswood bolts to Green Bay.

June 1888 The schooner Blazing Star had been wrecked on Tantalon Reef(Pilot Island?) and the lumber from her was being sold at Washington Harbor dock for $5.00 per thousand. "Going like hot cakes!" Someone had stripped and removed all the rigging and equipment the previous winter. The Captain said if they were found they would "pay dearly."

July 1888 The woodmarket was good with cordwood at $3.25 a cord "clear of pierage". Hemlock bark brought $5.50 per cord and was scarce.(This bark was largely used for leather tanning, but fishermen also used it to tan gill nets so they would not rot.)

7/22/88 Schooner Lucy and scow Laurel loaded cordwood in Washington Harbor, while the Madonna took on cordwood in Jackson Harbor.

8/6/88 Schooner Lucy Graham loaded tanbark and 4 Brothers from Racine loaded Garrett's and Gislason's cedar.

9/8/88 City of Nicollet(sic) took a load of bolts for a de Pere factory.

Nov. 1888 Captain Peter Hansen bought the five year old Schooner O.M. Nelson for $4500. She is very sound and will carry 140 cords of wood.

Jan. 1889 Lots of cedar and cordwood already cut. Wood is $2.50 a cord. Hanson Bros. planned to bank 2000 cords and lots of cedar. Teamsters rushed cordwood, etc. to piers at Detroit Harbor, Washington Harbor and other shore places. Peter Hansen had the biggest force, 20 men, working in the center of the Island. All told there were about 200 men cutting trees and hauling.

Feb. 1889 Peter Hansen had 15 horse teams hauling wood. Banking grounds could not hold all the wood that had been cut.

Nov. 1889 Wood prices were too low to warrant cutting. Nearly half of the primeval forests remained and were considered to be one of the Island's most valuable features. Most of the timber was on the east side and the principal owners were James Morgan and John Furlong from Milwaukee. Morgan owned a whole section (1 square mile) and several fractions of sections. Furlong owned nearly as much.This included some of the finest pine timber, but they would not cut it. Many offers had been refused. Morgan talked of establishing a "city" on the Island in the near future and was preserving the timber for its building.

1900 The statement was made, "Another few years will doubtless see the last of timber removed on the Morgan lands." (South of Jackson Harbor.) By 1895 the farmers were changing from dependence on cordwood to farm products.

Jan. 1890 Captain Peter Hansen planned to cross the ice to the mainland with a horse team, when the ice was safe, to buy 3000 cords of wood.

Feb. 1890 Because of low water, Ole Christianson was building a large lighter, with shallow draft, to haul cordwood from Detroit Harbor. Not as much was being cut due to low prices. Most of the merchantable timber near the harbors had been cut and they were now concentrating on Detroit Harbor and areas interior from Jackson Harbor.

April 1890 LaBrooks was building a vessel for A.A. Koyen to be named Edith Koyen. Her dimensions were: 50' keel, 16' beam and 6' deep hold. She could carry 35 cords of wood.

This was a poor season for maple syrup and the price was $1.75 per gallon. Schooner Laura loaded with bolts for Green Bay.

June 1890 A scow in tow of City of Green Bay capsized off Jacksonport. The cargo of 10,000 RR ties drifted ashore and onto Door County islands.Some people collected at least a thousand. It was said that if the owners did not claim them they would be sold to parties on this island and shipped to Chicago.

Aug. 1890 Captain August Koyen took the Edith Koyen, loaded with wood to Milwaukee on her maiden voyage.

Sept. 1890 Scow I.A. Johnson loaded wood in West Harbor and the O.M. Nelson took cordwood. Others loading that week were Lucy Graham and Edith Koyen in Washington Harbor; Laura, Nellie and Annie, Laurel, Arrow, Lily Ammiot and Mariner in Detroit Harbor; Emily and Eliza in Jackson Harbor. The Edith Koyen, built here last winter by Joseph LaBrooks now had her third captain.

Feb. 1891 Large quantities of timber and cordwood were being cut and hauled to landings. A busy and profitable season was expected.

May 1891 Schooner Lucy Graham took cordwood to Milwaukee and the scow Edith Koyen made her second trip to Milwaukee with a load of basswood bolts.

Dec. 1891 Schooner Laurel, loaded with wood, dragged her anchor at entrance to Detroit Harbor and grounded. The load was taken off by the Iris. The bones of the 40 year old Laurel will probably remain right there.

Schooner O.M. Nelson sailed from Sturgeon Bay to the Island in exactly 4 hours setting a new record.

Sept. 1892 David Bowman bought sawmill machinery in Milwaukee to be placed at Jackson Harbor.

Dec.1892 Schooner Dreadnaught, Captain Lawrence Figenschau, brought Bowman's boiler while Arrow hauled the rest of the machinery here. By the end of 1892 lots of men were cutting trees, but there was too little snow for hauling by sleigh.

Feb. 1893 Bowman's mill started, but a piece blew out of the boiler, which will need repair or replacement.

Mar. 1893 Boilermakers finished repairs for Bowman and he will add a shingle mill. There was lots of pine and cedar stock still available, probably enough to keep Bowman busy year round. By April 1893 Bowman was making up to 10,000 board feet daily.

April 1893 John Aznoe went to Sturgeon Bay on the schooner Oneida to buy an edger for the sawmill.

June 1893 Christian Saabye erected a new sawmill at Washington Harbor.

Aug. 1893 Cordwood was being sold at below market prices. One Island captain said, "The name of each vessel peddling wood below market prices is being kept tab of and will be boycotted when business is back to normal". Bowman's and Saabye's mills operated full-time and produced good quality lumber. This was a great benefit to the Islanders.

Oct. 1893 Cedar and tan bark business was dull, with few sales.

April 1894 logging article reported: Wages for loggers was $26 to $45 per month while the foreman got up to $100 per month and board. Some of the log buildings to house cutting crews were about 60' x 20' and were caulked with mud.

June 1894 Ole Christianson planned to have the rebuilding of schooner Madonna finished in two months. It was said she would be "as staunch and trim a packet as ever touched the Island." He hopes to "roll the greenbacks in through the hawsepipes" when she gets out.

Sept. 1894 Schooner Madonna took a load of RR ties and potatoes to Chicago for John Gislason.

Nov. 1894 A large fleet of "coasting" vessels owned here was shipping nearly all the cordwood to market.

Dec.1894 David Bowman sawmill was sold to August Koyen. Bowman owed August a sum of money and rather than lose it, August gave Bowman promissory notes for the balance of the selling price. Bowman, who still owed many persons, did not distribute the notes to any creditors, but pocketed them and left the Island. It was said that Bowman had put $1200 into the mill, but very bad management and poor sales caused his failure.

Mar.1895 Sawmills were powered by steam engines, but all were idle due to very cold weather freezing and bursting pipes. James Morgan still refused to sell his timberland unless he got his price of about $10,000. The 1200 standing virgin pines and a lot of cedar would probably more than pay for the land. It was reported that Two Rivers Mfg. Co. was looking longingly towards the Island and may become owners soon. Morgan had acquired the lands from Sturgeon Bay Canal Co. This was part of a 200,000 acres granted to them by Congress in 1866.

Mar. 1895 Nor Shellswick built a deep water dock in "Pottawatomie Bay" (Detroit Harbor?) and banked hundreds of cords of wood and several cargoes of RR ties and posts.

Mar. 1896 Nor extended his dock and had banked hundreds of cords.

May 1897 Schooner O.M. Nelson bent sails for her first seasonal with wood for Milwaukee.

Apr. 1898 No sale of Morgan land and timber yet. Buyers claimed the price was too high at $12,000 for a thousand acres whose principal value was the pine trees.

May 1898 Schooner Madonna loaded her fourth load of wood for the season for Milwaukee.

June 1899 James Morgan land sold to a New York syndicate that was reported as "not disposed to sell."

Feb. 1900 Morgan and Furlongs timberland sold to Forster Lbr, Co., Milwaukee. Morgan's sold for $10,000, but there was no report on Furlong's sale price. This encompassed nearly 1,900 acres, however, Furlong still had 240 acres in Washington Harbor. Thomas Setright from Menominee came here to prepare for logging and to protect company interests. Logs would be towed in rafts to a large Menominee sawmill. Building of a pier in Jackson Harbor was planned for shipment of cordwood, RR ties, etc. Nor Shellswick and August Koyen contracted to get the logs out and banked at Jackson Harbor. For cutting and hauling cordwood they got $2.50 to $2.75 per cord. Setright said they would also cut cedar telegraph poles. RR ties would be sawn at the mill from the remaining cedar.

Mar. 1900 Forster's wages for this winter's work was between three and four thousand dollars.

Apr.1900 Supt. Setright was well satisfied with the progress despite a late start and poor sleighing. Posts and poles were now peeled in Jackson Harbor and soon men would be peeling hemlock logs for tanbark.

May 1900 Log rafting from Jackson Harbor to Menominee began. Forest fires had raged for at least 10 days in Jackson Harbor. Lots of timber and fences had been destroyed.

Cream City Brick Co.(Milwaukee) crew peeled posts and poles that were cut here last winter. Their company planned to bring a portable sawmill here to saw lots of pine and hemlock trees which they own.

May 26,1900 Heavy forest fire in Section 5. Score of men out last night in partly cut-over cedar swamps. Timber damaged and lots of August Koyen's RR ties and posts were destroyed.

6/19/1900 A raft boom gave way in a heavy storm and many logs floated out of Jackson Harbor. Capt. August Koyen, tug Unknown, was hired to recover as many logs as possible.

Aug.1900 Cream City Brick Co. was building a large pier at Lobdills Point out to 14-15 ft. of water to accomodate large steamers. When the dock is finished, the mill will be brought in.

Sept. 1900 Some of the Morgan land in Jackson Harbor, from which merchantable timber had been removed, was now for sale.

Oct. 1900 It was said that in a few years the last of the Morgan timber would be removed. This stoney, gravely land likely would never be used for agriculture or grazing. Last heard of "Jim" Morgan, he was selling life insurance. Poor Jim!

Nov. 1900 Friis and Jensen prepared to log the Flannigan lands and the hardwood and logs would be sold to the best advantage. Capt. H. Erickson was ready to get out hundreds of cords of wood on Cream City Brick Co. land near the entrance to Detroit Harbor.

Feb. 1901 The winter was very favorable for wood cutting, fine weather and enough snow for sleighing meant plenty of work.

April 1901 Patsy Ryan reported that all of 1,400,000 board feet of pine, plus oak, basswood, hemlock, etc. had been harvested. This ended Pankratz Co. business on the former Forster Lbr. Co. lands. This 1800 acres had been sold by Furlong's heirs and Morgan.

June 1901 The Lobdill's Point mill was set up and running at full blast.

Aug. 1901 Cream City Brick Co. expected to harvest at least 500,000 board feet of lumber and hundreds of cords of wood.

Oct. 1901 Emil Leist was getting shingle mill parts from a closed mill in Menominee. Lobdill's Point cedar would supply this mill. Capt. Erickson was having a hard time getting choppers, even with much better wages than paid on the mainland.

Feb. 1902 Cream City now had a large crew taking out lots of logs and cordwood.

Jessen, Schmidt & Co. opened a turning factory to make cedar floats for fishermen's gill nets. Machinery was bought last fall in Racine and their floats were selling as fast as they could make them. William Jess, who had a business interest in the company, was the superintendent.

June 1902 Schooners Madonna and Iris each had already taken four loads of wood to southern markets. Iris made a trip from here to Sheboygan and back in four days.

Aug. 1902 Lobdill's Point mill, now owned and operated by Emil Leist, will shut down as the timber for Cream City Brick Co. is exhausted. Likely the mill will move to the mainland.

Feb. 1903 The bulk of the Forster lands has been sold, mainly to settlers. Bo Anderson and Ole Christianson got about 500 acres and are building a dock near the Jackson Harbor entrance. It will have two gangways to the main structure which will avoid the need for backing or turning of horse teams. Three vessels could lay at the dock at the same time. The owners planned to remove the shallow bar at the harbor entrance, this was only a few yards wide.

Several land owners on the northeast side offered to help pay for dredging. There were thousands of cords of wood ready for shipment and this business was expected to be lively for years.

Aug. 1903 Jessen, Schmidt & Co.dissolved by mutual agreement. Schmidt kept the market. Jessen and Nelson kept the hall and the float factory. They still, jointly, owned timber land bought from Forster.

Dec. 1903 After 8 months of being idle, the cedar float factory was running full blast as Wm. Jess & Co. business.

Dec. 1903 Emil Leist, Lobdill's Point business, was busy cutting hardwood lumber and cordwood.

Jan.1904 Leist started sawing shingles. Logs too tough to be split with wedges were rip-sawed in the mill and cut into 4' lengths for cordwood. This was Capt. Erickson's innovation.

Mar. 1904 Leist turned out 25 cords of "patent" wood daily. Most choppers had quit due to the very deep snow. Heaviest producers of cordwood were Anderson and Christianson, Nor Shellswick, Jacob Bowman and Alfred Hansen. They had former Forster lands and cordwood was in good demand.

July 1904 Ole Christianson, Madonna, was busy hauling wood from Jackson Harbor to Milwaukee. Schooner Lucy Graham had taken her sixth load of wood to Manitowoc. Yards were filling rapidly.

Aug. 1904 Lobdill's Point land was turned over to a Sturgeon Bay estate agent to sell. It was swampy and rough.

Oct. 1904 Last cargo of wood brought $6.50 per cord at Milwaukee. Anderson and Christianson put a mill on the land recently bought from City Investment Co. Stove wood will be cut and shipped to market on the Madonna. Last year the former owners cut lots of beech and maple cordwood from remaining limbs and butts. These had been ignored by the original cutter, who were most interested in logs.

Dec.1904 Anderson and Christianson's portable sawmill is being set up. Many are hiring them to saw via steam instead of the laborious, slow hand cutting. Hand cutting was done with a five foot or longer saw with a man on either end to take turns pulling it back and forth through the wood. It was often referred to as the "I got it, you got it" crosscut saw.

Jan.1905 Lots of cordwood, obtained from the former Forster Lbr. Co. land, is banked in Jackson Harbor.

Leist Bros. contracted with Anderson and Christianson to take out cedar on Lobdill's Point for shingles.

Mar. 1905 Lobdill's Point log boarding house burned while the men were absent. Some lost clothes, watches and money. Fire origin was unknown.

Apr. 1905 Lots of cordwood banked on Rasmus Hansen's and Anderson and Christianson's docks in Jackson Harbor.

3/23/05 Sheriff Minor came to sell logs on Rock Island belonging to Sebold Fichtner to satisfy a judgment secured by George Larson & Co., owners of the Jackson Harbor mill. Fichtner owed Larsons a substantial amount and the jury's findings were heartily approved by every Islander. "Certainly working men should be paid for their hard labor."

Apr. 1905 Bo Anderson and Julius Jensen started a sawmill in Detroit Harbor. They had recently bought the Iris to carry lumber, etc.

May. 1905 The Madonna was carrying wood to Manitowoc from Detroit Island for William Gierke. He had been offered $4.50 per cord last fall, but now must take much less.

The Iris, back from Racine, reported poor sales of shingles & wood.

July 1905 Hardly any wood was shipped, this with other shortcoming, made money "tight". Leist mill, Lobdill's Point, burned. It was totally destroyed with a loss of at least $1400. It was thought that a spark from the forge ignited sawdust. Leist and his crew were about to go to St. Martin's Island to tow a raft of logs back when they discovered flames coming through the roof. Bo Anderson lost about $70 worth of lumber. Several others suffered losses.

Sept. 1905 The failure of Two Rivers Co.hit some farmers hard as they had contracts to get out logs. It looked like the timber would rot on the ground. Maple wood was $3.25 per cord, about a dollar less than last year.

Dec. 1905 George Larson & Co. was getting their Jackson Harbor mill ready to begin sawing in February, when they would have a good pile of logs stacked. There was lots of cordwood stacked here. The price was high and many city people had switched to coal which they considered more economical.

Feb. 1906 Christian Saabye added a shingle department to his saw and planing mill. Nor Shellswick was logging on the south-east side and Geo. Pankratz Lbr. Co. said they would buy his logs if enough was cut to warrant sending a tug and raft boom. Geo. Larson Mill, Jackson Harbor, was in full time operation sawing for farmers who planned to build. Two Rivers Woodware Co. commissioned Jens Jacobsen to ascertain the amount of logs gotten out last winter by their predecessor, Two River Mfg. Co. They will take and pay in full for these logs which is fortunate as it was anticipated they would just lie there and rot in piles.

May 1906 Geo. Larson & Co. sold their portable sawmill to a syndicate consisting of Rasmus Hanson, Charles Anderson and Mads Svensen, all from Jackson Harbor, for $1600. Much wood and other forest products was hauled to the water during a recent cold snap.

April 1906 Captain Thomas Guinen supervised the re-building of Furlong's wharf in Washington Harbor.

June 1906 Schooner Madonna took wood to Port Washington where a much better market was found than in Milwaukee.

Sept. 1906 Hanson & Co.,Jackson Harbor, sawed lots of lumber for Jacob Bowman, then rigged up for sawing laths. Chris Saabye's mill was running and August Koyen would be soon sawing.

Oct. 1906 Schooner Harvey Ransom took a load of hardwood lumber for Jacob Bowman from Jackson Harbor to Green Bay where a good demand prevailed. Several hundreds of cords of wood cut in the winter of 1904-05 was still stacked near Nor's pier on the southeast side. The great blow in October last year carried the pier away, but it was now nearly re-built. No vessels were to be had and unless the wood was shipped that fall its value would be much less. Main wood owners were Nor Shellswick, Gus Jacobsen, William Jess and August Koyen.

Nov. 1906 Few men would work cutting cordwood as more money could be made in pine and cedar logging. Anderson and Christianson planned to make cordwood. Jacob Bowman was anxious to clear more land for sheep pasture. He said nothing paid better if rightly pursued.

August and Volney Koyen erected a new sawmill on Nor Shellswick's land in Section 17. There was enough timber to keep busy for at least a year. Koyens recently bought 68 acres of timbered land from Jessen, Schmidt & Co. near the mill for $1300. They feel they got a bargain.

Cedar, to be made into ties, was in good demand at a good price.

Feb. 1907 Very cold weather and Milwaukee yards lack of stocking heavily caused a scarcity of cordwood resulting in a heavy demand and good price.

Mar. 1907 William Larson, Green Day, was here seeking timber lands on the three islands. He got a 60 day option on land belonging to Rasmus Hanson with a selling price of $5000.

May 1907 Schooner Joses of Racine loaded maple cordwood at Shellwick's dock. This wood, cut in 1904-05, was still in good condition and brought the owner $3.75 per cord.

June 1907 Martin Dredge & Towing Co., Escanaba, brought a tug and scow here to load several lots of logs which were cut two to three years ago by Two Rivers Mfg. Co. Martin claimed to have a bill of sale, but refused to show it. There was something quite inexplicable about this as the last word had been that Two Rivers Woodenware Co. had bought the logs.

Aug. 1907 Schooner Joses hauled 160,000 board feet of mill-run hemlock lumber which Rasmus Hanson had sold to Racine parties at $15 per thousand board feet. Schooner Stevens carried wood from Jackson Harbor to Sheboygan.

Oct. 1907 Capt. Goodletson, schooner Lucy Graham, in Jackson Harbor, reported cordwood was getting scarce.

Oct. 1907 Captain William Auger and crew tried to make a log raft for Sturgeon Bay parties, but bad weather made their efforts futile.

Charles Anderson, Mads Svendsen and Ben Jensen will move a sawmill from the west side to a new structure on the south shore of Jackson Harbor. Much wood was banked and shipped to market on the schooner Madonna, Capt. Ole Christianson.

Capt. Erik Lunde, schooner Harvey Ransom, sold cordwood without middlemen to consumers in Manitowoc at $7.50 per cord.

Jan.1908 There was still lots of cordwood being harvested on former Forster Lbr. lands on the northeast side. There was still much for subsequent years. The three Kincaid brothers, Dave, Armar and Willie, broke a record by felling, sawing, splitting and stacking 9 1/2 cords in ten hours.

Apr. 1908 At least a dozen cedar float factories ran a good part of the winter with gas engines providing the power. These floats sold to commercial fishermen at a good price. Fine cordwood was available in Jackson Harbor. Three sawmills were busy cutting lumber, mainly for farmers.

June 1908 August & Volney Koyen moved their mill to the east side where they had lots of logs in stock. Magnus Johnson shipped basswood stave bolts to Two Rivers on the schooner Lucy Graham.

Mar. 1909 Lots of cordwood, banked in Jackson Harbor, will keep the schooners busy this summer if the price is right.

Aug. 1909 Sam Newman had a large amount of oak lumber piled at Washington Harbor dock. Lucy Graham had already taken a couple of loads to Algoma and probably the rest would go there. Cost to the owner was only $9 per thousand laid down in Algoma.

July 1910 A large wild fire had raged for over a month on the east side in slashings and standing timber. Rain was desperately needed.

Sept. 1910 Nearly all the cordwood and forest products had been shipped to market. Sam Newman's mill on his quarter section of land was making lumber.(Across from Sportsmen's Club.)

Jan.1911 With good sleighing prevailing, over a score of men were lumbering and hauling logs to the Jackson Harbor mill. Sam Newman expected to complete logging on his 1/4 section in a month or so. He was sawing 25,000 board feet daily and planned to stack 1,000,000 board feet in Jackson Harbor for shipment.

July 1911 Bo Anderson filled his contract to supply 50 cords of wood to the U.S. Lighthouse Service at St. Martin's Island. He would deliver like amounts to Poverty and Pilot Island lighthouses.

Aug. 1911 While doing road work, Bill Garrett found a primitive ax. Several years before, Morton Jorgenson had found six such axes on Detroit Island. A relic collector said it was the style used by the Hudson Bay Co. when collecting furs. On Detroit Island there was evidence of ancient gardens and it was concluded that the fur company had a station or settlement here. Judging from the size of the trees that had since grown in these plots, at least 150 years had elapsed since that time.

Sept. 1911 Nearly all the lumber sawed and banked in Jackson Harbor by Newman had now been shipped to Algoma. His force of men had also cut lots of cordwood which was destined for the same port, much was carried by the Schooner J.H. Hall.

Oct. 1911 Sam Newman now had a cordwood saw powered by a gasoline engine.

Dec.1911 Dave Kincaide, Sr, Newman's foreman, had a crew cutting the remainder of the timber. The cordwood was destined for Algoma and other ports. Ole Christianson's Flotilla took a cargo of lumber to Kewaunee.

Feb. 1912 saw more cordwood cut and banked than for a number of years. Newman of Algoma was the biggest operator.

Robert Gunnerson sold five 40s of timberland for $4000 cash to outside parties.

Feb.1912 From 6 to 8 gas powered rigs were busy sawing stove wood. (All the time I lived on the farm all cooking was done on a wood fired range. The house was first heated by a cast iron "box" stove, later we had a wood-fired, jacketed stove that naturally circulated the warmed air. Most farmers and some fishermen cut hardwood trees into 4 foot lengths, split the pieces with a pointed sledge or wedges and stacked the wood where it was cut. When good sleighing came, they hauled the cordwood home using a team of horses. The sawing rigs were hired to cut each piece into 12 or 16" stove wood. Normally a three man crew was needed, one to bring the pieces to the sawing table, one to work the hinged table and one to take the sawed pieces away from the saw. Usually a one-cylinder "hit and miss" gas engine with two large flywheels and a flat pulley was used for power. A leather belt was connected from the engine to the saw arbor pulley. Next to that pulley was a large flywheel and about a 3 foot circular saw blade on the other end of the shaft. After sawing the stove wood was usually stored in a shed near the house and "seasoned" more before being used. A regular chore was splitting the larger pieces so the wood could be fitted into the firing part of the kitchen stove.)

Feb. 1913 Haulers were busy taking Newman's wood to Jackson Harbor. Wood cutters were way ahead, there had been a lack of good sleighing.

Apr. 1913 The three Island sawmills were going "full blast".

June 1913 Captain Chas. Hanson's new gasoline schooner, Marion, hauled 30,000 board feet of lumber. This 62' vessel is rated at 25 tons.

Dec.1913 The gas vessel Flotilla carried wood to Sturgeon Bay.

Mar. 1915 Much cordwood was banked in Jackson Harbor.

Nov. 1915 There were several forest fires.mostly on Rock Island, but an all night rain nearly extinguished them.

Dec. 1915 George Mann offered wood to anyone who would cut trees to help clear his land. Many were getting their year's supply. At the Bethel Church 50th anniversary it was pointed out that when the church was built, there were no farmers, roads or horse teams here. Ranney, Washington Harbor, donated 80.acres and lumber & other materials were hauled by yokes of oxen.

Apr. 1916 Jackson Harbor Mill Co, was sawing, but it was felt that lumbering was nearly a thing of the past. The stock of logs was small and many wondered where they came from.

Oct. 1919 The Schooner Petrel took a load of wood from Gislason's to Algoma. Previously she'd made several trips from Jackson Harbor.

Dec.l, 1919 Captain Jepson's Wisconsin left for Baileys Harbor to load 1600 Christmas trees for either Milwaukee or Chicago, depending on which market offered the best price. It took 2 days to load them. The Diana took a load of Christmas trees to Chicago.

April 1920 Hagen Bros. and Ted Gudmundsen took out so many logs that they decided to buy a sawmill. They wanted to place it near the Washington Harbor dock.

June 1920 Hagen Bros, with carpenter John Johnson, were building a sawmill on the West side.The mill was moved from Jackson Harbor. The large boiler was hauled over the new road (Jackson Harbor?) built through the swamp.

March 1921 Hagen Bros finished hauling logs and would begin sawing in a few weeks.

April 1921 Hagens hauled 30,000 board feet of lumber to the schooner Oscar Newhouse which would take it to Manitowoc.

May 1921 Schooner Oscar Newhouse took 52,000 board feet of lumber to Manitowoc for Hagens.

June 1921 The Oscar Newhouse hauled a load of lumber slabs to Manitowoc(probably to be cut into firewood).

Mar. 1922 over 300 cords of wood were cut and banked in Jackson Harbor.

April 1924 Nels Zinc and Nels Jepson bought the small schooner Union at Fish Creek. They paid $500 and it will haul 35 cords.

Jan. 1925 Many farmers and fishermen were cutting wood for their homes. Some with timberland were offering $2.50 per cord for cutting wood.

Feb. 1927 With an unusual high demand, good stove wood was selling at $3 to 3.25 delivered.

April 1927 The Jackson Harbor mill was busy with an unusual stock of logs on hand. Heavy winds the previous summer had blown down lots of large trees.

June 1927 The wood shingle roof of Saabye's mill caught fire. The fire call, via the party line telephone system, was credited with saving the building. Because of the very quick response and assistance, the fire was extinguished with a loss of only about 100 sq. ft. of shingles. (Saabyes reported the fire to "Central" operator who immediately plugged in to the circuits closest to Saabyes, rang 10 short rings and announced the location of the fire. "Central" would continue on other circuits until everyone with a telephone would be notified. Men immediately sped hastily to the scene to provide assistance.)

Feb. 1929 Very little wood has been cut because of the very deep snow. A scarcity is expected next winter, even for home use.

Oct. 1929 Wood was scarce and high priced, therefore many homes converted to coal which was cheaper.

Mar. 1930 Blaine and Roy Olson contracted with George Hanson to cut 100 cords for $250. By this time it was unusual to be able to cut 100 cords in one place. As soon as they finished they were hired to cut for others. Forty years earlier woodsmen were paid from 5 cents to $1 per cord and it was the only way to earn money in the winter.

Sept. 1930 Volney E. Koyen & Sons started a box factory. Many thousands of boxes were needed annually to pack iced fish in to be shipped to market. Previously most of these boxes were made elsewhere. The 40 acres on Deerlane Road, which they bought from August Koyen was covered with hemlock, pine, balsam, cedar, beech, birch and maple. They moved Mads Svendson's mill to the site and drilled a well for water for the steam boiler. (Floyd Koyen told me sometimes they made and sold 1000 boxes per month at 35¢ each. Most were of hardwood and they even planed the boards. George McDonald asked, jokingly, why they didn't paint them. The mill made boxes and did custom lumber sawing until about 1945.)

Feb. 1932 Jens Jepson hauled logs to Koyen's mill. (Last mention in the Door County Advocate on sawmills.)

In 1935 Marvin and I cut hemlocks and balsams which we took to Koyens to have made into lumber. We used this to build the two car garage on the farm. Second-growth trees had reached a size where they could be made into lumber. Consequently various mills in various locations have operated through the years doing custom sawing and making fish boxes. Recently portable band-saw mills have made it convenient to take and operate the unit at the logging site rather than having to haul heavy logs from the forest to the mill. While mature hardwood trees are still being cut for firewood, most of these are logged off by Algoma Lumber Company and shipped off the Island on big trucks. They have logged many sites on this island as well as doing extensive timbering on Detroit and Plum Islands. Too bad this natural resource does not provide labor for Islanders.

The accompanying "Historical Interest" map shows Island docks known to the Milwaukee office of the U.S. Engineers. Cooperages to make barrels for shipping fish existed on Rock and St. Martin's Islands before any were in operation here. Eaton's map shows a cooper's shop on Indian Point slightly north of where Swenson's dock appears on the map.

The "Wood Dock -1873-5" in Washington Harbor was Nolans. This was later Hannes Johnson's fish dock and finally Rusings. I have placed an asterisk (*) on the map on the west side just north of Denny's Bluff to show where McDonald's wood dock was.

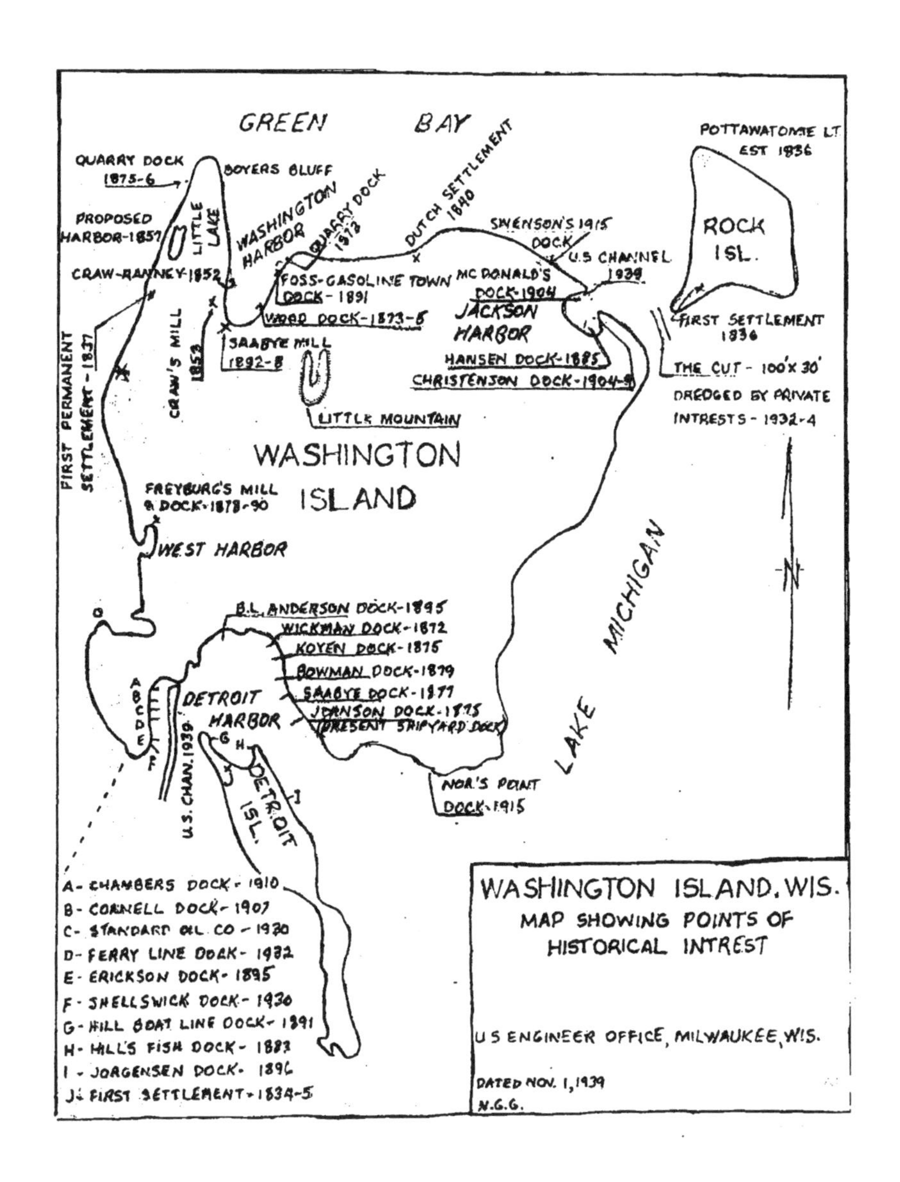
GREEN BAY
POTTAWATOMIE LT EST 1836
QUARRY DOCK 1875-6
BOYERS BLUFF
PROPOSED HARBOR-1857
LITTLE LAKE
WASHINGTON HARBOR
QUARRY DOCK 1873
DUTCH SETTLEMENT 1840
SWENSON'S 1915 DOCK
U.S CHANNEL 1939
ROCK ISL.
CRAW-RANNEY 1852
FOSS-GASOLINE TOWN DOCK-1891
MC DONALD'S DOCK-1904
JACKSON HARBOR
WOOD DOCK-1873-5
FIRST SETTLEMENT 1836
FIRST PERMANENT SETTLEMENT-1837
CRAW'S MILL 1853
SAABYE MILL 1892-8
HANSEN DOCK-1885
CHRISTENSON DOCK-1904-9
THE CUT - 100'X 30' DREDGED BY PRIVATE INTRESTS - 1932-4
LITTLE MOUNTAIN
WASHINGTON ISLAND
FREYBURG'S MILL & DOCK-1878-90
WEST HARBOR
N
LAKE MICHIGAN
B.L. ANDERSON DOCK-1895
WICKMAN DOCK-1872
KOYEN DOCK-1875
BOWMAN DOCK-1879
SAABYE DOCK-1877
JOHNSON DOCK-1875 (PRESENT SHIPYARD DOCK)
DETROIT HARBOR
U.S. CHAN. 1939
DETROIT ISL.
NOR'S POINT DOCK-1915
A- CHAMBERS DOCK - 1910
B- CORNELL DOCK - 1907
C- STANDARD OIL CO - 1930
D- FERRY LINE DOCK- 1932
E- ERICKSON DOCK- 1895
F- SNELLSWICK DOCK- 1930
G- HILL BOAT LINE DOCK- 1891
H- HILL'S FISH DOCK- 1883
I - JORGENSEN DOCK- 1896
J- FIRST SETTLEMENT- 1834-5
WASHINGTON ISLAND, WIS.
MAP SHOWING POINTS OF HISTORICAL INTREST
U S ENGINEER OFFICE, MILWAUKEE, WIS.
DATED NOV. 1, 1939
N.G.G.

FARMING ACCORDING TO THE ADVOCATE

(This series will attempt to cover Island farming from its beginning to the present. Most of the information is gleaned from the Island Archives copies of the *Advocate* and other publications dating back to 1862.)

Population: 1860--632 1865--267 1870--384

1869 189 acres had been cleared. There were 13 farms and 69 dwellings.

1870 There were 10 horses, 16 milch cows, 4 working oxen, 11 other cattle and 14 swine. Farms produced: 15 bushels of spring wheat, 15 bu. winter wheat, 1151 bu. potatoes, 1628# butter and 53 tons of hay.

Sept. 1876 100 acres of grain produced well. Potatoes produced a good crop whose quality and flavor "could not be beat".

June 1877 Garden crops and fields of Marrowfat peas were chewed by bugs and cut worms.

July 1877 160 acres of land was growing grain. With a bad infestation of potato bugs, farmers were using Paris Green poison. One tablespoon in a pail of water was applied to each plant. A Canadian farmer reported having used 300# per acre.

Aug. 1877 An agricultural survey showed: 27 horses, 100 "neat" cattle, 35 sheep and lambs, 2 mules and asses. Two-legged "mules and asses" were not counted. Wheat and rye were harvested and the sound of "flails"(hand threshing) on the threshing floors greeted one's ears. Resident mechanics had nearly made a new threshing machine locally.

Oct. 1877 Nine "Murphy" potatoes weighed 18#. Godfrey Kalmbach marketed his potatoes in Cleveland,Ohio. Because of the high quality of Island potatoes, many Green Bay parties sent here for their winter supply.

Nov. 1877 Mads Hanson had turnips weighing over 20# each and huge carrots and sugar beets.

1877 A survey showed these farming results for the year: 262 bushels of wheat, 2195 bu. oats, 595 bu. barley, 195 bu. rye, 1505 bu. potatoes, 3165 bu. "root" crops and 3000# butter.

Aug. 1878 Farmers here received a 6 horsepower, first-class threshing machine from Pitts Sons in Chicago. They also got a feed (grist) mill.

Oct. 1878 J.P. Hanson got 35 bu. winter wheat off 1 acre. D. Saucie averaged 26 bu. wheat per acre on his land. 5000 bu. of grain were harvested with two threshing machines at work. 0ne machine did nearly 4000 bu. 500 bu. of wheat was loaded on Ole Christianson's schooner Quickstep, to be taken to Sister Bay and made into flour. Before sailing a storm drove the vessel on the beach and the wheat was ruined.

June 1879 More acreage was planted in grain than ever before.

Oct. 1880 Wheat produced about 20 bu. per acre.

Oct. 1883 There was a good grain crop with 22 bu. produced for each bushel sown. H.0. Saaby got 85¢ a bu. for wheat and 55¢ a bu. for barley which he shipped to Sturgeon Bay. Farmers were improving their livestock by buying a number of "blooded" (purebred) cattle. Also they found a good home market for beef.

July 1884 Because of a rain shortage,farmers were importing hay.

Oct. 1884 Wm. Malloch's “White Star” seed potato produced 40 bushels. Farmers now had threshers, horse rakes and reapers.

March 1885 Hay and straw were scarce and farmers were hoping for navigation to open early so feed could be imported. Hay was selling at $20 per ton and hard to find even at that price.

Sept. 1885 Hay crop was nearly a failure, but St. Martin's, which had enough rain, had a good hay crop.

Oct. 1885 F.M. Hanson harvested 600 bu. of wheat from the 50 bu. he had sown, 10 acres of oats produced 300 bu. and 4 acres of buckwheat yielded 100 bu. He sold all but 90 bu. of wheat to a Green Bay miller at 73¢ a bu. He got flour for his own use at $4.50 per barrel. Later the Green Bay miller bought surplus wheat from other farmers at 73¢ a bu. A man from Michigan bought potatoes at 35¢ a bu. and butter at 16¢ a lb. Farmers imported hay because of the poor crop here. 800 people lived here. 70 of them were Icelanders.

March 11, 1886 W.O. Bradshaw tried to cross on the ice to Garrett Bay for hay, but it was unsafe to do so.

Aug. 1886 No shortage of hay this year.

Sept.1886 While the general grain yield was better than expected, the short-stalked oats was hard to reap and bind. There was a good fruit crop with Kalmbach and Saabye having "the finest apples grown in the state." The Duchess of Oldenberg variety was unequaled in size and flavor.

April 1887 It was said that a veterinarian wasn't needed to find the ribs on many Island stock. Feed scarcity and a very cold winter was hard on animals.

May 7,1887 Schooner Mariner arrived in Detroit Harbor from Milwaukee with hay and feed. Hay sold for $17 per ton. The tug Bruce, Escanaba, got 500 bu. of potatoes.

July 1887 H.O. Saabye, who had the finest 20 acres of wheat seen in years, was erecting a flour mill.

Oct. 1887 F.M. Hanson harvested 1500 bu. of wheat and oats.

Nov. 1887 A Green Bay firm bought all the surplus wheat and gave flour in exchange.

July 1888 Grasshoppers were so bad that H.M. Hanson turned his cattle in to graze on 20 acres of oats. He knew the field would not produce ripe grain. Millions and millions of these pests had ruined all the gardens and then turned to eating tree leaves. A Sturgeon Bay man was here taking fruit tree orders.

Aug. 1888 50 young folks on six sailing boats went to the Squaw Creek area of Little Bay de Noque, north of Eacanaba, to pick huckleberries. Later a huckleberry dance was held at Cornell's hall. A dance was also held at Saabye's grist mill.

April 1889 Grasshoppers hatched in a warm spell in March and it foreboded a bad pest season, but the cold April undoubtedly killed millions of them.

Oct. 1889 Chris Saabye sent to Springfield, Ohio for a portable steam engine to power his feed mill and thresher. Straubel and Ebling, Green Bay, bought grain at a low price. F.M. Hanson had 1140 bu.

Dec. 1889 Saabye's feed mill and house burned. Local farmers lost 800 bu. of grain.

Jan.1890 St. Martin's Island was uninhabited except for an old horse and bull that had been left to "fend for themselves."

Aug. 1890 A group of farmers met at Charles Jess' and decided to build the first Island cheese factory.

Sept. 1890 A Jacksonport man was selling fruit trees and nursery stock here. The Island had 100 families, 400 children and 3 schools. The grain crop was the best in years. Mr. Ebling, Green Bay, was expected here with a load of flour and feed. He would be buying grain. Chris Saabye bought a new steampowered threshing machine.

May 1891 The Island cheese factory association received the equipment from Tifft and Hay, Sturgeon Bay. An 18' by 40' building was being erected. The factory will be "one of the best in the county."

Sept. 1892 Lawrence Klingenberg bought a hay press and was busy pressing for farmers. Apples were plentiful, even though the trees were young. "Hooker" vessels were transporting them to Green Bay's west shore where they readily sold.

Cabinet maker Samuel Hanson applied for a patent on the potato digger he invented last winter. Castings were now arriving and it was being assembled. It was said to be a "reversible" kind that would bring two rows into one. Farmers had trouble finding enough pickers for the crop.

Dec. 1892 schooners Idea, Dreadnaught and Arrow had each taken a load of potatoes to market, while the Nellie and Annie had hauled two loads. There were also smaller shipments. Moneys from the fine crops allowed farmers to make many visible improvements. The scow Edith Koyen took potatoes, livestock, poultry, etc. to Escanaba.

Oct. 1893 A large quantity of potatoes was shipped to the Milwaukee market at 50¢ a bushel. Schooner Iris carried 3000 bu. for John Gislason.

In 1894 Assessor showed land on tax rolls as follows:

Year	1869	1882	1893
Acres	4064	11,456	14,316
Value	$17,192	$40,621	$56,170

DAIRY FARMING			
Acres		223 1/2	720
Hay-acres		182 1/2	800
Milch cows		67	285
Butter-lbs.		4385	12,250
Cheese-lbs.			6500

CROP HARVEST

Buckwheat	1896 bu.	130 Acres-2323 bu.
Corn		6A.-200 bu.
Barley	27 1/2 A.-628 bu.	12A.-249 bu.
Oats	141 1/2 A.-2340 bu.	350A.-8050 bu.
Rye	17 1/2 A.-56 bu.	10A.-108
Potatoes	8 A.-1402 bu.	170A.-18,303 bu.

July 1894 Grasshoppers were so bad that many farmers were cutting their grain crops to use as winter feed for animals.

Nov. 1894 Since Delta and Menominee Counties in upper Michigan were now raising lots of potatoes, the Island crop was shipped to southern Lake ports. Ahnapee, Kewaunee, Manitowoc, Sheboygan, Two Rivers and Port Washington were better marketing areas than Chicago or Milwaukee.

Dec,1894 Oats and hay crops were a failure. Bo Anderson brought in $700 worth of hay, oats, feed and flour which he readily sold. Corn, rye and potatoes produced a fair crop. Jessen sold a boat load of potatoes in Sheboygan at 55¢ a bushel. One firm handled 1000 bu. in Two Rivers at 60¢.

Aug. 1895 Several farmers were growing summer rye for fodder. It was mowed when the kernels were in the "milk stage" and as high as two tons per acre was harvested on unfertile land. John Aznoe sowed 2 bu. of rye seed per acre. This produced a thick crop with thin stalks. Grasshoppers had plagued crops for the last 3 to 4 years, but by the time they emerged, the rye matured enough to be safe from heavy onslaught.

By Sept 1895 a decided change from using yoked oxen to horses had occurred. Heavy, fine-looking draft horses were now being seen more and more.

Oct.1895 Besides Saabye's steam thresher, a.horse-powered thresher was at work here. Power came from a circular power “sweep” with four or five horse teams hitched to spoke-like projections from the central hub. Through gears, shafts and pulleys this provided the power in a manner similar to the steam engine. A long, flat belt extended from the "sweep" pulley to the thresher as was the case when the steam engine provided the power.

Schooner Medora took a 4000 bu. load of potatoes to a southern Lake port. William Jess, the largest single producer, shipped 1500 bu.

Nov. 1895 Three schooners hauled potatoes to market. A.A. Koyen bought potatoes at 18¢ a bu. and sent a boat load to Milwaukee where they sold for 20 to 28 cents, but freight and sales commission ran 5-8¢ a bu. Farmers were very disappointed as potatoes had become their principal cash crop. They hoped for a better price in the spring and many dug earth pits to store them over winter. Last year 25,788 bu. brought $10,984 and this year's crop was twice as big.

Mar. 1896 Eggs sold for 9 to 10¢ a dozen and butter was 12 to 16¢ a lb.

Aug. 1896 Army worms, in their first appearance here, destroyed some corn fields. They caused no big damage to other crops.

May 1897 Eggs were 6¢ a dozen and it was suggested that the chickens go on strike.

Oct. 1897 With a big potato harvest, A.A. Koyen was contracting at 33¢ a bu. and doing much better than last season.

May 1898 John Aznoe sold 700 bu. of potatoes at two times last fall's price. Many farmers sold several boat loads to Milwaukee and upper Michigan.

Sept. 1898 There was a good ripe pea crop. L.P. Ottosen harvested 83 bu. on 21 acres of land.

Sept. 1899 Two meat markets were operated by George P. Andersen and Jessen and Schmidt. Schmidt's sales averaged 1200 lbs. per week in the summer and he also bought livestock for the Escanaba market.

Dec. 1899 Bo Anderson moved the idle cheese factory to Detroit Harbor to serve as a warehouse for his store. In order to move it had to be cut in half and each part moved separately.

May 1900 At least $500 worth of nursery stock arrived here with most of it coming from New York.

Aug. 1900 The pea louse is here and most of the Island is infested.

Sept. 1900 August Koyen and Chris Saabye were threshing good crops of wheat and oats, but peas were a failure.

Oct. 1900 The second crop of clover was much better than the first one and there is an abundance of fodder. Wheat was producing 30 to 40 bu. per acre. Years ago Gus Swenson sowed a bushel and a peck of wheat and harvested 71 bu. His crop was so thick and heavy that it took a man three days to "handcradle" it. Thos. Launders got 90 bu. oats on 1 acre.

Nov. 1900 Three vessels loaded 12,000 bu. of potatoes for Chicago.

Aug. 1901 The apple crop was so heavy that the limbs had to be supported with props so they wouldn't break. John Aznoe had divided his 220 acres into eleven 20 acre plots.It required two tons of wire to do the fencing, but he felt it was the best investment he had made as he now had perfect control of pasture. Sept. 1901 oats was producing up to 50 bu. per acre.

Nov. 1901 Because of heavy rains, about 1/3 of potato crop rotted in the ground, still a good crop resulted. The price on the Island was 45-50¢ a bu. Schooners Iris, Madonna and Pride hauled loads south, while several smaller crafts took potatoes to upper Michigan,

Aug. 1902 The hay crop, which was the biggest ever, was "simply immense." Contract peas were nearly ripe and a heavy crop was expected.

Nov. 1903 At least 7 schooners and "hookers" were busy carrying potatoes and other produce to northern markets at fair prices. Schooners Madonna and Iris were taking loads south. Iris made a round trip to Manitowoc and back in 52 hours.

Mar. 1904 Hay and feed for animals was badly needed. Several farmers hitched their horse teams to large sleighs and traveled over heavy ice 30 miles to Escanaba for fodder. They reported no "traffic" problems on the journey.

Oct. 1904 45 acres of sugar beets was planted here for the first time under contract with a Menominee mill. 15 tons per acre was the best yield with a price of $4.50 per ton at the dock. Contract peas were $1 to $1.20 depending on the variety and they yielded an average of 25-30 bu. per acre. Most potato planting, spraying and digging was now done with horse teams. 250 bu. per acre was the average crop. Improved farm land sold for $20 to $35 per acre, while unimproved land went for $10 to $15 per acre.

April 1905 Peas and oats were the "mainstay" crops. In the last few years very little wheat was raised. Macaroni variety was being tried.

Nov. 1905 Schooner Madonna took potatoes to Waukegan for John Gislason. He got 65¢ a bu.

Oct. 1906 Carl J. Schmidt shipped 4600# of beef, veal, mutton and sausages to Escanaba. The schooner Lily Amoit recently took a consignment of meat to Menominee for Schmidt where a satisfactory price was obtained.

Nov. 1906 Four schooners were busy shipping potatoes to southern markets for John Gislason. Four "hookers"were delivering spuds to Green Bay's west shore ports. Price was 40¢ a bu.

May 1907 Ole Erickson, who had spent two years at a Madison agricultural college, brought a two-year old, 1400# Percheron stallion to the Island with plans to improve horse stock.

July 1907 Grasshoppers by the millions were devouring everything, leaving only stones and old hay fields.

Aug. 1907 Ole Bowman (now Lonnie Jorgenson's) built the first silo on the Island. This stone structure was 14' in diameter and 25' high.If successfull, others will also be building silos. (Prior to this time, some farmers had "pit" silos dug into the ground.)

Oct. 1907 With dairying now the principal farm business, this Island will be able to support double the population. Grain raising is no longer practical except for home use and even this hardly pays compared to what other crops the acreage could produce. There was a bumper crop of potatoes with several farmers harvesting at least 1000 bu.and many others getting 500 or more bu. The quality has never been better and if the price is not below 35¢ the farmers will do well.

Gustav Jacobsen invested $85 in a potato digger and he was busy at several neighbors. 40,000 bu. was ready for sale and all the local vessels were making repeated trips to markets. Vessels mentioned were: Schooners Joses, Lily Amoit, Madonna, Stevens, G. W. Wescott, Rose and steam barge Suet. Price- 45¢ a bu.

Nov. 1907 The first attempts at raising alfalfa here were unsuccessful. The first season it flourished, then withered and died. Some wondered if the seed was inferior or the soil presented problems. It was doing very well in the rest of the county where soil and climate was very similar to here.

Mar. 1908 Bo Anderson drove a team across the ice to Menominee and he expects to make another trip.

April 1908 Several farmers are preparing ground for planting of cherry trees.

May 1908 Eight horses brought here by a dealer sold for about $200 each. He plans to bring 7 more. Due to warm weather, young grasshoppers are already in evidence. Old age seems to be the only thing that kills them.

June 1908 Last year Gunnar Sigurdson harvested 75 bu.of potatoes from a planting of one bu. of Banner variety.

Aug. 1908 About 20 acres of cherry trees were planted last year. Enough orders have been placed for 20 acres more. The trees will be delivered this fall and planted next spring.

Oct. 1908 Carl Schmidt sold his meat business and 9 acres, plus his house on 2 acres to George Anderson for $2200. He was looking for another place, either here or in the county. Later in the month he bought Charles Jess' farm and personal property for $3600 and was already hard at work.

Nov. 1908 In the last 2 years over 5000 Ostheim variety sour cherry trees had been planted. There was talk of having a cannery here. Ole and Jens Hanson and Wallace Bowman attended agricultural school in Madison.

Dec. 1908 The Washington Island Local Union No. 5438 was organized with 22 farmer members and more expected to join. This was a branch of the state farmer's Union of A.S.E.

The tax roll by school district for $100 valuation was announced: District 1 (Washington Harbor) = $2.53, District 2 (Detroit Harbor) = $1.89, District 3 (Jackson Harbor) = $2.20, District 4 (Eastside) = $2.31.

Jan.1909 Treasurer Gudmundson reported that two-thirds of the tax money had already been collected.

April 1909 At the annual town meeting a big discussion centered around whether cattle should be restrained or allowed to roam freely as they had to date. The vote was 93 for restraint and 58 against it.

Gustave Boucsein and Jens Hansen traveled to Wyoming to inspect irrigated government land that was being offered at $15 per acre. Later Jens reported he was so pleased that he bought 60 acres.

Oct. 1909 Several thousand cherry trees were on order. So far nearly 10,000 had been planted here. The good, average price for cherries was $55 per hundred.

Gus Boucsein,Ole Erickson and Haldor Gudmundson, who had studied scientific farming at Madison, were introducing others to new farming methods, seeds, grasses and blooded stock, Registered Holstein cattle, Percheron horses, special breeds of hogs, sheep, ducks and chickens. Alfalfa was now being raised successfully. Yields of peas, oats and barley were the greatest in Island history.

Oct. 1909 Islanders winning first prize at the Door County Fair were: John Malloch for citrons, Sigurd Sigurdson for sunflowers and Arni Gudmundson two prizes for his Astrachan Red and Iowa Beauty apples. It was said that many Island grains would have won if they had been entered.

Nov. 1909 40,000 bu. of potatoes were available for sale and there was a good demand for them. At Kenosha they brought 38¢ to 45¢ a bu. The growers would get $15-20,000 for the crop, the best the Island had ever done. Capt. Peder Hansen had 2200 bu. of the finest ever seen.

July 1910 The farmers again cut their oats for hay fodder to save them from the grasshoppers.

Aug. & Sept. 1910 Ole Christianson on the Flotilla was bringing hay and other feed here to supplement the poor crops. At least 200 tons of hay from Kewaunee and much corn, oats, etc. was needed. The hay sold for $20 per ton.

Nov. 1910 The pea crop was a failure with many not even getting their seed back. Schooner Petrel took a load of potatoes for John Gislason, the Lily E. took 10,000 bu. for George Mann and the Geo. A. Marsh took 14,000 bu. for the local farmer's union. A.A. Koyen planned a shipment, but the schooner skipper changed his mind.

July 1911 Vernie Richter was the first of the local strawberry growers to supply the home market when he picked and sold 50 quarts on the 13th. Other commercial growers were: Mrs. Mads Svendsen, Squire Gudmundson, Ole Hagen, G.F. Paulig, Thos. Launders and John D. Johnson. Some picked 50 cases.

July 1911 Over 1000 cases of strawberries were gathered and sold here. Quality and flavor were excellent.

Sept. 1911 Large loads of apples were shipped on Ignatius Kiss' vessel. Corn was being cut and was now one of the farm staples.

Oct. 1911 There was a scarcity of wooden barrels to ship apples in. 40,000 bu. of potatoes would go to market.

Dec. 1911 Schooner Grace M. Filer carried 11,500 bu. of potatoes to market, this equaled 23 carloads. Jens Jacobsen sold these to a commission man on W. Randolph Street, Chicago for 7O¢ a bu. net. The man pronounced that it would just be enough potatoes to furnish breakfast for the western metropolis. This was the best ever for a large quantity shipment.

May 1912 Potatoes were $1 per bu. About $1000 worth of nursery stock was planted. Several plum orchards were set out.

Aug. 1912 Several boats carried people to upper Michigan to pick huckleberries. There was a big demand and they brought 12¢ a quart. (I remember picking some blueberries and huckleberries in a wood clearing south of our present home.)

Nov, 1912 Ole Hagen harvested 2000 bu. of potatoes. Schooner Grace M. Filer loaded 13,000 bu. in 2 1/2 days. 80 loads had passed over the Koyen scales by 8 AM and a procession of wagons nearly 1/2 mile long waited to unload. One day 142 loads, totalling between seven and eight thousand bu. was put aboard. The schooner Arendal followed and took nearly as large a consignment for George Mann and it loaded 6000 bu. in one day. Mann's load netted 34¢ a bu. Schooner Belle Brown was prepared to load and would be followed by a fourth vessel.

Dec. 1912 The schooner George Marsh was reported missing with a load of potatoes shipped by the Farmers Union and Jens Jacobsen in charge. However, it was later learned that she managed to reach a port on the eastern shore of Lake Michigan.

Oct. 1913 The yield of potatoes for shipment was 45,000 bu. George Mann had 7000 bu. load on the schooner Arendal. He would either pay 50¢ per bu. outright, or take them to market for whatever they would sell for. The best yield was 400 bu. from 18 bu. planted.

Nov. 1913 Booth Fish Co. dock in Washington Harbor was the only practical one for loading potatoes on vessels. They demanded a cent a bushel for passage over their dock. Eventually the Railroad Rate Commission was called in and they lowered it by 40 percent. This seemed satisfactory to all. However, a diversion of freight to Matt Foss' dock, across the harbor, began.

Gasoline schooner James H. Hall took on 3000 bu. of rutabagas and 1000 bu. of potatoes here and stopped at Baileys Harbor for the rest of their load.

Dec. 1913 Jens Jacobsen got 43¢ per bu. net for the load he accompanied to market.

May. 1914 Peter Yudin, Marinette butcher, bought and shipped over $2000 worth of livestock here. Christ Hansen's 1940# bull brought 6¢ a lb.totalling $116.40 -the largest price ever. Christ replaced this bull with a pure bred Holstein that was one year old. A large number of fruit trees were planted.

June 18, 1914 Last Monday a heavy frost did vast damage to crops.

July 1914 J.W. Cornell, the Island's biggest cherry producer, expected 300 crates and had 60 picked the first day. George Nelson, who planted 200 trees 3-4 years ago,had the prettiest orchard.

Sept. 1914 There were lots of wild blackberries and hazel nuts.

Oct. 1914 A 30,000 bu. crop of potatoes brought about 35¢ a bu. Capt. Peder Hansen's nephews raised 1100 to 1200 bu. for him.

Nov. 1914 Lots of second crop clover went to seed, but only Ole Hagen harvested about $50 worth. Few farmers knew that Pete Jensen had an attachment for hulling clover seed on his thresher.

Mar. 1915 Anticipating a big fruit crop, Chris Saabye had his fruit box factory running full time.

June 1915 The creamery was being built and hoped to be running in 60 days. $5000 worth of stock had been subscribed and an agreement had been made with a Chicago promotion company who would build a 26' by 40' structure and equip it for $4575. If desired, they would also furnish a buttermaker at $75 per month. The balance of the money raised was to go into a sinking fund for the local company. The land (site of present Chalet) was bought from L.W. Hansen.

July 1915 Lots of cherries were picked. Workers were paid 24¢ for filling a 30# crate. The creamery machinery arrived on the Goodrich boat from Chicago and they hoped to be ready to receive milk in about a week. Koyens drilled a well for the creamery.

Aug. 1915 Hastings Industrial Company, that promoted the creamery, had no difficulty collecting for the shares sold. Those short of cash took bank notes and the W. I. Creamery Co. was incorporated. The first day 1411# of cream was churned into 550# of butter. Some 30 farmers began shipping, but this was expected to increase to about 50. Cream was received on Mon., Wed. and Fri. from 7 to 11 AM. Later 1100# of butter was made in one week.

Aug. 1915 1300 cases of cherries and about 10 cases of small fruit, including strawberries and currants, were shipped. Also several hundred cases were sold locally.

Sept.9, 1915 Heavy frost occurred last week. Farmers expect the largest crop of grain ever. Oscar Nichol was at the creamery learning the trade. The creamery made the second butter shipment last week consisting of 12 tubs. (Butter was shipped in large, wooden tubs, "ferkins", to market where it was re-worked into cubes, packaged and sold to retail markets.) Also about 200# had been sold locally. The first shipment in August was between 1300 and 1400#.

Sept. 23, 1915 The farmers received their first checks from the creamery. They were paid 23¢ a lb. for butterfat.

Nov. 1915 The Farmer's Union was busy getting ripe, Marrowfat peas ready for shipment with an unprecedented price of $3.35 a bushel. Oscar Nichol took over as buttermaker and the farmers agreed to keep shipping to the creamery as long as butterfat was above 20¢ a lb. Presently it was 24¢.

May 18, 1916 Last Saturday 600# of butter was shipped to Gladstone and Escanaba. They would take any that could be spared.

June 1916 800# of butter was made in one day and the following Monday 1300# of cream was received at the factory.

July 1916 Checks for two weeks supply of cream totalled about $600.

Nov. 1916 20,000 bu. of potatoes were ready to be shipped. This was about half of the usual crop. As potatoes were scarce, the price had risen to $1.30 per bu. Peas were bringing $1. per bu., which was still considered a good price.

April 1917 A prospective potato buyer was here offering $2. per Bu., but none were available.

Oct. 1917 The Farmer's Union, with Art Wickman in charge, sent 60 cattle to market. The motor vessel Arrow took them to Escanaba where they were loaded in rail cars and sent to Chicago.

Nov. 1917 There was an abundant potato crop with prices of 75¢ to 80¢ a bu.

April 1918 Two cargoes of cattle were shipped to market. The motor vessel Wisconsin went to Sturgeon Bay while the Marion took a load to Menominee. A third cargo will be shipped in the near future.

May 1918 35 pure bred Holstein heifer calves were bought in Sheboygan County, shipped by rail to Green Bay, then trucked to a dock where they were lifted by canvas slings onto Ole Christianson's gas schooner Flotilla. Many spectators were amused by the animals antics while being loaded. This was the first shipment under the Island Holstein Breeder's Assn. 14 of these calves were being raised by Island boys and girls who planned to compete in a calf show in the fall with winners going to the county fair.

Nov. 1918 The motor vessel Wisconsin took 15,000 bu. of potatoes to Racine for Mac Gudmundson and Co. Freight at 18¢ per bu. was the highest ever.

Feb. 1919 The county agent and a doctor from Madison analyzed many soil samples and reported most of them showed acidity. They recommended pulverizing limestone and spreading on the fields. They feel this is the reason alfalfa crops here have failed although clover is grown successfully. The following year lots of marl was found in the "big marsh" (Hemlock Dr. north of Lakeview Rd.). This tested 97% calcium carbonate which would sweeten acid soil and fertilize. A lady, who had a sickly house plant, put two spoonfuls of marl into the plant's soil and it became large and healthy. Marl looks like yellow clay and is very sticky. It dries into hard lumps which can be crushed into fine powder.

April 1919 An agricultural survey of the Island showed:

Year	Cows	Heifers	Steers	Bulls	Total
1918	408	267	231	49	955
1919	482	424	164	59	1129
Increase	74	157	67	10	174
Percent	15	37	**28.6	13	16

** Number of steers had decreased as there was more money in dairy cattle. The Island was the only dairy area in the state that was free of cattle tuberculosis. Holstein Breeder's Assn. members proudly displayed signs reading "Pure Bred Bull Used on This Farm". Within a year there were no "scrub" bulls on the Island. Butter was advertised as coming from TB free herds.

Dec. 1919 There were plans for a cheese factory on the Island. One man had bought the equipment and the old Detroit Harbor school which he planned to move and use as the factory. The creamery owners ordered the equipment to make cheese at the creamery. As there was less profit in butter, they planned to make cheese 5 days a week and butter one day a week. There was not enough milk to support two factories. The old Detroit Harbor, one-room school was bought and moved by Ted Thorarinson to its present site (Vagabond) and opened as a grocery store.

Apr. 1920 Oscar Nichol, buttermaker earned about $1300 per year.

Nov. 1920 Schooner Oscar Newhouse took two loads, 5O00 bu. each, to market for Mac Gudmundson. Art Wickman and Jens Jacobson were taking about l0,000 bu. of potatoes and apples to Chicago to sell for the farmers.

Mar. 1921 The creamery planned to open soon as a cheese factory. It re-opened May 2, 1921.

Dec. 1921 At the present 74% of the Island dairy cattle were pure bred Holstein, while in 1918 44% had been.

Many farmers had raised over 1000 bu. of potatoes on 6 acres.

Feb. 1922 At the annual creamery owners meeting it was decided to sell the cheese making equipment and make only butter. The demand is much greater than the supply. Several tubs of butter, which were tested by the state in Madison, scored 92 to 93. This was the best that could be obtained from "gathered" cream. Patrons and shareholders were busy.using up to 16 horse teams, filling the icehouse at the creamery,

Mar. 1922 Farmers were delivering about 1300# of cream to the factory twice a week, 92 score butter was being made consistently. The University Dairy Department scored it among the highest.

June 1922 A farmer's meeting was held to discuss reviving the Island Holstein Breeders Assn. In one churning, the creamery produced 1100# of butter. This was becoming one of the most successful seasons.

Sopt. 1, 1922 Apparently the Breeders Assn. was revived as they held their first annual picnic (later called the "Bull" picnic)

Many committees worked to prepare for a big affair.The picnic meal was served at the ball park and Ole Hagen's grove. Horse races followed. In the girl's saddle race the winner was the Camp Hellanic's dietician riding Dr. Leasum's horse. The camp director of riding came in second on a camp-owned horse. In the boy's race Roland Koyen won riding Lawrence Gislason's horse. Bert Tiebold was second on Wilfred Koyen's steed and Ben Malloch finished third on Dr. Leasum's horse. The most exciting was a sulky race. Mac Gudmundson won with his own pacer (formerly a professional racing horse) and Charles Boshka placed second using Lawrence Gislason's pacer.

There were many children's races. The most exciting was a “chicken” race which 10 girls entered. Charles Jensen gave the winner a fine.spring pullet.

A "slow ball" game was played between the regular Island team and the "Scrubs", who gave the regulars a run for their money. No results were known as they quit counting when the score reached 50.

In the evening six reels of movie film from the University of Wisconsin were shown, interspersed with local talent vaudeville acts. A dance followed into the wee hours. Fully 500 persons attended the afternoon activities and at least half stayed for the evening events. They voted to make this an annual affair. About $200 was netted by the Holstein Breeders Assn. largely due to the generous contributions of most of the material. This very successful event was held each August for many years and was popularly known as the "Bull Picnic".

Oct. 1922 The potato yield was below average with about 125 bu. per acre. However, Jens Hanson was getting 240 bu. per acre from certified seed potatoes. The produce company paid only 15¢ per bu.

May 1923 Jens Hanson was the proud owner of triplet calves born to a pure-bred Holstein.

June 1923 Small pigs arrived on nearly every boat. This will eliminate the pork shortage which existed last year.

July 1923 a survey showed 2400 farms in Door County with over 200,000 bu. of potatoes annually, grown mostly in the northern part.

Aug. 1923 The second annual "bull picnic" had a program similar to the first one. Several persons were expected from Sturgeon Bay and other places. Besides the two regular ferry runs at 7 AM and 12 noon, a special boat would return visitors to Ellison Bay that night. The ball game was between "Fats" and "Leans".

May 1924 On Rock Island, Thordarson had a three-ton tractor pulling trees to clear for planting a fruit orchard.

May 1925 THe creamery closed after a turbulent existence of about 6 years. Too many were shipping cream off the Island making the overhead too great for the volume produced. After the closing nearly all the cream would be shipped away until the building re-opened as a cheese factory. The first buttermaker's name was not given. Oscar Nichol followed and the last one was a man named Holmes, who married Elsie Boyce, a local lady. A 30' by 30' concrete block addition was being built. More profit was expected from cheese.

The Island became the first place in Wisconsin to be accredited to ship cattle anywhere in the United States for 3 years without further testing. There was nearly 1000 head of cattle here. Also, carload lots of hogs from here brought a premium of 10 cents per hundred-weight over the market price.

June 1925 A new strain of Alaska peas called "Huntlers" (early maturing) was being tried here. The Sturgeon Bay and Ashland agricultural experiment stations had developed this fine type of canning peas which will be raised here for seed. Wisconsin was now heavily involved in growing canning peas. Previously peas here were the type used for such dishes as pea soup.

July 1925 most of the cherries were shipped to Escanaba. They sold for $2 per crate here.

The town crew had a big operation going at Anderson's sawmill where plenty of sawdust was available. In one day between 6 and 7 tons of grasshopper poison was mixed. Water and salt was hauled to the site and, along with molasses and poison, this was mixed into the sawdust. Several men were busy distributing the sacked poison around to infested areas. Usually the farmer's families then spread it on the fields. Hopefully.this would kill the grasshoppers before they reached the egg-laying stage. This was started in northern Door County last year and will be repeated here next year.

Aug. 1925 At the "bull picnic" Judge Grasse from Green Bay was the principal speaker. The chief of Wisconsin county agents and a representative from "Hoard's Dairyman" magazine also spoke.

Oct, 1925 The cheese factory re-opened with twelve farmers bringing about 1500# of milk daily, but within a month 25 farmers were bringing over 3000# daily. Andy Justinger came here as the cheesemaker and remained here for years and years. Before long over a ton of cheese was shipped and Islanders were enjoying its fine quality.

Ole Erickson had five swarms of honeybees and had sold over 150# of honey. There was still plenty in the hives to keep the bees over winter,

Oct. 1926 Islanders were planning to raise Yorkshire bacon-type hogs which bring a 75¢ per hundred-weight premium.

8/28/1925 Oats and mixed grain crops on the Island are excellent and nearly all has been harvested.

10/16/25 August Koyen lost a valuable horse last week when his team ran away.The horse came in contact with a fence brace which went two feet into the horse's chest .The horse was shot to end its suffering.

The cheese factory is selling excellent cheese locally and has shipped over a ton to market with good returns.

Bee keeping is a new industry here.It was tried about 1910,but the winters were too severe. Ole Erickson bought two swarms last spring. He now has five swarms and has sold about 150 lbs. of honey, with plenty left for the bees this winter. All wish Ole success in this venture,

10/30/25 Farmers spent an afternoon and evening at Tom's Hall with Professors Humphrey and Delwiche, arranged by County Agent Bailey. Discussion centered around the possibility of raising more cash crops and the Island livestock situation. In the evening Humphrey gave a very interesting lecture on his trip through the Argentine Republic where farms are up to 600,000 acres in size. Island farmers learned that orderly marketing of produce can increase income by 11%,while producing higher grade cheese, butter, fruit or vegetables can bring 36% more profit. Further through selling border producing cows and hens and farming the best land more extensively can add up to 72% to farm income. These on milk production costs were presented:

Annual milk production per cow	Production cost per cow
5000 lbs.	$2.67
6-7000 lbs.	2.10
8-9000 lbs.	1.81
10-11000 lbs.	1.67
12,000 lbs. and over	1.55

In 1925 the annual milk production per cow averaged about 5000# and that means a loss to the owner if milk is bringing $2.67 per cwt. A cow producing 8000# or more annually is a profit maker even if the price for milk is $2.00 per cwt. Farmers were urged to keep records of the production and butterfat content for each daughter of the purebred bulls and compare this to the record of the dam of each, also plan to test the amount of butterfat in the milk regularly.

The first year's results of "Hustler" seed pea raising was highly satisfactory. The Island has an excellent opportunity to develop a specific trade in this line.free from becoming mixed with other varieties. Also, farmers could install a small flour mill and raise enough wheat to supply local needs.

11/6/25 25 patrons are bringing over 3000# of milk to the cheese factory daily - formerly 12 patrons were bringing 1500# daily.

In the last 10 days one farmer patronized the Island creamery he netted $17 for his milk, but in the first 8 days he took milk from the same herd to the cheese factory he netted $22, even when the factory had only 12 patrons and the same overhead. About 2000 bu. of potatoes were shipped this year in place of the usual 20-40,000 bu. usually shipped. Most sold at $1.15/bu.

3/19/26 Four horse teams took about 5 tons of cheese from the Island factory to Ellison Bay, across the ice. Patrons claim about 20% more for milk in cheese versus butter.

4/16/26 The cheese factory is growing and this poem was submitted:

Try to co-operate and continue to squeeze
The teats of the cow that produces-the milk
That brings you the money that buys shirts of silk.

Although just at present returns may be small,
I'm sure we'll do better in Summer and Fall.
While winter was on, with me you'll agree
The freight was sure high and small was our fee.

So we must co-operate in this factory for cheese,
Results will be greater and all will be pleased.
And now just a favor we ask of you all
"Tis: Please take your whey in cans big or small."

5/28/26 35 cattle, a mixture of milch cows and fat beef cattle, was shipped last week for Peter Youdin of Oconto. He also bought some horses, but since there was a full load of cattle, the horses weren't taken away that day.

6/25/26 There was an active campaign to get rid of flies. The Dept. of Agriculture no longer issues free bulletins on fly control, but a place is found that sells them for about $100. It is expected that about 200 copies will be distributed to Island homes. Read carefully and put the recommendations into practice. By everyone co-operating we can materially reduce the danger of disease spread and relieve homes and animals of this tormenting pest.

6/18/26 There are rumors that the John Aznoe farm iaay become a golf course with the spacious home becoming-the clubhouse.

7/23/26 Professor Humphrey, Wis. College of Agriculture, met with Island dairymen at Charles Hansen's farm. About 50 attended showing that interest was greatly stimulated through the use of the Association's purebred bulls for the past several years. A big judging contest event is planned the 1927 "bull'" picnic. President George Hanson, of the Holstein Assn., suggested that each farmer train his best cow so she can be readily, handled in the show ring before next year's event.

The bacon hog industry was discussed by Fred Hansen, Wis. Livestock and Meat Improvement Council. A number of Island farmers intend to increase their pork production as a side line to dairying. The bacon-hog production is built up largely around the Yorkshire breed. The farmers will meet again on Sept. 30 when Fred Hansen will demonstrate the difference between a "bacon side" and a "lard-type side"

7/30/26 Two severe storms hit here last week. The first, about 6 A.M. Tuesday, assumed tornado proportions in some places. It demolished the creamery icehouse and destroyed considerable timber on Louis Hansen's and Martin A. Andersen's property, close to the creamery. At 3:30 A.M. the next day the second storm came in from the west. This spouted incessant lightning, rain torrents and intermittent hail resulting in heavy damage to crops and gardens. Nearly a dozen buildings were damaged. August Koyen's large barn was moved about 3' off its foundation and twisted out of shape. George Hansen's smaller barn was moved some and out of shape. Jake Lindahl's old landmark barn which had weathered many storms for over a half century, was unroofed. Much timber was blown down all over the Island. This was considered the most severe storm in old inhabitant's memory. Hail did much damage to the cherry crop. 12 of George Madsen's cherry trees were badly broken. Besides two severe storms last week, there seems to have been a little one Saturday which demolished a telephone pole midway between Detroit and Washington Harbors on Main Road. Evidently there was a car passing about that time as there was a Ford light found near the pieces of the-pole. Otherwise the storm seems to be a mystery.

8/20/1926 There is a wonderful abundance of wild raspberries with thousands of quarts being picked and preserved.

8/27/26 The Farmers Picnic, under the auspices of the W.I. Holstein Breeders Assn, was held yesterday and is now an annual affair with considerable importance. New features are added each year and now it is a veritable little fair with races, livestock judging, athletic games, public speaking and discussion of farmer's various problems. Many people visit from other parts of the county and state. The Holstein Assn. realized a modest profit through the day and from the movie and dance in the evening.

Nearly four inches of rain fell last night. Several grain fields had been cut the day before and many fields were ready for harvesting. Fortunately damage was slight.

9/24/26 Rainy weather made it difficult to harvest late peas and the second crop of alfalfa.

10/10/26 A meeting regarding bacon hogs was held with Fred Hansen, Wis. Livestock and Meat Improvement Council, Lloyd Larson, Cudahy Packing Co., and County Agent E.G. Bailey. Plans were made to buy a Yorkshire boar to sire next spring's pig litters. Possibly the boar will be bought at Jefferson Bacon Hog Show on Oct. 14. The United States has lost much of the foreign market because Denmark and Canada are concentrating on bacon-hog types. These hogs bring a premium of $.75 per cwt. The best bacon sides are obtained by crossing Yorkshire sires with sows of other breeds. Feeding barley and skim milk (soured) with alfalfa pasture and enough digester tankage and oil meal to balance makes an ideal ration for bacon production. U.S. bacon-hog raisers habit is to market heavily six months of the year, namely: April, May, June, October, November and December. However, Canadians have stabilized the pork flow to where fluctuation is only a few thousand animals per month. Hansen cut a bacon side and a side of fat pork. The bacon side was fully three inches longer, yielding a larger percentage of high priced bacon, loin and chops.

10/22/26 Farmers are hindered from harvesting their potato crop. Lack of frost to kill tops so potatoes ripen and over-abundance of rain, which makes difficult digging, are to blame.

10/26/26 Island seems to be a magnet that draws teachers here who marry Islanders and now it has drawn our cheesemaker into the fold. During the creamery's history it had three buttermakers, two who were already married, and Walter Holmes who married Elsie Boyce, an Island girl. Andrew Justinger, cheesemaker, came here a year ago last July when the place began to operate as a cheese factory. From Sheboygan Falls, he worked here continuously until last September when he took his first vacation. With him on the trip was Miss Myrtle Andersen, daughter of Mr. and Mrs. John O, Anderson. It proved to be about a two weeks honeymoon trip with visits to his old home and several other places. This week over 200 invited guests helped celebrate their nuptials at Nelson's Hall.

Last Friday a freak electric storm with blinding lightning, almost deafening thunder and torrential rain mixed with hail lasted about 2½ hours. About one week before Ole Erickson's barn was struck by lightning with very slight damage.

10/29/26 Farmers still digging potatoes. Geo. O. Mann bought 5000 bu. one day at $1./bu. The crop is light, but not affected by rot like in some other places.

10/21/27 Farmers are busy filling silos with corn and digging potatoes. Fortunately there's been no heavy frost yet.

12/2/27 The local cheese factory should be well patronized, not only when the cheese price is high. Lately butterfat is over 60¢/lb.

12/16/27 Farmers on the Island began growing seed peas in the early 1870s, so they have been grown here for at least 50 years. There is a special prominence for Islanders raising seed peas as a cash crop. Several years ago Toweles and Brandeis, Sturgeon Bay, bought 40,000 bu. from the Island, mostly Marrowfat variety and they took first prize at the International Grain Exhibit. Each fall the pea harvest companies rush agents here to contract next year's crop. About three years ago, some Island farmers formed the W.I. Seed Pea Growers Association, primarily to grow Hustler variety peas. This Alaskan variety is best known for being canned by factories. This fall V.O. Richter's Hustler peas took 1st prize at the county, state and International exhibits. Other samples were sent in by George Hansen, Chas. O. Hansen, Lauritz Klingenberg, Wilfred Koyen and Ole C. Erickson. 5 of the 6 specimens took prizes, sweeping all places for that type. Much credit is due E.G. Bailey, former county agent, and the farmers who formed the association. This year 14 tons of Hustler peas shipped produced about $1700.

2/3/28 At the annual meeting of the Island Creamery Co. reports showed that 1927 was the most profitable year in history. It started as a creamery and made butter for several years.

This proved to be a "rough voyage", although the first year over 30 patrons produced $32-33,000 worth of butter and paid about 6% dividend. Following this, for several years the stockholders received no dividends and finally operations were suspended for a summer. Then more stock was issued and cheese making equipment was installed. By the end of the second year as a cheese factory there were 34 patrons(now 36) bringing milk to the factory. Almost $35,000 worth of cheese was made and patrons received much more for their butterfat than neighbors who shipped cream off the Island. Much new equipment was installed, yet they still paid 6% dividend on all stock. More peace, harmony and satisfaction is the most promising feature. Production would increase at least 50% if all Island farmers were patrons. Very little more overhead expense would result. Farmers would get a still better price for butterfat and dividends would rise. Company directors were: Rob Gunnarsson, Carl Nelson, Jens Jacobsen, Louis Gunnlaugsson and George Hansen. President - Gunnersson, V.P. - Carl Nelson,, Secty. - Jens Jacobsen, associates - Gunnlaugsson and Hansen, Cheese Maker - Andy Justinger and Clerk - Anna Gunnlaugsson,

3/2/28 In making farming a business proposition, nearly 200 county farms have registered names with Bert Carmody, Registerer of Deeds. Local registered names and owners are:

Claradell ----------------------Charles O. Hansen
Circle Ridge ------------------George Hansen
Evergreen ---------------------Christ A. Hansen
E. Randolph-------------------Jens Jacobsen
Fairview -----------------------Ole C. Erickson
Happy Hollow ---------------Harry Hansen
Happy Home -----------------Hans B. Hansen
Pleasant Valley --------------John Aznoe

5/11/28 A new enterprise started May 1st. Brothers Chas. O and Henry.(sic) Harry Hansen started a door-to-door milk and cream route. This has been a long felt need. With adjoining farms, good herds and facilities, these men of integrity will treat their patrons right. There is no reason why success should not lie in their path..

6/15/28 Beetles, which appeared on the shore have been working their way inland. If not coped with immediately they will become a real crop menace. B.F. Rusy, county agricultural agent and Dr. Granovsky, Madison, swiftly made plans to alert farmers and begin action to control this infestation.

6/22/28 A committee of 5 men is searching for suitable farm land for an aircraft landing field on the Island. According to Nor Shellswick, four tracts are available as follows:

Peder Hansen farm	63 acres	$6,000.
Robt. Gunnersson farm	80 "	5,000.
Hans Hansen farm	98 "	10,000.
Geo. O. Mann farm	60 "	4,500.

Other- fields being considered are those of Jens Hansen, George Hansen and former Dr. Boucsein with no selling price set.

Aug. 1928 Over 500 people attended the annual Holstein Breeders' "Bull" picnic. Cherryland Airways plane, from Sturgeon Bay, arrived at the new airport at 8:30 AM. Because of high seas there was no ferry and the phone connection to the mainland had broken. For a half day the only communication with the mainland was Cherryland's plane. The meeting was held in the wood grove on the south side of the airport. Association President, George Hansen, called on Mr. Rusy to bring the meeting to order. Nearly every Island farmer was present along with a large number of summer and outside visitors. Then Mr. Goff commended the Association for their progress in breeding, as it celebrated its tenth year of existence. Arle Mucks, Secty. of Wisconsin Livestock Breeding Association, urged a maintenance of high breeding standards and said the Island would become famous as a breeding place of dairy cattle. Frank Swoboda, general manager of Natl. Cheese Production Federation of Plymouth, Wis., urged continuous herd improvement and cooperative marketing. Mr. Reeves, "Wisconsin Farmer" magazine, said the dairymen should not lose any chance for favorable publicity. He said the cherry business got lots of free and valuable publicity by taking advantage of every opportunity that arose. A tug-of-war was held between 10 farmers and 10 fishermen. Finally the "net pullers" gave way and the "teat pullers" won. The baseball game was followed by a pie eating contest. Cherryland Airways took many Island people for plane rides. Wm. Jess rode to Sturgeon Bay on this plane. Henry Fetzer and E.M. LaPlant who-had come by this airplane, also rode back home in it.

9/23/28 Snow flurries and on the 25th a real white blanket settled on parts of the island.

Oct. 1928 There are no farms for rent, except where a father rents to his son. Occasionally the son buys from the dad or heirs, or buys adjoining property with a price of about $100/ acre. Farms average under 100 acres with much timber.

1928 population a little over 1000, with 50 farmers. The oldest living farmer settled here in 1868 and came from Chicago where he was a ship's carpenter. There was a very good grain crop.

Magazine Writes Up Good Story on Washington Island. Has Over a Full Page of Interesting Pictures.

This article appeared in the Sept. 27, 1928 "Wisconsin Farmer". A representative of the magazine attended the annual picnic in August. Two pages of pictures showed the picnic crowd and County Agent Rusy and former agents Bailey and Goff. The caption on the latter picture is "Three boys who deserve a lot of credit". This article, one of many about the Island, is very interesting. Read it:

"The Indians called it "Death's Door". The French called it "Porte Des Mortes" and the present inhabitants call it "The Door" when referring to the strip of water off the Door County peninsula where Green Bay and Lake Michigan meet. This has been a favorite spot for archaeologists for years, containing as it does much Indian lore of great interest. "Death's Door" is so-called by the Indians because of a battle waged between the Winnebagoes and the Potawatami in this channel. While engaged in fighting, the wind rose and canoes were capsized and it is said that some 300 "braves" were either killed or drowned. It is from this legend that Door County gets its name.

Off the Door County peninsula are several islands: Plum, Rock, Chambers, Horseshoe, Washington and others. Washington is the largest and is the only one on which there has been any agricultural development. It is a part of Door County and is about eight miles from the mainland. In 1816 Col. John H. Miller, with several hundred men, was stationed at Green Bay.

This one was called Washington after the Father of our Country and also after the flagship of their fleet. Up until about 1880 fishing and lumbering served as the main occupation. Fishing is still an important industry and millions of dollar's worth of fish have been caught around the islands.

FIFTY FARMERS LIVE ON ISLAND

Washington Island has a population of a little over 1000 and of these 50 are farmers. We are advised that the oldest man on the island is Chris Saabye. He settled here in 1868, coming from Chicago, where he was a ship's carpenter. He followed his trade here and also worked in the lumber camps. As time permitted he cleared a little land, and today he has one of the good farms on the island.

In the early eighties several pioneers came to the island, most of them from Chicago or Milwaukee. Naturally in those days they worked in the camps and mills, but soon they realized the possibility of developing land and making homes of their own.

While attending the "Bull Days" celebrations a representative had the opportunity to meet some of the men who have contributed a great deal to the agricultural advancement of the island. S. Siguerson(sic) and Andrew Severson came to the island in 1884. Chris Hansen landed in 1882. John and Chris Peterson arrived in 1881 and Jens Jacobsen the same year. Oddur Magnusson is one of the "Old-timers" for he has been there since 1874. These men still live on their farms and in most cases on the original farm which they cleared, for few farms change hands on Washington Island.

(1928 "Wisconsin Farmer" article-continued.)

THEY ARE- GOOD CO-OPERATORS."

Co-operation has been the keynote. Several years ago co-operative organizations were formed. One of them was a branch of the Equity and Chris Hansen and Jens Jacobsen have been President and secretary since its inception. One year they shipped 70 carloads of potatoes to Chicago. A few potatoes are still raised, but the main industry of the island at the present time is dairying. Alfalfa predominates as the hay crop and a great deal of sweet clover is being used for pasture. Oats are making a good yield this year and most of the corn is put in the silo and there is one on almost every farm.

The county agents of Door County have had wonderful co-operation from the islanders with the result that great progress has been made. In a recent issue of the Wisconsin Farmer there was told something about the work accomplished by D.S. Bullock and County Agent M.B. Goff in organizing the Holstein Breeders association. The association purchased a well-bred bull and since then other bulls have been brought to the island, all of which have been owned by the association and each member pays a nominal service fee.

E.G. Bailey followed Goff as county agent and served in that capacity during the depression following the war (WWI). The farmers were hard up on Washington Island the same as in other localities and Mr. Bailey had his troubles. But during that time he got a lot of interest aroused in alfalfa and sweet clover with the result that they are being benefited now.

The present county agent, Ben Rusy, has carried out many projects started by the boys who preceded him and has added others. During a recent visit it was found that the farmers are 100 per cent for their county agent and Mr. Rusy advised us that he could always depend on the co-operation of the farmers on the island.

BREEDERS HAVE GREAT OPPORTUNITY

The Holstein Breeders of Washington Island have an opportunity to do more than has been accomplished by any other like number of farmers. As yet there are only a few pure-breds, possibly 25 females, but they are good. There are some excellent grades, in fact it is doubtful if one could drive over any other township and find fewer poor cattle than can be found in this isolated region. If the breeders would develop one certain family and stick to one line of breeding, in a few years they would have Holsteins to offer that could not be purchased elsewhere. It is a clean area and there is not much danger of getting any infection on the Island. During the past few years there has been a noticeable improvement with each succeeding generation. The daughters have produced more than their dams and the dams more than the grandame, but now comes the critical time. There are many good producers on the farms and it is going to be necessary to buy another bull in the very near future. The next bull must be one of outstanding individuality of known ancestry. One poor bull can ruin the dairy industry of the entire island. It isn't the same as if he were to be used on one herd only. The association will and should pay more for the next bull than they have ever paid before.

A better bull is needed to continue with the herd improvement idea. The breeders are alive to the situation and we know they will go ahead and not do anything that will cause them to drop back in any way.

(1928 "Wisconsin Farmer" article continued.)

THEY ARE STRONG FOR EDUCATION

It is interesting to know that there are six short course boys on the island. One of them, O.C. Erickson finished in 1907 and besides his advanced knowledge of agriculture, he took back a pure-bred heifer. He now has six pure-breds on his 125 acre farm, all progeny of his original purchase. The third generation will soon be ready for higher education and in all probability many will attend the university.

There are excellent schools and good gravel roads. All farms are connected by telephone, and of course this connects with the mainland. Each family is assessed $10 per year to maintain a doctor on the island. The taxes amount to less than $1 per acre. One sees a lot of stone fences and of course some old log houses, but as a whole the farm homes are modern, the land is well fenced and the buildings are in good repair.

GOOD PLACE FOR STATE PICNIC

If the Wisconsin Holstein Breeders Association is looking for an ideal place to hold its summer meeting, let us suggest Washington Island. From a scenic view point the peninsula and the islands cannot be duplicated in the state. Other than the help from county agents the Holstein Breeders on the island have had no outside assistance or encouragement and if the state association wants to hold its meeting where it would really do the industry the most good this would be the logical place.

PUT AN OLD SLOGAN TO WORK

The time-worn slogan,,"United WE Stand, Divided WE Fall" certainly rings true on Washington Island. As a result of their united efforts, it is a tuberculosis free area, the first in the country.

Only pure-bred bulls are used. All scrubs have been eliminated from the island and they test their cows regularly.

Jim Hill was right when he said: "See America First", but to Badger folks, let us suggest that you see the Door County peninsula and the Potawatomi islands before you say you have "seen Wisconsin". Another thing, if any of our readers suffer from hay fevers they can get relief in Door County and especially on Washington island.

(End of "Wisconsin Farmers" article.)

10/12/28 Pete Peterson just completed a new barn on the old Lindstrom property which looms up as an ornament on Main

Road. This is one of the really old farms. Almost 20 years ago a house was built here and conceded to be the finest on the Island at that time.(The old, original part was of early stove-wood construction.) The old barn had been in very poor condition and did not even exist for the last several years. The new structure is very noticeable and a welcome improvement.

10/26/28 Andersen Bros. finished threshing last Saturday and this was one of the best crops the Island has ever raised. There is an exceptionally large potato crop, but rain has hindered the harvest.

11/2/28 Incorporation papers were filed at Madison definitely establishing the Washington Island Airport with a $5000 capitalization. Pres. Geo. Mann, Vice-Pres. Dr. Chas. Colebaugh, Secty-Treas. Wm. Jess, Directors - Tom Goodman and Ted Gudmundsson. Movement for an airport started last spring and enthusiasm was boosted by the presence of North America Airways plane at the Door County Cherry Blossom festival. It was realized that if the Island wanted aircraft larger than small open-seaters it needed a modern field. In short order a group of men put the new field in shape. The 55 acre tract (part of Peder Hansen farm) had been purchased and tractors and graders made runways.

October 1929 Island potatoes had a good name and sold readily, while others were "a drug on the market."

Eventually potatoes grown elsewhere adopted the the name "Washington Island Potatoes." As their quality was inferior to Island grown ones, the good name was lost. Resorters still buy their winter supply here and say they can't get such good quality in the Chicago markets.

February 1929 Annual Creamery Co. meeting reports showed that over $35,000 worth of cheese and over 2000 # of whey butter were produced last year. Patrons averaged over 52¢/lb. for butter-fat, which was better than they would have received from selling the cream. Vernie Richter and Robt. Gunnersson attended the Holstein Friesan Breeder's Association state meeting in Madison.

March 1929 Nearly all Island roads are fairly passable for horse drawn vehicles, while main thoroughfare's are used by auto.

May 3 1929 The Holstein Breeders Association met to plan entertainment for the Wisconsin Holstein Friesan Breeders Assoc. Convention to be held here on July 25th. Special statewide interest is being manifested.

July 12, 1929 Jens Jensen's new barn was struck by lightning before it was finished. The bolt entered the cupola, followed the hay carrier track, branched off and shattered several studdings and did an estimated damage.of about $25.

July 12, 1929 The Holstein Breeders Assoc. is sparing no effort to have a large crowd at the annual summer outing on July 26th.

The Advocate was given a copy of the article sent to all Wisconsin members.

July 12, 1929 Advocate article: WASHINGTON ISLAND GETTING MUCH PUBLICITY ON PICNIC

Article Sent Out Last Week Praises Site Selected.

The Wisconsin Holstein-Friesian Association is sparing no efforts to have a large crowd at its summer outing which will take place July 26 on Washington Island and incidentally is giving the Island wide publicity. The Advocate has received a copy of the mimeographed article sent to all members of the association last week and publishes it in full as follows:

The annual summer meeting and picnic of the Holstein-Friesian Association of Wisconsin holds an unusual appeal this year in that it will be held on the interesting and historic Washington Island. Washington Island is located at the north end of the Door Countv peninsula and is separated from the mainland by the waters of "Death's Door." It is reached by driving north from Sturgeon Bay to Gills Rock , where ferry service will carry the breeders to the Island.

Washington Island has a circumference of about 37 miles. The population is about 1000 people of Norwegian, Swedish, Danish and Icelanders origin. In former years this Island was the home of the Potowattomie Indians and its various harbors and cliffs have interesting tales of Indian lore connected with them.

The two main industries of the Island are fishing and dairying. Holstein breeders attending this picnic will be given the opportunity to see commercial fishermen at work, and to do some bass and trout fishing themselves.

In a Holstein sense the Island is of particular interest. Washington Island was the first T.B. free area in the United States. Abortion is unknown there. The Holstein-Friesan cow rules supreme, and the average cow of the Island is a fine individual and a heavy producer. The reason for this development lies in the cooperative spirit that permeates this Island. Only good, purebred bulls have been used, and these have been used cooperatively in bull "blocks" or "rings" with an. exchange of bulls within the members of the ring every 18 months.

The program of the day will include speeches by Earl J. Cooper, Director of Extension of the Holstein-Friesan Association of America, and W.E. Wintermeyer from the Bureau of Animal Industry, Washington, D.C.

W.W. Bird, Cambria; Emil Tital, Plymouth; Fred J. Southcott, Oconomowoc and S.H. Bird, South Byron, will be given honorary recognition and will be presented with canes in honor of their achievements and records as Holstein breeders.

Residents of the Island are arranging an interesting tour that will show their Holstein herds and fishing industry.

Every effort is being made to arrange a good outing. All are invited to Washington Island on July 26th.

7/12/29 Everyone is anticipating a great time at the big farmers picnic, the 26th inst. (This picnic was as popular then and as well attended as the Island Fair is today. It was held at the Island Airport and usually Pilot Wally Arentsen, from Escanaba would be offering "barnstorming" rides at a reasonable price.)

Jens Jenson's new barn was struck by lightning before it was finished. The bolt entered the cupola, followed the track of the hay carrier, branching off and shattered several studdings, doing and estimated damage of about $25.00.

3/7/1930 Advocate - GLIMPSES OF EARLY DOOR COUNTY --Christian Saabye

I see that the Advocate wants to know about the old fellows of the county. Well, I'm not one of the first, nor am I of the last to come to Washington Island. We came in 1868 and I am the last one living of those who came in the spring of that year, 62 years this coming year.

We went through just about everything that old settlers had to go through. Carrying water one-fourth to three-fourths mile and tripping when we were pretty near home and that, of course, made it necessary to go back and fill up again. I well remember when we came to the Island, Mrs. Malemberg kept a boarding house at the Booth dock, where we stayed the first day, and then moved into the house that is now used by Mrs. Jeanie Garrette. Later we lived in a house on the other side of the harbor.

The first thing to do now was to find the land that we entered at Madison, but that was not very easy as there was not one straight road to go by. The road from Washington Harbor to Detroit Harbor was supposed to follow the line but it was 10 rods out of the way, so, of course, we got that much out of the way when we measured east from that road. We started cutting an opening in the woods so the sun would shine down, and here a few potatoes were planted but most we got was tops, they grew all tops, and the potatoes were the size of hazel nuts. The following year we made a big hole in the woods and more air and sunshine came down and then, of course, we had raised real potatoes.

In June of 1868 they found what they thought was the right place in the woods to start a building, so a log house, 14' x 36' was started. The logs were up and the roof on and then my dad. had to .get back to Chicago to earn a few dollars before winter.

He came back in November and finished a room 10' x 14' in one end of the newly built log house. In this room we lived for 2 years before we were able to get any more done to the house.

One day in early fall of 1868 my chum, Hans Mackerson and myself, were strolling on the dock at Washington Harbor. We were called into the store and each of us was fitted with boots by the good storekeeper, Mr. Ranney. Now here sure was a good man. He saw what poor footwear we had and knew the winter was soon to be here and he knew our circumstances and his good heart went out to us. He treated all the settlers right. He told them to bring their wood for which he paid $2.50 on the bank. But it took $1.50 to get the wood to the bank and my dad could only cut one-half cord per day for the first month. The next month he did better, three-fourths cord per day. He finally got so he could cut a cord. It surely was slow work getting started. Two years to got the first cow, 4 years to get the first yoke of oxen; in 7 years we finally got a small horse team. Three years following we had lots of grasshoppers and sometimes they left but little. We also had dry seasons when nothing would grow. One thing we had plenty of and that was hard work. But we never went hungry.

Old Grandpa Cornell hauled-our first wood to Washington Harbor, for which he received 1.50 per cord. His good wife was blind, but she was not idle. She was knitting all the time. One day in the fall of '69 she called me in and put on-my cold little hands a pair of wool mittens. My, but that felt nice! Yes we had many nice and generous people in those days., Fishermen were most liberal too. You could go to the harbor and bring home a bag full of fish and they would pick out the best and not charge a cent.

(Advocate Article on Saabye Cont'd)

I will say people, as a rule, were just as happy, just as contented, and maybe more so than now. Now they never are satisfied, always scrambling for more, If you have to follow the crowd you surely got to have more than we used to get. From 1880 to 1885 I freighted the farmer 's wheat and rye to Sister Bay mill to have it made into flour and feed. This was cold work. Most of it was done in November and we had no stove in the boat either. The boat was an old sailboat, 29 feet long.

In the fall of 1886 George Moe and I took the boat to Garrett Bay where we were to wait for my dad to come down from Sturgeon Bay, but before he came a storm came up and damaged our boat. It was blown high and dry on the shore and a stone went through from the outside. Well, when the wind went down I made up my mind that I was going to sail the boat home again, so I patched up the hole and shoved her to again and started for home. It went well for a while, but then the wind died and the water in the boat gained on George no matter how much he bailed, so of course, he wanted to go to shore. Well, the fact is I didn't mind getting on shore myself, so there was nothing else to do but head for the nearest dock and that was Weborg's. We could not have struck better people than the Weborgs. First, old man Weborg helped us salvage our boat, brought out his tackle and ropes, and he knew how to get at it, too, and our boat was safe for the winter.

George and myself stayed there a week and the board and lodging was either $1.50 or $ 2.50. I cannot remember which. This was in the good old times, when people were good.

At another time I went to Sturgeon Bay in a 19 foot skiff with a sail, and brought home 6,000 shingles. Anyone who now wants to try this is entirely welcome. --CHRISTIAN SAABYE

10/18/29 Eastside School was closed for a week, beginning 10/4, so children could help to harvest potatoes.

11/21/29 A two-day farm Institute discussed local farm problems. Ole Erickson, Vernie Richter and George Hanson made arrangements, assisted by County Agent Rusy and R.A. Kolb. County-farmer Taylor was the principal speaker.

4/25/30 Farmers had started to work the soil, but with the temperature low Tuesday, the ground was frozen hard and a snowstorm followed.

5/16/30 More cherry trees were set out this spring than for many years. Art Wickman, Vernie Richter, Mads Swenson, Conrad Andersen and Christian Anderson planted large orchards.

5/30/30 Recent frosts caused considerable damage here, but it was much less than farther south in Door County. Fruit trees are not yet fully in bloom. Some garden crops like potatoes, beans, cucumbers, etc. were killed.

Albert Olson has added 20 feet or more to his barn. The new part, built by John Johnson and son Charles, has steel siding.

6/13/30 Monday was about the first real summer day. It has been so cold that apple trees and lilacs are just blooming and cherry blossoms peaked a week ago.

6/27/30 Home-grown strawberries are coming on the market this week.

7/11/30 Recent rain has developed the strawberries and grass to where a bumper crop of fruit and hay is expected.

8/1/1930 Falling from the hay load on the way to the barn, Torje Johnson, 70, for 40 years an Island resident, was killed. His head struck a rock causing instant death. Henry Peterson stopped for a little gas for the car and found the body. The horses, frightened when the hay rack gave way, ran a couple rods and stood whinnying for someone to come.

8/8/30 many shade trees and groves are being stripped by short-lived worms larvae with leaf color and segmented body. Some large woods are nearly bare.

8/15/30 County Agent Rusy came and said the worms would retard tree growth, but not kill the trees.

8/29/30 The worms have disappeared, but evidently many trees will die since they have been so badly eaten that all buds formed for next year are gone. The condition is serious.

11/14/30 As a result of Halloween vandalism, two injured parties went to the authorities and demanded action. A peacemaker suggested giving the children a chance to apologize, make restitution and promise no further molestation. Except for a few, the children agreed to do so. Albert Olson, a quiet, good natured, good hearted bachelor, living alone, had been pestered for years with considerable damage, repair and expense. He met with the boys and sternly demanded a sum of dollars in settlement. Among other things, his neatly piled stone fence was scattered all over the field. Albert refused to let the boys fix the fence. Unknown to him they fixed it nicely, so the other damage he forgave.

5/8/31 One of the dreams of Islanders finally has come true. Charles J. Schmidt has converted his farm to golf links. It is predicted the golf course will be one of the greatest drawing cards for tourists.

7/10/31 A radical campaign against grasshoppers was conducted last week. Most of the ground has been covered with poison The last poisoning did a good job and there is confidence this will happen again.

7/24/31 Cherry picking began Monday with an abundant crop, but prospects for good prices and ready sales are not encouraging.

7/31/31 The golf course-is very busy with large patronage. Worms have ruined thousands of trees much worse than last year. The beech trees have been badly hit. The grasshopper poison is less successful owing to lots of green grass. The previous year the ground was dry and barren, so they ate the poison.

7/3/31 Henry Hanson has established an ice cream parlor and serves cake, candies, root beer and other delicacies, all home-made.

7/31/31 The-early cherry crop picking was finished this week. Late cherries will be ripe in a week to 10 days.

8/21/31 Berndt Gunnlaugsson has begun grain threshing. His machine is hauled and powered by a Fordson tractor. It has a bundle conveyor to carry the grain into the machine which eliminates the danger of feeding the sheaves directly into the cylinder. Nearly all the grain now is a mix of oats and barley for dairy cattle feed. Production averages 10 bushels to the acre.

10/16/31 The first killing frost hit the pumpkin leaves. Potato vines need frost to kill growth and ripen the tubers. There is an excellent crop of late potatoes, some of the finest ever raised. Berndt is also filling silos for farmers, but the crop is so abundant that the silos will not hold all of it.

12/4/31 Peter Yudin of Mariette bought a truck load of Island cattle.

5/6/32 Farmers are busy hauling potatoes to Young's Washington Harbor dock where the Milwaukee freighter "North Shore" will take a load to market.

8/12/32 Eighteen women enjoyed a housewarming at the re-built Ole Bowman cabin. His niece, Anna Wickman and three nephews, William, Arthur and Arnold and their wives had supper and talked of early Island days. In 1872, at about 21 years of age, Ole took a one-quarter section homestead and built a small, one room cabin. While waiting for their homes to be built, many pioneer Island families used the cabin as a temporary dwelling. Some of these were: George Lucke in 1879, "Swamp" Olson in 1883, Henry Immel in 1884. Others included Ole Eastman, Arni Gudmundsson, Tom Bessie, Mr. Stockwell, Dave Kincaide and a sister of Mrs. Nichols. An old wooden ox yoke witi iron pins found on the Bowman farm hangs beside the stone chimney. On the walls hang all the old chromo pictures which belonged to Ole Bowman.

2/22/35 Recent survey figures show Island farming is - declining. In 1930 there were 75 farms, today 1/3 of them are idle. In 1920 there were over 200 horses, now there are 110. One reason is there is no market for cordwood. Farmers formerly relied on cutting and selling wood to supplement their income. When this business stopped, except for a very few, farmers could not show a profit. For years Washington Island was noted for fine potatoes until about 15 years ago. They were shipped handily by vessels and the Island Farmers Union used to ship from 9000 to 15000 bushels every fall. In 1913 sixty-seven horse teams lined up for 3/4 mile in Washington Harbor with high wagon loads of potatoes and these were loaded into schooners at the dock and in the harbor. There were more horses in that line than are owned by Island farmers today. In November 1916 the ripe,seed pea crop sold for nearly $11,000. The Island population in 1920 was 932, in 1930 it was 775 and in 1935 about 776.

April 1935 Jens Hansen moved from his Jackson Harbor farm and now rents the late Jake Bowman's on the East side.

The huge barn on the old Boucsein farm is being razed to improve the property.

4/26/35 Peter Yudin, Marinette, left last week with 90 head of cattle he bought from Island farmers.

May 10,1935 The Island dairy and cheese factory burned two days before the arrival of the Island's new fire truck. Pleck Ice Cream and Dairy Company, Sturgeon Bay, will supply milk for consumers, while Evangeline Milk Co. is receiving milk from Island farmers. The fire loss is about $15,000.

THE ED ANDERSON POTATO GROWING STORY

(Gathered from archive files and conversations with former Anderson employees.)

Gladys Jepsen wrote "The History of the Irish Potato" many years ago. She told of early Spaniards finding potatoes grown in Peru and in the Bolivian Andes where Indians used them for food. Dried spuds and drawings of the plant on pottery have been found in early graves showing they were used for food at least 1800 years ago. Spaniards carried taters to Spain and they were spread throughout Europe and Asia. As they were not mentioned in the Bible, many thought they were a creation of the devil and refused to eat them. Soon this superstition was forgotten and nearly everyone ate them.

In 1586 Spaniards introduced potatoes to England and a few years later they made their way to Ireland. Soon the Emerald Isle economy nearly depended on this starchy tuber's abundant yield which provided food for both man and animal. In 1825 potato blight hit Ireland and many deaths resulted from starvation, cholera and other diseases. Relief food that was shipped in was of little help. Homemakers only cooking skill was boiling spuds, thus they did not know how to use unfamiliar foreign foods.

In 1719 a Scottish preacher, Rev. James MacGregor, led 16 Irish families to North America where they settled in Derry, New Hampshire. Here the first potatoes in North America were grown on 2½ acres and they saved the settlers fram starvation their first winter.

Ever since the first land was cleared by early settlers, potatoes have been grown on the Island. In 1876 Postmaster Severs, also Town Clerk, reported, "The potato crop promises well except for a few Colorado varmints (beetles)". The next year Severs harvested a 9" long Peerless variety that weighed 18 lbs. In 1878 twenty-five acres yielded 1505 bushels and in 1879 the clerk reported 37 acres in potatoes.

In Ed Anderson's letter to Mrs. Burgoon he stated that from 1895 to 1932 about 80 Island farmers had from 2 to 10 acres annually in spuds. Forks were used to dig them and they were-hand picked bagged, stored and then shipped to market by schooners from Booth's Dock on the west side of Washington Harbor. Loaded wagons stretched for over a half mile waiting to unload into the vessels. George Mann and the local Farmers' Union were the principal sales agents. This potato raising continued until the nitrogen, phosphate and potash was depleted from the soil. Ed had the soil tested and found it sorely lacking phosphate and potash. Many Islanders advised him not to try potato farming, but he knew that plants, like humans, needed food.

Ed's young years were spent on the family farm on Main Road to the right of Zink's hill, Washington Harbor. At 14 years of age he left and began working in Chicago as a tailor's delivery boy for $3 per week. His board cost $2 and carfare was 60 cents weekly, leaving him with 40 cents. Shortly he returned to Door County to work for Door County Fruit Growers Co-op, run by Jim Langemak, his former 8th grade teacher. After trying a life as a Great Lakes sailor, he went back to Chicago and earned $50/ week at Stewart Warner Company. However, he wanted to buy and sell so he quit and took a $25/ week job in Chicago Commission Row.

Ed Anderson's older brother sent a carload of potatoes for him to handle. On the Island they would have netted $125, but Ed got $462 for the farmer's load. It was 1920 when Ed began working for a potato broker and the next year he opened his own brokerage which was continuous from then on. Soon he averaged an earning of $30 to $50 per day selling carloads of spuds. By 1941 he was the biggest operator in the business handling 7 to 8 thousand carloads a day (700 bu. to a carload). He moved 5 million bushels a year. The Franklin Park, Illinois processing plant packaged 50,000 bags daily.

By the mid 30s Ed was moving several million bushels per year and he began looking for a summer home in New England, Michigan, Wisconsin and Minnesota. On a visit to the Island he realized his boyhood home was the most beautiful place, so he bought it and began to spend summers from the first of June to Labor Day. This was too long for him to be idle so he began buying Island land. His first idea was to plant cherries. but he decided to stay in his own business. Luckily he hired Jim Hansen with whom he had many things in common. Both had a love of the sea and sailing. In World War One Ed had been a wheelsman on a Lakes ore carrier. Jim had 10 years sailing on freighters and in the Merchant Marine in World War Two. Jim was an excellent potato grower and Ed, 45 years a broker, knew all aspects of selling.

In 1947 Ed joined with Carl Roder, Sturgeon Bay who was a university trained agriculturist, to test the possibilities of large scale potato farming here. They planted 15 varieties and quickly learned that Idaho Russets were best for this soil because it has a very high PH factor - 6 to 8. This causes scabs to form on smooth skinned spuds, but is perfect for russets.

By working the soil from 8" to 10" deep and with proper application of one-half ton per acre of 6 - 24 - 24 fertilizer, coupled with a good spray program to eliminate insects and blight, the average yield per acre would be 450 to 500 bushels. Farmers from 1895 to 1932 averaged 75 to 125 bu./acre.

In 1919, when Ed started brokering potatoes in Chicago, there were 100,000 potato farmers in the USA, by 1974 there were 15,000 left. Except for 1973 and 1974, production costs exceeded the market price for 20 years. This also applied to most farm commodities. While the Island had wonderful soil for russets, it was still necessary to bring the market price above production costs. By 1974 the cost of lumber, insecticide, fertilizer, equipment, taxes, etc. amounted to $4/cwt. Costs of, farming increased 100 to 150% in the last 18 months.

Oct. 1948 news article said "Washington Island Eyes Title of State's Potato Capitol". 45,000 bushels of seed potatoes, grown on 150 acres, was harvested by 60 Island workers, Partners in this enterprise were Roder Bros., Sturgeon Bay University-trained farmers, and Ed Anderson, Chicago Potato King. A 40' by 90' warehouse was built to store 15,000 bushels and 30,000 bushels were shipped to Maplewood and Nasawaupee warehouses for storage and railroad transportation. The Washington Island Certified Seed Growers Association, composed of independent Island farmers will send seed potatoes throughout the USA.

At first potato picking was done by hand on Anderson's farm. Pickers were given as many basket tickets as they thought they could pick in a day. These tickets were placed in the full baskets that were collected and tallied. One day an Island woman picked 300 bu. and received 6 cents for each bushel. High school students earned money picking on weekends. After the work day ended, Islanders were permitted to glean left-over spuds for their winter supply. Ed also had deliveries made to people who could not pick their own. Besides this, Ed did a great favor to Islanders who had either farmed or fished all their life. Many were first enrolled in Social Security when they were hired and consequently they received benefits in their later years which they otherwise would not have been qualified for.

A good crop needed the normal 4" rainfall in July and 3" in August at the right time. Average day temperature was 70 to 80 degrees and 55 to 65 at night. As the rainfall could not be totally depended on, it became necessary to irrigate and originally this was by water pumped from Detroit Harbor. As the operation grew 400 acres were irrigated using 3 man-made lakes, wells and Lake Michigan water. Portable large aluminum pipes carried water to the fields in 1961. That year a crew of 60 conducted the harvest. About 35, mostly Texas Mexicans, hand-picked in the soil which was too stoney to do the harvesting by machinery.

By the mid 50s Ed was farming some 1400 acres, half owned and half rented. A three year crop rotation system was employed. Potatoes one year, grain the next year and hay the third year.

Processing had required handling the potatoes 14 times before they got into the consumers hands. This caused lots of bruising and expense. The volume had grown to where it was no longer feasible to ship by truck and rail, so Ed purchased two former carferries. The "City of Cheboygan" had been "Ann Arbor #4" until 1948 when the State of Michigan bought her and the "City of Munising" to serve as auto, passenger and freight vessels in Mackinac Straits and to Detour and Drummond Islands until the bridge was built. He paid $25,000 for the "City of Cheboygan", 259' long and 54' beam. He re-named her "Edward H. Anderson" but she was usually called "No. 4" while the "City of Munising" was called "No.2". These two vessels cut the handling in half. Large, hopper wagons, using old bus axles and holding 210 bushels were built on the farm. Many old Island stone fences wound up as part of the big dock where these boats were berthed. The spuds now went direct from the field to the boats. These ferries when empty had a draft of 7' forward and 11' aft, but fully loaded they drew 16'. During the October harvest the 210 bushel wagons arrived at the dock every 12 minutes and were pulled across the ramp into the hold where a Jeep would "snake" them into position . The wagon's conveyor belt in the bottom was started and the spuds rolled out onto an elevator and to the mounting pile in the hold. The "No. 4s" hold (53' by 208') could handle 70,000 bu., while "No. 2", nearly 100' longer, held 105,000 bu. The business's best annual crop was 250,000 bu. of taters and 750,000 lbs. of grain.

In Feb. 1960 the crop was washed and bagged on the Island, but this was very costly as the packaged potatoes had to be loaded onto large trucks which were transported to the mainland on Island ferries. Subsequently, in the fall, the loaded ferries were towed to Sturgeon Bay where they wintered while the crew processed the spuds for market. In later years the full boats went to Benton Harbor, Michigan.

In April 1960 #1 Russet Burbank potatoes brought $5.50 / cwt. on the Chicago market. Of the 15 -million lb. crop 80% were No. 1s and according to Ed 40% of those came from Idaho. Ed owned 500 acres on the Island and planned to expand to 1000 acres. His brands were "Pinebrook" and "Washington Island", but soon all would be "Washington Island".

In late 1960 the full vessels were towed to Sturgeon Bay where they were docked for the winter. 20 workers on board washed, sorted, bagged and shipped the harvest. A cold storage warehouse was planned at the Sturgeon Bay dock. Orrin Gunnlaugsson was manager on the boats and Jim Hansen managed the Island farm. The filled bags slid down a chute by gravity into waiting trucks. Ed was now buying in 43 states. The Island crop represented just 4% of his total volume. In 1959 the local crop produced 450 bu./acre.

"C" grade spuds, the little ones were tossed out. "B", or No. 2 Grade, the "Utilities"(with nobs) and No.1 Grades were sorted out, packaged and weighed in one continuous operation. Where formerly it cost $25/ ton to get spuds to market, it now cost just $1.75. Ed's holdings had swelled to 1800 acres with about one-third in potatoes and the rest rotated in oats and clover. In later years tugs pulled the two loaded boats to Benton Harbor where railside facilities were available. Here 5 to 6 months was spent on board preparing the potatoes for market. 5, 10 and 25 lb. bags were filled, then placed in 100 lb. bags for shipment. The ferry's boilers supplied heat for the winter with supplementation by propane heaters. The trip from the Island to Benton Harbor took two days. Two blocks below the North Avenue bridge, the Schooner Stafford sold spuds at Wright Coal Dock, Fans circulated air in the holds which were kept at 40 degrees, In May both vessels were returned to the Lobdell's Point pier with fertilizer, agricultural chemicals and other supplies needed for the coming crop. Potatoes kept for seed were also aboard.

At one point Ed considered the feasibility of a French-fried processing plant. After the 1970 season, market conditions and personnel circumstances forced the closing of the Anderson potato business in Chicago. This ended the large scale potato operation here.

Eventually, a Canadian firm bought the boats, loaded them with scrap and one tug towed them to Italy, where they were reduced to scrap.

For several years Ed studied the feasibility of operating a French-fried processing plant on the Island, based on resumed potato growing here. His dreams were cut off by his death in 1978.

Ed purchased a large portion of the northern part of Detroit Island, had it surveyed into building lots and sold many of them in his last years.

In 1961 red Pontiac potatoes were planted in 125 acres, while the balance of the crop was again Russets. His 14 tractors, three harvesters, plows, sprayers and grain combines were then worth $250,000.

No. 202

6/28/35 Geo. O. Mann recently lost three head of cattle on pasture land.

8/2/35 Island farmers are about through hauling in, hay, which was a very good crop this season. Some will harvest a second crop. (That year we threshed alfalfa seed from the second crop, the only year we were able.to do that.)

7/16/35 The Island Garden Club held their second annual flower show in the basement of Trinity Lutheran Church. there were over fifty entries.

12/20/35 If Rock Island already radiates the atmosphhere of Iceland, it will be even more so next spring and summer. Hjortur Thordarson, the genial owner of this palatial estate, has a 100 lb. box of 50 to 75 varieties of flowering plants-from Iceland, to be transplanted in his huge rock garden that covers the slope of an age-old beach, the length of nearly two city blocks. He makes flowers his hobby and attends them personally. The shipment will be in the estate's huge greenhouse until they can be set outdoors. He says they amount to only one-sixth of available Iceland varieties.

4/30/36 Nate Abrams, cattle buyer was here last week on business.

4/17/36 A number of farmers are busy tapping trees and making maple syrup. Quite a number of gallons already have been made.

5/22/36 Lawrence Anderson, Jackson Harbor, is building a new barn on the Anderson farm.

11/6/36 Lawrence Anderson has been very successful in raising a crop of over 200 bushels of potatoes and 300 bu. oats.

10/15/37 Slive Gunnlagnson(sic) Steve Gunnlaugsson has purchased the Sam Newman farm of 160 acres for the amount of $600. A new barn and a new butcher shop (now W.I. Elec. Co-op office) have been built here in the last two years,

11/26/37 "Farm Relief" is again being discussed. Everyone hopes that Congress will manage to create a sound "farm aid" plan during this special session. However, if past precedent is any arbiter, the odds are 100 to 1 that in the future, as in the past, more good comes out of things the farmer does for himself, than those done for him by any political or outside group. During the past ten years there were a number of farm relief measures and everyone wholly or partially was a failure. During the same years a farm co-operative marketing has steadily gone ahead. The result of farmer organization to stabilize production and marketing has been in a near-record 1937 agricultural income. Self-help is still the best help.

12/10/37 Art Wickman, who sold and shipped a great many of his Thanksgiving turkeys, will soon prepare for the Christmas rush. Many of these birds will be shipped to Chicago.

5/6/38 Art Wickman bought a fine work horse from Green Bay, which was delivered here Sunday.

7/15/38 Cherry picking began in a few orchards last Monday, while others started on Wednesday. Many local people and outsiders are picking.

7/22/30 Because of blight, cherries are not as good as usual.

7/29/38 early cherries (Richmond) are being picked. Next week the late ones (Montmorency) will be ready. Hay crops on the island are very good this year.

4/18/1919 A survey of cattle on the Island showed the following:

YEAR	COWS	HEIFERS	STEERS	BULLS	TOTAL
1918	408	267	231	49	955
1919	482	424	164	59	1129

Friday last week, Captain Christianson's boat, Wisconsin, took away 16 head of cattle condemned by State Tuberculosis Testers, At Thursday's Holstein Association meeting it was decided that steps will be taken to eradicate "scrub" bulls with the same thoroughness that the State used in eliminating cattle that tested positive to TB. It is predicted that within a year there will be no "scrub" bulls on the Island.

Holstein Association members display signs reading "Pure Bred Bull Used on This Farm". Each member agrees in writing to use only pure bred bulls and if he fails to do so, the Association may remove the sign. Because of this attention to having pure Holstein cattle, Island butter is in much greater demand on the market. No other creamery, except a few private herd plants, can advertise butter made only from the milk of tuberculin tested cattle.

The Autumn 1951 Surge News ran interesting comments on Island Dairying such as "In about 1980 Olafur Hannesson (my grandfather) brought a pure bred Holstein bull here."

Also George Mann & Sons had the largest herd here in 1951--about 130 cattle and Andrew Justinger, cheese maker here for 25 years, also pasteurizes milk and cream for local use. He makes an average of 600 lbs. of cheese daily.

(About 1949 Jack Hagen and Alex Koyen, who were farming together, bought the-first Surge milking machine to be used on the Island. The Surge milker can be seen at the Island Farm Museum)

As previously mentioned the first Island cheese factory association erected an 18' by 40' building on what is now Michigan Road (1st house on left going east past Airport Road) in 1891. In December 1899, Bo Anderson moved the idle factory building to Detroit Harbor to serve as a storage shed behind his store (now Holiday Two).

June 1915 The first creamery to be built on the present site of the Chalet was a 26' x 40' structure, built and equipped by a Chicago promotion company for $4575. They provided the buttermaker at $75. per month.

With more money in cheese than butter, the factory re-opened May 2,1921 as a creamery. However, by Feb. 1922 the owners decided to sell the cheese making equipment and make only butter.

May 1925 the creamery closed. 1925 it re-opened as a cheese factory and Andy Justinger came here as cheesemaker. In 1949 he bought the factory, three months later it burned to the ground a few days before the first fire engine arrived on the Island. 26 farmers depended on milk for their income. The factory made 100,000 lbs. of cheese annually. 10 lbs. of milk make 1 lb. of cheese, thus one million lbs. of milk was needed to make that 100,000 lbs. of the annual cheese production. Cheese was 8¢/lb. Andy spent one depression year away as a galley porter on a Great Lakes oil vessel. As Andy's son, Dudley, grew older he worked with his father in the factory. In 1960 Myrtle Goodlet worked at the cheese factory for $100/ month in May, June, Sept., and Oct.; while in June and July she got $50/week, as there was a much greater volume of milk delivered in those two months.

5/7/49 Following the $15,000 loss of the factory by fire Andy Justinger had gotten cheese making equipment for a temporary plant which was soon in operation in the low farm building at Launders farm(1st farm on right side of Eastside Road, north of Lakeview Road). Plecks Ice Cream and Dairy Company, Sturgeon Bay, provided milk and other products and Evangeline Milk Company agreed to take the farmer's milk. However, in short order Andy was making cheese in the temporary quarters while the new factory was being erected.

An interesting record which showed "'The Island Dairy - Peter H. Eiler, Prop." and Jens Jepson's delivery of milk to the factory:

DATE	LBS OF MILK	BUTTERFAT	PRICE PER CWT. of BUTTERFAT	TOTAL
8/46	3839	3.0	$3.85	$126.89
8/51	1220	4.0	3.32½	46.36
10/51	3018	4.2	3.39	121.73
6/53	4438	4.2	3.15	167.76
6/55	5480	3.85	2.94	177.24
6/56	4923	4.15	3.01	175.70

(Jens Jepson's farm was on the right side of Gasoline Town Road, just north of Jackson Harbor Road.)

Andy Justinger bought the cheese factory early in 1949 and ran it until 1959 when his health was going bad. On April 9, 1959 twelve farmers met and agreed to start "The Washington Island Co-operative Dairy". Lake to Lake Dairy had agreed to buy cheese, eggs and other farm products. The Co-op would handle their ice cream, etc. on a commission basis. Door County Co-op would put in a line of feeds to be sold here.

5/5/59 The farmers met and elected the following officers:

President - Jack Hagen
Vice President - Marvin Andersen
Secretary - Conrad Anderson
Treasurer - Ray Briesemeister

William Jacobsen, in addition to the above four officers would serve on the Board of Directors.

8/6/59 The settled price for the plant was $11,300 plus $3500. for the equipment with $5000 down payment. It was suggested that the $5,000 be raised on the basis of the number of milking cows each patron had at the time of the plant purchase. Ray Briesemeister had ceased milk production and left the Island, so Maynard Gunnlaugsson was chosen to fill Ray's place on the

Board. A check was made to see if Marjorie Bjarnarsson would act as Treasurer, and she agreed to do so. Elmer Arneson will be the cheese maker.

9/22/59 Attorney Herman Leasum will draw up the Land Contract. It was agreed that the factory be bought for $15,000. The $5,000 down payment to be raised on the suggested "per cow" basis by the patrons. The Bank of Sturgeon Bay agreed to make loans to the farmers needing money to make the down payment for any farmers having loans with them. The $10,000 balance in Land Contract would be paid off at $150 per month to Andy and Myrtle Justinger.

The Washington Island Co-operative Dairy, Inc. issued both Class "A" Stock and Class "B" Stock. At the beginning the following patrons bought a share of Class "B" Stock at $1.

Jack,Hagen	Marvin Andersen
Conrad A. Anderson	Maynard Gunnlaugsson
Gilbert Falk	William Jacobsen
Alex Koyen	Irvin Goodlet
Leroy Andersen	Raymond Jensen
Russell Gunnlaugsson	Magnus Gunnlaugsson

Those patrons who joined later were:

5/2/60	Russell Gunnlaugsson	Magnus Gunnlaugsson
8/20/60	Fred Koyen	Wallace Jensen
12/31/60	Lloyd Launders	8/1/61 Raymond Andersen
11/30/61	Duane Jacobsen	7/17/62 Lonald Jorgenson
9/2/62	Leila Hagen	12/12/'62 Carroll Koyen
12/12/62	H. R. Anderson	3/20/63 Leonard Ruel
7/20/62	Charles Jorgenson	8/16/65 Thorsten Williamson

The Articles of Incorporation stated the Capital Stock would be $20,000 worth divided into 1990 shares of non-accumulative Class A Common Stock with a par value of $10 each and 100 shares of Class B common Stock with a par value of $1 each. Each holder of Class B Stock is entitled to one vote on each question, but loses that right after discontinuing to deliver milk to the Co-op for one year. Class A Stock has no vote except as provided by law. The board may declare dividends of not more than 4% per year on Class A Stock.

However,when the books were closed on the Washington Island co-operative Dairy, Inc. on June 30, 1969-they showed the following redemptions:

Redemption of Class A Stock	$4250.
Redemption of Class 8 Stock	$26.
Redemption of Equity Reswerve	$3516.09

Leaving Total Assets of $15.83.

Person receiving redemption	"A" Shares	Total	Equity Reserve
Jack Hagen	57	$575	$406.20
Conrad A. Anderson	30	300	143.60
Maynard Gunnlaugsson	50	500	108.35
Gilbert Falk	45	450	251.68
William Jacobson	55	550	72.41
Marvin Andersen	40	400	195.98
Alex Koyen	45	450	430.21
Irvin Goodlet	25	250	246.39
Raymond Jensen	40	400	68.07
Carroll Koyen	37	375	103.59
Russell Gunnlaugason			266.84
Roy Andersen			123.22
Lawrence Anderson			3.61
Raymond Andersen			34.63
Steve Gunnlaugsson			5.03
Raymond Gunnlaugseon			123.25
Lonald Jorgenson			125.90
H. R. Anderson			181.69
Magnus Gunnlaugsson			86.84
Lloyd Launders			104.24
Leonard Ruel			106.93
L. D. Jacobsen			260.77
Wallace Jensen			14.97
Thorsten Williamson			35.08
Leila Hagen			10.63
Fred Koyen			3.84
Charles Jorgenson			.14

10/20/59 Arbutus Greenfoldt was named Trustee.

The cheese factory operating license was applied for with the Wisconsin State Dept. of Agriculture.

11/13/59 The Oct. 1959 gross income from bottling milk was $3894.39, expenses were $862.94 prior to paying patrons for the milk they delivered, butterfat was $.82/lb. Cheese maker Arneson was permitted by the State to make whey butter and to bottle milk.

5/17/60 Myrtle Goodlet was hired as a helper for May, June, September and October at $100 per month, while in July and August she would receive $50 per week. Cheese price to local retailers dropped to 45 cents per lb.

6/30/60 The report for fiscal year 59-60 showed the following:

GROSS RETURN	Cheese	$23940.82
	Bottled milk	$ 8925.62
	Bottled cream	$ 2334.69
	Butter	$ 9902.35
Lbs. of milk received		832295
Average butterfat in milk		3.55%
Total lbs. of butterfat		29574.9
Butterfat in whey cream		1429 lbs.
Whey cream butterfat test		30.6%
Whey cream sold to Lovit		4660 lbs.
Pounds of cheese manufactured		63,293

9/20/60 Auditor's report showed these values:

Lot	$250.
Well	$450.
Building	$10600.
Equipment	$3700.

12/19/60 The Co-op decided to borrow $1000 from the Bank of Sturgeon Bay for one year so they could set aside cheese to age it.

1/4/61 Patrons, factory help and retailers may buy butter, cream or milk in less than case lots, while casual buyers must buy cases of factory products. Purchases of over 5 lbs. of cheese will be at wholesale price, while smaller cheese purchases will be at approximately store retail price.

Patrons discussed buying a-truck for $400. to haul cheese to Green Bay, etc.

3/16/61 The factory will soon be bottling skim milk.

4/16/61 Ray Hansen inquired about buying surplus whey for mink feed.

6/16/61 Factory cheese prices were set at:

Aged cheese under 5#	----	65¢/lb.
Aged cheese over 5#	----	60¢/lb.
Fresh cheese under 5#	---	60¢/lb.
Fresh cheese over 5#	---	55¢/lb.

July 1961 Factory cheese price was set at 60¢/lb. for all sizes and ages.

8/6/61 Cheese maker Arneson is leaving Sept. 1. Cheese maker Alan Weiss agreed to take over for $450 per month, provided housing was available. A picnic dinner was held at the factory with patrons, their families and the Alan Weiss family attending.

8/23/61 The Co-op will buy a milk carton bottling machine for $2850 with $450 allowed for trading in the old one. $2400 borrowed from the Bank of Sturgeon Bay and will repay the combined loans-of $3400 in three years.

9/l/61 The price of products at retail outlets was set at:

1/2 gal. homogenized milk	38¢
1 qt.of homogenized milk	19¢
1 qt. regular milk	18¢

9/27/61 The Co-op agreed to sell ½ and ½ cream.

1/30/62 Well to be chlorinated as soon as possible. It was done.

3/14/62 Well water tested and it is safe.

6/6/62 The Co-op agreed to act as a distributor for Morning Glory products with a 5% service charge. Alex Koyen to bring these products from Green Bay, while delivering our cheese there, for $32.50 per trip. Weis had wanted a raise but this was not possible so Tom Winters was hired as Cheese Maker at $450 per month, plus milk and cream for his household.

9/14/62 It was decided to buy Duane Jacobsen's truck for $400.

12/12/62 It was decided to buy a 9500 lb. vat, whey separator and 40 H.P. boiler from Bingham and Risdon for about $4640.

12/12/62 President--Marvin Andersen, Vice Pres.--Jack Hagen, Secretary--Conrad A. Anderson

1/l/63 Larry Young hired as helper at $10 per day part-time, and $50 per week full-time, plus expenses for taking cheese to Green Bay.

4/15/65 Discussed with Jack and Cecil Andersen hauling cheese feed, Morning Glory products, etc, during the navigational months of the year.

6/30/63 GROSS RETURNS,.

Cheese	$53,600
Bottled milk	$10,160
Bottled-Cream	$1,212
Whey Cream	$2,742

8/22/63 Co-op decided to bottle quarts of milk in glass during the winter months.

9/24/63 Lorraine Andersen selected as alternate trustee; Arbutus Greenfeldt was still regular trustee. wages for cheese maker Kent Borcherding raised to $400 per month.

10/15/63 President--Jack Hagen, Vice Pres.--Marvin Andersen, Secretary--Conrad A. Anderson

12/16/63 The cheese maker was authorized to price and purchase curd knives.

1/16/64 Co-op will borrow $9500 from Bank of Sturgeon Bay to refinance outstanding obligations.

Since 1959 milk production has doubled and '64 looks like a good year

4/14/64 Cheese maker John Hamilton is authorized to ship whey cream to whatever creamery he sees fit.

Wind damage to the factory will be covered by the local insurance company.

If Co-op can meet the USDA Inspection requirements the extra income could go in a fund for repairs and maintenance. A 700 lb. capacity drop tank and milk spouts was ordered.

5/15/64 Motion was passed to retain John Hamilton as cheese maker for two years from 6/1/64. It is understood that if he is released by us he gets one month's wages from the date of notice. If he quits he forfeits wages due as of the day of quitting. 60 days notice is required in either case.

6/15/64 Plans are to buy H.R. Anderson's truck for $300 for whey disposal away from the plant.

6/27/64 The above motion was rescinded because the truck was in bad condition. Co-op will buy a trailer with a tank instead.

6/27/64 A sign will be posted at the ferry dock promoting milk and cheese,also inviting persons to visit the factory. Bottling milk in glass was resumed.

8/17/64 Ice cream and cheese will be sold at the Island Fair. Letters of appreciation were sent to Vi Llewellyn and Kay Curtis for promoting our cause.

The Fairmont representative will be called to discuss distributing their products.

9/8/64 After a thorough cleaning of the plant by Mr. & Mrs. Hamilton, the Association's report shows:

1. Over 80% of our cheese meets State Brand quality with the balance being Junior and Undergrade. A vast improvement over July, when 33% was State Brand and over 50% was Undergrade. August had been even worse. It is an established fact a factory can not continue to be in operation if under 90% of the cheese produced qualifies for State Brand.
2. Milk sales for August 1964 amounted to about $800 worth, while in August 1963 it had been about $2400 worth, a 66 2/3% drop.
3. The State field man reported that the cause of so much Undergrade cheese rests with the factory, not the farms.
4. At the recent State Inspector's visit he reported we were definitely not keeping up with the production of hi-grade products, whether bottled milk or cheese.
5. There was an instance of failure to bottle milk without previous notice to customers.
6. The disposal of whey on the premises prior to establishing the present disposal system resulted in numerous flies and a stink that was well known about the Island.
7. A reflection that a sign had been placed at the ferry dock inviting visitors to see our plant and buy cheese, but if the smell wouldn't keep them away, the fact that often the doors were closed for most of the afternoon would deter them.
8. Pulling the well pipes confirmed the otherwise apparent fact that the well was contaminated with whey drainings from the plant area.
9. Careless piling of cans containing cream on the "American Girl" dock resulted in the spilling of most of the cream

from three cans, average value of each can's contents was $25.

10. Other irregularities were not as apparent, but there was no logical reason for their presence.

Following a discussion, a motion was passed to terminate the present cheese maker's services at the earliest possible date.

9/14/64 The August shipment of cheese was 5% State Brand, 34% Juniors and 61% Undergrade. This resulted in a loss on Undergrade of $648.

A motion was passed to express the Co-op's appreciation to Arbutus for all her work and dedication for her years as Trustee.

9/15/64 Bottling dairy products was discontinued and the cheese maker's salary was reduced $100 per month.

9/21/64 At a special meeting there was a report on applicants for the cheese maker's position. Out of 11 votes, 9 were for Alan Weis. He could come on several days notice.

Alex Koyen reported $4300 turned over to the factory account from the morning Glory account.

10/30/64 At the annual Co-op Dairy meeting the handling of butter was discussed.

11/17/64 A motion was passed to drill a new well at the plant. Bottling milk will be resumed after the new well is in operation.

12/15/64 A "boxholder" letter will be sent to all Island people asking their support in buying our products.

There were 318 cattle and 222 other live stock on the Island

1964 CROP REPORT

Land Owner	Total Acres	Acres Plowed	Non-Plowed
Potato Farms	1500	1300	200
Conrad A. Anderson	80	73	7
" " "	40	30	10
Ray C. Andersen	19.5	17	2.5
Leroy Andersen	19.5	17	2.5
Marvin Andersen	174	80	94
Gilbert Falk	169	132	37
Ervin Gunnlaugsson	108	85	23
Mac Gunnlaugsson	60	60	0
Raymond Gunnlaugsson	200	75	125
Russell Gunnlaugsson	216	102	114
Jack Hagen	165	107	58
Ray Hansen	10	8	2

Duane Jacobsen	196	124	72
Wallace Jensen	60	40	20
Lonald Jorgenson	100	145	25
Alex Koyen	140	120	20
Carroll & Myra Koyen	227	100	127
Leonard Ruel	113	101	12

1/14/65 Co-op will get plastic milk carton filler and 30 days supply of plastic cartons from Bingham and Risdon for a trial run.

2/18/65 Are considering a bank loan to buy bottling machinery and possibly a pasteurizer for pasteurizing the milk that will be made into cheese.

3/15/65 A resolution was passed to authorize the Board to borrow $1200 from the Bank of Sturgeon Bay to buy a carton bottling machine.

5/17/65 Will buy a pump for pumping the septic tank.

7/15/65 Jack Hagen resigned, H. R. Anderson was chosen to be Board Chairman and Marvin Andersen was appointed to fill the vacant place on the Board.

A vote of thanks was extended to Alan Weis for building up the bottled milk business.

7/15/65 Gary Kostichka was hired as cheese maker at $450 per month, to be raised to $500 when he assumes the bottling operation. Mrs.Caroline Lindahl will bottle milk in the interim for $1.25 per hour. Gary was guaranteed a minimum of six months salary.

3/2/65 Atty. Toft advised the Co-op to place the matter of garnishment of Leonard Ruel's account in the hands of the county judge to decide who was to receive what he claimed from that account.

The Co-op was advised to continue to handle Morning Glory products.

A motion was passed to allow no credit extension to those who no longer ship milk to the factory. This applies to either Morning Glory or Factory products.

8/16/65 Berns Bros. estimate for plant roof repairs is about $1000 and they were hired to do the job.

A motion was passed to pay for Mr. Hamilton's cheese maker's license for the balance of the year so we can have a licensed cheese maker in Gary's absence.

9/14/65 The need for better maintenance of motors and equipment was discussed and the decision was made to hire someone to do that.

10/13/65 Russell Gunnlaugsson will check the boiler for needed repairs.

A $5 advertisement will be placed in the High School Annual. The high school Senior class was given a price of 25¢ per half gallon of milk which they had bought for their turkey dinner.

11/15/65 A boiler reserve tank was purchased from Door County Co-op. A motor for the factory washing machine is needed.

12/15/65 At the annual meeting the Morning Glory account showed a profit of $941.44.

4/15/66 Three stainless steel milk cans and Blue Milk test equipment was bought at an auction in Vignes.

8/15/66 Things most needed at the plant are a set of stainless steel agitator forks and better rodent control.

9/14/66 We can get the franchise to handle Lake to Lake products. We will need a refrigerated truck and the Door County Lake to Lake representative has one in good condition for $800. A motion was passed to buy the truck if the franchise is gotten.

11/1/66 At the annual meeting Thor Williamson was elected Director for 3 years, replacing Russell Gunnlaugsson.

11/18/66 Fairmont has offered a sound proposition for the. Co-op to handle their products and they have a truck in excellent condition for $250. A motion was passed to contract with Fairmont and buy their truck.

12/13/66 There was a discussion about water getting into the freezer and damaging some Morning Glory products.

The Bethel Church will be paid $25 for a washing machine.

Motion passed to sell Fairmont products to factory patrons, restaurants and stores.

1/18/67 John Hamilton will receive $2 per day for the 15 days that he made cheese in December during the regular maker's absence.

A motion passed to close the Morning Glory account and open a new account named Washington Island Co-operative Dairy, Inc-Fairmont Account. Thor Williamson was authorized to make deposits and write checks against said account. Thor will be paid $2 per hour and 8¢ per mile for the use of his vehicle in connection with ordering and delivering Fairmont products from Green Bay.

$10 was paid for the pumping of the tank and floor drains.

2/3/67 In regard to the Fairmont account, Thor was placed on a commission basis as of 2/l/67. After minor monthly expenses (gas, oil, license, minor repairs) the remaining monthly profits will be split evenly between Thor and the Co-op.

4/17/67 There was a discussion regarding the small amount of State Grade cheese that was produced for much of the month. There was no conclusion as to the cause.

5/15/67 Thor turned over $400 of Fairmont profits to the General Account.

When the present factory stock is depleted, no more sales from the factory will be made. Thor was approved as Farm Inspector. A meeting will be called to discuss milk shipping to Lake to Lake.

6/19/67 It was agreed to pay 85¢ a lb. for butterfat for May and the first five days in June. On June 6th milk shipments to Lake to Lake would begin. Thus ended the manufacture of cheese on the Island.

8/25/67 A motion passed to renew the cheese factory license.

11/8/67 At the annual meeting, after conferring with Atty. Koehn we decided not to renew the bank note. We renewed the truck insurance and agreed to continue the ad in "The Cheese Reporter". Thor will be paid $10 to drain the factory whey tank. Floyd Koyen is hired to drain the factory equipment.

The following letter was received from Lake to Lake:

24 November 1967

Washington Island Shippers

The total volume of milk from the Island has been averaging under 1100 lbs the past two weeks. There are still 7 shippers involved so the average per shipper is about 150 lbs per day. With winter weather approaching and experiencing difficulty with pickup mainly with the ferry being late in windy weather perhaps it would be best if other arrangements could be made to handle the milk in the winter.

The transition to bulk milk pickup has been rapid with over 75% of the milk coming in is in bulk tanks. You can see that the cost of handling milk in cans will continue to rise and there-for any waiting time becomes more costly. This poses a problem that you folks will have to face in the near future and handling of milk in cans will cease entirely.

We would appreciate any suggestion you have to offer and certainly want to help if we can.

Sincerely,
William Tong, Fieldman
Lake to Lake Dairy Co-op

12/13/67 Fairmont discontinued the Co-op's franchise for handling their products as of 1/13/68. The reason was they had received numerous complaints from local customers.

4/15/68 Thor reported Fairmont earnings as follows: $175-January, $140-February, $110-March.

At the Co-op meeting a motion passed that as of May 1st Lake to Lake was to cut to 10¢ per cwt. of milk the withholding from each patron's account which was turned over to the Co-op to help make the monthly bank payments.

5/18/68 A special meeting was called to vote on two propositions.

1. To sell the building known as the Island Dairy, its contents and property for $8000.
2. If the above was passed, then a resolution should be passed to dissolve the corporation known as The Washington Island Co-operative Dairy, Inc. and distribute the net profits.

12 votes were cast.
To sell the factory--- Yes-8, No-4
Necessary for passage 2/3 of 12=8 Proposition passed.
To dissolve the corporation--Yes-6, No-2 Not voting-4
Necessary for passage 3/4 of 8=6 Proposition passed.

The Board unanimously voted to sell the factory and all property to Thorsten Williamson for $8000.

6/30/68 The final audit showed:

Sale of buildings	$8000
Bank Mortgage	$1461.34
Truck ' Sale	$350
Cash From Assets Sale	$6888.66

9/10/68 At a special meeting of the Co-op Dairy Board these motions were passed:

1. The Co-op was dissolved as authorized at the special meeting held on 5/8/68.
2. Arbutus is authorized to sign checks for the purpose of liquidating the Co-op.
3. Arbutus to be paid $25 for keeping and storing the Co-op records for five years. She will also receive $75 for work involved in dissolving the Co-op.
4. The Secretary will arrange for a "Satisfaction of Mortgage" to be delivered to the Co-op.

12/21/68 Class A and Class B Stock were redeemed.

12/30/68 The "Notice of Dissolution" was completed and sent in duplicate to Mr. F. Haugh.

8/3/72 The last, large dairy herd, belonging to Irvin Goodlet, was sold and shipped away on the ferry and the last milk cans were returned to the island. One by one the farmers had given up dairying until there was too little milk for the cheese factory. Later the plant building was rented to the Department of Agriculture for Entomology Research. I'm told that the day Lake to Lake refused to accept any more milk in cans there was a sudden scramble to re-activate the old cream separators and some churned butter, while others made ice cream. A few dairy cows were kept for home milk and cream consumption, but I do not believe there is a single dairy cow on the Island today, My brother, Marvin, kept one cow and unfortunately this led to his untimely demise.

Three State men studied dairy farming on the Island and reported these problems:

1. With 1300 acres of farm being used for potato production this greatly reduces the amount of land for dairy farming.
2. The quality of the milk is low.
3. The quantity and quality of feed produced is poor.
4. Buildings, equipment, water supply and management do not meet Grade A standards and some are below minimum standards for cheese manufacturing purposes,
5. At present Island cows average a production of 5000 lbs. of milk per year while the State average is 8400 lbs. per year and good herds produce over 10,000 lbs. per cow per year.

Today it appears that small farms, and even dairy farms larger than any on the Island are a thing of the past. From 1988 to 1999 a total of 10,000 farms disappeared in this State. Mega farming is taking over with long metal buildings housing thousands of animals. You can find a million chickens under one roof and cows wearing electronic necklaces. The old silo attached to the small red barn, if still standing, is idle as a feed storage bunker five times bigger and cheaper to operate has replaced it.

By spring of 1999 at least 19 more huge livestock farms, either by expansion or new construction, will each have 1000 or more animal units, which is the equivalent of 700 milking cows, or: 5 000 calves, 1,000 beef steers, 100,000 laying hens or 2,500 hogs.

The 37% increase in the number of huge livestock farms, from the present 51, is a record for any year in this state.

On these Wisconsin Mega farms, in order to milk all cows twice a day, milking continues throughout the 24 hours. When the cow enters the position for milking, the electronic ID on her neck identifies her and the computer triggers the proper amount of feed for her to eat as a very sophisticated machine milks her. Some of the biggest dairy farms in this state produce more than 110,000 pounds of milk daily. Some have as many as 1,400 milking cows.

In northwest Indiana a 12,000 head dairy operation encompassing four farms, costing sixty million dollars, plans to be in operation this fall. This will cover 9,500 acres with 120 employees. A major concern of their Dept. of Natural Resources is the proper handling of the thousands of tons of animal waste. They have only five animal waste specialists to cover 65,000 farms of all sizes. The 51 biggest operations receive the most attention, yet complaints and investigations grind on for years. People, including farmers, are appealing to local governments to put the brakes on what they call "factory farms". Neighbors are concerned about drinking water wells becoming contaminated and thus land values will drop. This has happened in southern states where huge hogs farms exist.

The mega farms are coming under closer scrutiny from the U.S. Environmental Protection Agency, which is formulating rules requiring the biggest farms to get operating permits and adopt waste management plans by 2003.

Today Wisconsin has 23,000 dairy farms, some of them smaller and mid-size run by the same families for generations. However, the future of "old MacDonald's farm" appears bleak.

If you think this is progress, an article in the Wall Street Journal entitled “Milking Technology is an Udder Breakthrough” tells what has developed in the Netherlands. You can't say that this Holland farmer's cows have above-average intelligence, but they can milk themselves. On a farm in Vijfhuizen the cows line up like so many customers in a post office. One at a time Trijnte, Catie, Janke, Zoeki and others march into the milking parlor without so much as a moo, deposit their milk-and return to the herd.

With a computer chip in her collar for ID, she approaches the machine whenever she feels the urge for a milking. A robot does the rest. A beeper alerts the farmer if anything goes wrong. A farmer no longer has to get up with the cows and is saved about 4 hours of work a day, plus a reduction of labor costs. The cows relieve their udders 3 times a day, instead of the usual 2, promoting a 15% increase of milk. It also reduces udder disease and boosts cow longevity.

A cow enters the stall, encouraged by a sweet snack released if the computer (reading her ID chip) decides it is time for a milking. Gates close around the cow as the robotic milkmaid slides underneath, its sensors spinning like a ship's radar. It finds the "reference teat" first, then hooks to all four with a rubber pulsating vacuum. Presently one machine can handle a herd of under 100 cows. The robotic three-stall milker sells for about $250,000 dollars, double the price of conventional machines which are attached to the cow by hand. After 12 years of research, Prolion began selling its device in 1992. 15 Netherland farms and others in Canada,, France, Japan and Britain, have these machines. Prolion's "Liberty" brand's slogan is: "Freedom for the cow. Freedom for the farmer." Thus ends my story on farming. No more “pulling teats and hollerin' whoa.”

In 1852 the Door County Advocate began business with 106 subscribers. The County had 3000 fishermen, loggers and a small number of farmers. It took 3 hours to print 160 copies of a four page paper on a hand operated press. Today a metal replica of the front page of the first issue is on the outside wall of today's Advocate headquarters. Then a year's subscription was $2, also payable in cordwood. Advertisers were known to pay in muskrat skins or other barter. Sometimes up to $1000 per year was made by running legal notices for the County. Name-calling and sarcasm were then common. The Door County Board of Supervisors once was called "Board of Asses". An apology appeared in the next issue "to any asses who were offended".

Island Archives records show that in addition to the Advocate the County's other newspapers were Republican, Expositor and Independent, eventually two of these merged and became Expositor/Independent.

Each correspondent had an interesting unique style of writing and until about 1900 it was common for them to sign their names, initials, or nickname. The first Advocate bearing Island news was dated Sept. 7, 1862. Here is a list of issue dates and the correspondent's signature:

6/24/1875	F.E.L.	4/2/76	E.W.S.
9/7/76	Robert Severs	3/1/83	MAL
4/12/83	Severs	3/19/85	Little Chick
1/7/86	L.B.	1/16/87	AMICUS
3/10/87	C.S.	6/25/87	PICKWICK
10/1/87	JUMBO	2/11/88	DON
6/2/88	TURK	3/30/89	MUGWUMP
8/30/90	Ben Fagg	4/25/91	R.V.
1/16/92	DOC	4/30/92	Myrtle Hope
12/31/92	A.L.B.	1/14/93	B.L.A.(Detroit Hbr.)
12/8/94	Oscar Hale	3/23/95	Bo L. Anderson
10/2/97	R.S.(Wash.Hbr.)	9/16/99	A.G.(Detroit Hbr.)
9/6/90	Ben Fagg	9/25/90	Robt. Severs
4/30/92	Myrtle Hope	12/8/94	Oscar Hale
9/16/99	A.G.		

It appears that the newspaper REPUBLICAN existed for just a short time. The dates and correspondent in the Archives were:

7/10/90 Liberator	7/17/90 Amateur	8/28/90 Roadster
7/17/90 Amateur	8/19/90 Liberator	8/28/90 Roadster

March 4, 1887 is the beginning of Island articles in the paper INDEPENDENT. Here is the list from that newspaper:

4/6/88	POTTAWATTAMIE	5/11/88	AMATEUR
6/15/88	J.F.P.	8/31/88	"BEN"

8/31/88	Y.E.C	10/12/88	JIM-JAM
11/9/88	PUSS	2/15/89	Lola
2/15/89	DOLORES	3/15/89	TIM
4/15/89	STUB & TWIST	4/12/89	RAMBLER
5/31/89	OLLE ANDERSON	6/14/89	FORGET-ME-NOT
7/12/89	Renegade	8/2/89	Nails and Ribs
8/2/89	What-Not	9/13/89	Nobody
10/4/89	Somebody	10/18/89	PIG
11/15/89	DO U NO ME	12/29/89	CZAR
4/4/90	Liberator	4/8/90	Once Again
5/23/90	Liberator	5/30/30	Your Correspondent
6/6/90	Liberator & Your Correspondent	8/30/90	Ben Fagg

From the Island Archives it appears that the paper EXPOSITOR was published from 1874 through 1876 with these correspondents:

5/22/74	W.H. Gibson	1/2/75	Teacher
5/9/75	B.G. Hannan	4/7/76	Anonymous
4/14/76	H.D. Miner	7/21/76	S.W.E.

Then 2 County papers merged becoming EXPOSITOR-INDEPENDENT with these persons writing Island news:

6/8/77	J.L.M.	5/10/78	Scribbler
5/9/79	Delta	6/13/79	Scribbler

It appears that this merger did not last very long as the INDEPENDENT again appeared under its original name while we now see the WEEKLY EXPOSITOR with these writers:

7/16/80	Scribbler	12/24/83	Erastus
1/25/84	Scribbler	5/9/84	Shoo Fly
5/21/84	Little Bo Peep	10/31/84	Topsy
3/10/85	Scribbler	4/3/85	Anonymous
12/18/85	Alto		

5/10/49 Big Dairy, Cheese Plant Burns on Washington Island. Fire destroyed the Washington Island dairy and cheese factory Thursday night, just two days before the arrival of the Island's new fire truck.

The flames of unknown origin swept the one-story plant in less than 2 hours, doing damage estimated at $15,000 by the owner, Andrew Justinger. Insurance covered part of the loss.

The Island's dairy output and bottled milk supply were only temporarily disrupted, and Justinger said that a new plant would be built immediately.

The Pleck Ice Cream and Dairy Co., Sturgeon Bay, took over the task of supplying milk and other dairy products to the Island, delivering its first load to the ferry Friday morning. Island farmers meanwhile sold their milk to outside dairies. The burned plant handled all the Island milk output and provided all of the dairy products in the town.

Flames were discovered by Dudley Justinger, son of the owner, at about 8 PM Thursday and he immediately turned in the alarm. The telephone alarm system brought volunteers to the scene, but little could be done to combat the fire.

The firefighters made an attempt to save the newly added receiving station, but were driven off by the flames. The Island had, at the time of the fire, only a chemical apparatus and some fire hose. It was impossible to reach the lake from the scene, which is near the center of the Island, so it was necessary to haul water in barrels and milk cans and pump it by hand in an attempt to quell the flames.

Destroyed in the fire were all the plant's equipment and the goods on hand, including 3000 lbs. of cheese and 500 lbs. of butter. Five tons of coal had been delivered the day of the fire and went up in flames along with a large shipment of supplies received on Wednesday. The firm's records were at Justinger's home, where he did the book work.

The owner said the new plant would be built on the same location, with work starting immediately. The Lloyd Launder's garage is being used temporarily to produce cheese with equ ipment that arrived on the ferry Friday night, less than 24 hours following the blaze. The new machinery came from a Kiel factory by truck and more was to arrive Tuesday.

The factory was built in 1914 as a farmer cooperative and began as a creamery. In 1925 an addition for cheese making equipment was erected. The plant had operated full time since its opening with the exception of short periods in 1939 and 1940-41. Peter Eiler, DePere, bought the dairy in 1942 and operated it until Jan. 1 of this year when he sold it to Justinger, who had been manager for Eiler several years. The new owner built a receiving station making the building about 40' x 60' in size, located at the intersection of Rangeline and Townline Roads.

10/11/1949 Island Thresher Completes His 55th Year; Started When 15.

Martin Anderson's first threshing machine was powered by a5 HP Steam engine. He owned this jointly with the late Christian Saabye, and they operated as a team for several years. Next was a 12 HP steam engine owned jointly with the Koyen Bros., Volney and the late August Koyen. The Anderson Bros., Martin A, Conrad, Maurice and Anton, bought out the Koyens and ran that outfit for many years.

For this 12 HP outfit water-was supplied by a team drawn tank. The straw was removed by hand.

About 10 years ago the Andersons purchased a new separator, with self feeder and straw blower, which they now use. Although the outfit is owned by three of the brothers, Martin is the only one engaged in running it. Anton is the brother who sold his share.

There are usually eight men in a threshing crew. On the Island they thresh largely oats and barley for the farmers' use.

One thousand bushels is the day's record. Mr. Anderson attributes this fall's relatively small grain crop to the cold, wet spring weather.

Born in Denmark, Mr. Anderson came to this country as a boy with his parents, the George Andersons. He was married on the Island to the former Christine (Stina) Peterson; and they have three children, Victor, sailing on the Great Lakes; Lillie, at home and Marcella, Mrs. Jack Hagen. Mr. Anderson runs a 40 acre farm located along Townline Road just east of the cheese factory.

12/l/1949 Appleton Firm Buys Valuable Timber on St. Martin's Island.

An Appleton firm has purchased a huge quantity of valuable timber on historic St. Martin's Island according to Earl LaPlant, realtor.

Knoke Bros,Appleton, bought the timber rights from an Island family which has owned the island for many years. Purchase price was not revealed.

St Martin's, a part of Michigan's Delta County, lies-in the mouth of Green Bay between Washington Island and the upper peninsula. The 1100 acre island is 12 miles from Washington Island and 6 miles across the passage from Rock Island, Door County's northernmost point.

St. Martin's is uninhabited except for a federal lighthouse keeper who is linked with the outside world through a telephone cable from Washington Island. The Jess Bros., Will, Harvey, Alton and Orville, own practically all of the island,having inherited it from their father.

There are an estimated 3,500,000 board feet of timber on the island, most of it hardwood. Only the hardwood was involved in the transaction. The island has no wildlife, according to Michigan Conservation authorities who inspected it several years ago.

The Appleton buyers have not revealed their plans for lumbering the island although they did say they would build an airstrip provide access for planes. A dock is now located on the side nearest the Door peninsula.

An old cemetery with markers between 1874-1880 are reminders that once more than 100 people lived there prior to Washington Island's early settlement.

10/20/1949 The Island, which had to import potatoes last year to supplement the local crop, had an extensive harvest. The development involving 150 acres of land and labor of over 48 Islanders in harvesting has been created by Roder Bros., Nasewaupee, and partner Edward Anderson, Chicago. The Roders are experienced county farmers who have put Door County potatoes on the map.

Anderson was originally an Island youth whose success as a national potato distributor earned him the title of "The Potato King". His company handles millions of bushels annually. Roder's "practical know-how" and Anderson's business contacts and capital were brought together when the two devised a development for Island potatoes and in 1948 ran a test plot on the Island. This plantings success led to the expansion this year. The potatoes raised on the Island are strictly certified seed, the highest grade on the market.

While the general county crop was poor, the Island harvest was excellent. Roder Bros., who personally suypervised the harvest, stated that the Island is ideally suited for potato cultur because of its climate, which is moderate and cool, the greater amount of rainfall, compared to the mainland and the excellent soil texture.

About 40 years ago there were large scale potato operations on the Island, but like on the peninsula, poor seed, low yields and a depressed market, caused a let down from which the Island never recovered.

The Island yield equaled 45,000 bushels with an average yield of 300 bushels per acre.

Of this 15,000 bushels were stored in the new Island warehouse and the remainder was shipped to Sturgeon Bay by boat. At Sturgeon Bay the potatoes were taken by truck to the Roder's Maplewood and Nasewaupee warehouses for storage or railroad shipment.The harvest was completed last week.

The "American Girl", "Welcome" and "Wisconsin" have been familiar sights in Sturgeon Bay waters during the harvest. A new 40 x 90' warehouse has been erected on the Anderson farm to store part of the potatoes till spring for shipment. This completely modern structure and storage is accomplished through a forced draft ventilation system operating with electric blower fans. Large bins hold the potatoes which are dumped in through trapdoors on the roof of the warehouse.

Banked up three-fourth of the vertical distance on three sides, the warehouse also includes a 24 x 30' wing which incorporates a grading room. The building started August 1 and was completed in two months.

Potatoes raised here are the Irish Cobbler, Triumph and Red Warba, early varieties, and Russet Rural, White Rural and Pontiac, late varieties.

About 65 persons were employed in the harvest. "Potato Vacation" at the schools made it possible for the Island youngsters to participate and all the pickers were island folk. Those from off the Island in the harvest were the trained and experienced operators of machines necessary in the harvest-- the vine beater, diggers and other equipment.

The youngest Island picker was three-year old Russell Jorgenson, who helped his mother Mrs. Leonard Jorgenson.

The oldest pickers were Chris Jacobsen and Chas. Schmidt, both 75. A three generation family, Mr. Jacobsen, Mrs. James (Doris) Cornell and Jackie and Jerry Cornell was among the pickers. Champion family group was the Bjorn Gunnlaugsson family, Mr. & Mrs.Gunnlaugsson and their seven children, Peter 23, Everett 15, Nathan 14, Murray 13, Orin 11, Danny 10, and Rosalie 8 picked more than 2,000 bags in a single week. On their best day they picked 437 bags.

When the Door County Advocate started, the first entry concerning the Island was dated September 7,1862 and it read thus:

OUR ISLAND FISHERMEN

. From D.H. Rice we learn that recruiting has been very successful on Washington and Rock Islands; over 20 volunteers have enlisted from there. Mr. W.P. Ranney, who everybody knows to be a whole souled patriot, has been giving $15 bounty to every volunteer from the town of Washington.

Town of Washington list of names drafted on Nov. 20,1862:

James Love	Samuel Love	Thos. S. Cornell
W.J. Nolan	Thos. Stenson	H. McFadden
Spencer Haines	A.J. Ward	

The next March exemptions from this draft were announced:

Samuel Love	Alienage
Thos. S. Cornell	Non-resident
Thos. Stenson	Heart disease
Wm. J. Nolan	Over 45

May 7,1863 Elected Town of Washington officials:

Supervisors- Chairman D.H. Rice; W.J. Nolan; P.McBride
Town Clerk- S.P. Drew
Town Treasurer- W. O'Neal
Town Assessor- J. Westbrook
Justices of the Peace- S.P. Drew; W. Ellis
Constables- T. Coffee; J. Folwell; S.Love

Washington Island 1865 census:

145 males 122 females 80 foreign born

Door County 1865 census:

1665 males 1431 females 1279 foreign born

In those days the constables maintained law and order and these offices were filled by election well into this century. Justices of the Peace held court for many misdemeanors. Serious offenses brought the County Sheriff here and those cases were tried in County Court. In the history of the Island there was only one convicted murderer who served a long term in Waupun State prison.